Reflections on American Music

CMS Monographs and Bibliographies in American Music
No. 16

Monographs and Bibliographies in American Music

Michael J. Budds, SERIES EDITOR
University of Missouri—Columbia

MEMBERS OF THE EDITORIAL BOARD

ॐ

Publications

1. Charles Schwartz, *George Gershwin: A Selective Bibliography and Discography* (1974).

2. Hans Nathan, *William Billings: Data and Documents* (1976).

3. Donna K. Anderson, *Charles T. Griffes: An Annotated Bibliography-Discography* (1977).

4. H. Earle Johnson, *First Performances in America to 1900: Works for Orchestra* (1979).

5. Irving Lowens, *Haydn in America* (1979).

6. Wilma Reid Cipolla, *A Catalog of the Works of Arthur Foote, 1853-1907* (1980).

7. John G. Doyle, *Louis Moreau Gottschalk (1829-1869): A Bibliographical Study and Catalog of Works* (1982).

8. James R. Heintze, *American Music Studies: A Classified Bibliography of Masters Theses* (1984).

9. William Phemister, *American Piano Concertos: A Bibliography* (1985).

10. Edward Brookhart, *Music in American Higher Education: An Annotated Bibliography* (1988).

11. Ernst C. Krohn, *Music Publishing in St. Louis* (1988).

12. Thomas E. Warner, *Periodical Literature on American Music, 1620-1920: A Classified Bibliography* (1988).

13. Kenneth Graber, *William Mason (1829-1908): An Annotated Bibliography and Catalog of Works* (1989).

14. Clayton Henderson, *A Charles Ives Tunebook* (1990).

15. David P. DeVenney, *Source Readings in American Choral Music: Composers' Writings, Interviews, & Reviews* (1995).

REFLECTIONS ON AMERICAN MUSIC

The Twentieth Century and the New Millennium

ॐ

A collection of essays
presented in honor of
The College Music Society

and co-edited by

James R. Heintze and Michael Saffle

CMS MONOGRAPHS AND BIBLIOGRAPHIES IN AMERICAN MUSIC
No. 16

Michael J. Budds, series editor

Pendragon Press
Hillsdale, New York

Library of Congress Cataloging-in-Publication Data

Reflections on American music: the twentieth century and the new
millennium: a collection of essays in honor of the College Music
Society / and co-edited by James R. Heintze and Michael Saffle
    P. Cm.--(CMS monographs and bibliographies in American Music;
    no. 16)
    Includes bibliographical references and index.
ISBN 1-57647-070-9
    1. Music--United States--20th century--History and criticism. I.
Heintze, James R. II. Saffle, Michael Benton, 1946- III. College Music
Society. IV. Series

ML200.5 .R45 2000
780'.973'0904--dc21

                                                                      00--47899

CONTENTS

ॐ

Part I
CONCERNING THE COLLEGE MUSIC SOCIETY

Part II
The Twentieth Century and the New Millennium

Contents

Contents

Contents

ILLUSTRATIONS

❦ Acknowledgments

F EW books reach press "unaided"; this one is no exception. In addition to the individual contributors whose thoughtful and often provocative efforts comprise the substance of this volume and whose generosity made its publication possible, the editors would like to extend thanks to Michael J. Budds, general editor of the *Monographs and Bibliographies in American Music* series, for editorial assistance and valuable suggestions regarding details and design issues; to Robby D. Gunstream, executive director of The College Music Society (CMS), for invaluable help in securing copyright permissions and providing information about CMS history; to Richard Kurin (director) and Charlie Weber of the Center for Folklife Programs and Cultural Studies, Smithsonian Institution, for facilitating the inclusion of the B. B. King/William Ferris interview; to Perry Martin, Center for Interdisciplinary Studies, Virginia Tech, for transcribing the King/Ferris interview; to David Sanjek, BMI Archives, for his help with Frances W. Preston's essay; and to Patricia A. Wand, University Librarian, and Ivy Broder, Dean of Academic Affairs, American University, Washington, D.C., for their ongoing assistance and support.

The authors also want to thank American University, which awarded Jim Heintze a sabbatical leave to complete his work on the present volume; and Virginia Polytechnic Institute and State University, which provided in-kind support. Finally, they want to thank their wives—Yolanda Heintze and Sue Saffle—for their patience, encouragement, and love.

JAMES R. HEINTZE
MICHAEL SAFFLE

4 July 2000

Born in Salt Lake City, **Michael Saffle** today is professor of music and humanities with Virginia Tech's Center for Interdisciplinary Studies. Saffle took his undergraduate and master's degrees at the University of Utah, Harvard University, and Boston University and completed his Ph.D. at Stanford University. The author of two books about Franz Liszt, he has published articles and reviews in JAMS, *Acta Musicologica, Notes*, and other musicological journals and serves as an editor for and contributor to the new edition of *Die Musik in Geschichte und Gegenwart*. Saffle has received fellowships and awards from the American Philosophical Society, DAAD (the German Academic Exchange Service), the Fulbright Foundation, the Alexander von Humboldt-Stiftung, and the Rockefeller Foundation. During the 2000-2001 academic year he will hold the Bicentennial Chair of American Studies at the University of Helsinki, Finland.

Born in Washington, D.C., **James R. Heintze** has been music librarian at American University since 1969 and has taught in the Music Department and American Studies program there. Heintze has written numerous articles and reviews and published nine books on a wide range of American music and culture. He has presented papers at the American Association of Recorded Sound Collections, American Musicological Society, Music Library Association, and the College Music Society. On behalf of the College Music Society, he served on its Board of Directors for CMS Publications, Inc. (1989-1992). From 1985 to 1994 Heintze was editor of the CMS series "Bibliographies in American Music" and from 1994 to 2000 co-editor with Michael Saffle for the Garland Publishing series Essays in American Music.

❦ PREFACE
About a Book Called
"Reflections on American Music"

MICHAEL SAFFLE and JAMES R. HEINTZE

A CENTURY ago our nation boasted a musical culture few of us today can imagine and none of us can remember. In 1900 ragtime was still a novelty, and Scott Joplin had not yet written "The Entertainer," the piece that remade his reputation after it appeared in an orchestrated arrangement in the 1973 Hollywood feature film *The Sting*. In 1900 performances by African-American musicians were relatively rare on American stages, although theater-going New Yorkers had at least heard of *Clorindy, or The Origin of the Cakewalk, A Trip to Coontown*, and other early efforts at bringing African-American music to the Broadway stage. In 1900 Antonín Dvořák had only recently returned to his native Bohemia (then part of the Austro-Hungarian Empire); his visit increased America's infatuation with "the classics" and set the stage for a long line of distinguished musical visitors from abroad: Gustav Mahler, Arturo Toscanini, Vladimir Horowitz, Igor Stravinsky, and Pierre Boulez, to name a few. In 1900 sheet music was sold in the thousands and tens of thousands and hundreds of thousands of copies; one sentimental ballad, Charles K. Harris's "After the Ball" had already become the first popular song to sell more than a million copies. Phonographs were becoming more and more common in 1900, but "jazz" remained a dirty word that few people outside New Orleans knew (and that had, as yet, little to do with music). And in 1900 a young insurance man named Charles Ives was already living and working in New York City, playing the organ at a Manhattan church on Sundays and gearing up to write some of the century's most remarkable experimental music; he'd already achieved some notoriety for the numbers he tossed off for student shows at Yale.

A most exciting and progressive century followed these events: one of spectacular scientific discoveries, the invention and manufacture of new products that led to more comfortable lifestyles, explorations in space, and telecommunications breakthroughs (including the World Wide Web and E-mail). Truly this has been "the American century," although not all of it deserves respect and praise: the unspeakable horrors of economic depression, world-wide war, and genocide are aspects of its—*our*—legacy. Whatever happened, however, American music went along for the exhilarating ride, exploring, seeking, pushing, and always experimenting. What emerged were new forms, styles, sounds, media, and expressions. We, the editors, view the 1900s as the most musically exciting and complex period in the history of this great nation.

Now, at the turn of the new millennium, it's time to take stock, to reflect, to learn more about what exactly happened. And, in doing so, what we discover may answer some questions as to what the future may hold for music. Hence *Reflections on American Music: The Twentieth Century and the New Millennium*.

To help us in our quest, we invited over seventy-five composers, corporate executives, critics, performers, scholars, technicians, theorists, and educators to submit their assessments and opinions of our nation's music— past, present, and future. The responding forty-two participants (excluding ourselves) range in age, location, and professional specialty—from their twenties to their eighties, from Maine to Florida to Colorado to Alaska, from graduate-student status to directorships in multi-million-dollar firms, and from limited recognition to international celebrity. The kinds and methods of their contributions vary too: from musical compositions to diary entries to "how-to" pieces to poems to speculative (but commercially oriented) "projection pieces" to fully documented scholarship exhibiting various academic attitudes and methodologies. Pleasantly, not all of our contributors agree with each other. What *Reflections* is all about, therefore, is not one interpretation of yesterday, today, and tomorrow, but the many necessarily different views about American music.

In addition to heralding the onset of the new millennium, this book has been compiled to honor The College Music Society (CMS) for its contributions to and impact on the musical world since its founding in 1959. No other music-related organization of college and university educators, performers, and scholars has played such an important part in America's music history. Part I of this volume is devoted to essays about the history and achievements of CMS; it also contains a revised version of a lecture presented originally at a CMS meeting several years ago. With the editors' sincere appreciation, the CMS provided its support and acknowledgment of the importance of making public the varied perspectives of the contributors contained herein.

In editing our contributors' work we have left much alone, relying on authors to address their topics in a careful and understandable way. Some of the authors make use of endnotes as well as lists of supplementary sources (books, articles, sound recordings, and so on); these we have recast when necessary to achieve consistency of presentation. Editorial explanations and clarifications inserted into quotations or added in the form of occasional foornotes are identified by square brackets; parentheses in quotations are the authors' own.

A notable feature of *Reflections* is an actual musical composition presented as the final "essay," one that directs the attention to the idea of self-expression, the new and different.

Ours is an age that prides itself on the appellation "postmodern"; we like to feel we can put things in different ways, to see things from different angles, to "construct" our own syntheses of reality. Composer Judith Lang Zaimont does that every bit as well with chamber music as John Luther Adams with diary entries, or Ann Kilkelly with comments on gender and tap dancing, or Marilyn Kielniarz and Jerold Ottley with thoughts about the future of religious music in millennial America, or William Velez with observations on music-rights organizations in today's United States. All these are different takes on American music yesterday, today, and tomorrow: they range in style from David Amram's meditations to John Cotner's aesthetic analyses to John Kander's and B. B. King's reminiscences to Patricia Shifferd's description of the Continental Harmony project sponsored, in part, by the American Composers Forum—the last a project underway at this volume goes to press.

This is not meant to imply that the present volume is in any sense comprehensive. A glance at the Index reveals the name of Elvis Presley, for instance, but not that of Little Richard; the volume itself contains only one unindexed reference to Frank Sinatra (in a contributor's biography: that of Ethel Ennis) but nothing about, say, Dean Martin or Ella Fitzgerald or Willie Nelson; and *Reflections* as a whole contains far too little about gospel music or Hispanic-American music or electronic music. No single publication, of course, could begin to encompass the staggering quantity and variegated qualities of twentieth-century American culture, much less the possibilities the possibilities of the new millennium.

No wonder the year 2000 looks so different from 1900. In this year, the last of the old millennium, ragtime music—now "antique"—nevertheless continues to be bought and sold, albeit on compact disks; some of it is even traded electronically (along with more commercially valuable digital "content") on Napster and other Internet sites, now being challenged for apparent violations of our nation's copyright laws. Black performers remain not only essential to America's musical life, but have become perhaps our most important contribution to world-wide twentieth-century popular culture. This does not mean, though, that so-called "classical" music is *passé*. Far from it: this year America's arts-oriented symphony orchestras and opera houses will perform before record-breaking crowds (although that achievement may seem to vanish in the face of the gigantic success of rap albums, metal-music concerts, and MTV). Sheet music is becoming scarce these days; on the other hand, personal computers, MIDI keyboards, and laser printers may be turning hard-copy music publishing into a thriving cottage industry. In 2000 jazz still holds its fans and connoisseurs in thrall, and so do blues and gospel—all three of them musics few Americans had heard, or even heard of, a century ago. And this millennial year, somewhere in America, there may be living and working the Charles Ives of the twenty-first century: a young Hispanic woman, perhaps, whose destiny it will be to contribute to music history something none of the rest of us today can imagine.

In 1996, in a letter praising the work of the Music Educators National Conference (and, one must assume, similar organizations, including The College Music Society), President Bill Clinton stated:

> Music is a universal language, bringing people together across barriers of culture and geography. The study of music opens a new and exciting world for young people and enriches the quality of their education. By playing an instrument or singing in individual or group performances, young people learn to express themselves creatively, to think critically, and to discipline themselves to achieve excellence in their art.... I commend the educators, parents, and community organizations [that] are working in partnership to ensure that music is a part of every American child's education.[1]

These words are as true, at least in spirit, in the year 2000 as they were in 1900; they are as true of the work college and university professors do today as that done by public- and private-school teachers throughout the "American century."

We hope you enjoy *Reflections on American Music: The Twentieth Century and the New Millennium.*

NOTE

[1]Published in *Teaching Music* 3/6 (June 1996): 45. The letter itself is dated 29 February 1996.

Reflections on American Music

Part I

CONCERNING
THE COLLEGE MUSIC SOCIETY

Dale A. Olsen is professor of ethnomusicology and director of the Center for Music of the Americas in the School of Music, Florida State University. He holds degrees from the University of Minnesota and took his doctorate in ethnomusicology at the University of California, Los Angeles. Olsen has lived, worked, and researched as an ethnomusicologist in Brazil, Colombia, Peru, and Venezuela; he has also performed as principal flutist with the Philharmonic Orchestra of Chile. In addition to holding other positions with professional societies, he is currently serving as president of The College Music Society. Among his publications are *Musics of Many Cultures: Study Guide and Workbook* (now in its third edition) and *Music of the Warao of Venezuela: Song People of the Rain Forest*; the latter volume won the Alan Merriam Prize. During the 1990s Olsen was recording review editor for *Ethnomusicology* and, with Daniel Sheehy, co-editor of *The Garland Encyclopedia of World Music*, Volume II (republished in part as *The Garland Handbook of Latin American Music*).

❦ American Music and The College Music Society
An Introduction

DALE A. OLSEN
President, The College Music Society (1999-2000)

ON behalf of The College Music Society (CMS), I am happy to introduce this book, *Reflections on American Music: The Twentieth Century and the New Millennium*, to CMS members and interested readers from around the world.

The term "American" means many things to many people. Because of the Italian merchant and explorer, Amerigo Vespucci, the entire Western Hemisphere is called "the Americas." Nevertheless, for some reason, in Latin America only the people of the United States are called "Americanos." Therefore, while the words "American music" can also refer to all of the musics of all the Americas (i.e., to all continents, subcontinents, and other land masses in the northern and southern portions of the Western Hemisphere, including the islands of the Caribbean), the present volume is mostly concerned with concert music—often called "art music"—and popular musical traditions of the United States. While I, as an ethnomusicologist, use a broader application of the term "American music" to mean "music in the Americas" (because the history of music and the music cultures in the "New World" share many origins, characteristics, aesthetics, and influences), the terms "American music" and "America's music"—*vide* Gilbert Chase—are a part of the scholarship within the United States. Furthermore, an approach that would embrace the entire Western Hemisphere would require many books.

It should be understood, however, that the United States is a microcosm of the world and that probably most of the world's cultures are now a part of, and contribute to, American culture. Therefore, in the broadest sense the term "American" must be used to embrace this cultural pluralism so as to eliminate the possibilities of internal strife. In spite of its motto *E pluribus unum* ("From Many, One"), the United States has never become the "melting pot" our forefathers dreamed about. Rather, it is a cultural and ethnic mosaic, in which the beauty of her design consists of a multitude of colors and a variety of musical textures.

The College Music Society has recognized this beauty and has had an "American" interest now for quite some time. It began in earnest when CMS emphasized the ethnic diversity of its annual national meeting sites. In this way The College Music Society has truly been innovative and broad-minded among scholarly music societies in the United States and Canada. Many of its annual national meeting sites have been held in large cities that are havens of multiculturalism where "Americans" from many ethnicities reside; these include Atlanta (1996), Miami (1986), Nashville (1984), Portland (1995), San Diego (1992), Santa Fe (1988), Toronto (2000), Vancouver (1985), and Washington, D.C. (1990). At all of these venues, "American" music has been emphasized: from blues to bluegrass, mariachi to matachines, and salsa to steelband. Another American interest, instigated during the term of President Phillip Rhodes, was to follow the routes (roots) of jazz by holding several of the Society's national meetings in cities along the Mississippi River and points beyond, beginning in New Orleans (1987) and including St. Louis (1989), Chicago (1991), and Minneapolis (1993).

Moreover, since the founding of The College Music Society in 1959, its journal, *College Music Symposium*, has always reflected a broad-minded interest in and approach to scholarship. Articles in one form or another can be found in almost every issue that include ideas and information about folk music, popular music, world musics, and ethnomusicology, along with every imaginable topic about European and American musics. The following citations provide just a sampling to show some of the articles that relate to the diversity of American music.

The first article in the *College Music Symposium* to reveal an American multicultural awareness appeared in 1962. It was written by Wilton Mason and entitled "Folk Music in a Changing World"; in it Mason explained that "we are now in rapid communication with every part of the globe ... we [Americans] have ourselves proven receptive, as never before, to ideas and impulses from abroad."[1] These were perceptive words written nearly four decades ago, and they are as true today as they were then. In 1976 Ralf Carriulo wrote the article "American Pluralism, the University, and Ethnomusicology," in which he discussed the need to include ethnomusicology in colleges and universities as a way of giving more exposure to America's cultural and musical diversity.[2] In the 1980s such diverse essays were published as "Carlos Castaneda and don Juan: Lessons in Sonic Awareness" by Heidi von Gunden, "The 'Indian' Operas of Charles Wakefield Cadman" by Harry D. Persion, and "From Yankee Doodle thro' to Handel's Largo: Music at the World's Columbian Exposition" by David M. Guion. In the 1990s a number of important articles appeared that addressed teaching issues relating to America's diversity; perhaps the most notable was Steven Cornelius's "Issues Regarding the Teaching of Non-Western Performance Traditions within the College Music Curriculum."

In addition, occasional issues of the series CMS Reports also pertain to American music, such as *Racial and Ethnic Directions in American Music*. Finally, one of the most important publication series in American music by any scholarly society is the series known as *Monographs and Bibliographies in American Music*, established in 1974.

Now that the twentieth century has almost ended, and the twenty-first century is about to be born, it is a time to reflect on our past, the present, and future. Truly, The College Music Society is devoted to the study, performance, and dissemination of musical traditions from the Americas. This book offers essays by a broad range of scholars, performers, composers, teachers, and others from the music world and industry, who speculate on the status of American music during the twentieth century and the new millennium. The College Music Society, in its long tradition of publishing materials and sponsoring institutes and workshops in American music, is proud to publish this important and timely book.

NOTES

[1]Wilton Mason, "Folk Music in a Changing World," *Symposium* 2 (Fall 1962): 33.
[2]Ralf Carriulo, "American Pluralism, the University, and Ethnomusicology," *Symposium* 16 (Spring 1976): 50-63.

ADDITIONAL SOURCES

Cornelius, Steven. "Issues Regarding the Teaching of Non-Western Performance Traditions within the College Music Curriculum." *Symposium* 35 (1995): 22-32.

Guion, David M. "From Yankee Doodle thro' to Handel's Largo: Music at the World's Columbian Exposition," *Symposium* 24 (Spring 1984): 81-96.

Gunden, Heidi von. "Carlos Castaneda and don Juan: Lessons in Sonic Awareness," *Symposium* 20 (Fall 1980): 117-124.

Persion, Harry D. "The 'Indian' Operas of Charles Wakefield Cadman," *Symposium* 22/2 (Fall 1982): 20-50.

Racial and Ethnic Directions in American Music. CMS Report No. 3 (1982).

A native of Illinois, **Barbara English Maris** is professor emeritus of music and coordinator emeritus of graduate degree programs in piano pedagogy at The Catholic University of America, Washington, D.C. A graduate of the Peabody Conservatory and the Ecole Normale de Musique, Maris served as president of The College Music Society in 1981-1982. Since 1995 she has held the editorship for articles and reviews of the *American Music Teacher*, the official journal of the Music Teachers National Association (MTNA). Maris's new book, *Making Music at the Piano: Messages to Adult Early-Level Students*, is scheduled to be published by Oxford University Press before the end of 2000.

❦ Facilitating Learning
The Role of The College Music Society

BARBARA ENGLISH MARIS

I T was in a limousine on the way back to the airport, after attending my second College Music Society (CMS) national meeting in 1973, at the University of Iowa, that I asked a stranger who was still wearing his CMS name tag, "And what do your students do after they graduate?" Even now I shudder when I recall the answer: "I dunno, but as long as they keep comin', I've got a job!" Was his the voice of cynicism or honesty? Surely, I thought (with the discomfort of an idealistic graduate student of the 1970s), he really didn't mean to say, "I don't know what happens to them after they pay their tuition, and furthermore, I don't care"? Or—and this thought still haunts me—perhaps he actually meant that he did not care about his students?

It is true, of course, that teachers cannot teach unless they have students. Unless students enroll in our institutions and show up in our studios and classrooms, we will not retain our jobs. But the rationale for the existence of the more than 1,800 institutions listed in the CMS *Directory of Music Faculties in Colleges and Universities, U.S. and Canada, 1998-99* has to be more than to provide jobs for nearly 35,000 music teachers associated with those schools.

7

Students as Learners/Teachers as Learners

Our college students typically include those who enroll for general or specialized music courses or activities. Our students may include music majors as well as those who choose to major in subjects other than music. (As I reread that somewhat convoluted sentence, I remember fondly the voice of CMS past-president Robert M. Trotter who refused steadfastly to define people in terms of what they were not, challenging us to remove from our vocabulary such phrases as "non-European," "non-Western," "non-White," "non-male," and "non-major.") As teachers in higher education, we work with some students who intend to make a career of music. We also work with some who are passionate about music but have chosen to prepare themselves to work in fields other than music. Some of our students have studied music for many years before entering college; others enroll for a required introductory course that may be their first formal study of music (and, all too often, also their last).

Although we work with a wide range of students enrolled in our colleges and universities, we never work with students who have no background in music or connection to some type of music. All our students have been in the presence of a tremendous amount of music throughout their lives. In the twentieth century, that situation became inevitable because of LPs, audio- and videotapes, CDs, radio, television, and computers.

As college teachers, we affect our students when they are in college and, directly or indirectly, we also influence them both before they enter the academic world and long after they leave school. Music learning begins before a young child enters nursery school or kindergarten. Learning a musical language begins when an infant is held and moved rhythmically, when a baby hears the comforting voice of a caregiver, and when a child realizes there is a correlation between the sounds she creates and the actions of people around her. Furthermore, musical experiences do not end when one leaves school or receives a diploma.

Every music student we work with will teach others about music. Music learning occurs in many situations—during radio broadcasts and television programs, as part of religious services and public concerts, through participation in festive occasions and family gatherings, while exploring MP3 and DVDs, in movie theaters, and at sporting events. The learning of music and the development of musical attitudes continue throughout life.

The academic world puts our students into neat little packages: music history or music theory, band or orchestra, vocal performance or music theater, contralto or lyric soprano, lieder or oratorio, piano performance or piano pedagogy, music business or music therapy, B.A. or B.M., Bach or rock, reggae or renaissance. In reality, however, most musicians wear many hats during their lives and careers. Their specific tasks may vary from year to year and season to season, but musicians' livelihoods depend on a variety of professional activities. Our degree programs make a sharp distinction between what we expect from students who major in performance and from those who major in education. In reality, though, all of our students will function as music teachers. Every time a musician performs, he teaches. And every time a teacher explains and demonstrates a musical concept, she is performing music. The Japanese composer Tohru Takemitsu suggested that the purpose of notation is to change the noun "music" into the verb "music." Music is not something that sits on a page waiting to be described and discussed. Music is an activity that invites us to create sonic patterns and produce effects that result from motions and emotions. It often has been said that we all are music "ed-ers." All of us teach others about music and what it means to us. Some of us do it with passion and compassion; others do it with frustration and fright. Some do it with enthusiam and pride; others argue that the real musicians are performers, not performance teachers. (Will we ever erase that archaic line: "Those that can perform, do; those that can't, teach"?) Some people argue we do not teach music at all. Instead, they suggest, our music students are people who have chosen to learn how to behave musically. But all musicians—all of our music students—demonstrate what music means to them, how they approach musical situations, and how they value the act of creating and responding to musical sounds.

Teaching involves three aspects of learning: teaching ourselves, teaching others, and teaching others to teach. Who will teach music in the twenty-first century? *All* our music students, whether or not they become certified as music teachers. All people who make music and listen to music will, whether by default or on purpose, influence others.

What music will our students come to know? Once upon a time that might have seemed like a rather easy question to answer. Songs our mothers taught us. Tunes our fathers whistled happily. Music created in our homes, neighborhoods, and communities. Once upon a time the music that people knew was the music they created and shared on a daily basis within a small circle of friends and family. Today's students, however, hear music that reflects centuries of artistic creativity and represents hundreds of musical cultures from around the world. No matter how much we love the songs heard at our mother's knee, we know that other parents have sung other songs in other languages to other children in other communities.

Research, technology, and the globalization of world culture have expanded the repertoire music students can hear today. But there are negative results as well from recent technological developments. The search for perfection affects music students as well as spellers and athletes. In music competitions, as in beauty pageants and spelling bees and football championships, we identify the "winner" by gradually identifying and removing all the "losers." In attempting both to encourage the best athletes and spellers and musicians and identify the most beautiful people, we risk discouraging the rest. Recordings of music and pictures of fashion models are edited routinely to remove squawks and blotches, alter the balance of sounds, and air-brush wrinkles and bulges. Is it any surprise that so many people conclude they can't sing and can't move rhythmically? Is it unexpected that people spend millions of dollars on cosmetics and surgery, hoping to improve their appearances? Do we wonder why our young people become depressed when they decide they are not as beautiful as the glamorous but doctored pictures of movie stars?

What if we refused to listen to any speaker who mispronounced a word or inserted "uhh"s or lisped or stuttered? What if we would not allow such people to speak at all? Who would be left to talk? Who would be left to listen? How would we communicate with each other? As someone once commented, "If only the best songbirds sang, the woods would be very quiet."

In spite of music competitions and Super Bowl Sundays, in spite of golf and tennis tournaments, many people do participate in sports and music. Most people find personal satisfaction in music that exists mostly outside of studios and classrooms; it is the music created and performed in garages, recreation halls, and village squares; the music involved with rock bands and folk groups; the music presented both formally and informally. Many of the music-makers in our world get along just fine, thank you, without the involvement of those of us who are music professors and go around professing our music.

What music will students learn in the new millennium? That question will continue to be discussed from many vantage points. Who will teach in our colleges and universities? What will be taught? What will we study? What will we include? What will we exclude? What music will be published and analyzed, performed, and memorized? How will music be disseminated? Every school-teacher and student will find their own responses to these questions, but it is clear that a tremendous quantity and variety of music will continue to be available to us and our students.

CMS as a Facilitator of Learning

The words of Robert M. Trotter, presented in his presidential report of Fall 1964, reflect the goals of CMS from its early years and throughout the twentieth century:

> In my opinion, as a society we must: be equally concerned with the most esoteric scholarship and the simplest primary-grade lesson in music; accept the Bachelor of Arts and Bachelor of Music as equally valid degree objectives for music students of differing orientations, and concentrate on improving the essential nature of both degrees; consider performance studies worthy of degree credit, when conceived as an opportunity to experience our musical heritage directly, in rehearsals that relate technique and understanding of musical styles whether or not they eventuate in public performance; recognize factionalism for what it is, a natural though regrettable result of two things, fear of encroachment on one's vested interests, and fear of loss of face, thus enabling us to work more constructively together; carry on conversation about music itself and how to teach it, in meetings and publications accessible to all college-music teachers; heed Donald Grout's admonition to stop thinking about subjects like this in terms of problem and solution. In my opinion [Grout's], it gives completely the wrong approach to the whole situation. In a problem, properly speaking, four conditions are present. First, all data are given; second, there is always an answer; third, there is only one correct answer; and fourth, when you have found the correct answer you are done with the problem. Not one of those conditions prevails in the kind of situation we are talking about, or in any kind of human situation.[1]

Throughout its existence The College Music Society has assumed responsibility and leadership for a wide variety of projects, based on the organization's underlying goals:

> to encourage and enhance dialogue among music teachers in higher education (including colleges, conservatories, and universities);
> to provide opportunities for professional development of faculty;
> to identify professional concerns of teachers and students;
> to encourage music research and creativity in various areas of specialization; and
> to enhance the quality of music teaching.

Frequently the decisions related to undertaking new CMS projects have been based on questions such as, "Does this need to be done by some person or some organization?" "Why is it needed?" "If CMS doesn't do it, will it be done?" The answers to such questions have resulted in such things as annual conferences, regional chapters and chapter activities, summer institutes on various topics, developmental conferences (such as the Wingspread and Dearborn conferences on music in general studies), scholarly publications (such as *College Music Symposium* and *Monographs and Bibliographies in American Music*), tools for communication within the profession (such as the *Newsletter*; the *Directory of Music Faculties in Colleges and Universities, in the U.S. and Canada*; and the "Music Faculty Vacancy Lists"), and various CMS Reports (a series of studies focused on professional issues). To meet special needs, CMS holds international conferences, provides mentoring opportunities, and establishes chatrooms and listservs. In addition, the Society represents college music teachers to professional accrediting organizations and government agencies.

The structure of CMS as an umbrella organization reflects the commitment to facilitating dialogue among members of various sub-disciplines of music: composition, ethnomusicology, music education, music in general studies, musicology, performance, and theory. CMS Board members represent their own disciplines, yet help all Society members understand and work with colleagues who specialize in other sub-disciplines. At CMS national conferences, held in different locations around the country, it has become traditional to highlight the music and culture of that geographic region, thus exploring various aspects of the rich heritage of American music. New works by CMS composers are also featured regularly at national and regional conferences. As music technology has developed, CMS has taken a lead in helping college faculty utilize new tools in communicating, researching, and teaching. By holding joint meetings with other professional organizations, CMS has encouraged dialogue with others involved in music study and performance. Acknowledging the importance of a global perspective in music education, CMS has also offered occasional teaching and learning institutes abroad.

Just as the music education of our students is not limited to what happens on our campuses, the continuing education of faculty goes far beyond what they took with them when they left graduate school. Learning to teach effectively is a process that continues throughout one's professional career, and much of that learning occurs informally.

Contents

**The contents page from the first issue of
The College Music Society's *Symposium***
(Fall 1961)

13

Earlier in this essay I used the heading "Students as Learners/Faculty as Learners." Those words reflect one of the biggest changes in education during the twentieth century. Today, learning is considered a lifetime process. Teachers often define themselves as facilitators of the learning their students will experience later on. Teaching is no longer a process of presenting historic facts, reciting figures, and pouring them into students' brains. We recognize that different people perceive and organize information in different ways. We know that the quantity of information in the world continues to increase exponentially. We acknowledge that "telling is not teaching," and we realize that what students do with information is more important than their ability to regurgitate isolated details. Just as our attitudes have changed toward the learning of students, so have they changed toward what we expect from teachers. No longer do we expect students to stay in school until they "know it all," then continue to work in the classroom, replacing teachers who had lectured them years earlier. Because teachers are expected to continue learning throughout their careers, the role of CMS becomes even more important. After I began attending CMS national meetings in 1972, my own horizons were broadened because of CMS meetings held in conjunction with other professional music organizations—among them the American Musicology Society (AMS), the Society for Ethnomusicology (SEM), the Center for Research in Black Music (CRBM), the Society for Music Theory (SMT), and the Association for Technology in Music Instruction (ATMI). At the regional level also, CMS chapters often schedule their meetings in cooperation with meetings of other professional organizations.

"Toronto 2000: Musical Intersections" (November 1-5, 2000) has been designed as a mega-meeting that will bring together many cooperating societies engaged in music research and teaching in colleges and universities, both in the United States and Canada. In Toronto the fifteen participating groups will present their independent programs, but all sessions will be open to registrants of all participating organizations. Several intersecting and joint sessions will be presented.

CMS and the Twenty-first Century

What will the role of The College Music Society be in the twenty-first century? That remains to be seen. Just as CMS has established a history of responding to change by making changes, however, I assume that the activities of the organization will continue to relate to needs of music students and music faculty. Within the Society, there is a commitment to high-quality research and other creative work, but there also is a strong commitment to the important work of helping students and faculty learn. CMS and CMS-ers care about their students.

As I reflect and as I project, I realize the values that drew me to CMS at the earliest stage of my college teaching career continue to be values that are needed, even in the new millennium. The aspects of the Society that most appealed to me when I was a student member still seem important now that we have entered a new century. These aspects include: valuing people at all stages of their development; valuing diverse aspects of music study and various areas of specialization; recognizing the interconnections of our lives; and seeking to meet the needs of students and faculty.

Although my academic degrees provided me with professional credentials, in many ways it was The College Music Society that showed me what it meant to be an academician. It was CMS that taught me how to be a college professor. By participating in CMS activities—attending national conventions and regional meetings, reading CMS publications, serving on committees, presenting and chairing conference sessions, accepting assignments, writing reports, working with other college teachers, and representing CMS to other professional groups—I learned what college music professors do. In working with my professional counterparts from other institutions, I discovered that certain frustrating conditions were not unique to my school. I learned that people on other campuses sometimes had developed responses to challenges that might be useful on my campus. Through CMS, I became more aware of many "non-academic" issues that are important concerns for students and teachers; these include staffing, class loads, budgets, tenure, copyright regulations, music study in the general education of all college students, the general education courses in the education of all college music students, student recruitment, faculty retrenchment, procedures for evaluating students and faculty, creative uses of technology, resources related to lesser known composers, and issues confronting colleagues in other areas of specialization.

Through The College Music Society, I came to think of myself not just as a piano teacher, but also as a teacher of college music students—a colleague of other teachers (both inside and outside of the field of music), and a member of a much larger educational community that goes beyond our college campuses. The Society has reminded me that all of the groups gathered under the CMS umbrella play important roles in music in higher education. CMS has broadened my horizons, helped me learn to identify conditions, guided me in asking questions, and pointed me toward appropriate responses. Perhaps even more important, CMS has introduced me to many tools that could be helpful in dealing with our changing world.

The ongoing challenges, both esoteric and pragmatic, that are considered year after year by the Society are issues CMS members encounter every day on their own campuses. As we pursue our work in the twenty-first century, those challenges will continue. For college music teachers committed both to their students and to their particular areas of expertise, I am convinced that, as we confront issues and deal with professional concerns, we will need to count on the Society to help us respond creatively to those conditions and challenges. It is not the responsibility of CMS to discover solutions to problems, but I believe that the Society will continue its on-going commitment both to music faculty and music students. I foresee that the organization will continue to seek creative responses to significant challenges. In the year 2000 and beyond, CMS will face the challenges both of helping college music teachers facilitate the learning of their students and also the task of enhancing their own continued growth. Although the specific responses will change, the basic challenges will continue. In the new millennium, we may expect that CMS will continue to facilitate learning and that music students and faculty will continue to define themselves as learners.

NOTE

[1]Robert M. Trotter, "President's Report," *College Music Society Symposium* 4 (Fall 1964): 14-15.

Leon Botstein is president of Bard College, where he holds the Leon Levy Professorship in the Arts and Humanities; he is also music director of the American Symphony Orchestra, the American-Russian Young Artists Orchestra, and the Bard Music Festival, and editor of *The Musical Quarterly*. After completing his undergraduate education at the University of Chicago, Botstein took his graduate degrees at Harvard. He has served as president of Franconia College and has taught at New York's Manhattan School of Music and Vienna's Hochschule für angewandte Kunst. Botstein's publications include *Judentum und Modernität, The Compleat Brahms, Jefferson's Children: Education and the Promise of American Culture*, and— forthcoming from the University of Chicago Press—*Music and Its Public: Habits of Listening and the Crisis of Musical Modernism in Vienna, 1870-1914*. He has also recorded on the CRI, Vanguard, Arabesque, Koch, and Telarc labels.

❧ Is There a Future for the Traditions of Music and Music Teaching in Our Colleges and Universities?

LEON BOTSTEIN

This is an edited transcript of an address given at the 1996 annual meeting of the College Music Society as part of its Robert M. Trotter Lectures series.

"Is THERE a future for music and music making at universities?" The answer clearly is, "Yes; there is a future, even if it may be a dismal one." In addressing what's happening to music teaching, I want to consider background issues that influence three areas: classroom music teaching and its subject matter in history and theory, scholarship (writing about music), and performance.

The College Music Society's report for 1990-1992 concerned issues we sometimes think constitute the main problem in all aspects of contemporary university life: diversity, gender, cross-cultural priorities. I would add to this list questions of sexual orientation and the exclusion of minorities. I think these are not the primary challenges in the teaching of music, however. I would also urge all of us to shutter our windows during invasions of not-very-helpful methodological fashions heralded by colleagues in other parts of the university. Our most pressing problems may be quite particular, so let us look at the music-teaching situation from an explicitly narrow perspective.

Many colleagues think things have changed for the worse from what they used to be. Senior faculty are nostalgic for the "good old days"; youthful radical colleagues and graduate students think these veterans have an outdated hegemonic, totalitarian grip on curriculum and standards. I believe there's some sort of "values" game-playing going on in these conflicts, none of which has much to do with music of any kind. The debate has become all about local cultural politics, turf, and the seizure of superior moral authority in front of a mythical audience. America's universities have become subject to a novel dislike of dissent; they have embraced a neo-Puritan politics. We seem more concerned about the categories each of us represents than about music of any kind.

Let us turn then to other sorts of issues that influence teaching and learning. First, consider the impact of popular culture. There always was something akin to "popular culture," but the mode of its access and distribution is radically different now than it was in prior historical eras. This situation influences various things, particularly listening habits. The student's ear is important, because in popular culture most of the crucial questions of diversity and gender are in the end wiped out. What is important about popular culture today, despite surface distinctions, is its immense uniformity that cuts across social boundaries. White, black, gay and lesbian constituents consume popular music together in a kind of crisscross fashion without any kind of doctrinal aesthetic coherence. We face an eclectic mix of ethnic, political, sexual, and regional attributes in popular music. Yet the uniformity imposed by mass commercial distribution remains most important.

The influence of today's popular culture on literacy in general is significant in terms of how we teach music. The way music is taught has always been contingent on the way ordinary literacy is attained, used, and distributed. Many psychologists believe musical literacy and cognitive functions are related. I believe there is a relationship between the way we ought to teach music and the way ordinary literacy is taught and retained.

There is a general problem with active literacy, particularly writing, and music literacy has followed suit. We are best at passive listening.

Therefore, the way music is consumed, produced, and adapted by young people needs to be better understood. It's not only the dominance of mechanical reproduction defined along the lines of the Adorno-Benjamin debate of sixty years ago that is at stake, but a matter of looking at modern technology as it really works and considering how people listen to sound and access and recall music. There is a dominant popular culture and mode of consumption out there that must be addressed no matter what distinct categories our students fit into, insofar as they have grown up in the United States.

Second, consider the larger acoustic environment; this affects issues crucial to music, such as memory, recognition, and how people process information. The acoustic environment in which people grow up concerns general environmental sensibilities regarding the relationship of space and time. Consider the street, the store, the home. Few of us worry about attaching meaning to musical phenomena, and we rarely take into account how the clock of daily life operates acoustically. What, historically, were "tempo" and "speed" in the early nineteenth century? How has the perception of silence changed? It is impossible to look at a score and derive from its conventional Western notation alone the exact meaning of "adagio" or "allegro con spirito." What was "allegro con spirito" to a society that never moved more rapidly than thirty miles an hour? It's hard to know, but the query is relevant. The important aspect about Beethoven's metronome *vis-à-vis* his music is how it was used in his era. Even those who have lost the ability to hear still hear sound internally in relationship to memory of prior-to-deafness conceptions of time, duration, and acoustic sound. In the early nineteenth century there was no habit of mechanical continuity. There was a fascination in the early nineteenth century with new automatic gadgets, but not with regularity. There was little interest in using the metronome to tick all the way through a piece of music. But this is how the device is used by conservatory students today. It's not that the metronome couldn't do it then. But no one viewed any mechanical device—even clocks—with quite the same expectation of regularity. There was no experience, even in lighting of consistency and evenness. Concepts of time and duration in history are important. They shape the capacity for memory.

If someone listens to a recording of a Mahler symphony day in and day out, that person will acquire an entirely different kind of musical memory than members of the previous generation had, because access to such an event did not exist. A concert audience listening today to Beethoven's Fifth Symphony is far more familiar with that symphony than any previous audience in history. If one could have attended every professional concert in Vienna from 1880 to 1900, it would have taken well over a decade to hear each of the nine Beethoven symphonies performed by a professional orchestra once. In an environment like that, the sense of relationship to the live concert and orchestral sound was different, and the acoustic memory and experience were different in terms of intensity.

A century ago, no one ever heard sounds comparable to a jet plane on a runway, or to an electric eggbeater, or to the hum of a refrigerator. We should pay attention to such things because they concern how people respond to sound. The same is true of the duration of sound and sight. People's tolerance of time, their attention span and sense of periodicity, and expectation (words used in talking about the perception of musical form) have meanings related to daily experience outside of music that inform the approach to music.

Charles Ives's recollection of hearing bands at an outdoor event and his use of that memory in a complex musical form are similar to the way a nineteenth-century novelist took real events spanning eighteen years or a few minutes and, through artistry, recreated in artificial reading time a parallel sensibility in the reader that distorts real time. Composer and novelist create comparable parallel narratives that don't have the same clocks. If we were to adapt a similar approach today, as music teachers in the late twentieth century (a century that has created its own clock), we would have to consider matters of the perception of duration in relationship to the use of absolute (but artificially calibrated) time in contemporary life. Changes in our society in respect to the experience of time are crucial to the expectations we place on music.

Consider the relation of sound and sight. Motion pictures with talking sound didn't exist before the 1920s. When we look at a nineteenth-century melodrama by Fibich, we gain a completely different conception of the possible relations between verbal narration and action to sound from that which we derive in a Wagner opera. Music can tell us something about the past no other art form can. The relationship of music to image is now ever more crucial. In the nineteenth century the success of a lot of music had to do with the societal function of the concert hall, in which people used listening to music in organized time to structure forms of internal visual hearing. People have always listened to instrumental music and imagined visual narratives of various kinds, some organized by the music itself and some by factors that have nothing to do with any anticipation that music can tell a story. These factors are different today and they must be taken into account as we teach music.

Third, let us look at the social structure of musical time itself, particularly its relationship to public and private functions. We must examine the social context for the way we make music in relation to the way we structure the everyday. What is the relationship of work to leisure? When is music listened to, in what context, and with whom? The social context of the use of music has changed dramatically. For some undergraduates this is a key part of their experience. We must know how they associate music to their daily routine of work and play, and to how they form themselves into groups using music. Schubert and his contemporaries learned to play and sing as part of ensembles. They recruited others and located needed colleagues when another singer or player was required. Is music today created collectively or heard intergenerationally, as it might have been in a village in central Europe in Schubert's or Dvořák's time? Or is it private or a peer- or age-segregated event? In what arena does it take place—public or private? Is it a family affair, or has the family structure *vis-à-vis* music changed dramatically? The dimensions of domestic living conditions, of neighborhood circumstances and social class—where music actually functions—are important.

Consider the late-nineteenth-century forums for listening to music. Students overlook the fact that a good deal of music in Vienna, a great center of a presumably "Eurocentric" and male-dominated art, took place in eating and drinking establishments. That is an important clue about the significance of various forms of music making and the relationship between musical art and social life and the role of different kinds of music. Public and private uses of music, music's social organization, and the space in which it was and is performed are crucial to the distinctions and relationships between "high" and "low" cultures. These important circumstances are very different in our time, particularly since the 1950s. Things then were different even in terms of the technology that we consider to be relatively recent. The design of concert auditoriums relates to the questions of such social habits and uses of leisure time. Our willingness to sit in fixed seats alongside strangers just listening has diminished. In the former Soviet Union, people flocked to concerts to hear standard repertoire played moderately well by ordinary Soviet pianists and orchestras. People cried. Why? Because sitting without fear in public in a social situation had real significance for them—a significance that, today, has been lost, at long last. But music still plays a special role in political conditions of unfreedom and repression.

Fourth, we must think about music in relationship to the life cycle. Music and music teaching have an important role in this cycle. Schubert died at thirty-one. To understand what that means, however, one has to understand the life cycle in historical context. In Schubert's day it was not unusual to die at thirty-one. What was his normal life expectancy? Forty-five, at best. What has been written posthumously about the metaphysical *Angst* of Schubert's late music is interesting. But what Schubert himself may have thought is a different matter. The issue of whether Schubert's angst was specific to him, rather than a daily experience for everyone his age living in Vienna in the 1820s, has to do with the overriding, mundane three "D"s: death, disease, and dirt in the pre-industrial urban world. The relationship of music to the fear of death, disease, and pain in every era must be examined.

When can young people learn music best? This has to do, in part, with fundamental changes in development and nutrition, in patterns of schooling, work, and old age, and with the life span. Perhaps it is important to realize that Fanny and Felix Mendelssohn experienced the onset of puberty three or four years later than someone born ten years ago probably will. When we teach young people music we need to ask what will that music have to do with the patterns of work, maturity, old age, health, child rearing, and death in a life span that extends to over ninety years in which maturation occurs at twelve years of age.

The links between music and social class are equally important. So are political contexts, which include the economics of music making and patronage. We need to explore the relationship of music to the industries of music making, institutions, patterns of support, and the political significance music is or is not given. It is important to recognize what the political function of music is in American culture. Is concert-classical music really a democratic art form? How does it fit in, or is it an uncomfortable importation of an aristocratic art form created by European patronage? To what extent is the question of music crucial to political leadership and a part of the political communication between a government and its people? These things differ in different countries and affect the musics produced and used. Certainly the issue of who supports music and why is important to consider. Our students know that music has little importance in presidential campaigns. Even if the National Endowment for the Arts functioned well, Americans wouldn't take to the barricades over it. In Austria, on the other hand, people *care* about who directs the Salzburg Festival and Vienna's Staatsoper. The same questions must be asked of church music in relationship to the state. The role of religion and shifts in religious practices clearly affect the teaching of music in schools and colleges.

If we think about how to teach music in terms of such issues, and set aside all the commonplace politically correct discourse, we may come to some interesting conclusions.

First, we might wish to consider students generationally rather than in terms of race, nationality, gender, sexual preference, ethnicity, and so on. We might conclude that what they need to do most is to learn how actually to make music. We might decide they need something like Hindemith's *Gebrauchsmusik.* We might ask them to use various technologies and produce music including pieces of "found music" from ambient sound using computers as well as other devices. We might use improvisation as the basis of beginning musical activity. Delay the teaching of notation. Delay the use of Schenker graphs. Schenker addressed a public whose habits of listening were quite different; he was showing those whom he considered philistines (piano-playing amateurs) that they didn't really hear properly what was happening in a Beethoven sonata. The Adorno-Schenker generations were fighting a different war. That war has become irrelevant except for those interested in historical analysis.

Training the ear is training in making music. Construct theory up from popular practice, not from the past, from Palestrina and Bach. Start with the periodicity characteristic of pop songs and work forward, or construct rhythmic and structural analyses based on jazz and commercial genres. Start with what's in students' ears and help them to grow beyond it. Use ordinary habits of hearing as a bridge to new forms of musical literacy. Understanding relationships between what's happening in their minds and ears and the less familiar traditions may lead to the development of different kinds of notation and ways of writing about music. The sound of a hunting horn can be notated *à la* Haydn, but one can't write down the sound of a car horn that way, and students have heard a lot of car horns, not to speak of non-Western musics.

The teaching of music history should be a bridge to what we call "theory": the critical analysis of sound and structure, the study of complex events. What if we helped students understand what they're already doing and how it can be illuminated by notation and analysis? Technology may be helpful. On some level, however, we are still prisoners of some kind of rigid ideology about who is and who is not musical. If you have "perfect pitch," you're musical. But the idea that the most musical person in a class is the one who can take perfect dictation without effort simply isn't exclusive or sufficient as a basis for determining talent or musicality. The traditional limiting assumptions about who is and who isn't gifted are harmful, not helpful.

Teaching music history from the present backwards, for example, and in other novel ways might help us find a good replacement for the music-appreciation course of yesteryear. In previous generations, especially in the Northeast, teachers like G. Wallace Woodworth at Harvard excelled at this kind of course. He played scratchy recordings of symphonies, and students learned to love music, attend concerts, buy records, and give money to the Boston Symphony Orchestra. But fifty years ago musicologists found such appreciation courses too lowbrow and insufficiently historical. Some composers in the university thought an audience was no longer important. These attitudes have undercut student interest in music.

A collapse has taken place in music education before college throughout the United States. Yet we produce more than enough professional musicians. What we need is a non-professional young public invested in making, hearing, and dealing with non-commercial music as part of their lives, because they consider music an important aspect of life and not mere decoration. One thing that's wonderful about teaching music history today is ironically the total lack of familiarity with it. This becomes a tremendous virtue. There is nothing as satisfying as introducing dyed-in-the-wool pop-music fans to Bruckner symphonies and Renaissance motets.

It is important to realize that surprise is, as a teaching tool, superior to detached respect. Surprise means, however, that we have to think about teaching music history in a different way. For starters, we have to teach pieces instead of dates. We also have to relate music history to history in general. For example, we might choose to discuss the relationship between Felix Mendelssohn's music and early-nineteenth-century neo-Classicism in art and architecture. Mendelssohn contributed to the Bach revival in 1829, but a year earlier he wrote music for a celebration of Albrecht Dürer at which an environment was created by the leading neo-Classic painters and sculptors of his time. What influence did that have on his music? Consider another example: What is significant about Mendelssohn's relationship with Goethe was Goethe's approach in the 1820s to romanticism. Which ideas did Mendelssohn incorporate from Goethe into his work as a composer? In other words, let us relate music to intellectual history. What if studying the relationship between Poulenc and *Les Six* to surrealism revealed analogous relationships useful in linking Brahms to the late-nineteenth-century German-Roman tradition in painting? What did the contact with American life and history mean to Dvořák? When we escape the European canon and consider other kinds of music making, these sorts of questions become especially important. If we fail to teach music history as a way of discovering history in general, our students aren't going to be interested in the historical repertoire, nor should they be.

The performance indications written in scores when they were created have different meaning today. The words Mahler wrote pertained to performance practice as realized sound; they meant something specific to the audiences and players he was working with. When we hear a Beethoven symphony and ask what his performance instructions meant to music audiences in the 1820s, we begin to treat musical texts as historically contingent. How would we achieve a comparable communicative result today? Theory is also a contingent discipline. But we must write music history not only as the history of texts as a clue to music making beyond motives of authenticity and period practices. To do that, we'll need to use a lot of resource materials few teachers and scholars have looked at.

Finally, consider the teaching of performance. We have to rethink its rituals, the relationships of musics to one another in performance and the repertoire we teach. We may even get youngsters to begin improvising on the violin, although the violin is not considered an improvisatory instrument. More of this kind should happen. I sit on juries and listen to violinists play the same sequence of materials I studied: the Mozart concertos—first the third, then the fourth, then the fifth. And then the Mendelssohn concerto, and so forth. Why not teach something else from the enormous literature that's available? Learning concertos should mean something in relationship to history; a few works shouldn't become canonic in fixed rituals of training. And we still fail to teach a differentiated approach to style and sound production.

If one thinks about all this in new ways and circumvents questions of gender, diversity, cross-culturalism explicitly—if one thinks simply in terms of musics—some interesting consequences emerge.

The music we seek to preserve and pass on in the university is now something strange, unknown, counter-intuitive. It isn't part of daily life. Perhaps that's an advantage. Yet, it has been appropriated in some limited way by everybody for every possible purpose, from jingles to film scores.

25

Perhaps we'll discover that certain divisions in music don't really exist. What we call ethnomusicology isn't really a separate discipline, but a way of working we need to integrate into our discussions of music as a whole. We really can talk about "world music," because of the fact that music is not linguistic in the strictest sense. That makes it accessible and universal through subjective appropriation. We might end up with subjectivity and objectivity unified without conflict in one field. We might find ourselves allied in our resistance to commercial culture. Universities are supposed to provide room for dissent, to introduce young people to things they wouldn't ordinarily stumble upon in daily life. In music we can do this quite powerfully by fighting the monopoly of the marketplace.

What we are doing, actually, is fighting against the onrush of fashion and thoughtless change. The university is properly a conservative institution by definition. We should see ourselves as re-inventing traditions in order to conserve them and the university itself. We may yet establish an appreciation for complex and endangered traditions of music. Music, in this sense, is a form of life—which, to everyone in the field of music, is a matter of life and death.

William Carlos Williams (1883-1963) practiced as a pediatrician for years in Rutherford, New Jersey, his home town. In medical school at the University of Pennsylvania he met and befriended Ezra Pound, who influenced his writing and arranged the London publication of *The Tempers* in 1913. Later Williams influenced Allen Ginsberg and other poets of the Beat Generation. Among Williams's publications are *Kora in Hell* (1920), *Spring and All* (1921), *Life Along the Passaic River* (1938), and *Pictures from Brueghel and Other Poems* (1963), as well as several novels and the introduction to Ginsberg's *Howl and Other Poems*; his correspondence with Denise Levertov appeared in 1998 in an edition prepared by Christopher MacGowan. In 1963, the year he died, Williams won the Pulitzer Prize for poetry.

🍎 The Rewaking

WILLIAM CARLOS WILLIAMS

Composed expressly for the first issue of the College Music Society's magazine Symposium, *"The Rewaking"[1] was graciously presented by Mrs. Williams. After conveying the poet's best wishes, Mrs. Williams added, "I know he'd like to do more, but his health does not permit." In an early issue of* Symposium *the College Music Society acknowledged the gift of this poem: "We are grateful for Dr. Williams's thoughtfulness and generosity and we wish him and Mrs. Williams heartiest thanks and good wishes."[2]*

THE REWAKING

Sooner or later
we must come to the end
of striving

to reestablish
the image the image of
the rose

but not yet
you say extending the
time indefinitely

by
your love until a whole
spring

rekindle
the violet to the very
Ladies Slipper

and so by
your love the very sun
itself is revived

NOTES

[1]Written 10 April 1961. ©1961 by The College Music Society, Inc.
[2]*Symposium* (Fall 1961): 110.

Reflections on American Music

Part II

THE TWENTIETH CENTURY
AND THE NEW MILLENNIUM

For the past twenty-five years composer **John Luther Adams** has
made his home in the boreal forest outside Fairbanks, Alaska. An
associate professor of composition at the Oberlin Conservatory of
Music, Adams has taught at the University of Alaska and
Bennington College; currently he also serves as president of the
American Music Center. He has written music for orchestra,
percussion, chamber ensembles, electronics, radio, film, television,
and theater, and his works have been recorded on the New World,
New Albion, and Mode labels. Adams has received awards and
fellowships from Meet the Composer, the National Endowment for
the Arts, the Rockefeller Foundation, the Lila Wallace Arts
Partners Program, Opera America, and the Foundation for
Contemporary Performance Arts. He has served as composer-in-
residence with the Anchorage Symphony, the Fairbanks
Symphony, the Arctic Chamber Orchestra, Anchorage Opera, and
the Alaska Public Radio Network.

❦ From "Winter Music"
A Composer's Journal

JOHN LUTHER ADAMS

The article below is an excerpt taken from Winter Music, *an unpublished collection of
essays, journals, and other writings.*

Winter Solstice 1998
COLOR FIELDS
For much of the year, the world in which I live is a vast, white canvas.

In the deep stillness of the Solstice, I'm profoundly moved by the
exquisite colors of the sub-Arctic winter light on snow. Reading art critic John
Gage's essay "Color as Subject," I'm struck by a parallel between the view out
my window and Mark Rothko's use of white underpainting beneath the colors
in his paintings. Like Rothko's translucent fields, the colors on the snow
suggest to me broad diatonic washes suffused with gradually-changing
chromatic harmonies.

Slowly, faintly, I begin to hear it: music stripped to its most essential elements—harmony and timbre floating in space, suspended in what Morton Feldman called "Time Undisturbed."

Christmas 1998
MUSIC FASTING

A life in music is a spiritual practice. As in many disciplines, my own practice sometimes involves fasting. From time to time, there are periods in which I listen to no music at all. I feel this as a physical need.

During busy periods of performance and teaching, I hear a great deal of music. And just as I might feel the need to fast following a time of feasting on rich foods, after several months of intensive listening my ears tell me they need a rest from music. My hope is that fasting may help me to hear sounds I haven't heard before, and to hear familiar sounds with new ears.

In her life and work, Pauline Oliveros practices an extremely difficult discipline: "Always to listen."

I admire this very much. And though fasting from music might seem to be a retreat from listening, I experience it as a time for listening to silence. Most of us are inundated with music and other sounds, these days. I feel very fortunate to live in a place where silence endures as a pervasive, enveloping presence.

New Year 1999
ENDINGS AND BEGINNINGS

Happy New Ears! — John Cage

Beginning to sketch a large new orchestral piece, I'm intensively studying the paintings of Rothko and Pollock.

Like Cage in music, Pollock made a radical new beginning in the middle of the twentieth century. Both artists opened territories they could only begin to explore during their lives. The questions posed by their work will continue to occupy others for a long time to come.

By contrast, Rothko and Feldman were endings. They both explored intensely private, self-contained worlds. And what Brian O'Doherty said of the one could apply just as well to the other: "Rothko was the last Romantic. But the last of something is usually the first of something else."

Which makes me wonder: Is it somehow possible to live and work in that timeless intersection between endings and beginnings?

January 20
FORGETTING THE NOTES

For me, composing is not about finding the notes. It's about losing them.

Although I'm still involved in writing scores, the most difficult thing is not knowing what to write down. It's knowing what *not* to write down.

I hope to discover music which sounds and feels elemental and inevitable. Before beginning to write, I want to hear as much of the new piece as I can, as it begins to take shape in my mind's ear. This is a slow, sometimes difficult process, but I've learned to trust it—even to savor it. I spend a lot of time thinking, reading, looking at art, walking, listening, sketching, trying to understand the essence of the new piece.

After six weeks in this mode, I now have several pages of notes for the new piece. But I've yet to start writing out the score.

January 22
FORM, MATERIAL, AND PROCESS

Over the years, I've moved away from working with audible compositional processes—an inheritance of Minimalism—toward an increasing focus on the fundamental materials of music: Sound and Time. My work is less and less a process of performing operations on notes, imposing compositional processes on sounds, or working within a syntax of musical "ideas." I now concentrate primarily on asking questions about the essential nature of the music—what is wants from me, and what it wants to be.

January 23
BIRTHDAY

Today, I'm forty-six years old.

By this time in his life, Ives had lost his physical health and had virtually stopped composing. But Feldman had left the dry cleaning business and was moving into his more expansive "middle" period.

Pollock was gone. But Rothko was poised on the verge of his major breakthrough into his signature style. That happened in 1950, when he was forty-seven.

Among my gifts today: the new score is underway.

January 24
DISAPPEARING LINES
After this, the lines disappear completely — Brian O'Doherty
What is line in music? This is a question I've pondered for many years.

In Pollock's poured paintings, long, fluid lines are multiplied into layered fields of perpetually-moving stasis and perpetually-frozen motion.

Much of *In the White Silence* (last winter's major project) is composed of continuously rising and falling lines, layered and diffused into an all-over texture of frozen counterpoint. In that piece, it feels as though at last I may have discovered a sense of line that is my own.

Now, in the new piece, I'm trying to take a leap I've contemplated for years: to let go of line and figuration altogether.

But what will be left?

January 25
ALL-OVER SOUND
In the new piece, individual sounds are diffused in a continuous texture, always changing but always with a minimum of what the art critics call "incident." This won't be easy to sustain. James Tenney, Pauline Oliveros, and LaMonte Young have all found it. So has Glenn Branca in his recent music for orchestra. And Morton Feldman achieved it most fully in his late orchestral works, *Coptic Light* and *For Samuel Beckett.*

Listening to all-over textures, it's difficult to concentrate for long on a single sound. The music moves us beyond syntactical meaning, even beyond images, into the experience of listening within a larger, indivisible presence.

January 26
THE MORE IT STAYS THE SAME ...
Monet's haystacks and water lilies, Cézanne's Mont Ste-Victoire, Rothko's floating rectangles, Diebenkorn's *Ocean Park* landscapes.... In the twentieth century, painters discovered (or rediscovered) working in series. By freezing a particular motive, the artist is free to concentrate on deeper nuances in other dimensions of the work.

As Robert Hughes observes: "One sees how absolutely Cézanne despised repetition, and how working *en serie* was his strategy for avoiding it."

It occurs to me that the new piece is part of a series of extended orchestral works, with *In the White Silence* and *Clouds of Forgetting, Clouds of Unknowing.* Some of the sounds are similar, even identical to those earlier works. But this is very different music.

Even within itself, the new piece embraces a series of sorts. Identical formal structures recur from section to section. The temporal relationships between sounds remain the same. Only the sounds themselves change. Rather than moving on a journey through a musical landscape, the experience is more like sitting quietly in the same place as light and shadows slowly change.

The longer we stay in one place, the more we notice change.

January 27
TOWARD THE LIGHT

It's 45° F. below zero, and getting colder. But it doesn't matter how cold it is. We're moving toward the light.

A month after the Winter Solstice the days are still very short, but noticeably longer. (We gain another seven minutes each day.) The low arc of the sun over the mountains is slowing expanding in height and breadth.

I'm working steadily and savoring the stillness.

January 28
DEEPER SILENCE

The cold deepens. So does the silence.

Down the valley, Fairbanks is wrapped in a dense cloud of ice fog. Across the Tanana flats, the peaks of the central Alaska Range have disappeared. But out here in the hills, the day is golden. The sun is rimmed in a spectral halo of ice crystals.

The temperature on my afternoon walk is 40° below. The only sound not made by me is the brief whoosh of wings as a lone raven flies past, in a straight line to the South. On the hillside, I encounter a young moose browsing on brittle alder branches. I stop. Speaking softly to her, I bow from the waist and move on, giving her a wide berth. She has enough to contend with, just staying warm and fed.

They're predicting 50° below or colder, tonight.

Back in the studio, at the writing table, I'm startled by a bright, metallic ringing—like a small bell. I look up to see a boreal chickadee at the feeder outside my window. In such deep cold and silence, the smallest sounds speak with singular clarity.

IN A TREELESS PLACE

After all these years, I'm still deeply obsessed with landscape. But the resonance of my musical landscape now is more interior, a little less obviously connected with the external world.

In art and music, landscape is usually portrayed as an objective presence, a setting within which subjective human emotions are experienced and expressed. But can we find other ways of listening in which the landscape itself—rather than our feelings about it—becomes the subject? Better yet: can the listener and the landscape become one?

If in the past the more melodic elements of my music have somehow spoken of the subjective presence, the human figure in the landscape, in the new piece there's no one present ... only slowly changing light and color on a timeless white field.

I remember the Gwich'in name for a place in the Brooks Range: "In A Treeless Place, Only Snow."

January 29
SIMPLIFY

The cold hovers in place. The ice fog thickens over Fairbanks. The sun still rises only a few degrees above the horizon, and today it's veiled in frozen mist. The snow is bathed in a strange slate blue-grey light.

Toward the end of a long day in the studio, I realize that one of the eight layers in the new piece may be a little too busy and unnecessarily detailed. As always, the hard part is knowing what to leave out.

For years I've kept near the piano my variation on Thoreau's dictum, a reminder of how I try to work: "Believe. Concentrate. Simplify. Simplify. Simplify."

January 30
WRAPPED IN CLOUD

The deep winter weather has completely changed the acoustics of this place.

A couple of days before the heavy cold settled in, it snowed. Since then, the wind hasn't blown at all. So those two inches of fresh powder still rest undisturbed on the branches of the spruce and birch trees. The ice fog has now enveloped the hills.

Snow and cloud mute the earth and sky. There's almost no ambient noise. Fewer people and animals are stirring. The air is less reverberant than usual, but sounds travel farther. On my afternoon walk, the few sounds I hear are vividly present. A distant dog team sounds nearby. My mukluks growl angrily in the soft snow.

February 1
THIS IS WINTER
I've taken a couple of days to step back from the new work. The extended weather forecast predicts no change.

February 2
FROZEN FIRE
The high temperature at the house today was minus 50°. But the clouds have thinned and the sun was back, so I went out for my afternoon walk. Even wearing snow pants, polar mukluks, double mittens, insulated cap with earflaps, and heavy parka with the hood up and the ruff pulled forward, my toes and fingers got cold.

In this extreme weather, the air almost becomes a different element —like the vapors of dry ice, like liquid fire. I love it. It makes me feel alive. Down with Global Warming! Long live the cold and the dark!

BRUSHSTROKES
Back at work on the new piece, I concentrate on the organ, the string orchestra, and the string quartet. Moving at relative speeds of 2, 3 and 4, these are the slowest of eight tempo layers. Relentlessly diatonic throughout, they are the sonic ground of the piece.

After two days away from the score, the erasing I thought I might need to do doesn't seem necessary. What I have here is a new texture.

In *White Silence* all the instruments of a given tempo layer changed chords together. In the new piece, one white cloud slowly dissolves one into another, tone by tone. This makes an unbroken diatonic field from beginning to end, over seventy-five minutes. To hear the individual tones changing will require very close listening. I think of these as the brushstrokes—the little discontinuities that articulate and emphasize the larger continuity of the whole.

The chromatic clouds—the colors floating on the diatonic ground—are played by three choirs of muted brass and wind instruments, moving in three different tempi. All the instruments within each choir change tones together. But many of the written notes are too long to be played in one breath. So the

players are free to breathe individually, as they choose. Brushstrokes, again....
Those breaths will impart a certain richness to the texture.

February 3
EDGES

Writing about Rothko, Brian O'Doherty asks, rhetorically: "Why all this blurring of edges?"

I'm asking myself the same question about the new piece. It might well be called *Colors on a Diatonic Ground,* or *Light On Snow.* Both light and snow have soft edges. But despite my enduring obsession with sounding images, this isn't tone-painting. It's music. The sounds don't grow out of the form. The form of the music grows out of the sounds.

The sounds of *Strange and Sacred Noise* were so complex—machine-gun snare drums, roaring tam-tams, howling sirens, thundering bass drums and tom-toms—that they lent themselves to the decisive articulation of hard-edged, geometric forms.

But this new piece is in equal temperament. And tempered sounds are more definite and declarative than noise. So to evoke the atmosphere of continuity and expectancy that I'm after, these blurred edges and more diffuse textures seem right.

A good day in the studio. The thermometer holds steady at 55° below zero.

February 4
BREAKFAST IN BARROW

I've broken my fast.

This evening, I boarded a jet in Fairbanks at 45° below and flew North—across the Yukon River, the Brooks Range, and the Arctic Coastal Plain—to Barrow, where it's a balmy 33° below. (Although with the wind chill, it's more like 80° below!)

I'm here for Kivgiq, the Messenger Feast—three nights of traditional Iñupiaq drumming, singing, and dancing. Groups from all the Iñupiat villages in Alaska and four villages in Arctic Canada have come to Barrow for this midwinter festival of feasting, gift-giving, and celebration.

After twenty years of listening to this music, it still sounds wonderfully strange to me. Yet it's also strangely familiar. By now, I know a few songs—at least roughly. And the angular melodic contours, asymmetrical rhythms, powerful unison choruses, and deep, explosive drums have become integral parts of the soundscape of my life.

Once, passing through a crowded airport somewhere down south, amid the noise of rushing travelers, I thought I heard an Iñupiaq drumbeat. Instantly, I was transported home. The memory of the sound of those drums took me there.

ESKIMO HEARTBEAT

These sounds can take us on all kinds of journeys. The high impact, full-spectrum sound of the drums—reiterated all night long—has an inescapable effect on consciousness. In some ways, the effect is similar to rock 'n' roll. But the rhythms in Iñupiaq music are always at least a little surprising. And even when the phrases are relatively predictable, the basic rhythmic cells—2+3 or 2+2+3—are asymmetrical. To my ears, this Iñupiat "heartbeat" (as it's sometimes called) is both more sophisticated and more energizing than the steady 4/4 backbeat of rock. After hearing a hot dance group from the Arctic coast, even the best rock bands sound rhythmically square.

The dancing tonight goes until 1 a.m.

February 5
ARCTIC SUNRISE

Just before noon, out across the tundra, a dirty yellow disk barely nudges itself above the horizon. Its outline is vague. It gives off no warmth.

Fairbanks is at 64° north latitude. Barrow sits on the 71st parallel. The days up here are still considerably shorter than in Fairbanks. But within seven weeks—on the Spring Equinox—they'll be the same length. In Fairbanks, for the past few weeks we've been gaining seven minutes of light every day. Up here, the rate of change is twice as fast. Although it's still dark most of the time, Barrow is rapidly spinning toward the light.

EARTH, SKY, SINGING SNOW

Sunrise turns out to have been the brightest moment of the day. In mid-afternoon I walk the mile or so from the lodge to the new Iñupiat Cultural Center. A vague fog has drifted in from the Arctic Ocean bathing everything in an eerie, blue light.

The flatness of the light mirrors the flatness of terrain. The sky feels enormous, all-encompassing. In this blue haze, it's difficult to distinguish the distant horizon. Sky melds into Earth, in an enveloping sphere—the center of which is everywhere, the circumference of which is nowhere. (Isn't this the way someone described God?) Standing, walking, being in such a place, it's not difficult to feel the presence of the spirit world.

On my return walk my mukluk breaks the crusted snow, sending shards sliding across the surface. They sing like broken glass.

RITUAL SPACE

Again, the dancing goes until 1 a.m. During the final performance of the evening, a woman from the audience walks up to join the dancers from Kotzebue. She doesn't notice that a small plastic bag has caught her mukluk, and she drags the bag with her into the dance area. The audience finds this quite amusing, especially when she finally notices the bag, shakes it free, and continues dancing.

At that moment, one of the young drummers puts down his drum, moves quickly out onto the dance floor, scoops up the bag, and stuffs it into his pocket. He returns to the drum line, picks up his instrument, and continues drumming.

All this happens amid smiles and good spirits. But it leaves no doubt about the fact that this is ritual space.

February 6
NUVUK

The day dawns (at 11:something a.m.) clear and colder. My friend Doreen Simmonds—one of my Iñupiat collaborators on *Earth and the Great Weather*—takes me out to the end of the road, to Point Barrow, the northernmost point in Alaska. The Iñupiaq name for this place is *nuvuk:* "a point of land which juts into the ocean."

Although the wind is fairly light and the thermometer probably doesn't read much below minus 30°, the cold feels intense. We scan for polar bears, but it would be difficult to see them even if they are there.

The low sun floods the ice and snow with a rich pink light. The feeling of endless space is exhilarating. *This* is what I want to find in music!

We return to Doreen's house, which is filled with her extended family—from young children to her elderly stepmother, bedridden with cancer. The old woman doesn't speak much English. Doreen tells me she weighs less than one hundred pounds. But the elegant beauty and dignity of her features are breathtaking, and her presence is commanding. Doreen makes a pot of caribou soup, which we share quietly with her mom.

BOX DRUM DANCE

Kivgiq is not held every year. Traditionally, it occurs following a prosperous hunting season, when there is enough material wealth to allow for widespread gift-giving. At the heart of Kivgiq is Kalukak—the Box Drum Dance. This elaborate ceremony is grounded in the myth of the Eagle Mother, who gave the gift of music and dancing to the People.

Tonight is the final night of the festival, and the highpoint of the evening is the Box Drum Dance. Traditionally, each community on the Arctic coast performs a different variation of the dance. Three years ago, at the last Kivgiq, the Kalukak was performed by the dancers from the village of Wainwright. Tonight, it's performed by the Barrow dancers.

Before the dancers enter, two men bring out a tall extension ladder. One of them climbs the ladder and lowers a rope, which has already been hung in place. A third man brings out the box drum and ties it to the rope, where it hangs, swinging freely. The drum is made of plywood, about 1x1x3 feet in size. It's painted bright blue and yellow. The top is finished with jagged edges (representing mountain peaks) and adorned with a single eagle feather.

The drummers, singers, and dancers enter, chanting in unison to the steady click of sticks on the rims of the frame drums. The box drummer sits on a chair, facing the wooden drum, his back to the audience. He wears a headdress made from a loon's head and wing feathers. Several young male dancers take their places, sitting on the floor, facing him.

The twelve frame drummers (all men) sit in a single, long row. They are dressed in bright blue qaspaqs. Most of the women, in vibrant red, sit in three rows behind the drummers. But several younger women stand facing the box drummer, holding long wands tipped with feathers.

When everyone is in place, as the chant continues the frame drummers begin playing full force, until the box drummer cuts them off with a wildly irregular beat.

In silence, he begins an elaborate series of gestures. He bows forward from the waist, extending his right arm above his head, full length on the floor. The male dancers do the same, and the young women extend their feathered wands.

The singers begin a new chant, accompanied by clicks on the drum rims.

Slowly, the box drummer pulls his arm backward, holds it there, then brings it rapidly forward, stopping just short of striking the drum. He does this many times, with stylized gestures of great formality.

When he finally strikes the drum, in a sudden unison with the frame drums, the sound is stunning. Tears come to my eyes.

As the dance proceeds, the box drummer begins to swing the drum on its rope. As he swings left, the male dancers move to his right, like puppets on a string. He performs an elaborate series of movements with the drum, which the dancers mirror in reverse.

Several minutes into the dance, another dancer appears, also wearing a loon headdress. On each drumbeat he hops, two-footed, moving around the Box Drum. Gradually he closes the circle, moving closer and closer.

Suddenly, in a marvelously fluid movement on his backswing, the box drummer hands the heavy mallet to the dancer, who becomes the new drummer. All this happens without missing a beat.

THIS IS NOT ART

This drumming, chanting, and dancing is not Art. It encompasses what we usually call Art. But it's more than that. This is not "art for art's sake." It's not social or political commentary. And it's certainly not self-expression. It subsumes all those things into the larger fabric of life—the life of the individual, the life of the community, the life of the land, and the life of the animals and the spirits that inhabit this place.

This is what so many of us have lost in the twentieth century, and what we so desperately need and desire in our lives. This is authentic. This has meaning. This is ritual.

Although this is not my culture, I would rather be here tonight at the Messenger Feast in the Barrow High School gymnasium than in any symphony hall, opera house, or church I can imagine.

About 2 a.m. the festival ends with a processional of all the dance groups and a few songs sung and danced by virtually everyone in the space. The sound of a hundred Iñupiat drummers playing in unison is a sound I'll never forget.

February 7
OUT OF THE FOG

On the morning plane back to Fairbanks, reading the arts section of last Sunday's *New York Times*, I'm struck again by how remote and moribund the "classical" music world seems. Even the term and most of what it implies simply doesn't apply to the music of most of the interesting composers working today. Embraced by the academy, the *avant garde* is dead, too.

By about 1950 many composers in America had figured this out. But it's taken another fifty years for the full implications to sink in. And by now we can add Postmodernism (whatever *that* was supposed to be!) to the casualty list, as well.

What a relief for composers. We can simply get on with our work.

A dense fog covers the Arctic coastal plain. But as we reach the northern foothills, the stark peaks of the Brooks Range rise up, clear in the pink morning light.

February 8

Back to work in the studio, feeling energized and inspired from Barrow.

It's still cold, but the light on my afternoon walk is exquisite. 50° below, tonight.

February 9

Another productive and satisfying day in the studio, working until after midnight.

The new piece seems very strange and extreme to me. The textures are so lush and amorphous and relentless. But that's exactly what I had hoped to discover. And at this stage in the process, the music is leading me wherever it wants to go. I'm just doing my best to keep up.

February 10
DIFFERENT LIGHT

The cold is slowly dissipating. After two weeks of 40° below and colder, 20° below feels absolutely balmy. The air is softer, now. The light is more intense.

The music continues to unfold almost effortlessly. I find myself a bit overwhelmed, even intimidated by it. That's probably a very good sign.

At evening, the progressive shades of blue—slate, indigo, midnight—are breathtaking. The aurora borealis begins dancing. If only I could find the sounds of *those* colors....

February 12
COLOR AND SPACE

I'm studying Ellsworth Kelley. A couple of years ago, Cindy and I visited the Guggenheim retrospective of his work. The next day, we took in the Jasper Johns exhibition at the Museum of Modern Art (MOMA).

Both shows made strong impressions, but I was overwhelmed by the richly tactile surfaces and the sheer creative fecundity of Johns' work. Although the whole body of Kelley's work was impressive, I wasn't as immediately enamored of individual pieces. By now, though, it seems that my own aspirations in music have more in common with Kelley than with Johns.

The big Mondrian exhibit at MOMA several years back also engaged me. Seeing the paintings themselves gave me a completely different reading of Mondrian. In reproductions, his paintings appear hard-edged and hyper-geometrical (without the obvious "painterly touch" of, say, Barnett Newman's surfaces). But "in person," Mondrian's canvasses seemed so fragile, so awkward, so human. Still, I've still never been able to completely warm up to Mondrian.

With Kelley, the obvious differences between the reproduction and the actual painting are size and fidelity of color. Beyond that, what you see in one is pretty much what you see in the other. There's little of that tactile element that so appeals to me in art and in music. As John Coplans observes, Kelley is more sensory than sensual. Still, I find myself more taken with Kelley than Mondrian. Maybe it's simply that he's more modern, more "American," and more extreme.

Like Kelley's paintings, my new piece emphasizes only color, form and space. Reading Coplans' book on Kelley, these words leaped off the page at me: "Since color and the canvas shapes are one and the same ... color itself takes on spatial characteristics. 'Color' becomes both color and space."

I imagine that at some point I'll work with harder-edged forms and more uninflected sounds. *Strange and Sacred Noise* is extreme in its geometric formalism. But the sounds themselves are much too rich and complex to be equivalents to Kelley's hard, flat colors. My guess is that I may find those equivalents in large harmonic blocks of electronic sounds. Silence, too, is likely to be a structural element in such music.

But that's another world, very different from the one in which I'm currently immersed. While the new piece is rigorously formal, my hope is that it will sound organic, even formless.

February 14
REMEMBERING THE DANCE

This evening, we attended a performance by musicians and dancers from Bali. The gamelan was *Tirta Sari de Peliatan,* modeled on the older *Semar Pegulingan*—appropriately, for Valentine's day, the gamelan of the love god.

My trip to Barrow and tonight's performance have reminded me that I too often think of music only in terms of metaphor or image, forgetting the fundamental role of the body. Maybe my next project should be a dance piece.

The memory of the bright, shimmering sounds of the gamelan warms and brightens the dark, subzero night.

February 16
EQUIVALENTS

I'm fascinated with equivalents, shared resonances between different phenomena: between landscape and mind, culture and ecosystem, painting and music.

Color and form, surface and texture, field and gesture: the equivalents between these elements of music and painting continue to fascinate me.

February 17
HARMONY, IN PERSPECTIVE

One of the defining currents of twentieth-century painting was the movement away from the detached viewpoint of perspective and its illusions of receding depth, toward a new emphasis on color and surface.

In music there's been a parallel movement away from the sequential development of relationships between sounds, to a new emphasis on the inherent qualities of sounds heard in the present moment.

Now, at the end of the century, Schoenberg's "atonality" appears to have been a dead end. The far more radical change in Western music was the fundamental shift—beginning with Debussy and Stravinsky, and continuing on through Varèse, Cage, and Nancarrow—from the primacy of Pitch to the primacy of Sound and Time.

In this new context, Harmony becomes simply—in Cage's all-encompassing definition—"Sounds heard together."

February 18
OUT OF THE BOX

After all the innovations of the twentieth century, most Western music continues to exhibit a perplexing two-dimensionality of Time. The bar lines are little boxes containing precisely measured portions of time. Even when the rhythms within those boxes are relatively complex, they're still bouncing off the measured walls that contain them.

Stravinsky railed against the tyranny of the bar line. By rapidly juxtaposing boxes of different dimensions (measures of different meters), he created a new illusion of depth in a flat temporal plane—much as Picasso and Braque did with cubist painting.

Ives was a pioneer of more truly multi-dimensional space. Although still narrative in conception, his music begins to move beyond the theatrical space of Berlioz and Strauss, toward a more complete physical space in which events occur with an independence more like that in nature. Varése attempted to abandon narrative form entirely, to construct like an architect, in abstract geometries of sound.

It was Henry Cowell who first postulated a unified theory of temporal harmony (in *New Musical Resources*). But it wasn't until Conlon Nancarrow that complete and rigorous temporal depth entered Western music. As the twenty-first century begins, we're just beginning to explore the possibilities inherent in Nancarrow's work with simultaneous dimensions of tempo.

February 20
GETTING LOST

What a joy it is to listen with curiosity and fascination as this strange music unfolds, each new sonority emerging from the last. The experience of working on a piece of this scale is like taking a journey through large, open country. I hope the experience of hearing it will be even more absorbing.

I want this music to be a wilderness. And I want to get hopelessly lost in it.

February 21-March 4
MORE LIGHT

We're moving into late winter. It's still quite cold, but the light is back, and we continue to gain seven minutes each day. The arc of the sun is higher and wider. It no longer sets behind Ester Dome, but farther to the west and north, behind the ridges of Murphy Dome.

For several nights, in early evening, Venus and Jupiter were so close to one another they seemed to be dancing. A week later, they've drifted far apart.

Three days of soft snow falling, and dusty grey light are followed by several days of sparkling blue.

As I drive home from the Festival of Native Arts in the wee hours, the aurora is so beautiful I have to whoop out loud.

NEIGHBORS

The animals are more active. The squirrel at the studio has emerged again. The redpolls have joined the chickadees at the feeder. The ravens seem to be more extravagant in flight, and even more vocal than usual.

The boreal owl has been calling since late January. And tonight, I hear the great horned for the first time this year.

Walking through the woods one afternoon last week, I flushed a snowshoe hare—a sudden apparition of white on white.

I feel fortunate to have wild animals as my neighbors.

March 8
AUDIBLE COLORS

I'm back at work on the new orchestral piece, moving into the home stretch.

I want the sound to be lush and transparent at the same time. The danger is that all the colors will run together.

The physical space, the distance between the instrumental choirs, is an integral part of this music. But I also hope to find a full and purely musical space, in which each of the seven layers of time/harmony and timbre is distinctly audible.

The diatonic ("white") layers can be lush. But the chromatics need to be more transparent—like veils of color floating over the surface. As the manuscript nears completion, I'm thinning out the chromatic layers and re-spacing the harmonies as widely as possible.

March 13
IMMEASURABLE SPACE

> *Time has turned into Space and there will be no more Time*
> — Samuel Beckett

It's finished, this evening: *The Immeasurable Space of Tones.* Seventy-four minutes of continuous orchestral sound, it's the strangest thing yet to come out of my studio.

After six weeks thinking and sketching, actually writing the notes took only about the same amount of time. The piece really did seem to write itself. I'm exhilarated and exhausted.

Twelve years ago, after the premiere of *The Far Country of Sleep,* my friend Leif Thompson made a prophetic observation: "I especially like that middle section," he said. "You know—the part where nothing happens. That's what you *really* want to do, isn't it?"

I've been trying to find the courage to do this ever since. My fear has been that by leaving everything out of the music, there'd be nothing left. Now that I've finally taken the leap and left everything out, my hope is that the only thing left is—the music!

Working on *Immeasurable Space,* I was continually amazed at how much is happening in the music all the time. What at first I thought was static and empty turns out to be remarkably active, full, and constantly changing.

We travel into new territory and slowly we begin to locate ourselves, to understand where we are.

Born in Pennsylvania, composer/conductor/multi-instrumentalist **David Amram** grew up immersed in music and mastered several instruments and styles, including jazz improvisation on the French horn. After military service he settled in Manhattan where, during the 1950s and 1960s, he served as music director of Joseph Papp's Shakespeare Festival; during its 1966-1967 season he also served as the first composer-in-residence for the New York Philharmonic; in 1971 he was appointed conductor of the Young People's, Family, and Parks Concerts sponsored by the Brooklyn Academy of Music—a position he held for almost three decades. Among Amram's compositions are more than 100 orchestral, chamber, and choral works, two operas, and scores for such films as *Splendor in the Grass* and *The Manchurian Candidate*; his autobiography *Vibrations*, published in 1968, will be reprinted in the near future. In addition to acclaim for his performances in countries as distant and different from one another as Brazil, Cuba, Kenya, and Egypt, Amram has received four honorary doctorates; in 1995 the City of New York recognized him "as a pioneer of multicultural symphonic programming" for young people.

❦ Music at the Millennium
America, the World, and the New Generation

DAVID AMRAM

TODAY American music is world music. This is because we have recently rediscovered and continue to rediscover, at the end of the twentieth century and the beginning of the twenty-first, what Columbis discovered in 1492: that there are, and have been for thousands of years, people *here*, too, with their own cultures and forms of music-making; and that the earth is not flat, that all of us can expand our personal horizons and travel around the planet, only to end our travels by returning to our places of origin.

As another millennium begins musicians and music-lovers everywhere (I call them "the new generation," although not all of them are young) have begun to realize that all of us can journey through music to times and places where we can feel at home. In this new and exciting era all of us can be more in touch with one another through the magic of music. We are learning that all the musics of all the cultures around the world are unique but still connected with one another—that all of them honor the rhythm of the heartbeat and the ways of singing the song that is within each of our hearts.

Every serious instrumentalist, singer, dancer, conductor, composer, improviser, troubadour, and listener understands that he or she is a keeper of the flame.

When we speak of America's music, we speak of the musical traditions created by the native peoples of this continent thousands of years ago. An amazing amount of Native American music has survived and is still being played today by the descendents of those who created it. When we speak of America's music, we also speak of the musical traditions that all the waves of immigrants and enslaved peoples brought and are still bringing with them to these shores.

From ancient Hopi chants to Benjamin Franklin's string quartet, from African-American spirituals to Portuguese fishermen's songs (some of them are still sung in New England fishing villages today); from King Oliver's and Louis Armstrong's trumpet stylings to George Gershwin's tone poems; from Haitian love songs to Vietnamese chants—we have enough varieties of music in America to provide sounds, rhythms, textures, and styles for the *next* millennium.

I write all this as a partial answer to the question I and most of my brother and sister musicians are constantly asked: What's the future of music in America? I always answer as diplomatically as possible: to deal with that future, one must first understand the present and why it is the way it is. And in order to do that, one must check out the *past!*

Without an understanding of our collective histories, those that we share by virtue of living with each other on this continent, we will always remain victims of the nineteenth-century mind-set of the Austro-Hungarian Empire and its stifling court system. This often unconscious victimization was something many of us brought over on the boats with us. Those of us with musical families in the Old Country inherited the attitudes of a caste system in which our ancestors struggled to see who would become doormen, head waiters, busboys, or janitors. (In the summer of 1951 I supported myself as a busboy *and* a janitor but still felt joy in knowing I was a musician, even if I couldn't get a job being one.)

In the new millennium those of us, young and old, who strive for excellence in music know that we will always be servants. But we know we shall serve the higher power of *music* and the Divinity that the many forms of true music reflects. And, because we humble ourselves to the music, we are servants of a higher power and are never *servile*. We show the world that we love our work. Our job is our passion. It always has been and always will be.

Donald Francis Tovey, the great musicologist and theorist, wrote about "the lost art of improvisation." Fortunately the genius of today's jazz and world-music artists has rekindled the flame of that art. Recent masters have added a whole new vocabulary for musicians of every kind, through the brilliance of their spontaneity. Through recordings, we can enjoy the discipline and compositional skill of magnificent music created on the spot, music that has enriched the entire twentieth century and will surely stand the test of time. When we speak of the future of music in America, we speak in part of catching up—by the classical-music establishment, the recording industry, and academia—and of accepting and understanding and studying the genius of jazz, Native American, Latin American, Middle Eastern, Asian, African, and Indian vituoso improvisers whose recorded work documents their phenomenal gifts.

Each cultural group and each of its individual artists has special sophistication and beauty. The study, participation, and appreciation of their musics makes Mozart, Beethoven, Berlioz, and Brahms sound fresher than ever. And, like the European masters, all of these musician-oomposers have their own personalities and flavors.

I was reminded of this in March 2000 when I visited Spillville, Iowa, where Antonín Dvořák spent three months in the summer after he completed his *Symphony from the New World*. On the walls of a small museum in Spillville are photographs of the Native Americans Dvořák met and spent time with, individuals who inspired his String Quartet, Op. 96, and String Quintet, Op. 97; Dvořák wrote about this himself, in letters displayed in the museum. In these letters he also mentions the beauty of African-American music and how it could provide a whole new vocabulary for American composers; photographs of Henry Thacker Burleigh and Will Marion Cook, both of whom studied with Dvořák in New York City, document his enthusiasm in another way. Many years later Cook served as mentor to Duke Ellington when Ellington composed his *Black Brown and Beige Suite*, his first major extended composition that brought the worlds of jazz, both notated and improvised, into a symphonic context. (Rubin Goldmark, another Dvořák student, taught George Gershwin and Aaron Copland.) Finally, in his letters Dvořák describes his enduring love of his native Czech culture; photographs document the Czech musicians he collaborated with during his idyllic three months in America's heartland. The tiny Dvořák museum in Spillville is a mecca for American music.

Dvořák gave us a blueprint, a plan for filling the hearts of all musicians forever: he told America to open its mind, heart, and ears. More than a century after he returned to Prague, we are beginning to pay attention to what he observed and wrote about.

Our future should involve making Dvořák's message known to every child who studies music. Appreciating both the treasures of our European tradition and the beauty and depth of the other traditions that have, all too often, been excluded from similar appreciation—this is a dream that is becoming reality. Those of us who have spent our lives trying to further this dream rejoice in seeing it become reality.

In America and many other countries symphony composers, conductors, opera singers, and performers of jazz and Latin American, rock, and folk musics are begining to realize that we are all connected. Rather than allowing themselves to be put into a big business blender and turned into mass-produced and deliberately mediocre techno-pop-shlock controlled by people with no love or knowledge of music, new-generation musicians understand that all of us should rejoice in our own knowledge, that we should share that knowledge with others, and that we should create our own styles even as we respect and help preserve the styles and treasures of the past. And, most important, as we respect and support one another.

This is a tall order. But sincere musicians have always been masters at overcoming adversity. That is our collective history. Today we are becoming our own anthropologists, ambassadors, and administrators—not necessarily because we want to, but because we *have* to. A growing army of young musicians of all kinds are meeting this challenge. These new musicians will fill the gaps that the million-dollar music industry has left open. It is the new generation that realizes no one is better equipped to determine our own destinies than we ourselves, and especially those among us who share their passion for all enduring forms of music.

When in 1971, as a composer/conductor/multi-instrumentalist, I signed a three-year contract with a major recording label, I met the company's promotions director. I had travelled to Atlanta to give a concert; during my visit there he drove me a few miles out of the city to a gigantic cement-lined pit the size of a stone quarry. It was an emormous graveyard for LPs of all kinds; huge machines with front loaders were scooping the phonorecords out of the pit into tractor trailers, at a cost of five cents per record. Those LPs not scooped up for sale were to be dumped in a landfill.

"You sure don't want your music to end up here, Amram," the promotions director told me.

"I sure don't," I answered. "I want my music and my recordings to last."

Many musicians today share this feeling. They will no longer be involved in music they know is designed to pollute our environment—music that, by definition, is created to add more instant trash to landfills, only to be replaced by more instant trash. They know they can make their own CDs if necessary and, by means of the Internet and World Wide Web, share their vision with kindred spirits around the globe.

As a composer of symphonies, opera, concertos, chamber music, and choral works, I was fortunate in 1963 to begin a lifelong association with C. F. Peters Corporation. Today Peters is one of a handful of publishers that follows the long road of quality and innovation. Most publishers have been merged with corporations run by people who have never played an instrument, sung a song, or attended a concert. This by no means makes them bad people, but their misfortunate in missing out on the joys of music does not qualify them to work in an area they know nothing about. (I don't know any composer, conductor, or multi-instrumentalist who would accept a position as CEO of a company that manufactured atomic-powered submarines or space satellites.)

Since there are scarcely any publishers left who make lifetime commitments to composers, the new generation is publishing its music itself, using computer technology; today's young composers can and do follow their hearts. Through the World Wide Web all of us can communicate with one another. Doors are opening and walls coming down. A new day is no longer a comin'. It's already here!

The new generation understands that all of us have a responsibility to become music educators in any and every way we can. Even if we are not affiliated with schools, we can share what we know with musicians and non-musicians alike. We are beginning to realize that the sense of sharing and spreading joy is the essence of all music built to last. Our art makes us *in*clusive, not *ex*clusive.

Musicians remain among the last craftspeople on Earth. In America's music the old and new, the written-down and the spontaneous are equally parts of the whole. Bach and Charlie Parker, Beethoven and Thelonious Monk are all role models for perfection, discipline, purity of intent, and expressive freedom. Ours is a garden about to blossom in a way no previous generation could have possibly imagined. As my seventieth birthday approaches, I'm grateful to be here to see and hear the extraordinary developments made every day.

In the last few years I have, for the first time in my life, been called a pioneer. Since the late 1940s I have played jazz horn and composed concert music; in both roles I used and continue to use the many musics I've learned about during a lifetime of travel. As a conductor I have combined and presented many of these musics together in concert. Sometimes I've programmed Beethoven and Brahms with jazz. Or I've combined music with the spoken word, which I did with Jack Kerouac in 1957 and which I continue to do with young writers today. But I never thought about pioneering anything. I just followed my heart, and, if I had a chance to be part of something beautiful, I leaped at that chance—and still do. Now that my operas, symphonies, chamber works, choral works, ballets, and symphonic band works are being recorded and performed, I seem to have been "discovered" by a new generation of artists. I hope my work will inspire younger composers and musicians and help them hang in there and never give up.

Now that my own dreams have become reality, I hope to spend the rest of my life encouraging others to pursue their dreams, to follow the drum and song they feel in their own hearts, and to remember the Navajo Twelfth Night prayer and walk the Trail of Beauty. The poet Keats wrote a long time ago that "a thing of beauty is a joy forever"; Charlie Parker said, "Now's the time." In America and throughout the world, time is of the essence. For those with purity of intent the doors are open and the possibilities unlimited.

Born in Texas and raised in Oklahoma, **Elizabeth Aubrey** is today professor of music at the University of Iowa; before moving to that institution she served as music director of A Newe Jewell, an early-music ensemble that performed and held workshops throughout the eastern United States during the 1970s. Her publications and recordings include *The Music of the Troubadours* and *Songs of the Women Trouvères* as well as articles for the "new" *New Grove Dictionary of Music and Musicians* and *Die Musik in Geschichte und Gegenwart* and a CD of troubadour songs. Aubrey has been a member of the council of the American Musicological Society and has served as president of that organization's Midwest Chapter; she has also served on the board of directors of the International Machaut Society and on the editorial board of *Historical Performance Online*. Among her awards are fellowships from the American Council of Learned Societies and the National Endowment for the Humanities.

❦ Medievalism in American Musical Life

ELIZABETH AUBREY

O VER the short span of seven decades, the Western world has rediscovered the music of an entire millennium. This has been an adventure for scholars as well as performers, for professionals as well as amateurs. Oddly enough, the United States has played a central role in resurrecting music that was created hundreds of years earlier on another continent. American interest in other cultures is voracious, perhaps because our young society is still a blend of immigrants, including European. For the oldest American families— those whose ancestors emigrated from England, Spain, France, the Netherlands, Italy, and Germany as many as twelve generations ago—to peer back another thirty or forty generations to the families of the eleventh, twelfth, thirteenth, and fourteenth centuries and to study peoples who never dreamed of the existence of a world beyond their Atlantic shores, is to glimpse cultures whose "otherness" is as foreign to us as are those of India, sub-Saharan Africa, or the Pacific Rim is to us today.

The twentieth century's fascination with medieval culture has roots in the nineteenth century, when scholars began searching European libraries for old manuscripts and reading the thousands of texts they contained: poetry and long epic tales of heroism and chivalry, scientific and medical treatises, encyclopedic tracts on philosophy and religion, historical chronicles, liturgies—and music. But the explosion of popular interest in early European culture, outside the walls of academe, has puzzled scholars. Not that historians don't understand the fascination with the history, art, music, literature, science, philosophy, and religion of earlier times: we medievalists sacrificed seven or eight years of our lives to the pursuit of Ph.D.s simply because the subject matter charmed and attracted us. In the course of our academic careers we have found the details of such arcana as paleography, iconography, textual criticism, scholasticism, hermeneutics, epistemology, motets, monophony, and modality as riveting as the castles, cathedrals, knights, and bishops that first excited our interest in the Middle Ages. There is, indeed, something inherently intriguing about the medieval world.

When we were in graduate school, however, most of us medievalists discovered—to our discomfort—that when we chattered excitedly to our friends and family about what we were learning, they smiled politely (or giggled, as my old high-school friends did when I told them the title of my dissertation), and changed the subject.* Thus most of us retired to our ivory towers, where we can talk paleography and epistemology to our hearts' content in the company of other fanatics, having resigned ourselves to the inexplicable fact that, outside our relatively small circle, practically no one cares if we discover a palimpsest that reveals a missing link in the evolution of neumatic notations.

Nevertheless, something about the Middle Ages has piqued the interest of the larger public, and the allure has spread into many corners of American life. The curiosity of Americans for medieval Europe has always been more than merely intellectual. Readers turn again and again to J. R. R. Tolkien's *Lord of the Rings*, replete as it is with medieval motifs, or to the detective stories of the Welsh monk Brother Cadfael—not only because they are wonderful reads, but also because they pull us into a world that seems so

---

*[*A Study of the Origins, History, and Notation of the Troubadour Chansonnier Paris, Bibliothèque Nationale, f. fr. 22543.* – Eds.]

distant and exotic, yet somehow nostalgically familiar. The enduring appeal of organizations like the Society for Creative Anachronism and of role-playing games like Dungeons and Dragons owes more to our desires to reincarnate characters and relive events than to an impulse to study them. Hundreds of high-school "madrigal choirs" and dozens of summer medieval and Renaissance "faires" have drawn in not only passive audiences, but also increasing numbers of participants. And the early music industry in CDs is booming.

To the dismay of scholars, the "Middle Ages" generally evoke in the minds of most people images of a society that was primitive, violent, superstitious or, at the very least, unenlightened. A modern staging of, say, the morality play *Sponsus*, which dramatizes the biblical story of the Wise and Foolish Virgins, often strikes Americans as quaint and almost humorous—a modern entertainment made all the more amusing by the realization that, to medieval minds, it was an intensely serious business, a didactic exercise whose fundamental purpose was to exhort and, well, moralize. From every indication, these spectacles found receptive audiences in medieval Europe, but for entirely different reasons than they do today, eight hundred years later.

So why do audiences pay money (a morality play would have been free to any and all during the Middle Ages) to experience such productions today? Why would *The New York Times*, *The Chicago Tribune*, and—of all places—*The Wall Street Journal* review early music concerts? How on earth can we account for a CD of Gregorian chant, recorded twenty-five years ago in an obscure Spanish monastery, which soared to the top of the charts; or four women singing thirteenth-century Latin polyphony before sold-out houses across the United States?*

§

Revivals of early music took wing in the 1960s and 1970s; these were led in this country by the New York Pro Musica, in Europe by the Studio der Frühen Musik of Basel, and in England by the Early Music Consort of London. Since the 1970s dozens upon dozens of professional and amateur early music ensembles have come and gone; today, nearly every university and many colleges have a Collegium Musicum whose purpose is to study and perform the

---

*[The CD is *Chant*, recorded by the Benedictine Monks of Santo Domingo de Silos, Spain (EMD/Angel 55138). The women's ensemble is Anonymous Four, also celebrated for recordings such as *Voices of Light* (Sony 62006). – Eds.]

music of the Middle Ages, Renaissance, and Baroque eras; musicians earn advanced degrees in early music performance practices.

My own first encounter with early music occurred at Grinnell College. During my sophomore year (this was 1970), the Collegium Musicum was directed by Jeremy Montagu, the percussionist for Musica Reservata, a British group that had been making LPs for several years. Montagu invited me into his office one day and played a recording of Jantina Noorman singing "The Prisoner's Song," a medieval English lament. Noorman's approach to this and much other early music was to sing with a forceful chest-produced sound, often sharply nasal. I was horrified. I assured Mr. Montagu that if I sang like that my voice would be ruined inside of a year; to this he replied that Noorman had been singing that way and also doing Schubert and Debussy in the "normal" *bel canto* style, for twenty years. I don't know whether it was to placate this imposing man or because I was beguiled by the intense emotion and sheer power of Noorman's singing, but I learned and then sang that haunting medieval song during a college concert at the end of the semester, using much the same kind of vocal technique. I still have a tape of that performance, and the applause that surprised me at the time with its length and sincerity still astonishes me. I was hooked.

So hooked that, after completing a double major in music and history (having also discovered a passion for research), I decided to undertake graduate study in musicology, hoping to earn credentials that would pave the way to a career as an early music performer. As a graduate student at the University of Maryland I joined the Collegium Musicum, founded a student Baroque Ensemble, and did a three-year stint in the peripatetic world of professional consort gigging, as music director—and singer, recorder player, and harpist—for the Washington, D.C.-based group A Newe Jewell (now defunct). I learned that professional performance of early music had to be undertaken primarily for the sheer pleasure of it; although we received a few small grants along the way and charged reasonable admission prices at our Georgetown concerts, we cleared only a few thousand dollars every year, most of which was consumed by operating costs. Even today few performers can make a full-time living in early music, the strength of the demand for CDs and concerts notwithstanding.

A doctorate and acceptance into the more secure world of academe for which it would accredit me grew more attractive as a career option. But professional experience was a major plus on the academic job market, which, would be 1 + 3; however, the context shows that they have to be divided as follows: 3 + 1 (imperfection of the following, instead of the preceding *L*). Example (b) shows a similar case of seven *B* which, according to the context, must be grouped 3 + 3 + 1, instead of 1 + 3 + 3. In both cases, a *punctus divisionis* after the first *L* would have been sufficient fully to clarify the rhythm:[1]

(a) cf. *GdM* II, 29, staff 5; (b) cf. *GdM* II, 35, staff 8.

An interesting license of Machaut is illustrated by the following examples of *imperfectio ad partem:*

Such use of imperfection does not correspond to strict theory, according to which imperfection may be caused only by a note which belongs to a perfect mensuration or, in modern terms, which is one-third of the next higher value. In the above examples, however, the 'imperfecting' note is one-half of the next higher degree. As a matter of fact, an example like the above is extremely rare in the sources of mensural notation. *
It seems that Machaut alone was open-minded enough to transgress the theoretical limitations and to admit a freer, yet perfectly logical and simple use of imperfection.[2] Two examples from the ballade *De petit po* are quoted by Wolf in *GdM* I, 171 (without indication of the MS source):

[1] In these two examples our thirteenth century scheme of transcription (*B* = quarter-note) is used because the entire mass is evidently written in *brevis*-beat. This fact is one of the various features proving that Machaut's mass is one of his earliest works, possibly written under the immediate influence of the mass of Tournay (see G. Reese, *Music in the Middle Ages*, p. 356). There should be an end to the story, inaugurated by Kiesewetter one hundred years ago and still repeated in modern books, that Machaut's mass was written for the coronation of Charles V in 1364.

[2] Machaut was known among his contemporaries for his freedom in the treatment of established principles of notation, as we know from his contemporary Johannes de Muris (see *GdM* I, 170). It is interesting to recall in this connection Glarean's similar remark about Josquin de Près, two hundred years later (see p. 108, footnote 2).

A page from Willi Apel's *Notation of Polyphonic Music, 900-1600* **(1953)**
Americans of various backgrounds, including immigrants like Apel, helped teach generations of graduate students about Medieval music.

even in 1982, was tight. The position I won at the University of Iowa attracted more than seventy-five applicants; fortunately, a central component of the job was directing the Collegium Musicum, and my performing skills were a deciding factor in my hire.

The "early music movement" has always been a peculiar mix of the popular and the scholastic. The creation in 1934 of the American Musicological Society (AMS), whose stated purpose is to advance "research in the various fields of music as a branch of learning and scholarship," was followed just five years later by the formation of the American Recorder Society, whose mission is

> to promote the recorder and its music by developing resources and standards to help people of all ages and ability levels to play and study the recorder, presenting the instrument to new constituencies ... [and] enabling and supporting recorder playing as a shared social experience.

There are now comparable societies for lute players and viola da gamba players that cater to professionals and non-professionals alike. The New York Pro Musica, whose numerous recordings brought early music into American living rooms, entrusted the staid AMS with bestowing the annual Noah Greenberg Award in recognition of the Pro Musica's founder, as "a grant-in-aid to stimulate active cooperation between scholars and performers by recognizing and fostering outstanding contributions to historical performing practices." Early Music America (EMA), founded in 1985 as a "service organization for the field of historical performance in North America," offers scholarships to attendees at summer workshops in early music performance and publishes a glossy, advertisement-rich quarterly magazine with circulation in the thousands. The EMA also confers two important annual prizes: the Thomas Binkley Award, named for the director of the Studio der Frühen Musik (and later founding director of the Early Music Institute at Indiana University); and the Howard Mayer Brown Award that honors one of the most important musicologists of the century. The broad appeal of early music to scholars, performers, and afficionados of all stripes is evidenced by countless pages on the World Wide Web, including The Recorder Home Page, The Crumhorn Home Page, The Harpsichord Home Page, Hurdy-Gurdy: The WWW Page, The Lute Home Page, Renaissance Racketts, The Shawm Home Page, Early Flutes, and—arguably the most useful of all (not least because of its wide array of links to sites of the most extraordinary variety)—The Gregorian Chant Home Page.

While scholars and amateurs have been executing a delicate dance with each other, there has been outright tension between early music scholars and performers. Both mistrust the other's goals and methods, even as they acknowledge their dependence on each other. Performers need the editions musicologists produce, the historical contexts they provide for composers and their works, and their reconstructions of instruments and studies of performance techniques; musicologists need performers to realize and re-create the sounds of the music whose scores they study. While most musicians can claim some skill in doing research, often creating editions of their own, and many scholars maintain active performing careers, there remains a divide. Particularly telling has been the brouhaha over "historical authenticity," a phrase that loudly and proudly claimed legitimacy for live or recorded performances of early music until about the mid-1980s. This imprimatur came under sudden and wilting condemnation when some scholars and performers questioned the very concept of authenticity, but for quite different reasons: scholars complained that it was simply impossible to know enough about actual sound, performing techniques, audience expectations, and composer intentions to claim any authority for a modern interpretation; performers asserted that *any* performance has its own "authenticity" if it communicates effectively. In early music "authenticity" is now the "A" word.

But, to the extent that every modern performance is a "re-creation," fashioned from a skeleton whose flesh and raiment have long since disappeared into irrecoverable dust, now fleshed and decked out anew by performers with new ideas and approaches, there *is* something fundamentally "medieval" about it. Scholars and performers alike are increasingly coming to appreciate that there was a certain fluidity in medieval culture, and nowhere more so than in music. Much medieval music was probably created on the spot by adroit performers, whether during liturgical celebrations before the altar or at court before a local duke—and only later written down (if at all). Medieval musicians, whether trained in the church or not, learned by ear, sang by ear, taught by ear. They relied more on oral transmission than written tradition, and, as anyone who has played the party game of "telephone" knows, no utterance passes unchanged from one mouth to another. The changes that so naturally took place in the Middle Ages were not perceived as changes at all; every subsequent performance was an occasion for variation on a theme, deliberate or not. All this points to one of the most insidious modern infidelities to medieval music, one for which American ingenuity bears a lion's share of the blame: the ossification of performances in recordings. Even more than performances of intimate monophonic songs that take place in enormous concert halls with sound amplification, the crystallization of a single performance—or worse (and, sadly, the norm nowadays), an edited conflation of innumerable "takes"—into digital memory is contrary to the very essence of early music.

§

Is the desire to make the Middle Ages "ours" a manifestation of postmodern America, an eclecticism that borrows images and voices from ages past and present, from cultures near and distant, and recombines them into a new whole? If so, this merely defines it; it doesn't explain why it is happening.

The Middle Ages included, of course, the turn of the first millennium; one might wonder whether modern medievalism is some weird echo of an eschatological scrutiny of life's meaning or of questions about where society is headed in the twenty-first century. Evoking eerie analogies to today's world, the turn of the first millennium was marked by many changes in the political, social, and economic make-up of western Europe. The centuries before had been characterized by considerable instability in society and thought. Nation-states had not yet coalesced; some peoples were still moving *en masse* from one locale to another; there was no stable monetary or trade system; regionalization reigned in governance, religious beliefs and practices, linguistic dialect, and societal norms.

As the tenth century drew to a close, centralized political authorities and ecclesiastical institutions—personified by kings and popes—began bringing equilibrium to the turmoil. Institutions such as feudalism developed, stabilizing some of the social chaos that had made daily life precarious. The practices of the Christian Church, from public worship services to administrative organization, became increasingly standardized, and the influence and power of the Church spread throughout nearly all of Europe. The new millennium was poised on the brink of an extended period of relative peace and prosperity, and indeed these significant changes led to such a surge of intellectual and artistic creativity that scholars often refer to the period from about 1050 to 1300 as the "high" Middle Ages.

The variety, imagination, color, and abundance of the literary, musical, and artistic works that burst into that new world teach us more about the medieval mind and way of life than do the treatises, chronologies, and documents from which we learn dates, names, and places. There are ample signs in medieval music, for instance, that sacred and secular were not as sharply separated as they are in our world. The mix of the religious and the profane is rather alien to us, and yet not altogether beyond our ability to understand and even appreciate. We may harbor suspicions, perhaps unconsciously, that the barriers we have constructed between the affairs of church and state, between faith and reason, between private morality and public citizenship might be a bit contrived. What we glimpse during a performance of medieval morality plays or of motets that mix erotic words in one voice with phrases from liturgical plainchant in another is a representation of human beings whose values we may not altogether share, but whose common ancestry we cannot disown.

I am not a futurist, and I have no predictions to offer about the direction that early music will take in twenty-first-century America. But I have a wish list. First, I hope that the growing awareness of and appreciation for the music of other cultures will always include the music of Europe; we have not yet exhausted the riches that are there. I hope that scholars and professional musicians will find new ways to draw Americans of all kinds into the world of medieval music; it should not be a rarefied phenomenon accessible only to the elite few. And I hope that scholars and performers will continue to seek ways to cooperate and learn from each other; each has strengths, insights, and most important, love for the repertoire that manifests itself in complementary ways. And I fervently hope that the number of live performances by skilled musicians in early music will grow, offering audiences opportunities to hear and see performers re-create medieval music on the spot. The artificial separation of audience from entertainers that is inherent in the creation and playback of recorded music robs both musicians and listeners of the joy of the moment, undermines any possibility of experiencing the music as the sacred-secular-popular-learned-serious-frivolous necessity of life that it was in the Middle Ages, and threatens to create museum pieces in place of an art that was once full of passion.

Barbara Wesley Baker supervises the Chamber, Women's, Men's and Gospel Choirs at Eleanor Roosevelt High School in Greenbelt, Maryland, a suburb of Washington, D.C. A former teacher at the Hartt School of Music, Western Maryland College, and Duke University, Baker studied at the University of North Carolina, Greensboro, and Teachers College, Columbia University; she took her Ph.D. at the University of Maryland, where she was named an American Association of University Women Research Fellow. She has conducted master classes at the Toronto International Music Festival and the Choral Music Experience/British Choral Institute, Hertfordshire, England; and her Chamber Choir performed with Dave Brubeck at the 2000 MENC national convention in Washington, D.C. Her articles have appeared in scholarly journals and several textbooks. In 1998 Baker was honored both as one of Maryland's Distinguished Women in the Arts and as that state's Outstanding Secondary Vocal Music Teacher. She is past president of the Maryland chapter of the American Choral Directors Association.

❧ Blending Choirs
A New Paradigm for High School Choirs with Odd Numbers and Strange Schedules

BARBARA W. BAKER

C AN you imagine a gospel choir singing a madrigal in addition to a Kirk Franklin song? Or a chamber choir singing "doo-waps" *and* Monteverdi? What can result from these parings may be more than the combining of two styles. The results can produce new paradigms for thinking about repertoire, scheduling, and meeting the artistic and social needs of students. This article explores the practice of "blending" ensembles of differing sizes and types by joining forces musically in cooperative ventures. This may seem strange to some choir conductors; for students, however, the results can be most rewarding. "Blending" provides exposure to a richer array of repertoire for every singer and can develop deeper respect and appreciation for each choir's music and musicianship.

As a choir teacher for over twenty-five years, I have noticed marked changes in the choral programs in high schools. One emerging trend is block scheduling, which limits the number of class periods in the school day by doubling the class periods for single classes. Many successful choir programs will be threatened by this trend. For example, many large choral programs consist of a select group (a chamber, madrigal, and/or show choir), a single-sex group (a women's and/or men's choir), a beginning, non-auditioned choir (a mixed chorus or gospel ensemble), and perhaps a concert or symphonic choir. Smaller school programs may only have two choirs: one select, the other non. In both settings, students could sign up for more than one choir without having to take classes in the summer (or go without a lunch period).

With block scheduling, reduced numbers of periods during school days forces some teachers to teach choirs during double periods one semester, then either have no choir the next semester or start over again with new students. As teachers of elective classes grapple for the same talented students, more and more choirs will be unbalanced in numbers or forced to rehearse at strange times during the school day. This surging trend to embrace block scheduling among school administrators and school-based management teams may decimate choir memberships or eliminate some choir teachers altogether.

What impact does block scheduling have on choir numbers and makeup? How can "blending" turn this trend around? When choirs become unbalanced because of scheduling difficulties, their teachers have to become more creative in recruiting and keeping students. Teachers may be forced to use class time for "sectional rehearsals" and to invite members from other choirs to attend these rehearsals. When these choices are no longer possible, teachers (may be forced to) use lunch periods for rehearsals, to rely on before- and after-school rehearsals, or, as a last resort, hold evening rehearsals. All these choices to keep their choirs balanced.

In the choir program at Eleanor Roosevelt High School, I allow students who sign up for choir to eat lunch during my class period if they do not have scheduled lunch periods. Supportive gestures like this one can help everybody involved. Students need to eat, and I need them to sing. In any event, they always know their music.

More troubling is the insensitivity of select-groups members. In many schools, members of select choirs wear the best uniforms, get to go on tours, and generally receive the accolades. This causes some members of these groups to "look down" on members of other ensembles.

What implications does "blending" have for establishing healthy relationships between choirs? At Eleanor Roosevelt High School there are five separate choirs: the select Chamber, Women's and Men's Choirs, and the non-select Concert and Gospel Choirs. Each choir has its own uniform and repertoire. Each year, at our spring concert, the choirs are combined to perform one or more selections *en masse*. In addition to that performance, I make a conscious effort to "blend" various groups of singers with other groups during the year. This practice provides a wonderful opportunity to expose singers of different abilities to music that their own ensembles might not be able to perform. I often pair the Chamber Choir (my smallest and most select group) with the Gospel Choir (my largest and least select), and our Concert Choir, a non-auditioned group perennially low on men, with the auditioned Men's Choir. "Blending" these choirs establishes healthy relationships between ensemble members and de-emphasizes competition.

Music educators cannot be immune to social climates. Teachers have to seek ways to work and live together in a more genteel and civilized way. Teachers should deliberately nurture mutual respect and civility in every encounter with students and between student groups; they must teach not only artistry and musicianship, but also show students how to have more and more positive shared experiences. There are few easy solutions to this challenge, but "blending" choirs allows for more varied musical, social, and—sometimes—spiritual experiences.

Years after their own graduations, former students have returned to our school and told me of their excitement and glee at having sung "Chamber Choir songs." Often graduates have told me how they learned to appreciate the different musics sung by other choirs when they, too, had to learn it. For many students, experiences like these can be watershed events in their musical lives. A young Jewish student, for example, decided to join the Gospel Choir after singing with them. He simply loved the energy and the rhythm of the music. Everyone benefits from collaborative and affirming behavior.

"Blending" can also have a positive effect on repertoire selection. For one thing, it allows choir teachers to re-prioritize their music budgets. "Blending teachers" can use music in their libraries that seems too difficult or requires larger performing forces available in any single choir. Many high-school teachers may have wonderful scores in their collections for which they never have enough sufficiently skilled tenors or sopranos. "Blending" a men's choir with another ensemble may result in performing forces large enough to perform works with four-part male or even eight-part SATB passages.

"Blending" can facilitate performances of great works and achieve musically satisfying sounds for conductors as well as students. Everyone gains from collaboration.

Music teachers must work closely with administrators, school-board officials, and guidance departments to maintain viable music programs. At Eleanor Roosevelt High School, there are nine, forty-five-minute class periods a day. Even with so many periods, students and teachers have to work hard to keep scheduling conflicts at a minimum. If music teachers can persuade administrators to schedule music students and classes first, there will be fewer conflicts. Even with preferential scheduling I have encountered instances when students could not participate in band or choir because of schedule conflicts. During summers my colleagues and I periodically report to school to work out difficult student schedules. We try to persuade administrators and guidance counselors to do what is best for the students themselves. When all else fails, "blending" choirs may do the trick.

"Blending" choirs can help teachers develop successful strategies to combat scheduling difficulties, lack of appropriate repertoire, and inadequate performing forces as well as expand the musical palettes of all ensemble members. I would never advocate obliterating all distinctions between choirs; instead, what I am suggesting is that "blending" choirs can provide meaningful and varied choral experiences for all singers. "Blending" de-emphasizes competitiveness between choirs and emphasizes cooperative aspects among the choirs. As Charles Fowler states in his book, *Strong Arts, Strong Schools*:

> The arts provide many opportunities for learning to work collaboratively with others. Through ... music, they learn how to mesh their own efforts with others to ensure a quality result. The arts can teach students to work together with a disparate group of individuals, something they will need to know when they join the workforce.[1]

Fowler suggests that cooperative learning is desirable behavior in the workplace, and I believe it is desirable in the choir room as well. "Blending" choirs allows singers of different musical skills and backgrounds to cooperate in collaborative ventures.

Only time will tell whether more choir directors will choose to "blend" choirs. I have been gratified with the results of "blending" as I have watched my singers develop and grow. When Gospel Choir members continue to ask to sing with the Chamber Choir, and members of non-select choirs sign up to audition for more select ensembles, I conclude that "blending" has had a positive impact on my choral program. I hope (with "blending") that I am sowing musical seeds among members of future church, college, community, and professional choirs.

NOTE

[1]Charles Fowler, *Strong Arts, Strong Schools* (New York: Oxford University Press, 1996), 163.

Arnold Broido is president of Theodore Presser, a music-publishing firm, and currently serves as chairman of the boards of both Presser and Elkan-Vogel; he also serves as president of the International Federation of Serious Music Publishers and as director and treasurer of both ASCAP and the ASCAP Foundation. Broido studied piano at the Mannes and Juilliard Schools as well as at Ithaca College, where he earned his bachelor's degree in 1941. After a brief stint as a music teacher in Binghamton, New York, he saw duty during World War II with the United States Coast Guard; a postwar job as head of the stockroom at Boosey & Hawkes proved to be the first in a series of positions with such music-publishing firms as Century, Mercury Music, E. B. Marks, the Frank Music Corporation, and Boston Music. In 1990 Ithaca College awarded Broido an honorary doctoral degree in recognition of his activities on behalf of contemporary music and intellectual property; in 1998 the American Music Center presented him with their Letter of Distinction "for his significant contributions to the field of contemporary American music."

🍎 Music Publishing in America

ARNOLD BROIDO

ALTHOUGH music publishing has existed in America since the 1700s, it was industrialization and urbanization after the Civil War that set the stage for explosive growth in the twentieth century. The forces of change were transforming a rural farming society into the dynamic powerhouse of America in the early 1900s. Mass production made it possible to produce inexpensive instruments, especially the pianos that became part of the normal furnishings in many middle-class homes. An increase in leisure allowed for more study of music as society strove to emulate European culture. Newly built opera houses and concert halls provided places for entertainment outside the home. Minstrel shows, vaudeville, variety shows, and traveling bands all spread the latest songs throughout the country. Sheet-music counters in dry goods and department stores throughout towns and cities brought the popular songs of the day to the public.

The stage was set, the time was right, and in 1893 the first great American popular ballad, "After the Ball," sold one million copies in its first year. Amazingly, one in every twelve families bought a copy!

This was long before broadcasting and recording, although mechanical reproduction had begun with the availability of primitive phonographs, gramophones, pianolas, and other "automatic" instruments. To take part in music one either performed or listened, and printed copies of music were necessities. Music participation required effort. Now, at the end of the twentieth century, the sounds of music are omnipresent; it bombards us from broadcasts, recordings, computers, and countless other mechanical means. Little participation is called for.

The events of the past century that affected music publishing are more complex than I can cover in these brief comments, but highlights stand out clearly.

Intellectual Property

Although protection of intellectual property is rooted in the Constitution of the United States, the Copyright Act of 1789 did not cover music. The 1831 revision did, but foreign works were not protected until the Act of 1891, which allowed reciprocal publishing contracts with other countries and was the legal basis needed to make international publishing possible.

Performance Rights

The Copyright Act for 1891 established performance rights in the United States for the first time. The concept of paying for the right to perform was not new; France had set up an Authors Society (SACEM) to collect performance rights in 1851. The American music community saw the necessity of such joint action to protect its rights under the law and, in 1914, established the American Society of Authors, Composers and Publishers (ASCAP). Constant battles to convince users—and Congress—that performances were not free for the taking helped ASCAP grow into one of the most important performance rights societies in the world. Today it is a leader in developing ways to cope with changing technologies and patterns of music use. In 1940 radio broadcasters formed their own society, Broadcast Music, Inc. (BMI), as a competitor to ASCAP, which they felt had grown too powerful. It too has grown and matured, developing into a full-fledged performing rights society of great importance. SESAC, founded in 1931, is the third United States performing-rights society. It is smaller, but still large enough so that most music users today need licenses from all three societies.

In the United States, societies split income available for distribution evenly between authors (composers and lyricists) and their publishers. This does not always hold true in other countries, where the split is sometimes two-thirds to the authors and one-third to the publishers.

Mechanical Rights

In 1908 the United States Supreme Court ruled that there was no protection under the then-existing copyright laws for recordings. The 1909 revision plugged this hole by providing the copyright holder with the right to grant permission to make the first commercial recording, after which, by following certain rules, anyone could make and sell recordings of any work. The statutory rate of 2 cents a composition for each record manufactured remained in place from 1909 until the 1976 revision. The rate then began slowly to creep up to the current figure of 7.55 cents for up to five minutes, or 1.45 cents a minute, whichever is higher. This legal recognition of the right to make mechanical recordings provided an income source from mechanical royalties roughly equal today to the money collected for performance royalties. In the United States, the Harry Fox Agency (HFA), a wholly-owned subsidiary of the National Music Publishers Association (NMPA), today licenses, collects fees, and distributes the royalties to the rightsholders for most recordings made in the United States. The HFA also handles synchronization licenses (e.g., right to combine music with film or television tape) and is beginning to license new digital uses, such as the Internet and multi-media productions.

In the United States it is customary for mechanical royalties collected by a society or publisher to be split evenly between composer (and lyricist) and the publisher.

Copyright

The developments summarized above culminated in 1986 when the United States signed the Berne Convention a century after it came into force in most of the rest of the world. Most recently, the 1999 Sonny Bono Copyright Act extended the life of copyright to seventy years after the death of the author(s) and brought the United States into harmony with the other signatories at Berne.

The importance of these protections to authors (composers and lyricists) cannot be overstated. Without authors there is little to protect, and publishers, ideally, serve as middlemen between geniuses and the public. Publishers act as filters by selecting, producing, and promoting material that serve their particular markets. The success or failure of any publication is the measure of how well these choices are made and how well the works are exposed and promoted. The grant of rights to a society by a publisher is non-exclusive; the publisher is thereby able to license both performance and mechanicals directly to the purchaser. The grant of rights by a composer to a publisher is by contract and is controlled by the terms of that contract, which the author (composer and lyricist) is free to negotiate.

Popular-Song Publishing

At the turn of the last century popular songs were promoted and sold by vaudeville, minstrel shows, and other live performance venues that provided most of the available entertainment. The stage in rural communities acted as a promotion tool for publishers. An entire industry of "song pluggers" was spawned to convince producers, band leaders, and singers that particular songs had to be included in the latest acts. "After the Ball," that first "million-seller" mentioned earlier, was promoted in just this way: it was introduced at the 1893 Chicago World's Fair by the Sousa Band and within ten years had sold ten million copies. A network of sheet-music dealers spread across the country and provided material for teachers, students, professional musicians, and the general public. Although a somewhat diminished group of sheet-music dealers survives in 1999, print has been relegated to second or third place; today sheet music is marketed for most popular-music publishers by a few giant print distributors, while recordings carry the brunt of promotion and sales. (The Internet is the latest promotional used by publishers and record companies.) Statistics indicate that only one in ten recordings sells more than 1,000 copies and that "hit" CDs must make enough profit to maintain the entire enterprise!

"Tin Pan Alley" (as it was called), the home of many early pop publishers, was located on 28th Street between Broadway and Sixth Avenue in Manhattan. As the business center of the city moved uptown, publishers and song-writers took over the Brill Building at 1619 Broadway, which became during the 1930s and 1940s the unofficial center of popular-music publishing.

The Great Depression, two world wars, and the emergence of the United States as the dominant world leader all affected musical taste. The sentimental narrative ballads popular at the beginning of the century were replaced gradually by the pop standards of the 1930s and 1940s; during the same decades ragtime and blues metamorphosed into jazz. Broadway and theater music grew in prominence after World War II, but rock 'n' roll swept all before it, as the buying audience for pop records grew younger.

As early as the 1940s country music, growing out of hillbilly and western music, was laying the foundation for rock 'n' roll. Its roots were in Nashville, which was the home of publishing and recording country music. The fledgling BMI established a foothold in Nashville, which gave them dominance in the most important new post-war area of youth music. ASCAP and SESAC soon infiltrated Nashville, but it was years before they were able to challenge BMI's position in country and rock.

The introduction of sound to the movies in 1927 created an entirely new use for music and caused most of the Hollywood and Los Angeles pop publishers to set up branch offices to fill the insatiable demand for film music.

In the 1960s the Beatles opened a new path as they demonstrated that it was possible for a group to take on all the roles by themselves: they wrote their own songs, controlled their own promotions and business affairs, and administered their own rights. The old publishing model would never be quite the same.

The latter part of the century has been increasingly concerned with maximizing profits as changes in popular taste diversified, ranging from rock to hip-hop and rap with a hundred variations along the way. Older catalogs have been bought up, merged, or amalgamated, as copyrights increasingly have been perceived in terms of product or software. The change from an analog to a digital world has meant that music, converted to numbers, can travel freely and without loss of sound quality around the world and reach a global market. Today content is king, and companies with the largest number of copyrights hold dominant positions. At the end of the century, five multinational companies dominate publishing and recording worldwide. It is thought that their combined income from rights amounts to approximately 80% of all money collected worldwide. The thousands and thousands of other publishers divide up what is left.

Serious Music Publishing

Sometimes called "concert music," "classical music," or "art music," serious music is both the star and the orphan of music publishing. It represents the symphonies, operas, concertos, ballets, chamber works, solo works, etc.,

73

that comprise music's more intellectual and cultivated branch. In 1900 this branch was almost totally European in origin, and it was the European repertory that was taught and listened to in the United States. Most serious American composers and concert artists studied abroad at the great conservatories; there was little need in this country to publish concert music by American composers. A few European publishers established American offices, but the needs of the market were met mostly by agreements with American educational publishers to distribute European publications to American markets. Of course the standard repertory of Mozart, Bach, Beethoven, and Company was reprinted in endless editions by American educational publishers. These libraries of classics provided a constant market of public domain (and consequently, royalty-free) material.

By the 1930s some American composers had emerged who were not satisfied with borrowed culture. Their experiments led to the beginnings of an American school of composition—one generally energetic and cheerful and was often influenced by the entire American vocabulary of popular music and jazz. There were few publishers during the 1920s and 1930s to consider their works, so several small groups of composers founded their own cooperative publishing companies. These were doomed to failure; they were underfunded and depended on patrons to keep them going. Brave attempts were made by a few composers to publish and perform works for their own small circle of friends.

World War I broke down many established publishing patterns and seemed to provide the energy for a cultural explosion. Before 1914 it was still considered essential for musicians to prepare for careers by studying in Europe, and many of the best American composers thus became truly international in their approach. After 1918, however, a new confidence in their own time and place began to emerge. World War II provided the final separation from Europe and provided the infrastructure for publishing concert music in America.

Publishers of concert music solved the practical dilemma of a limited market by establishing two ways of working. Because printed music was absolutely necessary for the study and performance of solo and small chamber works, publishers became adept at finding ways of printing small editions cheaply and profitably. Orchestral music, opera, and larger chamber works presented a different problem. It simply wasn't practical to print even a small edition (say, 500 copies) of the score and parts for a work that might receive at most one or two performances, so rental libraries handled most of the symphonic and operatic sheet-music (some of it hand-copied) available. This had the added benefit of allowing publishers to track all legal performances of a work and to make certain fees were paid. This problem became more important as illegal photocopies began to be made and performances that made use of them paid neither rental nor performance fees to composers or publishers.

BMI was first in the 1960s to license orchestras and concert venues. ASCAP soon followed and, miraculously, a dependable income stream emerged for both writers and publishers of performed serious works.

Philanthropic foundations viewed these developments as opportunities to support American culture; they provided funds for new concert halls and arts centers as well as for programs that sent serious young composers into the public schools to work with teachers and students. The government, not to be outdone, established the National Endowment for the Arts (NEA), which awarded grants as seed money for many arts programs. All this ferment made possible the viable publication of concert music; at last there were a number of places where a serious composer could submit scores and possibly have them accepted and promoted. Both educational and popular publishers established serious music departments. European companies set up well-staffed American offices. All this provided a real mix of musical styles available to an ever larger number of symphony orchestras established in response to the availability of both venues and funds. Public-school music programs flourished throughout the country; together with colleges and conservatories, they turned out an astonishing number of skilled musicians to staff the orchestras and opera companies.

European music had gone through a liberating process led by Beethoven, Liszt, and Wagner in the nineteenth century and, later, by Arnold Schoenberg and his followers in the earth twentieth. After World War II *avant-garde* composers rushed to experiment with sound on both sides of the Atlantic Ocean. New technologies in the form of tape recorders, tone generators, synthesizers, sequencers, and other machines were increasingly looked upon as ways to release music from what were perceived as the last shackles of tonality and traditional forms. Scales, rhythms, timbre—were all explored as the "new" overwhelmed what was felt to be the "old" or tired music of the past.

For publishers this was a moment of truth: they had to decide what and whom to support without enthusiastic audiences giving them clues. The general public still flocked to "old" music, and carefully nurtured subscribers and supporters of the arts voted with their feet against the "new." Commissions were still available for new works, but, with rare exceptions, few newly commissioned works received second performances. Conductors continued to depend on what was known and familiar, and there were few slots available for new or experimental music as orchestras attempted to keep auditoriums filled. In recent years public-relations and marketing gimmicks have become increasingly prominent operating procedures on the part of many orchestras and opera companies.

Publishing has always been a form of gambling; in the past, however, public support provided guidance. For fifty years publishers have had to figure out what might be ephemera and what real music, although ahead of its time, needed to be captured and made available for the future.

Technology came to the rescue with a partial stopgap answer: computers, rather than engravers, could be used to set musical type. Paradoxically, this occured during the late 1980s, precisely when copying machine (the same machines that destroyed so many educational publishers when schools and churches began using them illegally) became so sophisticated that it was possible to print acceptable editions of one or two copies. Music that would never have been "printed" before began to appear in publishers' print catalogs. Using computers, composers began to typeset their own scores and extract parts; thus they were able with little difficulty to provide materials for rental libraries.

For some publishers all this came too late. The oil crisis of the early 1970s that led to cuts in arts budgets revealed cracks in the economic infrastructure. In public schools music education, the backbone of the system that provided musicians for expanded professional organizations, was often eliminated; instead, educators concentrated on reading, writing, and arithmetic. Local financial support for performing-arts organizations often became based on how much income they generated. Music for the sake of music was facing growing resistance. "Pops" concerts and star soloists performing hit "museum" pieces of the past may have increased the entertainment value of orchestras but did little to help publishers who had to depend on libraries of music still protected by copyright. As always, the smaller, weaker publishers succumbed. The amalgamation of serious publishing through corporate mergers followed (a trend that had already begun in pop publishing), and by the end of the twentieth century the number of important publishers of concert music have once again dwindled to a handful.

Educational Music Publishing

Waltzes, marches, schottisches, sentimental ballads, and art songs—these were the stuff that formed the backbone of home entertainment at the turn of the last century. Method books were needed to fill the needs of an army of piano, violin, and voice teachers who made their livings in every town and hamlet by providing the training they themselves had received when they were young. Publishers could be found in most Eastern and Midwestern cities, where they ground out enormous quantities of music by local composers to meet market demands. Music magazines blanketed the nation's teachers with advice and news of developments at home and abroad; they also contained pieces composed especially for them. At one time *Etude* magazine, with more than 200,000 subscribers, had the largest circulation of any magazine in the country. Libraries of classics, in editions bearing the names of well-known soloists and teachers, were turned out by the grander publishing houses; there was fierce competition over which of these libraries was the best and most authoritative. As time passed, however, tastes changed and entertainment grew more sophisticated. The result was the consolidation of publishing companies until, by World War I, the most important were concentrated in a few Eastern cities.

The decades between 1918 and 1939 completely changed entertainment. Radio and the movies created a different kind of society; no longer was home entertainment so important. Public-school music started to expand and to include band and orchestra training. Publishers concentrated on producing music for new school uses and flourished. The end of World War I saw the return to civilian life of military bandmasters who seized opportunities to teach music in the public schools. This wave of interest led to the great Midwestern band contests that, in turn, stimulated instrument and uniform manufacturers to churn out the necessary materials.

By the end of World War II music had been fully integrated into public-school curricula and, in fact, had become a required subject in many states. Music-educator organizations held conferences, clinics, and reading sessions partly to examine new publications and partly to show off the best products of the best school systems. Private teachers also flourished; although they taught voice and many different instruments, the piano remained paramount. For private teachers too there were organizations and contests and festivals.

The only area music publishing did not tackle was elementary-school music textbooks; these had become the province of book publishers. Nevertheless, educational publishing expanded again to meet the needs of schools and teachers. New companies were formed, and old companies had new vigor breathed into them. Consolidation again began in the industry, and companies still in the hands of their founders' descendants were looked on as prime targets for acquisition by bigger, stronger firms.

Traditional music engravers began to disappear in the 1950s; they were not replaced when they retired or died because there was no longer an apprentice system. Music typewriters made brief appearances, but their products were crude and difficult to read. The Music Publishers Association of the United States (MPA), which had served the education houses since 1895, established the Paul Revere Awards for Graphic Excellence; these set new standards for both music notation and print quality. Various technologies were employed to improve the appearance of printed pages, with much of the work being done in Japan, Korea, and Hungary. Only the development and improvement of computer programs for music typesetting finally brought standards back to reasonable and affordable levels.

Church Music Publishing

In 1900 America's evangelical Protestant churches were served by a scattering of family-owned businesses and a few denominational publishing houses. Company ownership often passed from father to son, even as new companies were formed to meet special needs, such as those of 1920s evangelists.

In 1925 the Church Music Publishers Association (CMPA) was formed to discuss and defend common interests. Because their problems were similar to those of the educational publishers, CMPA and MPA members have always cooperated with one another, at least to some extent.

The 1960s and 1970s saw tremendous expansion among CMPA firms, some of which established record labels as well as continued to print books, magazines, and other materials for the churches and religious services. During these decades many denominations set up their own music-publishing divisions, and many of these flourished as they sold their wares to what in effect were captive audiences.

During the last twenty years, however, corporate conglomerates have moved into the field of religious music, acquiring some of the strongest independent companies and shifting the center of Protestant music publishing to Nashville. Traditional Protestant congregations continued also to be served by many independent educational publishers, while a few specialist firms produced materials for Catholic priests and their parishes.

In recent years the contemporary Christian recording industry has shown significant growth, and contemporary worship services can be found in nearly every denomination. These shifts from traditional church music to "new" music have transformed church-music publishing because revenues from sales of printed materials have been replaced by revenues from licensing copyrights for print and projection. Christian Copyright Licensing International (CCLI) was formed in 1989 and today licenses the catalogs of most of the major church-music publishers to more than 100,000 American churches.

The Next Millennium

Who knows? At a time when technology continuously changes the industry and the only limitations seem to be those imposed by the laws of physics and human imagination, it would be presumptuous to try to guess what the future holds. On the other hand, music serves human needs and is not going to disappear. As repositories of protected copyrights, publishers will continue to generate income for composers and themselves. Recently the industry's confidence in this fact was demonstrated dramatically when one of the six major international publishers purchased another for a sum in excess of ten billion dollars.

The World Intellectual Property Organization (WIPO) oversees international copyrights. WIPO has made a strenuous effort to lead the way in international protection by adopting model laws for nations to follow. The United States too is leading the way: in 1999 it was one of the first nations to pass new laws to protect copyrights in the digital age. A tremendous struggle is taking place today between telecommunications and service providers on the one hand and rightsholders on the other. The telecoms propose free access to intellectual property in the name of profit, while the rightsholders fight for control and payment for the use of their copyrights.

The Internet has created the latest challenge. The general public, and not for the first time, must be convinced that protected intellectual property is not free for the taking, even though that taking seems to be easy. The freedom with which music and other intellectual material move around the globe is daunting. Some of the best technological minds are grappling with ways to end thefts of copyrighted musical material, but the thieves and their booty keep moving. As fast as solutions are found, computer hackers find new ways to steal and to make those ways of stealing available to all. Of course this struggle will continue. Piracy is not new.

We are living in the earliest days when national borders can be breached by invisible technological means. The world community has rigorously guarded and fought to protect its borders. Eliminating digital theft will require a level of international cross-border cooperation that has not yet made itself evident. These and other power struggles will influence music publishers and the composers they represent well into the new millennium.

SOURCES

Dictionary of Contemporary Music, ed. John Vinton. New York: Dutton, 1974.

Feist, Leonard. *An Introduction to Popular Music Publishing in America.* New York: National Music Publishers Association, 1980.

Harris, Charles K. *How to Write a Popular Song.* New York: Charles K. Harris, 1906.

One Hundred Years of Hope: Centennial Edition. Carol Stream, IL: Hope Publishing, 1992.

Roth, Ernst. *The Business of Music: Reflections of a Music Publisher.* New York: Oxford University Press, 1969.

Sanjek, Russell. *From Print to Plastic: Publishing and Promoting America's Popular Music (1900-1980).* [Institute for Studies in American Music Monographs, 20.] New York: Institute for Studies in American Music, 1983.

In 1999 **Scott Cantrell** became chief classical music critic of the *Dallas Morning News*. A graduate of Southern Methodist University, Cantrell took his master's degree at Rensselaer Polytechnic; he has also performed as an organist and choral conductor and taught as an adjunct at the State University of New York, Albany. Among his publications are articles and reviews for the *New York Times*, the *Encyclopaedia Britannica*, *Opera News*, *Gramophone*, *Symphony Magazine*, *High Fidelity*, and *Musical America*; he has also worked for newspapers in Albany and Rochester, New York, and Kansas City, Missouri; his program notes have appeared on Deutsche Grammophon, Bellaphon, and other labels and in program books of the Philadelphia and Baltimore Symphony Orchestras. A two-time recipient of the ASCAP-Deems Taylor Award for music journalism, Cantrell has served two terms as president of the Music Critics Association of North America.

❦ Classical Music Criticism
Crises and Hopes

SCOTT CANTRELL

FOR AT least a quarter of a century there's been much hand-wringing about the future—indeed, the present—of classical music criticism. With all kinds of trends working against the profession, the concerns seem to grow with each year. The classical music critic seems more and more like the California condor: once numerous, but now threatened with extinction; still capable of grand flights, but on closer inspection not a creature that inspires great love.

The concerns start with the given that only in single-digit percentages do Americans have any substantive connection with classical music. Classical music represents a whopping three percent of record sales, and that's only if you include things like the soundtrack to *Titanic*. These are not irrelevant figures to newspaper publishers, in a business increasingly driven by bottom lines and focus groups. We can only hope that the attractive demographics of the classical music audience can be a force in our favor.

We're further tarred by the perception of elitism. And in America at the turn of the twenty-first century the very word "elitist" has become as charged as "child molester." Ours is also a virulently anti-authoritarian age, which spells further peril for those who would hand down the aesthetic law. This came home to me when I observed some focus groups my own newspaper at the time, the *Kansas City Star*, was conducting on its arts and entertainment coverage.

The reaction was much more pronounced among men than among women—a bit of macho posture there—but there was real bristling at the idea that any critic, whether of movies or restaurants or classical music, could tell *them* what to do. Loudly proclaiming that they would make up their own minds, many of them insisted that they never read reviews of any kind. Some of this may have been merely a cranky Midwestern go-it-alone mindset, but I suspect similar responses are cropping up in newspaper focus groups all over the country. And this doesn't suggest a rosy future for critics.

The current fetish for focus groups is only one of a number of interrelated trends in the newspaper industry—and in our lives at large—that don't look good for serious criticism. In the first place, study after study tells us that Americans are working longer hours. And everywhere you look, you see competition for those fewer and fewer leisure hours growing, at geometrical rates. From the Internet to sport-utility vehicles, from gambling casinos to time-shares and virtual reality, the siren calls issue from more and more leisure alternatives.

And let's not fool ourselves: the so-called "classical music audience" is neither monolithic nor exclusive. The couple that goes to the opera tonight may be at a football game tomorrow and on the beach the day after. Classical music and its appurtenance, including music critics, are competing in an ever more competitive marketplace.

So are newspapers. And across the country, for several decades, newspaper readership has been steadily declining. (A recent uptick at a number of newspapers is unlikely to be more than a temporary aberration.) Facing this reality, one after another, newspapers have been folding and merging. In the last decade major daily newspapers have disappeared in Houston (our fourth largest city), Dallas, Milwaukee, Indianapolis, Baltimore, and Phoenix. All these cities have become one-paper towns, and with each paper's demise has gone a full-time classical music critic. There's also a death watch on papers in San Francisco and Detroit.

Beyond the demise of individual jobs, the disappearance of competing newspapers spells other unsettling consequences. Tim Page of the *Washington Post* observes that, by a huge statistical margin, a young person has a better chance of becoming a movie star than a full-time classical music critic.

One effect is that in all but a handful of American cities, there is now only one review of any concert—if that. Gone are the days of sometimes wildly different, even contentious, voices in local criticism. Each community is stuck with a single critic's prejudices. This also places new and unsettling pressures on the critics who are left. If people complain about their reviews, neither the critics nor their bosses can point to the availability of alternative viewpoints.

Now that newspapers increasingly are singular voices in their communities, they feel obliged to be less partisan than in the past, to be less handers-down of the law and more forums for a variety of viewpoints. The trend really got going with *USA Today*, with its pro-and-con editorials side by side. Under the circumstances, this is probably a healthy adjustment. But it has made newspapers more and more wary of taking strong and unpopular stands.

A concomitant of this trend—and of focus group hostility—is a growing wariness of opinion in other sections of the paper, outside the editorial page. All across America, editors have been cutting back on reviews, in both numbers and length. This just seems to be what you do if you're a newspaper editor at the turn of the twenty-first century.

An extreme manifestation of this trend has been in place for some time in Atlanta, where, with few exceptions, the *Journal-Constitution* will only review concerts that have repeat performances. A one-off performance by Andrea Bocelli or Itzhak Perlman will get reviewed, but not, say, the Emerson String Quartet. As august a paper as the *Washington Post* routinely prints tiny reviews that barely give room to name the performers and pieces, let alone attempt any substantive critical analysis.

Outside the newspaper field, the news magazines *Time* and *Newsweek* have eliminated their full-time classical music critic positions and all but the rarest notice of the field. *The New Yorker*, where Andrew Porter used to set a lofty standard of in-depth criticism, has found a fine successor in Alex Ross, but his columns rarely appear. And consider all the American record-review magazines that have disappeared in the last decade and a half: *High Fidelity*, *Musical America*, *Ovation*, *Classical*, and *Opus*.

In newspapers and general-interest magazines, part of the coverage cutback has to do with sheer competition for space. Newspapers were slow to catch up with the imporance—and I say that without any trace of irony—of popular culture. But now the classical music critic must compete for space with the pop music writer and the television writer and the video games writer.

Now that newspapers and magazines must appeal to generations raised on television, movies, and music videos—and now that newspapers battle television for both audiences and advertising dollars—there's a growing emphasis on sexy visuals. The quality of the photograph is more apt to determine the "play" given to a story than the quality of its writing.

The sooner classical musicians realize this and give some real thought to livelier photo presentations, the sooner they'll get better print presentation. Alas, apart from opera and the occasional young violinist who looks fetching in *décolletage*, classical musicians tend to be visually impaired. As an agent once lamented in a meeting with newspaper critics, "Do you know how hard it is to get a sexy picture of Richard Goode?" And what do you do with a symphony orchestra?

And, of course, editors will press critics to profile big-name stars at the expense of up-and-coming artists who may have much more to say. Never mind that neither Perlman nor Pavarotti is likely to have anything interesting to say at this point: they're going to get the big-spread coverage over the young composer of the new piece being premiered this weekend by the local orchestra. Happily, that's not always the case, and a good writer—with a trusting and supportive editor—can come up with a story on that young composer that will have readers hanging onto every word. That, in fact, is the challenge.

Part of the problem for newspaper music critics is an ongoing generational change in editors. The editors in my own earlier years tended to have at least some experience and interest in classical music. I'd run into them at concerts, and they'd often have perceptive responses to what they'd heard. But newer generations of editors—starting with those in my own early baby-boom age group—are far less likely to have this kind of connection. Whether it's the result of declining music education in public schools or merely of the rising force of popular culture, the implications for classical music coverage aren't good. Having acquired an ex-rock critic as his entertainment editor, the classical critic at a major American newspaper recently sputtered, "We're getting smarter, but our editors are getting dumber."

That said, editors do tend to be interested in trend stories. Even during a six-month reign of terror by a fine-arts-unfriendly editor, I managed to get a huge package on opera onto the cover of a Sunday arts section, on the premise that opera had become the cutting edge of theater. I think there will always be a market for stories that somehow humanize what's widely imagined to be a most esoteric field. And I think this can be done in ways that still convey substantive issues of artistic expression.

Whatever the ostensibly negative trends, to some extent classical music criticism will rise or fall on the strength of its practitioners. Alas, critics usually are hired by people with next to no inkling of who's musically authoritative and who isn't. Of course, there has never been any way of certifying critics, and even the premier practitioners would be hard pressed to agree on how certification should be accomplished. In practice, critics both superb and appalling have come from a wide variety of backgrounds.

There's an unsettling passage about critics in Gunther Schuller's superb book *The Compleat Conductor* (1997). Schuller spends most of the book detailing how careless, or willful, even the most famous conductors of the twentieth century have been with the basic facts of musical scores—careless with note values, dynamic markings, and tempos. It's a shocking exposé. "I fault especially the critics for this situation," Schuller writes:

> In over 50 years of reading musical criticism in daily papers I have seldom read a review that mentions specific conductorial misdemeanors: a wrong dynamic in such and such a passage, a wrong tempo, an unwanted or exaggerated accelerando, an orchestrational distortion or deviation—not offered, by the way, as a mere opinion ("the conductor took much boarder than usual tempos").... Reviews of concerts consist usually of generalities, representing one performance ideology or another, but rarely are there specifics. No wonder conductors feel they can do more or less anything they want with a composer's music.

It *is* a challenge to write about this most ineffable of the arts, and for readers—even the most devoted concertgoers—so little versed in even its basic vocabulary. Personally, though, I love the challenge of writing about the concert I've just heard in a way that a reader—a nonspecialist as well as a professional musician—may be able to imagine what it sounded like. I love the challenge of writing about both living and long dead composers in ways that may make their music come alive. I once wrote about the controversy over tempos in eighteenth-century minuets, complete with phone numbers readers could call to hear side-by-side comparisons of recordings. I was delighted when a number of non-musicians said they had found it fascinating. (Readers are more intelligent that editors sometimes acknowledge.) Of course, far more sophisticated *son et lumière* presentations are possible with the Internet.

Focus groups keep telling newspapers that they want news they can use—consumer information. In a day of so much competition for people's leisure time and money, I figure music critics should be right up there with Ralph Nader as consumer advocates. As Virgil Thomson observed, critics may not be good for much, but they're the only corrective we have to paid advertising.

Part of our job is to keep ahead of the audience: to sniff out the up-and-coming composers and performers, to recognize and identify trends, to keep up with musicological scholarship—and sometimes to issue warnings. With so much money going into marketing sometimes marginal musicians, the marketplace needs critics to separate the wheat from the chaff. With so many performances on automatic pilot, we need critics who can illuminate the difference between the responsible and the careless, between the so-so and the compelling.

Except in the long runs of movies and theater, there's little evidence that critics have major impacts on ticket sales. But—with all the caveats about our anti-authoritarian age—critics do have pulpits for crusades. Whether for improved standards from the local symphony orchestra or for a much-needed new concert hall, critics can foster a raising of expectations and, ultimately, of standards.

At a pace no one could have predicted, the Internet is transforming the ways we communicate, and web sites offer vast new venues for critical voices—including sound examples and interactive opportunities. Whether what we know as the newspaper—printed on paper—will be around much longer is anyone's guess. But, whatever the physical medium of the future, I'm not ready to close the door on classical music criticism. At the moment, in fact, I'm heartened by the considerable expansion of arts coverage in the *New York Times* after a period of retrenchment. A rash of recent appointments to major newspaper jobs suggests they'll be in good hands for the foreseeable future.

I have a little secret: I get a perverse pleasure from those nasty letters to the editor calling me everything but a child of god. They tell me that people take music—and me—seriously enough to get up on their hind legs. In a world of too many mindless, makeshift performances and too much passive hearing, that's a good thing. And—dare I say it?—I couldn't *buy* that kind of publicity.

Criticism is by nature an arrogant profession. But, if you think about it, so are composition and performance. And, as with composers and performers, if critics don't stir up people's emotions from time to time, we're not doing our job.

Raised in Tucson, **John S. Cotner** is a graduate student in music theory at the University of Wisconsin, Madison; he also teaches music courses at the Madison Area Technical College and since 1993 has served as an announcer for Wisconsin Public Radio. As a child Cotner toured the United States and Canada with the Tucson Boys Chorus; later he played rock and blues guitar with local groups and took his bachelor's and master's degrees at the University of Arizona. Cotner's research interests include musical semiotics, post-Romantic extended tonality, and popular music studies. He has presented papers at annual meetings of the Society for American Music, Music Theory Midwest, and the Society for Music Theory, and his analysis of Pink Floyd's early music is scheduled for publication by Garland in *SoundChasers: Interdisciplinary Writings on Progressive Rock.*

❦ Music Theory and Progressive Rock Style Analysis
On the Threshold of Art and Amplification

JOHN S. COTNER

I BELIEVE we are in the midst of a Golden Age in popular-music research.

Today, particularly in contemporary academic circles, a variety of specialists are exploring new ways to deconstruct and reengage the cultural and aesthetic meanings of musical works and performances.

One effect of the scholastic "cross-fertilization" between, say, music theory and philosophy, is that explanations of popular and rock styles are breaking free from conventional music-analytic methods. Especially during the last ten years or more, musicologists and theorists have begun rethinking the ideological foundations according to which we discuss intra- and extra-musical dimensions of rock performances and recordings.

Progressive rock is one area of research that is receiving special attention. This interest stems in part from the fact that many of our most productive and groundbreaking thinkers on the subject were young adults

88

during the 1960s and early 1970s, and experienced first-hand the social and political turmoil of the times. Scholars such as John Covach and Walter Everett heard the musical revolution as it exploded around them: Dylan's conversion to amplification; the Beatles' new aestheticism in *Sgt. Pepper's Lonely Hearts Club Band*; King Crimson's ingenious syntheses of art-influences with the immediate, visceral energy of rock; and Jimi Hendrix's revolutionary sonic metamorphoses. All this, I believe, is one reason why the Beatles, Jimi Hendrix, and other contemporaneous rock artists continue to command the attention of music theorists, historians, and philosophers. In other words, we rarely concern ourselves with styles of music—or most any form of art, for that matter—with which we have no personal investment. To put it another way: we are inclined to internalize and contemplate the form and content of those artistic phenomena with which we sense a certain emotional ownership—those associated with own life experiences, feelings, and memories.

Music, more perhaps than other artistic medium (apart from, say, film), causes us to sense within ourselves the continuous tension between mind and body, between intuition and intellect, between instantaneous sensory stimulation and delayed, thoughtful reflection. This is another reason progressive rock continues to receive so much attention: artists such as the Beatles, King Crimson, and Jimi Hendrix were explicitly preoccupied with the substance of this mind/body opposition. Of course, other 1960s styles, such as soul and country-western, also expressed psychological tensions. Yet through the interplay between vernacular (oral) and cultivated (written) musical strategies, progressive rock seemed to express the mind-body opposition with unique range and depth. Progressive rock, through a range of related aesthetic and ideological codes, went further than most marketed styles of the 1960s and early 1970s toward actualizing the oppositional tension between mind and body in musical terms.

§

Consider three American styles of progressive rock: those of Frank Zappa and The Mothers of Invention, of The Jimi Hendrix Experience, and of The Velvet Underground. Compare them to three styles of British origin: those of the Beatles, of Pink Floyd, and of King Crimson. Building upon the general claims set forth in the previous paragraphs, I propose

that the growth of 1960s and early 1970s progressive rock occurred
within a dynamic continuum of two dominant reactionary
ideological trends: formalism and eclecticism; and
that Andrew Chester's concepts of extensional and intensional musical
construction suggest a useful way of analyzing the musical
techniques and practices involved in this interplay of style codes.

The need for an alternative conception of progressive rock obtains from
the fact that the descriptors "progressive," "art," and "classic" have lost their
usefulness during thirty years of mystification concerning how adequately to
codify rock's aesthetic and cultural inconsistencies. At issue is the widespread
notion that progressive rock was primarily a British phenomenon. Paul
Stump and Edward Macan have made a persuasive case for this view, pointing
to a 1970s British post-psychedelic genre "characterized by high degrees of
instrumental and compositional complexity."[1] By their account, this was a
style different even from those of 1960s forerunners like Pink Floyd, the
Cream, and the Jimi Hendrix Experience. Indeed, the Beatles' *Sgt. Pepper's
Lonely Hearts Club Band* (1967)—acclaimed for its exploration of recording
production technologies, compositional mentality, conceptual completeness,
and countercultural references—remains to this day, for the vast majority of
scholars, critics, and musicians, the locus of an ideological and aesthetic
transformation in 1960s rock. Also at issue is the notion that, as Macan
suggests, there is no progressive rock without the continuous and overt
assimilation of "classical music" into 1960s rock; there is no "progress"
without the expression of countercultural ideologies.[2]

These definitional criteria are problematic for reasons English author
Richard Middleton addresses in some detail. Middleton explains that
progressive rock occurred "in the middle of complex situational change,
where the social formation and the musical culture are characterized precisely
by heterogeneity and seemingly transient affiliations."[3] Further, he challenges
the argument that this music is a unique artifact of the counterculture. Even
if, as one line of reasoning has it, "the development of rock in the 1960s was
determined mainly by intramusical factors—from a desire to explore the
technological and musical possibilities of the new conditions of production set
up in the rock 'n' roll moment," this still does not explain, for instance, "the
evident fact that the techniques, modes of expression and performers claimed
by the counterculture as their own were apparently appropriated by the
established music industry interests." Nor does it explain how "the music

spread into every social corner and function." In fact, as Middleton asks, "Is progressive rock, then, a single phenomenon at all?"[4]

Middleton provides a series of analytic readings of recorded musical works by the Beatles, Cream, Pink Floyd, and Procol Harem in order to demonstrate that progressive rock contains the following attributes:

"eclecticism," in terms of instrumentation, electronic treatment, and reference to diverse musical heritages;

"'art' influences," evinced in the Beatles' "Strawberry Fields" (with its "heterogeneous texture") and "ever-changing relationships of instruments"), or the "influence of older art music sources" in "A Whiter Shade of Pale" by Procol Harem, which utilizes harmonic sequential patterns associated with J. S. Bach's cantatas; or Pink Floyd's "avant-garde experiments" in recordings such as "Astronomy Domine;"

"technical exploration" found in Pink Floyd's and the Beatles' music during the mid-1960s, and perhaps the most accessible characteristic; and

"clear countercultural references."

I argue that progressive rock is both stylistically and historically contingent and cannot be defined through references to either cultural or aesthetic criteria alone. Instead, progressive rock incorporates both formal and eclectic elements. It consists of a combination of factors—some of them intramusical ("within"), others extramusical or social ("without").

Although a unidirectional English "progressive" style emerged during the late 1960s, I also propose that, by 1966, the tempo of artistic dialogue between rock musicians in Great Britain and United States had already dramatically accelerated; and that, by 1967, progressive rock had come to constitute a diversity of loosely associated style codes. For groups like the Beatles, the Beach Boys, the Byrds, Pink Floyd, and the Jimi Hendrix Experience, the notion of stylistic "blending" and "borrowing" had become, to a lesser or greater degree, an aesthetic convention.[5] This situation suggests that, within the stylistic continuum of mid-1960s and early 1970s progressive rock, American and British styles were already interpretable "from without" in terms of dominant cultural typologies, or dialects; and "from within" in terms of musico-aesthetic perspectives concerning the recorded musical work.[6]

Figure 1. The Style Continuum of Progressive Rock, ca. 1966-1973

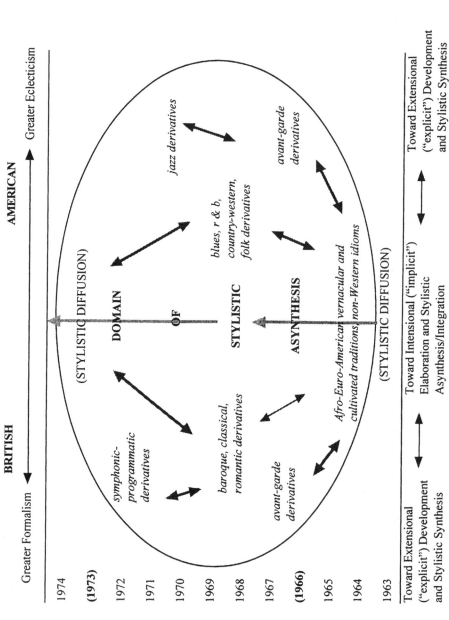

These ideas are expressed in Figure 1, which provides a working model of what I call the "style continuum of progressive rock." Along the top of the figure, I identify American and British dialects of principal post-World War II "popularized" styles; these can be distinguished from one another according to their geographical, national, ethnic, and social settings. Along the left-hand side of the figure, I identify the historical era in question: 1966-1973; this timeframe reflects my assumption that artistic experimentation was continuous across the domain of rock styles from roughly the mid-1960s to early 1970s.

Reading along the top of Figure 1, *formalism*—as I use the term here— refers to a preoccupation with established external compositional systems, structural unity, and the autonomy of individual art-works.[7] Regarding progressive rock, the central musical codes of this preoccupation are the following:

> syntactic and structural, such as the elaborately organized phrase grouping structures and resultant large-scale design of Genesis's "Supper's Ready" (1972);
> electronic adaptations of so-called "serious" music, such as Emerson, Lake, and Palmer's treatment of the fourth movement from Ginastera's First Piano Concerto in "Toccata";
> instrumental virtuosity, such as demonstrated by the guitarist Robert Fripp in works like "The Talking Drum" (1973); and
> combinations of these attributes.

Like formalism, *eclecticism* connotes a predilection toward style synthesis, or integration. Contrary to formalist tendencies, however, eclecticism foregrounds the discontinuities—the gaps—between historical and contemporary styles and electronic media. Sometimes these tendencies refer simultaneously to vastly different musical genres, idioms, and cultural codes within the same recorded sound-event. Examples include the Beatles' use of Eastern and rock idioms in "Within You Without You" from *Sgt. Pepper's Lonely Hearts Club Band* (1967) and Hendrix's sonic-timbral transformation of the "Star-Spangled Banner" at Woodstock (1969). Eclecticism of these kinds involves a technique similar in some respects to photomontage, in that the composite shapes of both songs result from the disjunction of symbolic associations between two or more dissociated musical media or systems.

How then do we measure the extent to which American and British progressive rock artists tended toward either formalism or eclecticism? At the bottom of Figure 1, I invoke Chester's discussion of *extensional* and *intensional* "modes of musical construction." Chester writes that extensional strategies "build diachronically and synchronically outward from basic musical atoms. The complex is created by combination of the simple, which remains discrete and unchanged in the complex unity."[8] Chester associates extensionality with the structural logic of Western art music ("classical music"), particularly baroque- and classical-period styles, compositional systems, and materials, and—more specifically—the sonata principle, contrapuntal devices like imitation, and rules of combination for motivic and sequential development, as well as genres such as theme-and-variations, rondo, the tone poem, fantasy, and the song cycle. Thus Chester draws upon a host of residual formalist value judgments deriving from traditional aesthetics. By contrast, intensionality is common to many non-Western musics, in which, Chester remarks,

> the basic musical units are not combined through space and time as simple elements into complex structures. The simple entity is that constituted by the parameters of melody, harmony and beat, while the complex is built up by modulation of the basic notes, and by inflection of the basic beat.[9]

Chester tells us that, for popular musical styles, complexity builds *inward to* minimal formulaic units; for "classical music," on the other hand, complexity builds *outward from* minimal motivic units. According to Allan Moore, extensionally-oriented musical strategies expand or develop by "accumulation," while intensional means increase or elaborate by "magnification."[10]

The shaded central region in Figure 1 indicates what I call the "domain of stylistic *asynthesis*." Neither predominantly formalist nor univocally eclectic, the aesthetic standard of this domain is signified by an impulse to create a composite sound that neither depletes nor neutralizes the diverse influences and preferred medium upon which it draws. In the domain of stylistic asynthesis the means of experimentation is primarily intensional rather than extensional, and it can best be located within the style of a specific individual (or band): the idiolect. The growth effect I describe is not synonymous with the notion of "development" or "progress" in any modernist sense, but originates in the creative impulse of performance and the improvisational moment. The musical and electronic media of stylistic

94

asynthesis struggle against, and periodically break through, the ideological and aesthetic power structures of mass culture.

The arrows in Figure 1, spreading outward from "1966," plot the increased degree of extensional elaboration across both American and British progressive-rock styles. The stylistic diffusion of the early- and mid-1960s reflected the multiplicity of rock styles deriving from African- and Euro-American vernacular and cultivated traditions; these included rural blues, r&b, jazz, beat, folk, and country sources and involved the influence of Muddy Waters, The Supremes, Miles Davis, the Beatles, Bob Dylan, Johnny Cash, and Elvis Presley, among others The influence of non-Western musical materials, such as East Indian modes and instrumentation, was essentially short-lived and primarily a source of novelty.[11] From this state of stylistic diffusion extended distinct and variably oppositional courses of style growth in the United States and the United Kingdom; these I call *avant-garde derivatives*.[12]

In the context of the growth of progressive rock styles during the 1960s and early 1970s, these derivatives involved the simultaneous influence of the visual arts, dada, chance music and minimalism, experimental electronic music, *musique concrète*, the compositional strategies and rules of the Western common-practice period (roughly 1600-1900), and the structural and improvisational codes of African-American jazz, r&b, and blues. Between 1967 and 1969 British groups like The Nice (proto-ELP), Procol Harem, and Genesis derived their own syntheses of Baroque and Classical compositional systems and genres. Around the same time in the United States groups like the Jimi Hendrix Experience, the Byrds, Jefferson Airplane, and Frank Zappa and The Mothers of Invention derived provocative syntheses of r&b, folk, and country-western styles. With these conditions in mind, the Beatles' *Revolver* (1966) and Frank Zappa's *Freak Out!* (1966) represent exemplary, although contrary, derivative subcodes of the 1960s "vanguard" in rock music.

At the outer boundaries of the style continuum in Figure 1, the differences between British and American progressive rock suggest sites of increased ideo-aesthetic tension. Edward Macan has shown that, by the late 1960s, a highly derivative "symphonic" or conceptual-programmatic style was established in the United Kingdom; the Moody Blues' *Days of Future Past* (1967) exemplifies this kind of formalist/extensional mannerism.[13] An eclectic/extensional counter-trend was established in the United States and is represented to this day by the specialized improvisational jazz-rock fusions of Miles Davis and Jimi Hendrix. Still, Billy Cobham's *Spectrum* (1972), with guitarist Tommy Bolin and keyboardist Jann Hammer, is an outstanding example of the kind of aesthetic standard of which I am thinking. I do not mean to suggest that symphonic- or jazz-rock fusions were exclusive either to America or Britain. On the contrary, these trends must be understood as distinct aesthetic forces that themselves interacted during the 1960s across a larger transcultural artistic milieu. On the other hand, the style-code of progressiveness that was 1960s jazz-rock provides evidence of what has been called "transracial fusion," which flourished largely in Great Britain and the United States. This kind of ideo-aesthetic tension calls to question the idea that an "authentic" genre of progressive rock can be established with certainty.

In order to explain the ideas proposed thus far, I shall turn to three case studies of American progressive rock, spanning the years 1966 through 1968.

"Hungry Freaks, Daddy" from *Freak Out!* (1966) by Frank Zappa and The Mothers of Invention

In *Freak Out!* Zappa presents his subversive, postmodern intellectualism in terms of musical parody.[14] "Hungry Freaks, Daddy," for example, alludes to the signature riff of the Rolling Stones's "(I Can't Get No) Satisfaction" by duplicating its rhythmic profile as well as the tone color of Keith Richard's electric guitar.[15] This having been said, meaningful expressive differences exist between the two riffs. In "Satisfaction" the riff departs from and returns to the dominant scale degree (B in E Major), which suggests that the two-measure figure is self-contained and closed. Further, the intervallic span of the riff is narrow, confined to a stepwise ascent through the minor third from fifth degree to flatted seventh. In "Hungry Freaks, Daddy" the opening octave leap encompasses the tonal-modal space of the song; the release of the octave from the unison is a rhetorical gesture, mocking the original riff by sharply accenting its rhythm. Moreover, the riff gains melodic-rhythmic emphasis through the change in intervallic motion into the syncopated weak eighth note on the fourth beat of measure 1. Finally, the harmonic openness of the progression from an A-Major tonic triad to the subdominant D-Major triad reinforces these intervallic processes of non-closure.

"(I Can't Get No) Satisfaction" originates in an intensional kind of musical creation: the song-form, rhythmic formulae, blues-based harmonic progression, riff structures, vocal nuances, and timbral-textural contrasts retain all the impurities and performative inconsistency that typify the Stones's preoccupation with authenticity. In "Hungry Freaks, Daddy," on the other hand, Zappa treats the riff from "Satisfaction" as if it were a composed motive subjected to continuous variation. Pitches, intervallic and rhythmic relations, tone color, and vocal and instrumental enunciations of the beat are exposed for their extensional potentialities; the original riff is transformed into a motivic template—a discrete, complex musical figure, open to compositional scrutiny and detached revision. Musical parody is built into the covert ideological distance Zappa and The Mothers of Invention place between themselves and their musical environment. In many ways *Freak Out!* foreshadows the crisis between extensional and intensional kinds of musical development so prevalent in early 1970s English progressive rock.

"Heroin" from *The Velvet Underground & Nico* (1967) by The Velvet Underground

Unlike the songs on *Freak Out!*, those on *The Velvet Underground & Nico* demonstrate attempts to develop musical materials through expressly intensional means. The sonic environment they create functions as a conduit for communal and individual expression within the context of Andy Warhol's fluxus-derived *Exploding Plastic Inevitable*; their role is organic to the total sensory—"intermedia"—experience. "Heroin" from *The Velvet Underground & Nico* exemplifies the aesthetic depth of the album as a whole.

Figure 2 illustrates how the song-form of "Heroin" grows through a series of textural build-ups and releases, gradually culminating in the horrific intensification from the end of verse 4 through the coda. Much of the song's aesthetic effectiveness is concentrated in the open-ended epistemological condition posed by the narrator, Lou Reed, and how this condition is evoked through the repetition of tonic and subdominant harmonies, versus textural progressions and recessions. Thus the ends of verses 1, 2, 3, and 5, correspond to iterations of the poetic hook "And I guess that I just don't know, and I guess that I just don't know."

As Figure 2 demonstrates, the large-scale design of "Heroin" emerges via an intuitive form of through-composition. Although the four-measure phrase groupings provide hypermetric and syntactic continuity, the structure of the song is generated through interactive processive formulae. Tempo, for example, is treated with a high degree of elasticity: in the introduction and coda ($\quarternote = 69$), with both sections markedly slower that the song-form proper. Verses 1, 2, and 3, on the other hand, begin "andante" ($\quarternote = 98$), and abruptly

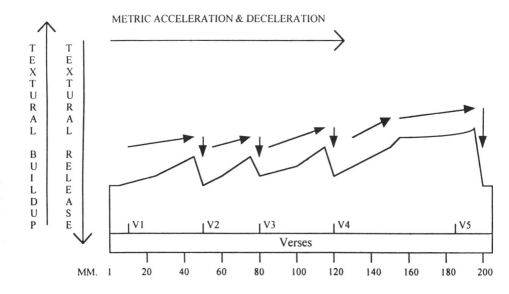

Figure 2. "Heroin" from *The Velvet Underground & Nico*

accelerate to "allegro" (♩ = 132); verse 4 begins at a moderate tempo (♩ = 108), then accelerates to ♩ = 132 and to ♩ = 144. This last, quickened tempo is maintained for the duration of John Cale's amplified, distorted viola solo, which itself exceeds the length of the previous individual verses. Finally, verse 5 is compressed temporally toward the song's climactic moment, at which point the instrumental texture is densest and closest to sonic rupture; at that point all layers of the musical fabric interact to create powerful forward momentum, and timbral, registral, and improvisational concerns supersede pitch and melody as primary parameters of intensional elaboration. Through these intensional means of material elaboration, the musical system in "Heroin" achieves its rhetorical and aesthetic alignments, fulfilling the fluxus effect of unity through the disunity of everyday experience.

"Voodoo Child (Slight Return)" from *Electric Ladyland* (1968) by The Jimi Hendrix Experience

Recorded during the spring and summer of 1968, the double album *Electric Ladyland* constitutes a compendium of Hendrix's stylistic mannerisms and innovations. The final song, "Voodoo Child (Slight Return)," crystallizes the rich history of his blues aesthetic and exemplifies the means by which he reshaped rural blues formulae in the context of the rock "power" trio. For the purpose of this essay, I shall focus on Hendrix's improvisational idiom in the two guitar solos.

One of the most powerful rhetorical and emotional effects of "Voodoo Child (Slight Return)" lies in our perception of continuity between the parallel guitar solos. By this I mean that the two improvised solos evince melodic trajectories of distinct, yet parallel, psychological impact. Hendrix, for example, initiates the second solo with a variant of the melodic-rhythmic formula that signals the beginning of the first; later, in the second solo, he imitates the over-arching ascent of the first but extends the latter solo to more than twice the length of the former.

In both solos Hendrix's obsession with surface-level rhythmic syncopation and phrase elisions are instances of what Rik Emmett considers a kind of "propulsion" unique to the guitarist's amplified idiom.[16] To put it another way, the rate of rhythmic transformation from beat to beat is maximal; the manner of timbral-articulative ornamentation extreme and capricious. Hendrix's irregular distribution of notes and rhythms, considered against the backdrop of his indomitable sonic metamorphosis, at times causes vivid syntactic destabilization at the musical surface-level.

Metaphorically, however, the second solo, like the first, suggests a defiant struggle to obtain the unattainable. The solo line, reaching upward, culminates with an even greater rise in pitch and polyrhythmic intensity. Simultaneously (and this takes place against the unrelenting metric-rhythmic consistency expressed by Redding's bass and Mitchell's drum kit), Hendrix's sonic-timbral-rhythmic tranformations seem to signify a provocative existential paradox: sonic "breakthrough"—evinced in Hendrix's rising, compelling, sustained high bends—never fully transcends the "will" of the metric substructure. Indeed, the conflict between background formal and syntactic continuity and foreground processive or improvisational discontinuity seems to suggest a semantic conflict between existential and spiritual motivations within Hendrix's mystical, escapist, psychedelic blues aesthetic. Furthermore, Hendrix's amplified improvisational idiom represents a radical and virtuosic synthesis of sound and noise; this intensional and extensional tension collapses Chester's view that style growth is achieved primarily through extensional modes of musical development. Considering these factors, I argue that Hendrix signifies the critical link between 1960s British and American progressive rock.

For these reasons I also argue that 1966, rather than 1967, marked the critical turning point in the emergence of progressive rock: the Beatles' *Revolver*, and Frank Zappa's *Freak Out!* were released for mass consumption within disparate listening audiences and dissociated subcultural contexts in 1966. In these albums "Tomorrow Never Knows" and "Return of the Son of Monster Magnet" introduced unconventional recording treatments and layered stylistic allusions into the idioms of mid-1960s rock. What's more, the *avant-garde* eclecticism of both albums not only foreshadows but necessarily counteracts the stylistic formalisms obtained by Yes in *Close to the Edge* (1972), King Crimson in *Larks' Tongues in Aspic* (1973), and Emerson, Lake, and Palmer in *Brain Salad Surgery* (1973).

King Crimson epitomizes the ideology of English progressive rock, also (and perhaps better) termed "art-rock." The group's tendency toward extensional development and greater formalism is clearly made manifest in numbers like "Larks' Tongues in Aspic" (1973), Parts One and Two, themselves related through motivic parallelism, techniques of sequential development, pre-composed phrase grouping structures, functional harmonic progressions, extended tertian sonorities, and treatments of dissonance uncommon to most other styles of rock. In large part King Crimson's aesthetic standard subverts technological experimentation and appropriates the mentality of intellectual rigor generally associated with Classical, Romantic, and neo-Classical Western art traditions.

The style continuum illustrated in Figure 1 demonstrates just one possible way of establishing a historical connection between 1960s and early 1970s progressive rock. In my own work the assumptions and premises surrounding this frame of reference are in continuous refinement, although my goal remains to address the ideological and aesthetic inconsistencies of progressive rock as a historically-contingent phenomenon, one of lasting appeal to contemporary musicians interested in the myriad ways that rock, as a vernacular formation, can conflict and meld with cultivated musical traditions.

§

At the turn of the twenty-first century the question remains: how can my research, and that of others, impact our understanding of rock music as an aesthetic and cultural phenomenon?

A momentary digression, followed by some provisional answers. Ultimately the so-called "progress" of 1960s British rock may be tied not only to the explicit preoccupation of groups such as Genesis and King Crimson with extensional "modes of musical construction," but also to an ideology allied with a modernist emphasis on structure rather than process, all-encompassing theories, and the autonomy of the work of art. By contrast, the so-called "progress" of American artists such as Jimi Hendrix and The Velvet Underground seemed to run counter to formalism: that is, the manner of stylistic eclecticism was less synthetic and unidirectional, the means of musical variation and elaboration predominantly intensional, foregrounding explorations of sound, noise, gesture, rather than genre and structure.

Further, due to the fact that artistic dialogue between British and American rock bands was rapidly increasing during the 1960s, the "asynthetic" dimension of progressive rock, specifically between 1966 and 1973, evinced tremendous tension between intensional and extensional kinds of musical organization. In this regard Jimi Hendrix and Frank Zappa carry a great deal of the weight of aesthetic advancement. Among their British counterparts, the Beatles and King Crimson assert a parallel "anxiety of influence" on the psyches of latter twentieth-century post-progressive artists. Indeed, many musicians and songwriters continue to mimic the compositional strategies and performance idioms of these and other 1960s rock artists. Yet their respective aesthetic impact has not been diminished, in part because their political stance with respect to society cannot be depleted.

What, then, is the state of music-theoretical research into rock and popular music at the turn of the twenty-first-century? To return to a point I made earlier, contemporary music theorists, historians, and philosophers, among others, are developing comprehensive critical-analytic approaches to musical works of art. Gino Stefani is one of the scholars helping us understand the value of music criticism that takes into account listener competence and the covert operations of our interpretive ideologies:

A competence measured upon the whole of society and its sound production is an adequate frame to describe production of musical practices, the contribution of the artists, particular competencies of musicologists, functions of institutions, et cetera. Such a description, moreover, might enable us to explain why and in what sense a certain practice or experience can be 'music' for some people and not for others. Finally, a model of general musical competence within a culture allows us to elaborate more clearly and firmly the aim of musical education—that is, the promotion of a certain competence.[17]

Susan Fast has demonstrated this very point: that our goal is not to "reify style" based on taste values and academic biases, but to increase our understanding—our competence—through meaningful comparison and analysis of musics representative of the "whole of society," overflowing with significance.[18]

Not too long ago I realized that all forms of music are worth our analytic and critical reflection. All of them reveal something about human behavior and the human condition, about our personal and public histories, belief systems, institutions, shared thoughts, and shared emotions. Musical artworks, be they scores or recorded performances, reveal something about the multifarious ways we perceive ourselves in relation to our environments, other individuals, and communities.

As a matter of critical reflection, I must also argue that progressive rock no longer exists as a viable socio-political movement within contemporary industrial societies of the West, because rock music in general no longer functions as a site of cultural and political foment in a way comparable to its function during the 1960s and early 1970s. At that time, the socio-economic environment in Britain and the United States functioned as a conduit for the subcultural revolution out of which progressive rock arose. The "progressive" style itself had a refractory political dimension: it not only "stood for" liberal ideologies and lifestyles, but implicated, in its rarified British and American dialects, a naïve utopian optimism and narcissistic cynicism unique to the times.

The goal of my work, however, is not to theorize how or why one musical style is or is not more valuable than another, or why one form of music is more worthy than another of critical analysis. This line of reasoning overlooks an invaluable opportunity: if we pay attention to the codes that correlate expression and content in musical works and performances of different cultural heritages, we shall be better able to uncover the social practices implicit in the musical techniques themselves. Subsequently, we shall come closer to understanding the expressive range of musical languages and the advantages and limitations of music theory-building itself, as well as our own roles in constructing and deconstructing value systems within private and public communities (not to mention institutions of higher learning).

As we enter the new millennium, we may be able to seize the opportunity I am describing. One way we can realize this opportunity is to engage musical artworks as both aesthetic and cultural entities, as markers of the human condition, and as artifacts and experiences that manifest properties of autonomy and structure, of feeling and motion, of intuition and intellect—and, as such, are worthy of critical reflection.[19]

It is possible, then, that 1960s and early 1970s progressive rock still calls for exploration and understanding in part because the aesthetic tension between formalism and eclecticism is so strongly evinced in the kinds of musical techniques employed by the artists (and others like them) discussed in the previous pages. What's more, this tension seems to signify a provocative process of socio-economic continuity and contradiction across British and American cultures of that time. As I demonstrate, 1960s progressive rock artists explored the conceptual oppositions between mind and body, matter and form, sound and noise, in unique ways, thereby crossing the threshold between art and amplification in ways that continue to influence musicians today.[20]

NOTES

[1]Paul Stump, *The Music's All That Matters: A History of Progressive Rock* (London: Quartet Book, 1997), 9.

[2]Edward Macan, *Rocking the Classics: English Progressive Rock and the Counterculture* (New York: Oxford University Press, 1997), 12-13. Macan's book is a comprehensive and well-conceived socio-musicological exegesis on English progressive rock.

[3]Richard Middleton, *Studying Popular Music* (Buckingham: Open University Press, 1990), 27. Originally stated as a question.

[4]Middleton, *Studying Popular Music*, 27-28.

[5]Simon Frith explains the market conditions that contributed to the establishment of a prosperous artistic dialogue between American and British record producers and rock musicians by 1968. I assert that the aesthetic codes of late 1960s and early 1970s English progressive rock were already activated by 1966; see Frith, *Sound Effects: Youth, Leisure, and the Politics of Rock 'n' Roll* (New York: Pantheon Books, 1981), 96-100.

[6]In *Style and Music: Theory, History, and Ideology* (Philadelphia: University of Pennsylvania Press, 1989), Leonard Meyer writes:

> Dialects are substyles that are differentiated because a number of composers— usually, but not necessarily, contemporaries and geographical neighbors—employ (choose) the same or similar rules and strategies.... Or a dialect may be defined by social class or cultural factor: folk music versus art music, military music versus dance music. But most often dialects are distinguished historically. (23)

While Middleton and Meyer generally agree that *dialects* classify artists according to geographical, national, and historical associations, the lower levels of code such as *genres* and *sub-codes* are marked by increasingly music-specific criteria for grouping. In the case of progressive rock, stylistic heterogeneity tends to ambiguate the criteria for classification as we move closer to the style of an individual or band (idiolect) and piece-specific analysis (idiostructure or intraopus style). For a clear delineation between the general and specific historical and cultural markers of popular musical styles, see Middleton's "levels of code" for syntactic and semantic analysis in *Studying Popular Music* (Buckingham: Open University Press, 1990), 172-174. These levels of code influence my view of progressive rock, yet the basis of his approach is more completely formulated by Gino Stefani in "A Theory of Musical Competence," *Semiotica* 66 (1987): 7-22.

Part of the problem with the idea of genre as it is applied to styles of 1960s and early 1970s progressive rock is that the verbal categories used to describe the new radical expressions of rock were themselves in transformation. One of the prominent markers of a progressive movement in 1960s rock was the trend toward movement-length conceptual works, and a conscious attempt to overcome the artistic limitations of the two- to three-minute radio-ready single. Thus I argue for a more functional concept of genre as it pertains to a broader rock aesthetic; an aesthetic that is nonetheless attached to a larger industry of "popularized" musics. Such a conception is signified on three fundamental levels: by the relation between single and album formats (and, within these, at the level of the subgenre or subcode); by a necessary distinction between live and studio venue (and, within these, at the level of the opus as "sound-event"); and by musical and recording techniques. The concept of style, then, seems to reside closer to the behavior of the performing artist/composer or band—the level of the idiolect. Thus style change is dynamic and continuous and resistant to categorical reductionism. The "style continuum" I develop in this essay constitutes one way of addressing these factors in a historical context. Bruce Baugh's notion of causal constructivity relates in interesting ways to the third point—viz., that of musical and recording techniques—as do John Andrew Fischer's views about the ontological quality of rock recordings (although I question the latter's thesis about rock musical style analysis). See Baugh, "Prolegomena to Any Aesthetics of Rock Music," *Journal of Aesthetics and Art Criticism* 51/1 (Winter 1993): 23-29; and Fischer, "Rock 'n' Recording: The Ontological Complexity of Rock Music," *Musical Worlds: New Directions in the Philosophy of Music*, ed. Philip Alperson (University Park: Pennsylvaina State University Press, 1998): 109-123.

[7]Modern formalism has a complex history that cannot be given adequate attention in this essay. For a brief though concise explanation, see Carl Dahlhaus, "The Quarrel over Formalism," *Esthetics of Music*, trans. William W. Austin (Cambridge: Cambridge University Press, 1982; reprint, New York: Cambridge University Press, 1983, 1988), 52-57. See also *Twentieth Century Theories of Art*, ed. James M. Thompson (Ottawa: Carleton University Press, 1990), especially Roger Fry's "Essay in Aesthetics" and "Pure and Impure Art" (subtitled "Formalism).

[8]See Andrew Chester, "Second Thoughts on a Rock Aesthetic: The Band," *New Left Review* 62 (1970): 78-79. The terms *diachronic* and *synchronic* are particularly abstract semiotic concepts connected with Structuralism, having their basis in the linguistic theories of Ferdinand Saussure and Roman Jakobson. Chester's definition of extensionality seems to equate the *synchronic* "mode of language" with the rules of selection for a certain compositional system, and the *diachronic* mode with the rules of combination and variation characterizing a musical work in its unfolding temporal

context. See Terence Hawkes, *Structuralism and Semiotics* (Berkeley and Los Angeles: University of California Press, 1977) for a cogent explanation of these concepts.

[9]Chester, "Second Thoughts on a Rock Aesthetic," 78-79. A point of terminological clarification is in order concerning the concept of intensionality: Chester's substitution of the letter [s] in place of [t] serves to distinguishes his term from the more abstract phenomenological concept of intentionality, as well as from the idea of author "intention." Further, a number of authors have indicated ways in which Chester's dialectic might be conceived as unique continua within a larger field of historical, cultural, and aesthetic relations. In "Some Observations on the Social Stratification of 20th-century Music," [John Shepherd, Phil Virden, Trevor Wishart et al., *Whose Music? A Sociology of Musical Languages* (London: Latimer New Dimensions, 1977), 155-177], Virden and Wishart suggest that "any musical production in the twentieth century might be arranged somewhere along a *continuum* ranging from almost totally extensional or explicit elaboration within the piece to almost totally intensional or implicit elaboration" (163 [my emphasis]); needless to say, I am indebted to them for conceiving of this interaction as continuous. Frith discusses Chester's terms in "Towards an Aesthetic of Popular Music," *Music and Society: The Politics of Composition, Performance, and Reception*, ed. Richard Leppert and Susan McClary (Cambridge: Cambridge University Press, 1987). Other scholars have demonstrated that, although Chester's formulation is imperfect, his fundamental ideas are still eminently useful for the critical analysis of popular music.

[10]From correspondence with Allan Moore, November 1999. Moore's article "Anachronism, Responsibility and Historical *Intension*" [*sic*], *Critical Musicology Journal: A Virtual Journal on the Internet* (1997) directly influenced my understanding of the historical and contextual implications of Chester's aesthetic dialectic.

[11]For an insightful theory concerning the period of diffusion across styles of rock and roll during the late 1950s and early 1960s, see Langdon Winner's essay "The Strange Death of Rock and Roll" in *Rock and Roll Will Stand*, ed. Greil Marcus (Boston: Beacon, 1969), 38-55.

[12]In the context of progressive rock style growth during the mid-1960s, *avant-garde* refers to a self-conscious experimentalism that foregrounds the aesthetic conflict between vernacular and cultivated musical traditions, as well as a preoccupation with innovations in electronic sound production and recording treatments. In another sense, the Beatles and Frank Zappa and The Mothers of Invention are considered *avant-garde* because both groups implicitly embody radical, totalizing oppositional stances toward the dominant social group.

[13]See Macan, *Rocking the Classics*, 32. The whole of his Chapter Two, "The Progressive Rock Style: The Music," presents an excellent historical account of the different "waves" of psychedelic and post-psychedelic genres and subgenres.

[14]In order for something to qualify as parody, it must not only refer to another contemporary or older style in satirical (not necessarily humorous) terms, but must take critical stock in the thing imitated. See Fredric Jameson, "Postmodernism and Consumer Society," *The Anti-Aesthetic: Essays on Postmodern Culture*, ed. Hal Foster

(Port Townsend, WA: Bay Press, 1983), for an eloquent distinction between parody and pastiche as effects of postmodernism.

[15]See Ben Watson, "Frank Zappa as Dadaist: Recording Technology and the Power to Repeat," *Contemporary Music Review* 15/1 (1966): 109-137. In this article Watson discusses Zappa's rearrangement of "(I Can't Get No) Satisfaction," writing that "In the [19]90s, sampling was to make such practices widespread: already in the [19]60s Zappa presented a music in which every sound was surrounded by quote-marks. Where most pop production aims to rationalize the production of music—making it cheaper and more standardized—Zappa used technology to create something unheard-of" (115).

[16]Rik Emmett, "Hendrix & the Art of Rhythm, 2," *Guitar Player* (December 1990): 114.

[17]Stefani, "A Theory of Musical Competence," 7-8. See note 6 above.

[18]Susan Fast, "Rethinking Issues of Gender and Sexuality in Led Zeppelin: A Woman's View of Pleasure and Power in Hard Rock," *American Music* 17/3 (Fall, 1999): 245-299.

[19]Two valuable recent collections of theoretical writings on culture are: *Critical Terms for Literary Study*, ed. Frank Lentricchia and Thomas McLaughlin, 2nd ed. (Chicago and London: University of Chicago Press, 1995); and *The Cultural Studies Reader*, ed. Simon During (London and New York: Routledge, 1993; 2nd ed. 1999).

[20]The arguments in this essay were originally formulated in a paper presented at the Twenty-Fourth Annual Conference of the (Sonneck) Society for American Music, Kansas City, KS; February 1998. They shall be developed in my dissertation, provisionally entitled "Archetypes of Progressive Rock, ca. 1966-1973."

Film composer **Carl Davis** was born in Brooklyn and studied composition with Paul Nordoff and Hugo Kauder at Bard College. In the mid-1950s Davis served as assistant conductor with the New York City Opera and as an accompanist with the Robert Shaw Chorale. In 1959 he won an Off-Broadway Emmy for *Diversions*, a revue, and went to England to supervise overseas productions; he has remained abroad ever since. Davis's commissions include ballet scores for Sadlers Wells, the English National Ballet, and the Northern Ballet Theatre; scores for a large number of silent films produced for Thames Television and Channel Four; recordings of American popular songs and classical operatic selections on the EMI and Collins Classics labels; scores for many BBC documentary series; and collaboration with Paul McCartney on *The Liverpool Oratorio*. Davis is married to actress Jean Boht.

John C. Tibbetts, associate professor of theater and film at the University of Kansas, holds a doctorate in interdisciplinary studies. Tibbetts served for four years with the Army Security Agency and later worked as a broadcast producer for KXTR-FM Fine Arts Radio and KMBZ News Radio, as an on-air host for KSHB-TV, and as a fine-arts reporter for KCTV (CBS). He has written about music for the *Christian Science Monitor* and the Monitor Radio Network as well as for Voice of America and National Public Radio. Tibbetts's publications include more than 250 articles for *The American Historical Review*, the *Journal of American Culture*, *Film Comment*, *Notes*, and the *American Record Guide*. Among his books are *American Theatrical Film*, *Dvořák in America*, and (co-edited with James M. Welsh) *The Encyclopedia of Novels into Film*.

❦ The Sounds of Silents
An Interview with Carl Davis

CARL DAVIS and JOHN C. TIBBETTS

"SINCE seeing my first movie at age four, I have been interested in films," remembers composer Carl Davis. "And to me that meant being also interested in film music. Even the so-called silent movies, which I saw as a boy at the Museum of Modern Art, fascinated me with the idea of putting music to images. Nowadays, with my television projects, concerts, ballets, and recordings, it's a regular part of what I do for a living."

Davis is the complete artist of the new millennium, a man of all media, a composer adaptable to any musical demand. Constantly in motion, this transplanted American has written scores for radio plays, Off-Broadway revues, the Royal Shakespeare Company, and the English National Ballet. For the BBC he composed music for several television documentary series, including Jeremy Isaacs's legendary *World at War* and *Cold War* as well as the forthcoming mega-series *History of Britain*. His motion-picture credits include scores for Ken Russell's *Rainbow* (1988) and Karel Reisz's *French Lieutenant's Woman* (1981). In the 1980s and 1990s Davis composed all of the music for the thirteen-part Thames Television series *Hollywood*, as well as for several documentary series about the silent film era for Channel Four Television and PBS: *The Unknown Chaplin, Buster Keaton: A Hard Act to Follow, Harold Lloyd: The Third Genius*, and *Cinema Europe*. Recent television projects include *Pride and Prejudice*, seen on PBS. Several years go he became artistic director and conductor of the Liverpool Orchestra's annual "Summer Pops" Season. In the last three years he has conducted the Royal Philharmonic Orchestra, the Philharmonia, the Royal Scottish National Orchestra, and the Scottish Chamber Orchestra. Davis has made numerous recordings and performed orchestral programs and "live" accompaniments for silent films at festivals in Florence, Barcelona, Tel Aviv, Rome, and the United States.

Millions of film enthusiasts around the world know Carl Davis best for his silent-film scores, most of which were written for the brilliant British film historian/producer Kevin Brownlow.[1] Davis belongs to a select company of classically-trained composers who have indulged in silent-film scoring; among them have been Camille Saint-Saëns (*L'Assassinat de duc de Guise*, 1909), Eric Satie (*Entr'acte*, 1924), Paul Hindemith (*Krazy Kat at the Circus*, 1927), Arthur Honegger (*La Roue*, 1922 and *Napoleon*, 1927), and Jacques Ibert (*The Italian Straw Hat*, 1927).[2] More unusual is the fact that Davis has composed for *both* silent and sound films, joining such luminaries as Dmitri Shostakovich (who not only worked in the silent period on *The New Babylon* in 1929, but scored Grigory Kosintsev's sound film *Hamlet* in 1963).

§

On a particularly bright January morning in 1998, Davis invited me to his home in the suburb of Barnes, just across the Hammersmith bridge on the north side of London.[3] It's an "odd corner," he says about the collection of winding streets and picturesque houses that surround him. Portions of a local church preserve authentic Norman architecture; other nearby dwellings date back to the early seventeenth century, when Queen Elizabeth and her entourage would sail up the river for a game of bowls. Up the street is the Olympic Building, where early "flickers" used to flash across the big screen at the turn of the last century.

Davis's home is itself a cross-section of local history. Its rambling structure dates back to 1910, but inside it has been recently refurbished and divided into living rooms and working areas ideally designed for both the family man and the working professional. Here, in the top-floor study, the cold sunlight of a January morning pours through the windows, burnishing the large black concert grand and glancing off the glass-framed poster announcing the 1980 London premiere of Abel Gance's 1927 French epic film, *Napoleon*. A second glance at the poster reveals something amiss: below the brim of Napoleon's three-cornered hat beams *Davis's* face, a characteristically elfin grin spreading across his puckish features—an inkling to one and all that this highly "respectable" composer possesses a maverick sense of humor.

As we share mid-morning tea, book shelves crowd around us, bulging with thousands of items ranging from recordings of Bix Beiderbecke to opera scores by Bellini and Delibes. An award from BAFTA (the British Academy of Film and Television Arts), in recognition of Davis's *French Lieutenant's Woman* score, adorns a side table. Strewn across the piano are manuscript sketches for a new work for Channel Four television, *A Dance to the Music of Time*, and for the documentary series from Ted Turner/Flashback Television, *Cold War*.

Poised between history old and new, music classical and popular, television and film, movies silent and sound, the sixty-four-year-old Davis keeps his options open. Although a native of Brooklyn, he's been living in London for many years. Yet—"I am emphatically *not* an English citizen," he declares. "I don't want to close the door. I still have very strong emotional ties to America."

Davis ruefully admits, however, that his education in America was a "chequered" affair. The years spent at one of the city colleges in Queens he categorizes

Carl Davis at work in his London home

categorizes as a "disaster." But later at the New England Conservatory of Music and at Bard College in upstate New York, he met two men who were to become influential mentors: Boris Goldovsky and the late Robert Shaw. "I was impassioned about opera in those days, and Goldovsky had a special talent for making it accessible to general audiences. That's something I've never forgotten.

"Then, in 1954, Shaw came up to prepare a chorus for a recording for RCA. I was only eighteen and very bold. So I got a job with him as accompanist. We toured the States in 1955 and 1956, and a few years later I worked with him on some recordings. I learned a lot about blending the popular and classical repertoires—which, come to think of it, I've been doing ever since! We continued to work together in the early 1960s when he toured Eastern Europe and when he went to Moscow to do the first performance of the Bach B-minor Mass. There are a lot of negative things you could say about Shaw, but he was brilliant at getting a chorus to *sing*. I mean, they became a united, organic instrument for him. And they always had a very distinctive sound, even though the individual members of the choir were always coming and going.

"Shaw always chose voices that he knew would work in an ensemble— not too wobbly, not too loud, not too shrill. They may not have been very distinctive solo voices, but they were very good. I remember when Shaw was starting an enormous tour of Eastern Europe in 1961, and his pianist was a woman named Harriet Wingreen, whose family had been destroyed by the Nazis in the War. She told Shaw she would not play in Germany, no matter what. So he asked me to come to Berlin and play for the Chorale, and I did. Very few members were the ones I knew from the mid-1950s. Yet the sound was the same and so was the virtuosity. I could not have distinguished between the two ensembles. Never mind what he did with his arms (which were not too helpful!) or what he thought about the music. He just had this way of imposing his personality on the chorus. I mean, that was really fabulous."

A defining moment for Davis came one day when the Shaw Chorale arrived in Philadelphia for a concert date. "It was a sort of mystical thing," he recalls, "at least for me. I was downtown, killing time, standing in the center of a music store where a lot of blank manuscript pages were laid out on a table. I looked at the white pages, and it suddenly struck me—'God, I want to fill that *up*; that looks very attractive to me!' To this day I can't stand to see empty staves! I'm superstitious about it!"

Working with contemporary film directors has sometimes tested Davis's abilities to assist collaboratively on a given project. For *The French Lieutenant's Woman*, based on the novel by John Fowles, he encountered formidable director Karel Reisz, an intellectual who came out of the Free Cinema movement in England in the mid-1950s. "Karel is a real poet," acknowledges Davis, "but like several directors, he has a terrible time articulating anything about music. He's quiet and rather withdrawn at times. I had to pull things out of him, to play things for him, to understand what he wanted. It's the sort of thing where 'he knows it when he hears it.' But he displayed a remarkable sensitivity in relating the music to the story. The movie was quite complex, you know—a film within a film, which interwove events in both Victorian and modern times. Karel would tell me sometimes to use a Victorian style of music for the *modern* sequences and, at other times to reverse that, to use a more modern sound for the *Victorian* scenes. I think this technique worked well to bind the characters together, old and new, fictional and real. As a result of our work together I was to have composed for another picture of his, *Sweet Dreams*, the Patsy Cline story; but it didn't work out."[4]

With director Ken Russell, Davis encountered an artist who has definite ideas about the musical needs of his pictures. Indeed, Russell's love for classical music has resulted in a number of films about famous composers, including Tchaikovsky (*The Music Lovers*, 1970), Gustav Mahler (*Mahler*, 1974), and Franz Liszt (*Lisztomania*, 1975).[5]

"Ken has this habit of piling up classical-music excerpts on the soundtracks of the first cuts of his films, just to get a sense of how picture and music might work together. But I was supposed to write an original score for *The Rainbow*, an adaptation of the D. H. Lawrence novel—which is not about music at all. Ken went ahead and compiled a test score for the first cut of the movie with stuff from Debussy, Bartók, and Rachmaninoff. That left me having to replace those masterpieces with my own stuff. It felt like I was coming out a loser! Ken told me once that he preferred the score to be written *before* he actually shot the movie. But you have to admit he is completely involved with music and picture; he's very passionate about it. I can also say he did listen to my own ideas too. That was when I tried to keep matters from being very 'Mickey-Mousey'—you know, where you imitate too closely every gesture and mood in terms of the music. I had to restrain him about that."

Davis's happiest and most extensive collaborations have been with historian/documentary filmmaker Kevin Brownlow. History was made—and re-made, as it were—when the two worked together in 1979 on the Thames Television documentary series *Hollywood*, a thirteen-hour celebration of the glory days of the American silent film. "It was an immediate success all over the world," says Davis. "In the euphoria of all that, I thought, 'Now that I've composed music for 300 to 400 movie excerpts, why don't I try to score a complete silent film?' Well, Kevin, in the meantime, had restored the complete *Napoleon*, a four-hour silent classic directed by Abel Gance in 1927.[6] Eventually, there would be two rival music scores to his restoration: Francis Ford Coppola's American version, scored by his father, Carmine [who had scored *The Godfather*], which had to be cut down to around four hours; and mine, the complete one, which would clock in at five hours. We got the 'okay' for the funding from Thames in August 1980, and the premiere was to be on 30 November. So I had to put together five hours of music in just three months!"

A daunting challenge, indeed—the longest score ever composed for a film. I glanced once again at the *Napoleon* poster on the far wall, the one with Davis's own features peering out from under the hat and realized this is no whimsical piece of identification. Davis, the upstart American, like the legendary Corsican, is capable of a few "Napoleonic gestures" of his own.

Under the supervision of producer David Gill and Brownlow, Davis worked in the fashion he continues to pursue to this day: For the strictly historical sequences he produced an eclectic blend of classical quotations from composers contemporary to Napoleon's time: Méhul, Grétry, Cherubini, Dittersdorf, Gossec and, of course, Beethoven. "Since Gance's film ended with Napoleon leading an army of liberation into Italy in the last years of the eighteenth century—before the time Beethoven grew disillusioned with him—I felt justified in quoting Beethoven's music. You can't avoid the fact that there is a good 'match' between Beethoven and Napoleon. Both were so dynamic, intense, and direct in their actions. I researched all the sources of Beethoven's 'Eroica' theme—the piano variations, the ballet *Prometheus*, and of course, the Third Symphony—and used all of them in the score."

In addition, Davis culled authentic tunes and folk songs from the Revolutionary period, as well as quotations from Honegger's 1927 score to the film. He juxtaposed Honegger's setting of Méhul's *Chant de depart* in counterpoint to the "Marseillaise." "I knew that silent film composers before me had always drawn upon the classics," Davis says, "so it seemed a valid thing to do."

Indeed, amassing the score was a veritable "research project," as he calls it. "I learned all sorts of things. For example, when I found out that Napoleon once remarked he could listen to an aria from Paisiello's opera *Nina* every day of his life, I decided to use it in the picnic scene in Corsica." For scenes of a more subjective nature, Davis composed original music of his own, such as the "Joséphine de Beauharnais" theme and the "Eagle" theme—a recurring *Leitmotif* deployed in tandem with Gance's repeated imagery of the Napoleonic bird as a symbol of the French "spirit of freedom."

Napoleon was premiered on a Sunday morning, 30 November 1980, at the Empire Theater in London's Leicester Square. "It seemed like all of London was there," recalls Davis. "The Wren Orchestra was in the pit, and I conducted with my back to the audience, facing the screen. Even after our rehearsals, no one knew if we would be able to stay in 'synch' with the film. I tried to cover that by including some 'escape hatches' in the score—fermatae where a tympanist or somebody would cover a gap if the music arrived ahead of a particular scene, for example. I'll never forget that day. It was momentous. People were amazed at the freshness and power of the total experience."

Emboldened by the success of the venture, Thames Television and Channel Four commissioned Davis to score more silent film classics being restored or reconstructed by Brownlow and Gill. Among more than thirty titles were D.W. Griffith's *Broken Blossoms* (1919), Chaplin's *City Lights* (1931), Douglas Fairbanks's *Thief of Bagdad* (1925), Erich von Stroheim's *Greed* (1923), Clarence Brown's *Flesh and the Devil* (1926), Victor Seastrom's *The Wind* (1928), and two Buster Keaton comedy classics, *Our Hospitality* (1923) and *The General* (1926).

"Well, it was a grand gesture," says Davis, "and what it meant was that every year from that point on we did several of these films. We're still doing them. I just finished scoring *The Phantom of the Opera* [1925], with Lon Chaney. It's a lot of music. Robert Shaw once told me that I'd written 'several miles of music.' I guess it really is a lot of 'mileage,' all right. But since *Napoleon*, I've gotten wise and have worked with assistant orchestrators, like Christopher Palmer, David and Colin Matthews, and Nick Raine. But I never tell them, 'Do it any way you want.' I'll prepare an elaborate short score and say, 'This is an oboe melody; this is a string passage; this is for the brass, etc. I'll get back a draft and mark it up, adding, changing."

"The man is uncanny," adds filmmaker Kevin Brownlow during a recent interview.[7] "Carl seems to belong to the silent-film era. You listen to the music, and you completely relax, knowing that he understands it, he's got it. It's not so with other composers I've worked with, believe me. And Carl's a terrific showman, very enthusiastic and completely reliable. I mean, it's amazing that he can do everything. But, he's too popular for the classical-music critics. He doesn't get the recognition he deserves."

No one is more fully aware of the slight than Davis himself. "People think of me as a film composer, but I'm really a composer who writes for films. I remember Miklós Rózsa saying the same thing: that you bring all your inherited or trained baggage as a composer into film. I do think music in itself has affective properties, although I wouldn't want to be too literal about that. It's a tricky issue. Stravinsky said that music in itself—say, the C-Major scale—doesn't mean anything; but when you play it 'slowly, with feeling,' it might elicit some sort of response. Even so, ask three different people and you get three different interpretations."

Davis's scores for *The Wind, Greed,* and *Our Hospitality* demonstrate (respectively) his instrumental ingenuity, methods of paralleling and counterpointing music and image, and his use of *Leitmotive* and theme-and-variation techniques.[8] A masterpiece from the late silent-film era, *The Wind* was directed by the Swedish master Victor Seastrom and starred Lillian Gish as a woman who journeys to the desert and goes mad under the pressure of the eternal wind and sands. "The movie was about a drought, about a very arid part of the American Southwest," says Davis. "Life was constantly uncomfortable for everybody. I wanted to express the sense of discomfort, to make the audience uncomfortable with the sounds they were hearing. So I cut out all brass and winds, anything that had color; and I limited my palette to the 'black-and-white' of strings, keyboard, and percussion. At times I used five percussionists, each with his own group of instruments. By the time you get the storm at its peak, you have five gongs being battered simultaneously, assaulting the audience. Much of the music was aleatoric, written without bar lines. The players have a lot of responsibility for making their own sounds based on just general directions, rather like a mass improvisation. But it actually is tightly controlled—I have to *teach* it rather than *conduct* it."

By contrast, Davis' music for *Greed,* an adaptation of Frank Norris's classic novel *McTeague* (1899)—itself a grim tale of avarice, madness, and homicide—runs counter to the atmospheric and emotional charge of Stroheim's stark imagery. "In one scene a cousin is saying goodbye to the dentist. Both are important characters, and soon they will be at each other's throats, trying to kill each other. Should I anticipate the oncoming villainy with my music? Well, I thought about it; but no, I finally decided to take my cue from the presence in the shot of a player piano. I just went with the sounds of a piano and sort of ignored the action. But if you listen closely, you'll hear that I injected a few dissonances into the piano performance and instructed my player to over-pedal some of it—just enough to convey a slight feeling of unease."

For *Our Hospitality,* Buster Keaton's masterpiece about a deadly family rivalry in the Old South, Davis utilizes the technique of linking specific themes (*Leitmotive*) with characters and situations. For example, there's a "fate" theme, first introduced in the prologue, that foreshadows the concatenation of events to come. Keaton has his own theme: a lovely, lyric melodic line that recurs in an endless variety of ingenious instrumental and rhythmic guises; in each instance it takes its cue from and in turn enhances the grand gestures, be they romantic, desperate, or heroic. "Films like

Keaton's have long gag sequences, where one small joke leads to another, and then another, until there's a culminating moment. I find that by using one theme and developing it through this series of gags I can participate in Keaton's method, maybe nudging the sequence along, following it, leading it, and so forth."

One has to wonder whether Davis has ever actually just sat at a piano and accompanied a silent film himself. "Yes, of course," he replies, "but not in a theater. When I was preparing for the *Hollywood* series, I'd go over to Thames Television every Tuesday around four in the afternoon and improvise in the screening room with all kinds of old films. Just to get ideas, you know?"

I wondered whether any other composers or musicians have started that way.

"Well," Davis answers, eyes twinkling, "off-hand, I can think of Virgil Thomson and Shostakovich. And Eugene Ormandy, too. That was in Russia, in his early years. He wouldn't talk about it, though. He never would admit it."

§

Does there emerge from Davis's eclectic musical pursuits a "signature" or idiosyncratic "sound" common to them all? "People have come to me claiming they hear characteristics of my music in ballets, movies, and silent film scores," he answers. "They think they are complimenting me, and I accept it for what it's worth. But I don't think about that sort of thing for a minute. If you do, you end up thinking, 'Well, I'll give a project my *World-At-War* kind of thing'; or, 'I'll use my *French Lieutenant's Woman* style.' If you do that, you are in an absolute dead end, creatively. I just try and do what's right for any given circumstance, whether it's for the stage, television, or the movies. It's a big responsibility. If the music is wrong, or overrides a visual image, or contradicts it, I'm disturbing the creative whole. On the other hand, if the music's doing something that is helping the picture, I'm enhancing the event. And that is all the reward any of us ever need."

Finally, as if all these pursuits were not enough, Davis takes time each year to conduct live screenings and concert versions of his film scores, as well as programs of film music by esteemed colleagues and mentors like Franz Waxman, Max Steiner, and Dmitri Tiomkin. "You are putting on a *performance*," Davis says. "There is a public out there, not a select group like a film society or a university club or an art-house crowd. You're suddenly doing *Napoleon* for three-thousand people in a big auditorium. I've done Chaplin reconstructions in Tel Aviv, in Los Angeles, in Seattle, and in Hong Kong for four thousand people, three nights sold out."

One wonders what lies ahead for this versatile artist. There is no doubting, however, that whatever may come, Carl Davis and his music will be ready.[9]

NOTES

[1]For accounts of Carl Davis's work on the Kevin Brownlow documentaries and film restorations, see Judith Palmer, "The Sound of Silents," *The Independent* (13 February 1999): 12; and Kevin Thomas, "Carl Davis' Forte Is the Sound of Silents," *Los Angeles Times* (24 April 1992): F16. For an overview of the Thames silent series, see Charles Champlin, "'Third Genius' Applauds Wit of Harold Lloyd," *Los Angeles Times* (16 November 1989): F3; Richard Corliss, "Silents Are Still Golden: *Cinema Europe* Is an Evocation of the Time When Pictures Were Really Moving," *Time* (1 July 1996): 64; James Monaco, "*Cinema Europe*: The Other Hollywood," *Cineaste* 24/2-3 (1999): 86-88; and Charles Silver, "Chaplin Redux," *American Film* (September 1984): 20-34.

[2]Music accompanied silent films from the very beginning, with the projection of a program of films by the Lumière Brothers in the Grand Café on the Boulevard des Capucines, Paris, on 28 December 1895. The Saint-Saëns score for *L'Assassinat de Duc de Guise* was later published as a concert piece (his Op. 128), scored for strings, piano, and harmonium. Satie's score for René Clair's *Entr'acte* (1923) has been cited by historian Martin Miller Marks as "the first original film score of consequence by an avant-garde composer" [Marks, *Music and the Silent Film: Contexts and Case Studies, 1895-1924* (New York: Oxford University Press, 1997), 167]. The film was originally inserted between two acts of the ballet *Relache*, which premiered at the Théâtre Champs-Elysées on 4 December 1924. The music is a unified, continuous piece, scored for a small orchestra, and lasting twenty minutes. For a detailed account, see Marks, *Music and the Silent Film,* 167-185.

Through-composed scores like Satie's were comparatively rare; the majority of silent-film musical accompaniments were compilations of previously published material, in which original composition was limited to bridge passages and, possibly, one or more distinctive themes. For more information about the role classical composers played in silent-film scoring, see Kathryn Kalinak, *Settling the Score: Music and the Classical Hollywood Film* (Madison: University of Wisconsin Press, 1992), 48-65; Roy M. Prendergast, *Film Music: A Neglected Art* (New York: W.W. Norton, 1977), 3-18; and Marks, *Music and the Silent Film.*

[3]The author wishes to thank Paul Wing for assistance in arranging the interview with Carl Davis.

[4]Charles Gross scored the film.

[5]For an overview of Ken Russell's composer biopics, see Robert Phillip Kolker, "Ken Russell's Biopics," *Film Comment* 9/3 (May 1973): 42-45; and John C. Tibbetts, "The Lyre of Light," *Film Comment* 28/1 (January-February 1992): 66-73.

[6]Davis began work scoring the film in September 1980. For a full account of the collaboration on the restoration and scoring of *Napoléon*, see Kevin Brownlow, *Napoleon: Abel Gance's Classic Film* (New York: Alfred A. Knopf, 1983), esp. 235-245. For a critical reaction to the event, see Jonathan Cape, "Restoration Drama," *The Economist* (28 May 1983): 99.

[7]From Tibbetts's interview with Kevin Brownlow, 20 July 1999, London.

[8]For information on *Greed*, see Herman G. Weinberg, *The Complete Greed of Erich von Stroheim* (New York: Arno, 1972); for information about *The Wind*, see Tibbetts, "Vital Geography: Victor Seastrom's *The Wind*," in *Passport to Hollywood: Film Immigrants Anthology*. ed. Don Whittemore and Philip Alan Cecchettini (New York: McGraw-Hill, 1976), 255-263; for *Our Hospitality*, see Jim Kline, *The Complete Films of Buster Keaton* (New York: Carol Publishing Group, 1993), 93-97.

[9]For a fine compilation of Davis's film and television scores, see *Carl Davis: The Royal Philharmonic Collection* (Tring TRP099); in this collection Davis conducts the Royal Philharmonic Orchestra in a program of music from *The World at War*, *Pride and Prejudice*, *The French Lieutenant's Woman*, and *Napoleon*.

David P. DeVenney is director of choral activities at West Chester University of Pennsylvania, where he conducts the Concert Choir and University Chorale and teaches courses in choral conducting and literature; he also serves as music director of the Reading Choral Society, one of America's oldest musical organizations. DeVenney has published widely on the topic of American choral music, opera, and musical theater, and has written articles on the choral works of Schütz and Brahms, among others. He serves as general editor of the Research Memorandum Series published by the American Choral Foundation.

❦ American Choral Music at the Millennium

DAVID P. DEVENNEY

IT would be difficult to find another segment of the American music scene more vital than that of today's choral world. Nearly every aspect of American choral music shows signs of great strength and vigor. Memberships in professional organizations like the American Choral Directors Association and Chorus America are expanding rapidly. The number of choruses, both amateur and professional, has grown exponentially in the past half century. The quality and number of new works commissioned by these choral ensembles is remarkable in its breadth; audiences for performances of new works are increasing every year. While there are some troubling signs below the surface, none at the moment seems capable of derailing the continued growth and vitality of American choral singing during the next century.

When asked to write this essay, I agreed for two reasons. First, I had recently completed a history of American choral literature that concludes with a discussion of works from the recent past.[1] Writing this article enabled me to step back a bit from that task, which focused solely on established literature, and take a wider view of choral music in the United States today. Serendipitously I talked about all this to colleagues from around the country; writing this essay helped me continue those conversations and expand them to include several recurring ideas. Most of the research for this essay was conducted via email, telephone, and personal contacts with a wide variety of American conductors and composers working at many levels and in diverse circumstances. I have been surprised by the similar views most of my colleagues espoused, perhaps even more so because they frequently coincided with my own perceptions. I have drawn heavily upon these many conversations below, although the ideas expressed herein remain mine.

While there are few hard facts to be found on this topic, Helene Whitson of San Francisco has compiled an admirable resource as part of her ongoing work with the San Francisco Bay Area Choral Archives. Her research has identified over 500 vocal ensembles of "varying numbers and interests" in the greater Bay Area, from "Monterey to Mendocino, San Francisco to Sacramento. Over 25,000 people sing on a weekly basis in community choruses and large performing church choirs."[2] Whitson traces the history of choral singing in the Bay Area back two hundred years. She has also identified an "explosion" in the late 1950s based on her discovery that 22 choruses, founded during that decade, still exist today; another 30 choruses were established during the 1960s, 98 during the 1970s, 127 during the 1980s, and 119 during the 1990s. The first edition of the *San Francisco Bay Area Directory of Choruses* (1985) lists 140 active ensembles; the second edition (1988) lists more than 300 organizations; the third (1992), nearly 450; and the fourth (1998), over 500.

These groups are diverse: they range from college and university groups, children's choirs, "performing" church choirs (i.e., choirs that give regular concerts in addition to performing liturgical services), community choirs, jazz ensembles, gospel choirs, professional choirs, select chamber groups, and symphony choruses. Particularly interesting is that, while some choirs have disbanded, most continue.

Alan Harler, director of choral activities at Temple University in Philadelphia and music director of that city's Mendelssohn Club, relayed a similar story that illustrates growth in another form. The Mendelssohn Club, a civic chorus, was first established over 125 years ago. Several years before Harler became its director, the organization split into three factions over disagreements about its artistic direction. One faction left the Mendelssohn Club and formed its own symphonic chorus, the Choral Arts Society; a second stayed to rebuilt the original ensemble; and a third left both organizations to start a group of its own. Today, all three choruses appear regularly with the Philadelphia Orchestra and present their own annual subscription series before large and enthusiastic audiences. From dissension sprang three choruses where one had existed before.[3]

Similar situations can be found in Los Angeles, Chicago, Houston, Phoenix, Cincinnati, Minneapolis, and numerous other locations across the country. Nor is the phenomenon confined to America's largest cities. Harrisburg, Pennsylvania (pop. 60,000) boasts two semi-professional chamber choirs in its immediate area; and Des Moines, Iowa (pop. 195,000) has not only a professional choir, but also a symphonic chorus, several select community groups, and an annual international children's chorus festival.

GALA, the national association of gay and lesbian choruses established in 1982, exemplifies yet another way choruses may be formed to meet special needs, one similar to the growth of gospel choirs during the 1950s and 1960s in response to needs and desires of African-Americans. There are now 180 GALA choruses throughout the country, in cities large and small, that not only serve the artistic, community, and political lives of their particular constituencies, but foster new audiences (and, incidentally, new singers) for other choral undertakings.[4]

Professional organizations devoted to meeting the needs of choirs and their conductors also continue to grow. Chorus America was established in 1977 by several dozen professional conductors and others who wanted to pool resources, share information and experiences, and foster the spread of professional-level choral singing. From these beginnings has evolved a national organization, with offices in Washington, D.C., that represents nearly 550 community, children's, symphonic, and professional choirs, in addition to over 500 conductors, board members, and others interested in the organization's goals.[5]

Obviously choral music in this country is flourishing. Conductors have spoken to me of their delight that choirs are growing. Most of them suggested that Americans at the end of the twentieth century are seeking ways to enrich the cultural and spiritual aspects of their lives and that choral singing is a proven, rewarding way of doing this. In an age when so much of our lives is conducted electronically and impersonally, the personal experience of submitting one's energies to the task of singing great music with other human beings is both refreshing and rejuvenating.

This tendency is not without historical precedence in the United States, either. Since the founding of the country by the earliest settlers in New England and by missionaries in California and the Southwest, choral music has provided a vital and ongoing way of creating a sense of community and fostering artistic experience. One has only to consider the impact of the eighteenth-century singing school movement in New England or the establishment of singing societies and music clubs across the country during the nineteenth century, and parallels to modern-day America become apparent:

> I think American choral music has always been an amateur art, and will continue to develop that way; professional choirs will need to continue to work hard to maintain and build on their current level of success. The activities of Chorus America will be essential if this is going to happen, but I don't think any amount of effort will turn us into a land of many flourishing professional choruses.... [This] view comes mainly from my attitude that the real rewards of choral music (like chamber music and lieder) are found in the doing of it, not as much in the listening. Our audiences often are composed of relatives of singers (of course) and other choral singers, who are singing the concert vicariously. And I think this is fine. In the same way spectator soccer has grown in this country as a generation has grown up playing soccer, our goal should be to raise generations who have the feeling of choral music from the inside.[6]

There are other signs of health and vigor in American choral music. Chorus America has sponsored a nationally-syndicated radio program, *The First Art*, that redresses the notion of choral music being given short shrift on classical radio stations. Although expensive to produce, *The First Art* has demonstrated steady growth; today each broadcast attracts 720,000 listeners over 281 stations nationwide.[7]

Outreach programs by professional choruses, like those of the Pacific Chorale (Orange County, California) and the Dale Warland Singers (Minneapolis), have been developed in order to educate the public about choral singing, particularly the very young through children's choruses. This movement is also partially designed to combat the effects of reduced public spending on music education in our elementary schools. The large and growing grassroots children's chorus movement is most encouraging and portends well for choral vitality in this country.

Finally, the healthy state of American choral music can be observed in the quality and number of recently commissioned works. Most professional choirs in this country have as a part of their mission statements the goal of fostering new compositions for choir. Indeed, several prominent professional choirs—the San Francisco Chamber Choir, for example—dedicate nearly all their resources to this effort. (It is difficult to conjure even one symphony orchestra or opera company with a similar mission.) A great many ensembles regularly commission one or more new works per season, and Chorus America annually gives monetary awards to those ensembles that commission and perform new American music. The professional choir movement has actively pursued this goal, but the mantle of new music has also been placed on the shoulders of community and school groups. Colleges and universities have commissioned music not only from composers on their faculties, but also from outsiders with national reputations and followings. GALA choruses have been amazingly busy commissioning new works—partly because they want to sing music that addresses their own needs (many works, for example, have been commissioned by GALA ensembles in honor of singers or directors who have died from AIDS), but also because theirs are mostly single-gender choirs that need appropriate music to perform. The same is true of the burgeoning children's choir movement in this country; their number of new commissions each year is astonishing.

Concomitant with the explosive rise in commissions has been a change in the nature of new music. Composers at the end of this century are returning to more conventional melody and harmony; they have moved away from atonal, serial, and other experimental styles. How long this will last is unknown, but the advent of neo-romanticism has reengaged and encouraged choirs and their conductors to commission and perform new music.[8]

All these things show signs of continuing. More choirs are being formed throughout the country every year. Our most gifted and able composers are receiving choral commissions, and their compositions are being given prominent and repeated performances. Ensembles like the GALA choruses are continuing to engage new audiences; so are programs that seek to include under-represented communities in joint concerts (e.g., "art" choirs performing with gospel choirs or vocal jazz groups); so are nationally-syndicated programs such as *The First Art*. Recent trends in popular music may also portend increased audiences and performers. Many pop music stars during the past two decades have belonged to or been groups: Menudo, Back Street Boys, Spice Girls, Boyz II Men. Youngsters have always wanted to imitate their idols; perhaps such youngsters may eventually make their way into choirs and, as adults, discover and explore other kinds of music.

Several problems loom in the background, however. Public-school music programs are under siege across the country. These programs should be strengthened because of the educational and aesthetic benefits they offer our children through making music together. Without school-music programs, the battle for future singers and audiences may be lost .

Several respondents to my queries voiced concern over the repertory of choirs in America's high-school and church choirs. Too many conductors are programming music that lacks artistic merit; in many cases they almost entirely eliminate "art" music from their programs. Some school conductors seem driven to engage students (on however superficial a level) and entertain parents and administrators, rather than educate their charges and audiences. I have attended far too many concerts even at colleges and universities that consist mostly of lighter pieces: humorous works, spirituals, folk song settings, and so forth. Performing lighter literature is worthwhile, and its appeal to performers and audiences is undeniable, but dining exclusively on "desserts" does not bode well for the development either of music literacy skills or a mature aesthetic sense.

Finally, more needs to be done to educate government, foundations, and the corporate world about choral singing and its benefits to the communities served by its choirs. One of my correspondents wrote that

> When legislators, foundations and corporate donors finally wake up to the fact that choruses are magnificent community builders in so many ways, then grants to our organizations will surely begin to catch up with those given to symphonies, ballets and opera companies. But if we in the choral world don't educate these grant givers, who will? And we must also convince them that music in schools not only makes kids smarter, it teaches them discipline, it bonds diverse groups together, and it gives all of them pride in their common achievements. When these truths become better known, our whole country will be singing.[9]

Whitson, in her *Bay Area Directory*, eloquently sums up the principal reasons why choral music is and will continue to be an important thread in the artistic tapestry of the United States. She points out that

> The types and styles of choruses [in America] reflect the variety of personal interests of a large number of community members. Looking at choruses and their activities—their musical emphases, their programs, their numbers, their supporters, their products, from CDs to t-shirts, their rehearsal and performance sites,—is one way of documenting aspects of how people live in our community, what they do in their leisure time. Choristers are unsung heros. They often are taken for granted as part of the musical experience. The choristers will be there— attentive, quiet, prepared, ready to rehearse and perform. They may have had to take a vacation day from work, but they are there. Community choristers are

volunteers who give of their time to come to rehearsals, buy their music, buy, rent or make appropriate concert clothing, and pay dues for the privilege of doing all this. Why? Because choral music adds great meaning and richness to their lives. In today's depersonalized world of rush and stress, choral activity is one source available to people to be inspired, refreshed and allowed to rejuvenate their natural emotions and feelings....

Involvement in choral activities is not limited to those who participate in the singing and conducting.... Many instrumentalists, from rehearsal pianists and organists to full orchestras, are involved in the production of choral music. Each of the choruses has friends and support groups, volunteers who want them to succeed. Those friends, colleagues, and acquaintances come to choral concerts, contribute money to support those choruses and offer their services in ushering, fundraising, building risers, holding garage sales, etc. Our communities have businesses who advertise in choral programs, put our flyers and announcements in their windows and even match employee contributions to different choruses. And, what about the institutions which provide the space for creating music? A community may have a concert hall, but most often it is the local church or school which provides the space for rehearsal and performance. All of these people and institutions participate on a regular basis in the production of choral music.

Choral singing is the most accessible form of music performance. People who wish to participate in the performance of music can most easily do so by joining a chorus.... Even today, with the incredible diversity of opportunity to attend cultural events or listen to recordings, people still want to participate, to create music themselves. Choral singing is a musical activity which continues to involve large numbers of people in our communities and contributes incalculable fullness to our cultural lives.[10]

NOTES

[1]David P. DeVenney, *Varied Carols: A Survey of American Choral Literature* (Westport, CT: Greenwood, 1999).

[2]Helene Whitson, "Introduction," *San Francisco Bay Area Chorus Directory*, 4th ed. (San Francisco: San Francisco Bay Choral Archive, 1998). This work was provided courtesy of Kirke Mechem.

[3]From a conversation in Philadelphia with the present author, 15 June 1999.

[4]Information taken from the GALA website, <www.galachorus.org>, on 17 August 1999.

[5]Information taken from the Chorus America website, <www.chorusamerica.org>, on 30 July 1999.

[6]From email correspondence with William Weinert, Eastman School of Music, University of Rochester, 5 August 1999.

[7]From the Chorus America website.

[8]To be fair, a few composers who have chosen to write in this style have received performances and commissions, even when their music was considered old-fashioned or even reactionary. Daniel Pinkham, Ned Rorem, and Gian Carlo Menotti have written (and continue to write) in accessible and traditional idioms and have achieved prominence and financial rewards by doing so. The current trend toward a neo-romantic aesthetic has simply encouraged more (and also good) composers to write in this style.

[9]From email correspondence with Kirke Mechem of San Francisco, 20 April 1999.

[10]Whitson, *San Francisco Bay Area Chorus Directory*. Reprinted by permission.

A native of Maryland, freelance jazz vocalist **Ethel Ennis** attended business school in the 1940s while singing with local ensembles. In 1955 she recorded her first album on the Jubilee label with Hank Jones, Kenny Clark, and Phil Woods; later she recorded for Capital and RCA. In 1958 Ennis performed with Benny Goodman at the Brussels World's Fair; fourteen years later, she launched a tradition when she sang "The Star-Spangled Banner" without accompaniment at the second inauguration of President Nixon. Praising *If Women Ruled the World*, her latest CD on the Savoy Jazz/Denon label, a critic for *Downbeat* wrote that Ennis's "voice runs deep, exuding the personality of a sage who has lived many lives"; Frank Sinatra called her "my kind of singer." Biographer Sallie Krabetz's *Ethel Ennis, The Reluctant Jazz Star* was published in 1984.

Born in Indiana, **Earl Arnett** grew up in a military family, graduated from high school in Tokyo, and later attended Wabash College, where he majored in philosophy and history. For fourteen years he worked as a reporter and feature writer with the *Baltimore Sun*; later he served as director of the graduate program in music-criticism at the Peabody Conservatory of Music. In 1980 Arnett resigned from the *Sun* to become a music entrepreneur with his wife, singer Ethel Ennis, whom he married in 1967. Together they produced concerts and a live album, then opened Ethel's Place, a music club and restaurant in Baltimore's Mt. Royal Cultural Center. Among other books, Arnett is the author of *Maryland : A New Guide to the Old Line State*, published by The Johns Hopkins University Press.

❦ The Music We've Called Jazz

ETHEL ENNIS and EARL ARNETT

IN 1955, when Ethel walked into a New York recording studio to make her first album, the term "jazz" still had a profane, semi-sordid connotation. The word echoed distant sounds of southern sportin' houses, bawdy strip joints, and city night clubs—music with unrestrained rhythms and melodies spawned by pleasures of the moment. In 1959, when Earl first heard the horn of Miles Davis on early morning radio, the restrained emotions of *Sketches of*

Spain, arranged by Gil Evans, spoke to his young Midwestern heart of individual freedom and passionate desire. In contrast to the church hymns that had inspired him earlier, this "jazz" spoke directly and immediately of contemporary life, what it felt like to be alive in America at that instant.

We didn't know each other then, but by the time we met and married in 1967, jazz had already moved to the concert hall, where critics were calling it "America's classical music." Opinion had traveled a long way from 1928, when H. L. Mencken wrote in *The American Mercury*:

> Most of our native minnesingers, like most of our native artists in prose, seem to labor under the delusion that jazz is music, and some of them even appear to think that it is better than the music written by Beethoven. [Ezra] Pound nurses no such folly: he is well aware that jazz, with its relentless thumping in four-four time, is no more, at best, than an expanded drum part, with an accompaniment for wind-machines, most of them defective tonally.

We wonder what Mencken would have thought of his old Saturday Night Club friend, Louis Cheslock—a venerable violinist, and for more than fifty years a composer and teacher at the Peabody Conservatory of Music—when he attended a Duke Ellington concert in the early 1970s. The setting was the Famous Ballroom (now demolished), an earthy vestige of the big-band era in Baltimore that featured Sunday afternoon concerts sponsored by the Left Bank Jazz Society. Dr. Cheslock sat enthralled near the rhythm section, where bassist Joe Benjamin thumped away in four-four time, smiled at Lou, and asked him, "How do you like that, professor?" The professor thoroughly enjoyed himself and later had Duke sign a composer's medal, part of a collection that included the famous European musicians Mencken so admired. (Mencken once wrote facetiously that there were two kinds of music: German music and bad music. Ellington maintained there were only two kinds: good and bad.)

When Ethel performed with Ellington and his band on national television in 1964, she sang "Love You Madly," a signature song Duke had published with Luther L. Henderson, Jr., in 1950. By the time he died in 1974, Ellington had received the Presidential Medal of Freedom and the French Legion of Honor and was recognized as one of America's foremost composers, although he never won a Pulitzer Prize for music during his lifetime. (A jazz composer wouldn't achieve this kind of recognition until 1997, when Wynton Marsalis won for his oratorio *Blood on the Fields*.)

Ethel remembers Ellington as a sophisticated gentleman, one totally immersed in the life of making and playing music. He wrote and arranged from musical sketches that only became formal arrangements after performances and recording sessions. In this manner, the music had room for individual players to impart their own feelings of the moment—not easy to do with a large ensemble, but Duke developed a family of musicians just for this reason. He wrote for them, and they played for him.

This kind of easy informality, combined with musical taste and discipline, fit an American century of chaos and change. In his pioneering book *Music in a New Found Land* (1965), English musicologist Wilfrid Mellers claims that Ellington combined folk art and commercial artistry to create jazz as "the representative music of our industrial world." Duke saw himself in less grandiose terms. The most important music was what he was working on, his favorite performer the one in front of him. He lived in the present and future, never looking back, charmed with life and charming to those he encountered along the way. In the process he created an enduring musical legacy that will give twenty-first century historians auditory clues to our time. We both feel that the Elllington of living memory will become a cultural icon to those who follow us.

Like many jazz musicians, Ellington and his band encountered ready appreciation and enthusiasm for their music in European countries when their own countrymen ignored them. But this fact isn't surprising; it's still true. When Ethel gave a concert in Bonn in 1999 (a gift to the citizens of Germany's former capital before the American embassy moved to Berlin), the audience listened and responded—not only to Ethel, but also to the special musicans with her: Marc Copland, Keter Betts, and Billy Hart. One critic even brought with him a newspaper clipping from 1958, in which he had written about Ethel's appearance with an all-star Benny Goodman band in Cologne.

Europeans always seem to have had an earlier understanding of contemporary American music—particularly jazz, blues, and rock—than home audiences, perhaps because we Americans have always been more class-driven in commercial categories than we like to admit. The roots of our popular music lie in the African-American experience, which, until the 1960s, was legally segregated from the rest of ethnic America. Ethel grew up in an era of "race records" created and sold to dark-skinned people in urban ghettoes and country towns. As late as 1963, when she signed a recording contract with RCA, Ethel was only the third Black singer (after Lena Horne and Della Reese) to receive star treatment at that label. In the past, RCA had regarded singers and musicians of color as unworthy of their attention.

As much as anyone, Benny Goodman changed this situation in the recording industry when he hired African-American musicians for his bands and insisted that individuals be evaluated only according to their musical ability. Ethel remembers Benny as a quiet taskmaster who wanted the music played correctly. Not a composer in the same league as Ellington, he nonetheless broke down barriers between "classical" music and "jazz." When Goodman played Mozart and Bartók with orchestras *and* led swinging big bands, he silenced critics from the Mencken school. Increasingly American jazz musicians explored a variety of styles across artificial boundaries, ranging from free-flowing improvisations to interpretations of difficult scores. Arguably, the word "jazz" has lost whatever meaning it had in the early part of the twentieth century, and we should now speak only of musicians and composers: their abilities, styles, and spirit.

However much we may object to the word, "jazz" conveys a tradition of the twentieth century that will have relevance for the twenty-first. It will remain a conversational "language," one the late Sidney Bechet called the "remembering song—the long song that started back there in the South." Making this song, musicians listen and play at the same time, waiting for moments when the music becomes greater than their individual parts, when it soars freely between players and listeners. In *Treat It Gentle: An Autobiography* (1960), Bechet described the process this way:

> There ain't no one can write down for you what you need to know to make the music over again. There ain't no one can write down the feeling you have to have. That's from inside yourself, and you can't play note for note like something written down. The music has to let you be; you've got to stay free inside it.

We never knew Sidney, who died in Paris in 1959; during the late 1950s, however, Ethel sang with his contemporary from New Orleans, Louis Armstrong. Ethel and Louis performed "The Song is Ended," an Irving Berlin tune from 1927 that adds "but the melody lingers on" to the title phrase. We're sure that, in the century ahead of us, we'll continue to hear the lingering melodies of Duke, Sidney, and Louis, along with the haunting refrains of Billie Holiday, the Baltimore singer who died a few months after Bechet.

Billie once telephoned Ethel in the middle of the night from New York and encouraged her to continue singing. "You don't fake," she said, "and you're a musician's musician." This description also applies to Billie, although she could barely read a note. She truly listened (to Louis and Bessie Smith) and distilled the vintage wine she heard into a rich, brown, mellow brandy that burned the ears as it penetrated listerners' minds. Here was true experience, even if transmitted through hackneyed, popular songs. Billie never sang songs exactly the same way from night to night. There were always subtle variations depending on the mood of the audience, the temper of the musicians, the overall ambience, and how she felt at the moment.

The late Carmen McRae, Billie's friend and disciple, performed several times at Ethel's Place, the 175-seat music club we operated in Baltimore from 1985 to 1988. On those occasions, she remained true to this vocal tradition by giving every lyric an original interpretation, infused with her own irony and world-weariness. She once got quite angry with Earl for an interpretive introduction that violated her commitment to the audience. Don't define me with words, she said; just introduce me and let the definition come from the performance.

Many musicians passed through Ethel's Place during its brief but intense existence: Dizzy Gillespie, Wynton Marsalis (and his father, Ellis), Clifford Jordan, the Modern Jazz Quartet, Stephane Grappelli, McCoy Tyner, Ahmad Jamal, Toots Thielemans, Paquito D'Rivera, Charlie Byrd, Flora Purim and Airto, Astrud Gilberto, Jan Garbarek, Claude Bolling, Phil Woods, Horace Silver, Freddy Hubbard, Gerry Mulligan, Max Roach, Louis Bellson, Mel Tormé, Della Reese, KoKo Taylor, Taj Mahal, Leon Redbone, Bela Fleck, Joe Williams, Jimmy Witherspoon, Les McCann, Doc Watson, and Yo-Yo Ma ... the list goes on. In all, hundreds of performers in musical genres ranging from bluegrass and country to jazz, rock, Latin pop, and European classical.

After the sale of Ethel's Place, we traveled to Xiamen, China, to represent Baltimore at an international arts festival for sister cities. The songs of Michael Jackson greeted us at the airport, but the audiences there had never heard live jazz until Ethel, accompanied by piano and bass, sang in several concert halls. When she "jazzed" a Chinese folk song, the audience reacted strongly to the familiar presented in a new context. Music provided the translation and made the connection between cultures.

Throughout this experience, we were conscious of music as another way of experiencing and describing the world, a non-verbal sound language that opens avenues to the unseen and unspoken realms of our common humanity. Ethel calls this energy "soft power," while Earl prefers to leave it unnamed, a mystery accessible to all but frequently ignored or forgotten. We both use the word "spiritual" to describe music's potential to heal, inspire, and comfort.

In the past, most of us have depended upon the professional maestros to demonstrate music's power, but we think that the twenty-first century offers a new world of individual potential. We will always have musical masters and teachers, but the future promises that each of us can tap the musician within. We now have all the tools.

In the 1920s, when Harry Partch discarded three centuries of western musical theory and started to explore music from ancient Greece and China, he was considered a crackpot or, at best, an iconoclast. When he invented new instruments to play the ratios developed in his personal musical system, audiences marvelled at their appearance and strained at their unfamiliar sounds. Now, in a computer age at the very beginning of a new century, we can appreciate the unconventional imagination of such a composer. The world in all its cultural variety has opened to us, from the polyrhythms of Africa and Asia to the harmonies of China and Japan. Even where language presents a seemingly insurmountable barrier, music creates common bonds.

As we begin to grasp the implications of such insights, music will re-emerge from its relegation to the professionals and become more accessible to amateurs increasingly linked through computer networks. Private aural worlds, hitherto sealed off because of lack of education or ignorance, will be released to expanded, electronic audiences around the world. At first, this new soundscape will seem a cacophony, an incomprehensible noise from millions of mindscapes. But we believe that, gradually, individual human beings will compose fascinating music in a global conversation that will enlighten us all. Musicians will continue to play traditional songs on old instruments, but they will be increasingly regarded as antiquarians, craftspeople who offer a nostalgic counterbalance to an electronic age. Nineteenth-century operas will be sung in performance museums along with Broadway songs and classic blues.

Sounds, the raw materials of musical culture, have become available to anyone with a sampling tape recorder. No longer do we need to spend years learning how to manipulate standard instruments. Sampled sounds from any source can be organized to create any instrument one can imagine. Do you want a flute that manipulates the subtle vibrations of butterfly wings? It's possible.

The implications of such democratization have already made music industry executives nervous. The promotion and sale of music in the United States alone involves billions of dollars. How will they and the musicians they serve (or exploit) continue to make money? Commerce won't stop, but the emphasis may change from quantity to quality, from excess to moderation. If more people are making music themselves, they won't be easy consumers to please. They'll demand excellence and will be willing to pay for it—although, perhaps, not as much as before, because they're more conscious of how much is freely given. And, for genuine artists, a new economic scale won't be bad. Like all creative people, the musical artist's aim is to explore and share. We ask only to make a living.

We suspect that the twenty-first century will be an age of composers rather than performers. We imagine music schools where the emphasis will be on composition, where students will attend classes in harmonies, melodies, and rhythms from many cultures, where new instruments will be created all the time, and where sounds will be pursued and digested like the prey of ancient hunters. The music they create will be broadcast instantly to an electronic network that will include hospitals, private homes, and virtual concert halls. Music libraries will contain thousands of performances—live and recorded—on assorted hard drives, accessible from any computer.

Amid such dramatic changes, several biological constants will endure in music. The human voice will remain the most immediate and flexible instrument for expressing our feelings and inspirations. The individual performer will always be challenged to communicate the essence of any music, to translate sounds into a human context with his or her body. And, wherever people want to be free, to thrust themselves into the joy and sorrow of the moment, the improvisational spirit of the music we've called jazz will always be present.

An enlarged understanding of our planet offers the possibility not only of new music, but of a new definition of humanity—a definition more inclusive, more spiritual, more interconnected. Our scientists have begun to confirm what the mystics have long told us: the world, including our bodies, vibrates with electromagnetic energies that seem "musical" in their patterns and cycles. As we pass through our lives, each of us—even those who consider themselves tone deaf—creates unconscious music that interacts with that coming from other people, animals, plants, even landscapes. What a hidden symphony!

Hailed by the *New York Times* as "one of the finest conductors of her generation," **JoAnn Falletta**—currently music director of the Buffalo Philharmonic Orchestra, the Virginia Symphony Orchestra, and the Long Beach Symphony Orchestra—also appears regularly with orchestras and chamber ensembles in Europe, Africa, Asia, South America, and the United States. A native of New York City and a graduate of the Mannes and Juilliard Schools, Falletta is the recipient of eight consecutive awards from ASCAP for creative programming, as well as the American Symphony Orchestra League's John S. Edwards programming award. She has performed nearly 300 works by American composers; together with the Buffalo Philharmonic, she recently recorded three "American Classics" CDs for the Naxos label. Among the prizes she has received are the Stokowski, Toscanini, and Bruno Walter Awards for conducting.

❦ The Twenty-first-Century Maestro

JOANN FALLETTA

ONE of the most vivid memories of my days as a young conducting student at The Juilliard School is of an article about the conductor of one of the top five orchestras in the United States. This individual, the newspaper maintained, was so important and so private that he was never seen anywhere in the city except on the podium. Even when he left the concert hall after a performance he retreated to a favorite restaurant where a secluded table in the back room was provided for him, away from his throng of fans. The orchestra itself seemed rather proud of this—it meant, of course, that one had to purchase a concert ticket in order to enjoy even a glimpse of this charismatic conductor.

For my four fellow conducting colleagues and myself, the description of the life of this conductor could not have been more different from our own harried existences—dealing with the scarcely concealed contempt of the Juilliard conductor's orchestra, the scathing (and uncomfortably accurate) criticism of our teacher, the humiliation of cajoling, pleading and bribing our classmates into forming reluctant and disorganized groups over which we could wield our incipient batons. For myself, fifteen years and four music directorships later, that conductor's enviable situation seems even further from reality than it did then.

I am convinced that no one leaves a conservatory with more than the sketchiest idea of what it means to be a music director. Musical understanding, analytical aptitude, and psychological skills develop slowly as one studies, works, and matures. But even the most profound grasp of a score, the most elegant technique hardly prepares any of us for the duties that descend upon his or her shoulders the moment the music-director search committee reaches its decision. The choice of a music director is probably one of the most significant decisions any orchestra can make; the thought that the chosen one—the maestro—may have little to no idea what the job is all about is cause for some alarm.

We stand at the gateway of a twenty-first century even the wildest visionary could not have imagined at the beginning of the twentieth. As our thoughts turn, not only to the end of our own century but also toward the millennium, it seems an appropriate time to acknowledge the extraordinary changes that the last one hundred years have wrought in the arts.

It has been a century to remember. Extraordinary artistic innovation has mirrored rapid developments in science and technology. Unprecedented social and political upheaval, spurred by international conflicts, has redrawn the world map time and time again. Yet composers have risen to the challenges of expressing our changing world, creating new and complex works that reflect life in this century. In this time of rapid and unpredictable change in the arts, it is no surprise the archetypal conductor, entering the twenty-first century, must shoulder responsibilities quite different from those of his or her nineteenth-century predecessor.

Today, across America, symphony orchestras are facing what appear to be the most difficult times in their collective history. Often the very survival of these institutions will hinge on the skills of a maestro—not only musical talent, but also leadership ability, interpersonal communication skills, and management acumen in planning, scheduling, interacting with staff and musicians, dealing with conflict, and fostering feelings of solidarity, community, and common purpose. Add to these requirements broad artistic vision, an understanding of a given organization's musical objectives, and the courage to explore new possibilities and options coupled with the wisdom to preserve tradition at its best. Some persons may recall candidate Eugene

McCarthy's response to a 1968 query whether he was qualified to be President of the United States; McCarthy replied that, when you got right down to it, probably nobody was qualified. The same might be said for music directors at the end of the twentieth century. Probably no one has all the skills the job demands. But a solid understanding of the responsibilities of the position can and should help individual conductors develop their personal resources within the framework of his or her unique personality and charisma.

Musical talent remains the most mysterious and least quantifiable commodity in terms of a music director. Certainly even an unsophisticated audience can surmise that a violinist plays with poor intonation or a pianist has problems with the technical demands of a concerto. But can most audiences assess the skill of a maestro? Does a flamboyant podium presence equate to a prodigious talent? Does conducting from memory insure deep musical understanding? Do exaggerated tempos and dynamic changes imply a unique and revelatory interpretation? The true assessment of a conductor's musical skill often rests with the musicians over whom he or she presides. Can they play comfortably and expressively, feeling neither confined nor abandoned? Perhaps the ideal performance situation is one in which each musician feels free to play as if on his or her own, yet simultaneously enjoy the support and comfort offered by an interpretation that makes complete musical sense. In such an ideal performance the audience senses (rather than defines) a "rightness" about the experience—a subconscious structure, a pacing, a unified artistic conception, an inevitability that creates more than superficial depth and excitement. Certainly such "ideal situations" are far from commonplace. The musical understanding—indeed, the human understanding that such situations presuppose—are the goals to which conductors should aspire all their musical lives. The deeper and broader an individual's background, the richer and more profoundly evident are both the specific, unique qualities of his or her work and its greater significance.

Leonard Bernstein once stated that "any composer's writing is the sum of himself, all his roots and all his influences." The same is true of the work of any music director. The value of the music stems from the life of the artist, his or her particular set of cultural and social values, the community in which he or she lives, the nation to which he or she belongs. The maestro's art must be both an expression of an inner and outer world, and his or her life must be dedicated to the enrichment of both. Any conductor who is not fully devoted to the constant development of musical understanding is failing to recognize the single most significant requirement of the profession.

Secondary to the depth of one's musical aptitude is the ability to communicate that knowledge—to an orchestra, to audiences, and to the whole of a community. The technical and personal communication skills required on the podium are enormous and completely individual. The often-mentioned but little-understood concepts of "charisma" and "chemistry" are part of the question, and it is acknowledged that not every conductor works equally well with every ensemble. Each music director hopes to establish a productive working relationship with his or her own orchestra—a relationship based on mutual respect, trust, and a desire to foster what is best in the organization. Each maestro is called upon to make extraordinarily difficult personnel decisions, to inspire dozens of diverse personalities, and to conduct Bach and Stockhausen with equal aplomb! The only hope for success, I am certain, is for each conductor to be completely him- or herself on the podium, whether that means being humorous, dignified, intense, energetic, tranquil, or otherwise. Integrity seems to be the one characteristic that no orchestral ensemble is willing to overlook. "Style"—as long as it is based on sincerity—can and should be as different as each maestro is to the next.

One of the most telling reflections of the music director's vision and personality lies in the choice of repertoire for the orchestra. Other factors may influence the final shape of the symphony's programming, but each maestro ultimately bears overall responsibility for the complexion and texture of a given season's offerings. Are individual compositions simply pieces the conductor would like to perform? Or do they reflect collectively a certain character, mission, or vision? As much as they may be somewhat constrained by financial limitations, choices should be artistically motivated. What repertoire will help the orchestra develop, grow, challenge itself, stretch stylistically? It need not be the repertoire with the greatest technical demands: a good performance of Mozart's *Jupiter* symphony, for example, is much harder to pull of than one of Orff's *Carmina Burana*.

A balance should be struck in presenting pieces from all periods, and a sense of overall logic and motivation behind that choice of pieces is critical. Selections should support and complement the expressed objectives of the orchestra and, in the long run, contribute to the vitality and vibrancy of the organization. In addition, music directors must seek the reintegration of living composers into society at large. The orchestra exists not only as a beautiful reflection of a musical past, but as an unerring mirror of current society. A living, breathing, dynamic institution, the symphony is constantly developing exciting repertoire. If we succumb to the suggestion that only music written between 1750 and 1900 should be performed, are we not invalidating the orchestra as an institution and ourselves as a culture? Certainly music directors should not embrace new music indiscriminately. Half-hearted performances of new work can drastically weaken the case for an ongoing repertoire. Isn't it possible, though, for each maestro to find a handful of living composers whose work speaks to him or her personally—and to champion those composers? Aaron Copland believed that the United States would only achieve true artistic maturity when composers feel themselves affirmed and buoyed by their communities, when "living music" means something, in the deepest sense, to everyone. Music directors can help their orchestras and communities celebrate the privilege of experiencing and appreciating music of all times—through thoughtful selection, inclusive presentation, and, most of all, committed and vivid performance.

Often the conductor becomes the focal point around which swirls the conflict of balancing artistic goals with monetary considerations. I am convinced that, in times of financial challenge, artistic integrity and vision must be even more clearly defined and upheld. The goal of any orchestra is to serve the needs of its community. To accomplish this, its music director must strive to forge a strong community within the orchestra family, fostering the concept of artistic integrity as a shared vision. No maestro, whether he or she spends eight or forty-eight weeks with an orchestra, can abdicate his or her responsibility to uphold the highest musical standards. There is no ideal situation. But through creativity and hard work, an environment can be created wherein artistic achievement can flourish.

Does artistic achievement necessarily equate to expense? I do not believe so. But it does equate to hours and weeks and months of planning, of prioritizing, of refining and polishing a vision for the organization. Artistic integrity is not about playing the most demanding pieces in the repertoire. It is not about featuring the most expensive soloists, nor about having the largest number of string players. For music directors, artistic integrity is helping to release the vibrant energy within each player, enabling each musician to achieve his or her musical best. Artistic integrity is recognizing that orchestras do not develop through the splashy applause of concert nights. Rather, they develop slowly—through every valuable minute of rehearsal, through every score that is tackled, through every audition held. Conductors must build artistic integrity into all the little bits and pieces of their orchestras' activities. This attitude, this search for excellence, does not necessarily cost more financially, but it does cost more in time, work, commitment, dedication, cooperation, and communication. The return, both individually and collectively, is beyond price.

Few conductors have significant marketing or development experience when they accept positions with orchestras. Even fewer are the music directors who do not spend, over the course of their tenure, countless hours with experts in those fields, analyzing, fund-raising, reaching out to community constituencies. The details of this kind of commitment are myriad: they may involve creating special programs or festivals, pre- or post-concert discussions, speaking at countless civic groups, designing and implementing educational activities, gaining media visibility and cooperation, and working at grant writing and corporate and individual fund-raising. It is only through a vital artistic partnership with the community that any maestro can hope to make his or her orchestra a vibrant thread in the tapestry of community life.

We as conductors must have the courage to rethink widely held assumptions. We may not know what the concert hall of 2050 will be like. But all of us have faith in the serious investigation of our art, of musical sound. As our organizations undergo striking metamorphoses, they will look to us, the music directors, for leadership—for artistic ability, honesty, vision, creativity, communication, energy, sense of mission, collaboration, and total involvement. In extraordinary times it is extraordinary action that makes the difference. The coming century will not be a time for maintaining the status quo; rather, it will be a time for making decisive and focused commitments to the values that are at the core of the art. To do any less would be to leave our orchestral world defenseless to those who perceive the arts as trivial and non-essential. The music director of the twentieth and the twenty-first centuries must be a teacher in the purest sense—a teacher who has internalized art so completely that its manifestation becomes his or her persona. As a leader and a communicator, each maestro must bring to artistic endeavors an energy that is as inspiring and compelling as the art form itself.

As artists in a pluralistic, competitive society, music directors cannot afford to remain aloof from their audience. Involvement is essential, not only in raising dollars but also in raising consciousness. Performing artists share a fundamental supposition that there is a significant community with an appetite for art, a discriminating, renewable public. The fearful reality is that this audience of expectant, appreciative listeners is at risk. If we are not careful, we may find that we have been diligently trained and scrupulously prepared to answer questions no longer being asked.

In times of financial and social challenge for orchestras, is there truly a valid place for the enigmatic and charismatic conductor of my Juilliard memory? Is it not imperative for music directors today—and tomorrow—to communicate through every possible means their belief that music is an integral part of our lives and of our community? We stand on the threshold of a new millennium, a temporal landmark that holds tremendous metaphorical and spiritual significance. As we move forward, the most exciting development for the twenty-first century may not be technological advancement but an expanding sense of what it means to be a human being. Conductors and their ensembles can eloquently and passionately articulate the conviction that music lies at the core of our continual reinvigoration of the human spirit.

Charles L. Gary completed his undergraduate work in American
history at Yale and earned graduate degrees in music education at
the University of Cincinnati. After teaching in the public schools
of Ohio and Tennessee, he served on the faculties of Austin State
University, Purdue University, and George Mason University.
For the past eighteen years he has been director of graduate
programs in music education at The Catholic University of
America. Gary is a former executive director of the Music
Educators National Conference (MENC); a past president of the
Alliance of Associations for the Advancement of Education, he
has also been assistant director of the Tanglewood Symposium
and has served a number of other professional organizations.

❦ Public-School Music Education in the Twentieth Century

CHARLES L. GARY

HOWARD Hanson was one of the outstanding American composers of
our time. He was the first winner of the American Prix de Rome for his
composition *California Forest Play*, premiered at California State Redwood
Park in July 1920. Director of the Eastman School of Music, founder and
president of the National Music Council (NMC), president of the Music
Teachers National Association (MTNA), board member of the Music
Educators National Conference (MENC), winner of the Pulitzer Prize and the
Ditson Award, Hanson was for seven decades an influential personality in
American music. In his later years he told a group of teachers that the loss of
the New York Phiharmonic, or the Philadelphia Orchestra, or the
Metropolitan Opera would be less catastrophic than the disappearance of
music from our public schools. What is the nature of the institution that was
so highly esteemed by such a man?

At the turn of the century, when Hanson was four years old, music was a
well-established part of the curriculum in most of large cities and many
smaller towns throughout the United States. Trained musicians, known as
"supervisors," helped elementary-school teachers show children how to read

music and sing. They directed high-school choirs; in many schools entire senior classes performed as choirs at their graduation ceremonies. Works by Handel, Haydn, and Mozart were learned in schools across the country. The success of this instruction is attested to facts like this one: it was possible to organize a chorus for the famous May Festival of Cincinnati because so many local singers had been trained in public schools.

In 1884 a Department of Music Education was created by the National Education Association (NEA), and many supervisors participated in annual meetings of the organization. The 1906 meeting was scheduled for San Francisco, but the earthquake forced its cancellation. When it was announced that the NEA would meet the following year in Los Angeles, Philip C. Hayden, then secretary of the Department, realized not many supervisors from the East or Midwest would be able to travel by train to the meeting. Instead, he invited any and all of them living close to his home in Keokuk, Iowa, to come investigate his system of teaching rhythm. Responses were positive and, through the *School Music Monthly* he edited, Hayden advertised the meeting more extensively; together with Edward Bailey Birge, music supervisor in the Indianapolis schools, he planned a three-day gathering in Keokuk. The president of the Department being ill, the assembly was presided over by vice-president Frances Elliott Clark of Milwaukee; some 104 individuals registered for the meeting. And, when Herbert Owen of Madison, Wisconsin, reported that the committee appointed by Clark recommended the formation of an independent organization, sixty-nine attendees signed up. Of them, forty-four were women, twenty-nine men.

It was never the intention of this new group to supplant the NEA's Department, but over the years music educators gravitated to the new organization, and it became the Music Supervisors National Conference (MSNC). In 1940 the NEA asked the Conference to represent it in music matters.

In its early years the Conference turned its attention to the high schools. When, at the 1910 meeting in Cincinnati, Superintendent F. B. Dyer asked for advice about music-appreciation courses and school credit for private lessons, a committee was appointed to develop a major in music. At St. Louis in 1912 the Conference advocated full-credit for music study requiring homework and half-credit for rehearsals. At the Rochester meeting in 1913 the organization discussed the issue of high-school orchestras.

By the beginning of the twentieth century, instrumental music could be found in a number of American schools. Frequently this was made possible by the presence of students, especially violin players, who were also taking private lessons. Some instrumental ensembles were even organized and led entirely by students; an orchestra in Easton, Pennsylvania, was one example. The mandolin, enjoying great popularity at the time, was sometimes included in such groups. An outstanding orchestra was organized by Will Earhart in Richmond, Indiana; during the early 1900s it had become a full-fledged symphonic ensemble and its reputation began to spread.

A notable event in 1910 was Albert Mitchell's visit to England to study methods of class violin instruction at Maidstone, Kent. On his return to Boston Mitchell's innovations proved so successful that he was relieved of his choral duties and made a full-time teacher of instrumental music. Piano classes were introduced in some schools a few years later. By the 1920s class instruction, both homogeneous and hetereogeneous, was becoming common. In defending class instruction, Mitchell told those who attended the 1920 Conference meeting in Philadelphia that he sought not to develop finished violinists, but to open the door to music and "educate the sense of touch, sight, and hearing." The following year in St. Joseph, Missouri, Earhart defended class instruction in instrumental music when he stated his belief that the schools' mission was not to "fit the pupil into a musical life, but to fit music into the pupil's life." These statements reflect Conference attitudes that persist to the present day, although at times its members complain that developing excellent performing groups is the real purpose of some programs.

A significant event occurred in Dallas in 1927 and had some interesting antecedents. In 1922 the MSNC met in Nashville, and the Richmond, Indiana, orchestra, then directed by Joseph Maddy, was invited to perform. The town of Richmond raised $1,000 and sent seventy-five students to the convention, where they made a tremendous impression on Randall C. Condon, one of the speakers. Condon, then superintendent of schools in Cincinnati, had been asked to speak on the topic: "A Supervisor as Seen by Superintendent." Elected president of the NEA's Department of Superintendence a few years later, he asked his supervisor, Walter Aiken, to invite Maddy's orchestra to appear at the convention he was planning for Dallas; in response, Aiken secured Maddy and his recently assembled National High School Orchestra. The 270 student musicians from thirty-eight states played programs that included Beethoven's Overture to *Egmont*, Wagner's Overture to *Rienzi*, the "Andante" from Tchaikovsky's Fifth Symphony, Sibelius's *Finlandia*, and excerpts from Hanson's "Nordic" Symphony. At the conclusion of its convention, the Department of Superintendence passed resolutions calling for the extension of music to rural schools and for "placing music on an equal basis with other fundamental subjects."

The successes of National High School Orchestras from 1926 to 1928 prompted Maddy and his associate Thaddeus P. Giddings, music supervisor in Minneapolis, to open a summer camp for instrumentalists. This National High School Orchestra and Band Camp, held at Interlochen, Michigan, was at first rather humble but managed to hold on through the Depression. It is today a full-fledged academy of the arts, boasting scholars and faculty from around the world.

There were few school bands in America before World War I. Famous trombonist Frederick Innes organized a Boy Scouts Band in Denver and within a year took them to England, where they received top honors at their "Jamboree" there. The formation of bands was given additional impetus by the patriotic fervor that developed during the war years; following the conflict, band directors—many of them trained by the Damrosch brothers (Frank and Walter)—had returned home and went looking for jobs in the schools. School administrators found bands of value, not only for educational and school-spirit purposes, but also for creating favor with the public. At the University of Illinois, Albert A. Harding developed outstanding marching and symphonic bands; these ensembles became another training ground for instrumental-music teachers and were soon imitated on other college campuses.

A school-band "tournament," held in conjunction with a music-trades convention, was held in Chicago in 1923; the winner was a band from Fostoria, Ohio, directed by John Wainwright. The tournament launched a contest movement that swept the schools and lasted more than ten years. Eventually the Conference's Committee on Instrumental Affairs took charge of these interscholastic events and established a ratings system. The quality of music performed was improved by lists of pieces considered suitable for festival competitions.

During this same period of time remarkable development took place in the area of choral singing. At the 1928 Conference convention in Chicago, the A Cappella Choir from Flint, Michigan, High School sparked an interest in unaccompanied Renaissance music, including works by Giovanni Pierlugi da Palestrina, Orlando di Lasso, Jacob Arcadelt, and William Byrd. At the time Russian and Scandinavian composers (including Pavel Tchesnokov, Alexandre Gretchaninoff, F. Melius Christiansen, and Edvard Grieg) were popular. In many schools enthusiasm for a-cappella singing in high schools became strong enough to replace or supplement accompanied choral music.

In 1930 the Conference determined that it could no longer depend on voluntary efforts by its officers to carry on the many activities the organization had developed. A business office was therefore convened in Chicago, with Clifford V. Buttelman serving as Executive Secretary. In 1932 the Conference replaced the word "Supervisor" with "Educator" and became—as we know it today—the Music Educators National Conference (MENC). The change reflected developments since 1907: most MENC members were music teachers working under individuals who coordinated activities on behalf of their respective cities or counties. Such individuals may still have been referred to as "supervisor" or "superintendent," but the most common title soon became "director."

When the NEA asked the Conference to become its music department, Vanett Lawler was sent to Washington to open a branch office. During the lean years of the 1930s she was loaned to the Pan American Union, where she worked with musicologist Charles Seeger. Her association with Seeger resulted in Lawler's visits to South America to help build stronger programs in music education there. At the end of World War II Lawler served UNESCO in Paris and became an important figure in establishing the International Society for Music Education. Since Lawler succeeded Buttelman, the MENC has entertained visitors from around the world seeking information about American music education in action.

By 1940 a well-established curriculum in music existed in many schools. This included not only performing groups (bands, orchestras, and choruses), but also classes in harmony, ear-training, music history, and music appreciation. Not all schools enjoyed such varied programs, but they were becoming more widespread, especially in the cities.

As early as the nineteenth century, cities like Cincinnati trained their own music teachers. By the beginning of the twentieth century this task had been taken over by conservatories and universities, as well as by normal schools that were rapidly becoming teacher colleges. Karl W. Gehrkens of Oberlin College in Ohio was the first to develop a full four-year college-level major in music education, one distinct from majors in performance and composition. Bachelor of Science in Music Education degrees were first awarded to three Oberlin students in 1922, and during the next twenty years or so this became the degree offered by most colleges and universities with music-education programs. Some college music departments, especially in state institutions, were established to serve large numbers of students eager to fill music positions then opening up in the expanding nationwide school system.

After World War II college music-education programs, spurred by continued interest in music and G. I. Bill monies available to thousands of veterans, continued to flourish. It was then that graduate programs in music education began to expand—and, with them, interest in music-education research. In 1932 William S. Larson established the *Bibliography of Research Studies in Music Education*. Most of that journal's contents consisted of masters' theses; later, doctoral dissertations were added to the list. By the 1950s the number of annual titles had grown enormously, and it was decided that only dissertations would be cited. In 1953 the MENC launched the *Journal of Research in Music Education*, with Allen P. Britton of the University of Michigan as its editor.

By that time other aspects of the MENC's publication program had grown. Members were supplied, for example, with lists of music worthy of study, with advice on dealing with the music industry,[1] and a series of "Source Books" that covered many phases of the profession. By May 1963 the list of subscribers to the *Music Educators Journal* totaled 42,240.

In the late 1950s composer Norman Dello Joio discussed with Vanett Lawler a problem he recognized: young composers were having trouble having their works performed. Together Lawler and Dello Joio designed the Young Composers Project, later underwritten by a grant from the Ford Foundation and administered by the National Music Council. Creative young musicians under thirty-five years of age were placed in school systems as composers-in-residence. To qualify to receive a composer, a school system had to provide opportunities for creating works for young children, bands, orchestras, choruses, and small ensembles. There was no difficulty in locating suitable sites, such was the vigor of music education at that time.

Almost simultaneously, the Russians launched Sputnik; within a few years many schools found themselves pressed to emphasize mathematics and the sciences. Lawler turned to MENC's old friend, the school superintendents. In 1958 the American Association of School Administrators devoted an entire convention to the arts, and its resolutions committee produced the following statement:

We believe in a well-balanced school curiculum in which music, drama, painting and the like are included side by side with other important subjects such as mathematics, history and science. It is important that pupils, as a part of general education, learn to appreciate, to understand, to create, and to criticise with discrimination those products of the mind, the voice, the hand, and the body which give dignity to the person and exalt the spirit of man.[2]

Under the Kennedy administration the U.S. Office of Education made grants to universities and school systems for educational research. In 1963 an institution returned grant money when it became apparent a contract could not be completed. It was too late in the year to advertise for more proposals, so the Office contacted Claude Palisca, a musicologist at Yale University who had already submitted a proposal of his own. At the Office's request Palisca changed the subject of a meeting he was organizing to "Music in the Schools." The Yale Seminar in Music Education was, on the whole, critical of what the participants believed was going on in public schools. Unfortunately, only a few participants (musicologists and college teachers) had any recent contact with some of the fine programs that did exist. Many of their concepts were based on music education in New York City, which, at that time, lacked exemplary programs. (Only a few years later New York eliminated music from the curriculum and did not replace it until Rudolph Giuliani became mayor.) Some of the comments made at the Yale Seminar, however, helped music educators who wanted to take advantage of the climate of change characteristic of the period.

One direct result of the Seminar was the Juilliard Repertory Project, supervised by composer Vittorio Giannini. The Project collected high-quality Medieval, Renaissance, Baroque, and Classical music. Contemporary works and folk music of instructional teaching were also included. A distinguished group of musicologists (it included Gustave Reese, Paul Henry Lang, Noah Greenberg, and Palisca himself) selected over 400 compositions later field-tested across the country. A group of distinguished music educators (including Allen Britton, Sally Monsour, Mary Ruth McCulley, and Louis Wersen) served as advisors. Some 230 works, both vocal and instrumental, were finally selected for the Project's library; the music itself was made available to schools through Canyon Press in Cincinnati.

Although the Juilliard Project and Yale Seminar were appreciated by music educators, the critical nature of the Project's final report irritated many of them. Among these was Wersen, music director for the Philadelphia public-school system. In 1966 Wersen became president of the MENC. Drawing upon a grant from the Theodore Presser Foundation and a considerable portion of the MENC budget, and with the cooperation of Boston University, he planned a symposium to be held at the Tanglewood Music Center during the summer of 1967. Robert A. Choate of Boston University was chosen by Wersen to plan the affair, one at which leaders from many sectors of society—philosophy, industry, labor, religion, psychology, and music—spent a week with a select group of music educators. The educators remained for a second week to consider what had transpired and seek answers to such questions as how can we better serve our students? and how can we make music education more useful to America today and tomorrow? A "Tanglewood Declaration" was written before the music educators departed. It consisted of (a) a statement that music should become part of every curriculum; and (b) eight statements that attempted to answer the questions identified above. (Several of the statements reflect criticisms of school music made at Yale.)

Meanwhile the Young Composers Project had impressed the Ford Foundation and was continued. The National Music Council that ran the Project had encountered difficulties because of unfamiliarity with the ways schools operated; the result was a $1,380,000 grant to MENC to organize the Contemporary Music Project for Creativity in Music Education (CMP). The Young Composers Project was continued as a part of a larger design that also included workshops and seminars, held at colleges across the country, that were intended to help teachers understand and feel more comfortable with contemporary music. Especially influential was the Seminar of Comprehensive Musicianship, held at Northwestern University, that helped improve the education of music teachers. Experiments in education took place at thirty-six institutions, many of which redesigned their curricula to deal with music as a whole rather than in terms of history, theory, ear-training, and analysis. The future of these experiments looked bright, but traditionalists in charge of some programs prevented their universal adoption. Nevertheless, the Seminar influenced teaching at other than college levels, and music teachers in middle schools and junior highs found its concepts useful.

In 1968 another grant from the Ford Foundation, to which MENC added $50,000 a year, helped CMP continue. Teaching comprehensive musicianship was still part of this endeavor; to it were added a program called "Professionals-in-Residence to Communities," as well as a number of complementary activities. Groups of music educators with special interests also organized associations that had considerable effect on school-music programs;

most of these were associated with the MENC. One involved Stan Kenton and John Roberts, the director of music in Denver and a jazz trombonist; together these men made a case at a Tanglewood symposium for America's indigenous music. In 1968 the National Association of Jazz Educators (NAJE) was formed "to further the understanding and appreciation of jazz and popular music, and to promote its artistic performance." Kenton's and Choate's "Tanglewood Declaration" helped make legitimate a music the schools had held at arm's length for years.

§

So much for earlier developments. What has the MENC done lately?

During the last twenty-five years string instruction in the schools has grown remarkably. Credit for this must be shared with the American String Teachers Association and the National School Orchestra Association; too, the influence of Japanese master Shinichi Suzuki has been substantial. School orchestras and community groups now perform much of the standard string and symphonic literature as well as pieces composed especially for them.

In addition to the wealth of music produced for school use by participants in the Young Composers Project, material currently in use by school groups has been contributed by other artists. Soon after Czech composer-conductor Vaclav Nelhybel came to America, he asked the MENC to advise him on marketing his works. Nelhybel was told there was a large audience for music in America's schools and that some publishers dealt only with that market; he was also informed that many schools had performing groups, both choral and instrumental, able to play standard literature. Nelhybel followed an MENC suggestion that he write for school groups and subsequently composed many compositions for band, orchestra, and chorus. Other institutions, including the high school at Ithaca, New York, have commissioned new music from such composers as Alec Wilder, Vincent Persichetti, Barney Childs, Leslie Bassett, Warren Benson, Armand Russell, Robert Ward, Samuel Adler, and Alan Hovhaness.

Through its Teacher Training Authorization, the Education Professions Development Act of 1967 awarded four art-education organizations grants that made possible a joint project. Named IMPACT (Interdisciplinary Model Programs in the Arts for Children and Teachers) by Charles Dorn, then executive officer of the National Art Education Association (NAEA), this project funded five sites responsible for infusing the arts into school curricula.

149

Those sites—located in Columbus, Ohio, and Eugene, Oregon—did most to show that the arts can benefit traditional school curricula.

One fortunate side effect of IMPACT was that it brought together over a period of time four professional arts-education associations. Calling themselves DAMT (for Dance, Art, Music and Theater), these associations sought out cooperative ventures that might advance their several causes. One such venture was the Arts Education Advocacy Project that brought to the Kennedy Center in Washington, D.C., school administrators and state school officers and produced a number of suggestions for encouraging support for the arts. The more formal name of Alliance for Arts Education was adopted at that time; its project director was John Mahlmann, executive director of the National Art Education Association.

A wake-up call for educational reform occurred in the 1980s when the United States Senate report *A Nation at Risk* was issued.[3] The report led to a number of books and other responses that focused attention on the knowledge and skills expected of school graduates. As part of this effort the Consortium of National Arts Education Associations received a grant from the U.S Department of Education, the National Endowment for the Arts, and the National Endowment for the Humanities. The money, administered by MENC, was used to underwrite the production of "National Standards for Arts Education." MENC had already produced two sets of standards for music education (in 1974 and 1986); these served as models for the larger work. With the passage of the Goals 2000: Educate America Act, which included the arts in the curriculum, the national goals produced by the Consortium were written into law.

There is no accurate way of determining the effects of school-music programs on American society. One can only speculate, and I shall. First, bigger is not always better; nevertheless, there is more music offered in schools today than in 1900. That music is also more varied, nor is it limited to the classical repertory of Western Europe. It is estimated there are some 2,000 orchestras in the country today. Certainly some of their players must have begun their activities in the schools. Church choirs appear to be having increasing difficulty in recruiting volunteers, but that may be because many singers participate in community or professional choirs.

In 1900 there were no Sweet Adelines. Nor did the Society for the Preservation and Encouragement of Barbershop Quartet Singing in America (SPEBSQSA) yet exist. The Young Men in Harmony program developed jointly by MENC and SPEBSQSA in the 1970s has introduced many boys to the joys of song. Many of them still participate in this unique American pastime.

One of the most telling expressions of support for music education may be found today in school buildings. Elaborate, acoustically designed music rooms loaded with expensive equipment are not unusual. These rooms have been funded by parents and other taxpayers because musical opportunities are considered valuable. Would such support have had such concrete manifestation if music education had not, in some senses, been successful?

NOTES

[1] *Music Buildings, Rooms and Equipment*, 5th ed., ed. Charles L. Gary (Washington, D.C.: Music Educators National Conference, 1966).

[2] American Association of School Administrators Official Report for the Year 1958. This publication includes a record of the annual meeting and work conference on "Education and the Creative Arts" (Washington, D.C.: American Association of School Administrators, 1959).

[3] Issued 5 May 1983. See also, Thomas M. Smith, *America's Teachers Ten Years After "A Nation at Risk"* (Washington, D.C.: U.S. Dept. of Education, 1995).

ADDITIONAL SOURCES

Birge, Edward Bailey. *History of Public School Music in the United States.* Boston: Oliver Ditson, 1928.

Boyle, J. David, and Robert Lathrop. "The IMPACT Experience: An Evaluation." *Music Educators Journal* 59/5 (January 1973): 42-47.

Documentary Report of the Tanglewood Symposium, ed. Robert A. Choate. Washington, D.C.: Music Educators National Conference, 1968.

Mark, Michael L. *Contemporary Music Education,* 4th ed. New York: Schirmer Books, 1998.

Morgan, Hazel Nohavek, and Charles L. Gary. *A History of American Music Education*, 2nd ed. Reston, VA: Music Educators National Conference, 1999.

Music Education Source Book, ed. Hazel Nohavek Morgan. Chicago: Music Educators National Conference, 1947.

Music in American Education. Chicago: Music Educators National Conference, 1955.

Wilson, Bruce, and Charles L. Gary. "Music in Our Schools: The First 150 Years." *Music Educators Journal* 74/6 (February 1988): 25-101.

Bob Goldfarb owns ArtsMedia LLC, a Los Angeles-based company that works with radio stations, the Internet, and the recording industry on projects related to culture and the arts. A graduate of Harvard College and the Harvard Business School, Goldfarb has also worked as director of United States Operations for Teldec Records and as a senior manager at radio stations KUSC and KFAC in Los Angeles. From 1995 until 2000 he served as executive director of the American Composers Alliance.

❦ The Invisible Art
New Music in America

BOB GOLDFARB

THE prospects for American composers at the start of the twentieth century looked unpromising. The United States had its great novelists and poets and painters, but no American composer had yet made an indelible mark on the nation's cultural life. In fact classical music generally, through institutions like symphony orchestras and opera companies, played no great role in nineteenth-century American culture, although the upper levels of society recognized European classical music as a part of their cultural patrimony. How much has changed in the last one hundred years? Arguably not a great deal.

America's musical life began in the eighteenth century with the first known concert given in 1731, but no enduring musical institutions were established until the nineteenth century. A musician named Gottlieb Graupner created a Philo-Harmonic Society in Boston around 1809 (it disbanded in 1826). New York's first opera house opened in 1833, and a predecessor of the New York Philharmonic was founded in 1842; the Metropolitan Opera was founded in 1883. These organizations primarily presented European music—German symphonies, Italian opera—with a very few exceptions. William Henry Fry's opera *Leonora*, with a libretto after Edward Bulwer-Lytton, was produced in Philadelphia in 1845, and *Rip Van Winkle* by George Frederick Bristow was staged in New York in 1855, but they were rare events.

These composers of nineteenth-century America are now largely forgotten, as are others such as Anthony Philip Heinrich and Louis Moreau Gottschalk. The first American composer of classical music to achieve popular fame was probably Dublin-born Victor Herbert, whose first concert works were published at the end of the nineteenth century. His fame, however, rested primarily on dozens of popular operettas, including *Babes in Toyland* (1903) and *Naughty Marietta* (1910), and he was a renowned cellist and conductor as well. What's more, Herbert established a pattern that other composers would follow in the twentieth century: he recognized the power of the media and the importance of the business side of music.

Herbert was a pioneer in recordings. He worked with Thomas Edison and later made recordings for the Victor label, including acoustic-era performances of *American Fantasia* (1898) and the "Dagger Dance" from his Wagnerian opera *Natouma* (1911). The opera enjoyed thirty-five performances in Philadelphia, Chicago, and New York. Celebrated singers Alma Gluck and John McCormack recorded a few of its arias, in what was probably the first instance of media exposure for serious music by an American composer (though Victor also released songs of George Whitefield Chadwick, sung by Ernestine Schumann-Heink, around the same time).

Victor Herbert also played an important role in the founding of American Society of Composers, Authors and Publishers (ASCAP), the first performing-rights society in America, in 1914. It was only in 1897 that the United States Congress recognized performance rights under copyright law, and Herbert was among those who realized that an agency was needed to collect systematically the royalties due to composers. No American composer before him had used his celebrity on behalf of his profession.

Herbert was also a faculty member at the National Conservatory of Music in New York. The Conservatory was one of several such institutions created after the Civil War, including the New England Conservatory (1867) and the Peabody Conservatory (1857). During the same period Harvard, the first American university to offer courses in music, appointed John Knowles Paine the first American professor of music in 1875. Other composers who found a home in academe included George Whitefield Chadwick, who became director of New England Conservatory in 1897; Chadwick's pupil Horatio Parker, who became a professor at Yale in 1894 and dean of the School of Music ten years later; and Edward MacDowell, possibly the most famous of them all, who in 1896 was appointed the first professor of music at Columbia

University. By the beginning of the twentieth century composers had unmistakably begun their deepening relationship with universities.

The new century raised millennial hopes that the world was on the verge of a great transformation. Just as science and engineering had remade the natural world in the Industrial Revolution, political, philosophical, and artistic movements believed that old ideas could be transfigured and supplanted by a new order. Where would it end? Would American music similarly supplant European music in the new century? Would it achieve the kind of national and international respect accorded to America's literary greats: Walt Whitman, Emily Dickinson, Nathaniel Hawthorne, Herman Melville? Would the music be popularly recognized alongside America's great paintings, sculpture, and other works of art?

The public was generally unaware of American composers when Aaron Copland appeared on the scene in the 1920s. Much like the American composers of the nineteenth century, Copland was trained in Europe: he went to France in 1921 and studied with Nadia Boulanger for three years. Just a few months after Copland returned to New York, Walter Damrosch led the New York Philharmonic in the composer's *Symphony for Organ and Orchestra* (1924). That concert immediately established Copland as the leading American composer of his generation in the press and in the minds of musicians.

Significantly, however, not much of Copland's music was recorded commercially until decades later. One of the first recordings, a 1935 Columbia release, offered the *Two Pieces for Violin and Piano* (1926) with violinist Jacques Gordon joined by the composer at the piano, but it was not widely noted. Serge Koussevitzky's recording with the Boston Symphony of *A Lincoln Portrait* (1942), with Melvyn Douglas narrating, was the first popular recording of a Copland work. Copland's public reputation until then relied more on his book *What to Listen for in Music* (1939) than on recordings. Later he won an Academy Award for his score to the film *The Heiress* (1948) and was nominated for three other film scores. It was not until the 1950s and 1960s that Copland achieved truly widespread recognition for his work as a concert-music composer.

Within the profession, however, Copland made a strong impact through his organizational work, first with the League of Composers in the 1920s. Later Copland was the principal organizer of the American Composers Alliance (ACA), established in 1937 to collect royalties for composers of serious music; a year later he helped found the American Music Center, a central repository for the scores of American composers. These activities also contributed to Copland's standing as the dean of American composers.

Nonetheless, a hundred years after his birth, Copland does not hold an unshakable place in the concert halls of his own country compared to European composers, though a number of his works are often performed. In Europe he is one of two composers (Gershwin is the other) who represent American concert music, but his works are not embraced as masterpieces on the same level as European works of the same era by Dimitri Shostakovich or Benjamin Britten.

Copland's European-trained American contemporaries—they include Virgil Thomson, Roger Sessions, Wallingford Riegger—appear only rarely on concert programs nowadays and are practically unknown to the public. So are home-grown American composers like Charles Ives, Roy Harris, and Carl Ruggles. To aficionados Ives, largely ignored during his lifetime, now appears prophetic in his uncompromising adherence to a personal vision, a value that has come to dominate the *Zeitgeist* of our own era. Ruggles's embrace of nature and Harris's evocations of the American frontier, like Copland's "prairie" music, delight Americans as aural pictures of America. But even their best works are rarely performed.

The general public has no acquaintance with the music of Milton Babbitt, Elliott Carter, David Diamond, Howard Hanson, Douglas Moore, Walter Piston, Elie Siegmeister, Halsey Stevens, or their generation. The composers who came to prominence after World War II have no greater claim on the popular imagination, with the exception of Samuel Barber's nostalgic, elegiac *Adagio for Strings* (1936), one of the few contemporary works conducted by Arturo Toscanini. Its use in a recent film soundtrack revived its fortunes. John Corigliano and William Bolcom have also written for film in recent years, but they are not so well known.

Nor is the public aware of more recent composers such as Stephen Albert, Richard Danielpour, Jacob Druckman, John Harbison, Aaron Jay Kernis, Christopher Rouse, Joseph Schwantner, Joan Tower, Charles Wuorinen, and Ellen Taafe Zwillich. Yet these composers' works are generally well regarded by their peers, critics, and performing musicians. Why is the public so indifferent? And is there any hope that this will change?

The signs are not encouraging. The sales of classical-music recordings amount to only 2% of all recordings sold in the United States, and contemporary music accounts for a minuscule share of the 2%. Where the nineteenth century canonized the accepted composers as part of a pantheon

155

of godlike creators, the late twentieth century adopts a few composers—mostly the same ones—as "brand names" that reassure the consumer of the product's quality. The vocabulary is different, but the effect is the same. The public remains skeptical of the untried and unproven in serious music, and its taste remains deeply conservative.

This is true despite the proliferation of musicians and music organizations. A hundred years ago there may have been a few dozen professional composers in the United States; now there are several thousand full- or part-time faculty positions at colleges and universities, created mostly in the years after World War II. There has been an explosion in the number of symphony orchestras and opera companies in the United States, especially since the 1960s, and in chamber groups as well. However, there are still few concerts in major halls where contemporary American music is heard to any great extent. As a result, publishers—who remain the strongest advocates of living composers—can publish only a fraction of the worthwhile scores they are offered. They can earn back their investment in a composer's work only if the music is performed, so the limited number of performance opportunities forces them to limit their publications.

In the end this is a reflection of the tastes of the audience: if the public wanted to hear more contemporary music, the composers and publishers and performing ensembles would be willing and able to furnish it. The demand, however, has never been there. The experience of the media confirms that conclusion: classical-music radio stations report that their listeners tune elsewhere when stations play new music. And classical music, let alone new music, is almost never seen on television except on PBS and arts-oriented cable channels.

It has been an article of faith for a generation of musicians that time was on their side: new works, they thought, would eventually be embraced by the public. After all, masterworks of the nineteenth century were greeted with incomprehension, ridicule, and even abuse, as Nicolas Slonimsky memorably documented in his *Lexicon of Musical Invective* (1969), but many of them are now part of the standard repertoire. Through faulty logic, some composers believed it was therefore a sign of originality if their works too were ignored or disliked. They expected that Schoenberg—and they themselves—would be appreciated a generation or two after their works appeared, like Beethoven and Brahms before them. But it never happened. Some new works have, of course, found acceptance among concert audiences, but they are few. Virtually no composer of the last fifty years has attracted a broad following or won enduring recognition.

By contrast, twentieth-century masterpieces in fiction, painting, theater, dance, poetry, and film have been widely acknowledged, even by people who do not personally enjoy them. Names like Eugene O'Neill and Arthur Miller, Frank Gehry and Philip Johnson, Twyla Tharp and Martha Graham, John Updike and Eudora Welty, Langston Hughes and James Merrill, Edward Hopper and Jackson Pollock, Alfred Hitchcock and Martin Scorsese, have a currency in the culture that virtually no twentieth-century composer can claim. (Igor Stravinsky may come closest.) Under the circumstances, support for contemporary music is often more dutiful than genuinely enthusiastic.

Some performing ensembles have tried to make new music—and the traditional repertoire too—more accessible to the audience through pre-concert talks and user-friendly program notes. Museums are similar means to make their exhibits more comprehensible to their visitors, but while museum attendance rises, symphony orchestras have more and more trouble selling subscriptions. One result is that they are even less likely to experiment with new repertoire than they once were.

There are some important exceptions to these generalizations. Philip Glass and Steve Reich, for example, have attracted large, new, and avid audiences. Those audiences, many of whose members are also interested in contemporary painting, theater, and dance, are not looking for the heirs to Mozart and Tchaikovsky. They simply respond to this music as a reflection of contemporary experience. It is not a coincidence that both of these composers work with other media, Glass in opera and film, and Reich with video: multimedia presentations that appeal to audiences who otherwise might not enter a concert hall.

The popularity of composers like Glass and Reich, and the simultaneous drop in the sales of recordings of traditional classical repertoire, has recently spurred a number of major record labels to record new music to an unprecedented extent. Contemporary music, which mostly appeared on small labels with limited distribution, now forms a significant part of the releases of the largest international labels, and exclusive contracts have been awarded to several American composers. If commercial record companies consider living composers to be a good investment, perhaps there is a new audience for contemporary music in the concert hall as well.

Until that audience materializes, the presenters of classical music concerts will face the same problem that characterized concert attendance in the nineteenth century. In that heyday of Romanticism the arts were viewed as a kind of secular counterpart to religion, conveying eternal verities through a canon that embodied civilization's best works. The pantheon of this secular religion included composers like Haydn, Mendelssohn, and Beethoven—all Europeans. It welcomed neither novelty nor innovation; even Brahms was too radical for many tastes in the late 1800s. Audiences were not particularly interested in music that was new or distinctively American.

Many of today's concertgoers also want an experience that is uplifting, affirming, and unproblematic. Audience members of an older generation—who constitute the majority of symphony subscribers—may also attend their local orchestra's concerts for social reasons, or to support an important cultural institution, or simply to maintain a personal or family tradition. Others may be looking for an educational experience or a change from the clamor of the frantic world outside. But the attitude in sum remains conservative, much as it has always been in the American concert hall.

In the visual arts, New York's Museum of Modern Art encouraged the creation and promotion of new works for decades and amassed a collection of masterpieces in the twentieth century whose appeal may well be timeless. By contrast, the creation of new music in America is fostered mostly through the efforts of widely dispersed performers and publishers (as well as universities). This process has not yielded a body of music comparable in the public mind to the permanent collection at the Museum of Modern Art nor a demand for most of the music that has been produced.

In the future, will concert halls become more like galleries that exhibit the new work of emerging artists? Or will they ratify the most important works of each generation, as the Museum of Modern Art has done? Or will they continue to present the same corpus of older works?

Perhaps that is the wrong question. Any composer now can singlehandedly function as a publisher by engraving and duplicating his or her own scores, act as a record label by making compact disks of music, and can distribute recordings and scores over the Internet. Perhaps traditional institutions will become less important as arbiters of taste and quality, and individual enthusiasts will play the most important role. Or possibly new institutions, or the media, will take over the role that symphony orchestras and chamber series have occupied for hundreds of years. The involvement of composers with local communities may also create a different and more lasting bond between the public and new musical works.

Inescapably, however, the fate of new music depends not on gimmicks or organizations or media, but on the music itself. Whatever role is played by intermediaries and institutions, it is the work of art that makes its own best case for acceptance and perpetuation. If American music in the twentieth century has failed to claim a pre-eminent place in the history of the era's culture, the explanation must ultimately lie with the works and their creators. Perhaps the new century will reinvigorate serious music in America, in ways we cannot yet foresee.

One thing will not change. Music is an indispensable means of expression, with a unique ability to communicate ideas and emotions wordlessly but powerfully. Over thousands of years it has expressed humanity's relation to God and the world, and it has looked into the individual's soul. It has marked great occasions and provided consolation and inspiration. Composers know that their work is essential because a culture without great music is inconceivable.

Jane Gottlieb is director of the library at The Juilliard School, New York City; she also teaches doctoral-level "Music Reference and Research" classes at Juilliard and holds the title "Associate Vice President for Library and Information Resources." Among her recent publications are *Guide to The Juilliard School Archives*, *Collection Assessment in Music Libraries*, *Knowing the Score: Preserving Collections of Music*, and *Pianist, Scholar, Connoisseur: Essays in Honor of Jacob Lateiner* (co-edited with Bruce Brubaker), as well as articles in *Notes*, *The New Grove Dictionary of American Music*, the *Dictionary of American Biography*, and *Scribner's Encyclopedia of American Lives*. Gottlieb is an active member of the Music Library Association and served as its president from 1995 to 1997.

❦ Music Librarianship
70 Years Back and 70 Years Forward

JANE GOTTLIEB

THE profession of music librarianship in the United States came of age in the twentieth century with the founding of the Music Library Association (MLA) in 1931. Although music collections existed in both public and academic nineteenth-century libraries, professional standards for acquiring, cataloging, preserving, and disseminating music materials within libraries did not really exist until the establishment of MLA.[1] Through its official purposes ("to promote the establishment, growth and use of music libraries; to encourage the collection of music and musical literature in libraries; to further studies in music bibliography; to increase efficiency in music library service and administration; and to promote the profession of music librarianship"[2]), the MLA is today the primary venue for discussion and action concerning all aspects of music in American libraries.

Carol Bradley, foremost chronicler of the MLA and of music librarianship in its first century, reported that there were nineteen people in attendance at the organization's founding meeting at Yale University in New Haven, Connecticut, on 22 June 1931.[3] Most of these individuals had been trained as musicologists and were responsible for music collections in major

160

academic and public research libraries; they included Eva Judd O'Meara (Yale University), Carleton Sprague Smith (Music Division, New York Public Library), Barbara Duncan (Sibley Library, Eastman School of Music), and Otto Kinkeldey (Cornell University; formerly of the Music Division of the New York Public Library). These founding MLA members helped build some of our country's major music collections and developed many of the standards for cataloging and bibliographic control of music materials still in use today.

In 1931 most music collections consisted primarily of paper materials: books and scores (both printed and manuscript). The predominant format for recorded-sound materials was the 78rpm disk. The political and economic upheavals that followed World War I helped create a "buyer's market" for European source materials, and librarians with a mandate to build collections could acquire major masterworks from European book dealers and auction houses at what even then were considered bargain prices.[4] The MLA founders considered "shared cataloging" of scores and sound recordings to be among their primary goals, but of course the development of standards for computer cataloging was decades away.[5]

Obviously, there have been monumental changes in the field of music librarianship during the last seventy years. The education boom of the 1950s led to the establishment of music departments in colleges and universities around the country, all of which needed their own music libraries to support research and performance activities. The development of automated library catalogs in the 1970s and the availability of vast amounts of information on music materials in bibliographic databases—including OCLC (Online Computer Library Center) and RLIN (Research Libraries Information Network)—have facilitated the shift in emphasis from development of individual collections to establishing systems of resource sharing among libraries.

Music librarians in the twentieth century have helped create, and have benefitted from, a wealth of extraordinary reference tools about music and music literature. Notably, the four international bibliographic databases— RISM (*Répertoire International des Sources Musicales*), RILM (*Répertoire Internationale de Littérature Musicale*), RIdIM (*Répertoire International d'Iconographie Musicale*), and RIPM (*Répertoire International de la presse musicale du XIXe siècle*)—all of which were developed after 1950,[6] provide a wide range of information about primary and secondary source materials. These tools give scholars access to resources held in libraries and repositories all over the world. They are also significant as models of international cooperation by scholars and librarians.

The explosion in music-reference sources in the twentieth century is also evidenced by the various editions of Vincent Duckles's *Music Reference and Research Materials*, "the" bibliography of reference tools used by several generations of music librarians and musicologists. The first edition of this book appeared in 1964 and includes 1,155 entries; the fifth edition, revised by Ida Reed (1997), includes more than 3,800 entries.

The sixth edition of *Grove's Dictionary of Music and Musicians*,[7] published in twenty volumes in 1980, characterized its departure from its predecessors by using the title: *The New Grove Dictionary of Music and Musicians*. The first year of the new century should feature the debut of the second *New Grove* edition, which will be available in both print (twenty-nine volumes) and electronic formats.

With this proliferation of sophisticated reference tools, it is interesting to note that the thorny problem of providing access to specific musical works contained in *Denkmäler* and other sets and series is yet to be completely solved. This undertaking was identified as a priority by the MLA's founders.[8] It was first addressed by Anna Harriet Heyer in her *Historical Sets, Collected Editions, and Monuments of Music: A Guide to Their Contents* (first edition, 1957; third edition, 1980). Heyer's successor is a large-scale project by George Hill and Norris Stephens entitled *Collected Editions, Historical Series & Sets & Monuments of Music: A Bibliography* (1997), which unfortunately has not yet appeared in its entirety, either in print or electronic form. Music librarians anxiously await completion of this important project, which will enable simplified access to the wealth of repertoire published in sets and series.

The vast changes in the music-publishing and sound-recording industries has had, and will continue to have, a profound effect on music libraries. The frequently discussed decline in classical-music literacy has brought with it a change in markets for printed scores and sound recordings: specifically, a reduction in the former and growth of the latter. It is now more difficult for music librarians to acquire printed scores of historical and contemporary music. Indeed, some music collections, particularly those in public libraries, consist primarily of recordings. And, because sales of popular-music recordings are overwhelmingly higher than those of classical music, some record companies are either cutting back on classical products or limiting their output to "popular" classical or "cross-over" titles. BMG Classics's recent announcement about cutbacks to their classical music output is just one example of this trend.

In his 1951 article "The Place of Gramophone Recordings in a University Music Library," Vincent Duckles wrote: "In a university music library there is nothing to be gained from isolating recordings from books and scores. On the contrary, every effort must be made to bring media together in a functional relationship."[9] More that fifty years later, we have come closer to Duckles's vision through the possibilities offered by streaming digitized audio and video across networks, both within music library walls and across campuses—and beyond. It is now technologically possible for users to gain access to a library's media collection from remote locations.

These technological possibilities are limited, however, by existing copyright legislation. Technologies that can replicate and transmit materials published in all media in digital form presents clear challenges to the U.S. copyright law. During the past few years legislators, librarians, information professionals, and representatives of the publishing and recording industries have been engaged in discussions about adapting existing rules to the digital age.[10] Libraries implementing electronic reserve systems must carefully develop institutional policies to insure compliance with copyright law. Recent lawsuits against MP3 and Napster, Inc., for copyright infringement of music transmitted over the Internet demonstrate the dangers of allowing uncontrolled access to copyrighted works.

The MLA's founders were able to acquire important collections of printed and manuscript music from abroad and focus their efforts on populating their libraries with treasures; today, however, music librarians must struggle with the overwhelming task of preserving these collections. Most printed music published from the mid-nineteenth through the mid-twentieth centuries was issued on highly acidic wood-pulp paper; the use of "permanent" (or acid-free) paper did not become standard until the last ten to twenty years. Added to this are the challenges of preserving more than a century of recorded music, preserved on a variety of media ranging from wax cylinders to compact disks, as well as those associated with preserving information transmitted in electronic form. The standard preservation medium for print materials is microfilm. Yet, although microfilm succeeds in preserving the informational content of a printed book or score, it is a difficult medium to access, particularly in the case of music scores: properly-formatted paper copies need to be generated from microfilm for the music itself to be of any use to performers. Although they provide a good means for access to rare or deteriorated items, digital copies are not long-term preservation solutions.[11]

The profession of music librarianship has also changed in the last seventy years. The MLA now has more than 1,800 members, plus an additional 700 subscribers to its quarterly journal *Notes*. The standard recommendation for the education of music librarians includes a degree in library science, an undergraduate (and, preferably, a graduate) degree in music, facility with languages (particularly western European languages) and, ideally, a broad-based education in the humanities. Although this background provides most professionals with the skills they need to do their jobs, today librarians must be fully adept with computer programs and Internet searching; they must also possess sophisticated administrative skills as well as the ability to manage a number of tasks simultaneously.

The MLA has been diligent in offering perspectives on the history of music librarianship and its future. Among its significant publications in this area are Ruth Watanabe's 1981 article "American Music Libraries and Music Librarianship: An Overview in the Eighties," Mary Wallace Davidson's "American Music Libraries and Librarianship: Challenges for the Nineties,"[12] and, most recently, "Music Librarianship at the Turn of the Century"—a set of essays that appeared in the March 2000 issue of *Notes*. The last has been cited several times in this article; it includes contributions on virtually all aspects of music librarianship today, from cataloging, preservation, and copyright to changes in the music-publishing and sound-recording industries and the central role of technology. It should be required reading for those interested in gaining a full view of the present state of music librarianship.

§

I too, came of age as a music librarian in the twentieth century; so did The Juilliard School Library, which I am privileged to administer.[13] How do some of the challenges and issues mentioned above work in my day-to-day administration of the collection, one designed particularly to support performers? What are the pressing future issues from a local perspective?

In the last year The Juilliard School Library underwent a major renovation involving expansion of its physical capacity as well as the creation of a state-of-the-art computer network to support current and (one hopes) future technological needs. We endeavor to integrate electronic resources fully into our services, but we do not expect them to replace the printed scores and books on our shelves.

Performers need scores to play from, and they usually need to obtain access to them quickly. When a student comes running into the library looking for a copy of a Debussy violin sonata, a Beethoven piano sonata, or a new work by Milton Babbitt, we must be ready to provide a physical copy of the desired work. I spend a fair amount of time insuring that the library shelves are well-stocked with copies of standard and non-standard repertoire.

Juilliard students are strongly encouraged to seek out and perform new compositions. When a student comes to me seeking a copy of a new work, it is frustrating to contact the publisher and find that either that work is not available at all, or—even in the case of solo or chamber works—that it is available only on a rental basis. Libraries have always been important promoters of new music; performers discover new works by browsing our catalogs and our shelves. The current music-publishing environment limits our ability to promote effectively the discovery and performances of new music.

I also spend a lot of time on user education, showing students how to use the catalog, helping them develop an awareness of primary source materials, and emphasizing the importance of "edition shopping." There are many important differences between various editions of a musical work. The Juilliard School Library houses more than a dozen editions of Beethoven's piano sonatas, all of which represent different approaches to editing and performance practice. It is important for performers to have access to *all* these editions, as well as to facsimiles of manuscripts and copies of early editions published in the composer's lifetime. The reprint editions published by Dover, Kalmus, and Masters Music publishers, while enormously useful, are generally reprints of nineteenth-century editions. These are the same "public domain" editions utilized in the few digital-score collections available at present. Because these editions are relatively easy to acquire and inexpensive, I worry about a time when libraries and users may rely especially heavily on them, either in print or electronic form, as their primary sources of historic repertoire.

In the current "web-centered" world, it is not uncommon for students to assume the web is their primary source for information on all subjects. If information on a subject isn't on the web, it must not exist. In our efforts to combat this dangerous misconception, we work hard to inform students about the wide range of printed information sources pertaining to the discipline of music. We also emphasize the importance of sensibly balancing print and electronic resources when searching for information. For questions concerning historic repertoire, students are encouraged to begin their searches in standard dictionaries and bibliographies, before continuing with electronic indexes and, finally, web resources. We caution them about the lack of editorial control on the web and remind them to evaluate carefully every source of information they come across.

The Juilliard School Library subscribes to all electronic music periodical indexes available at present, including *RILM, Music Index, IIMP (International Index of Music Periodicals)*, and *IIPA (International Index of Performing Arts Periodicals)*. We also provide access to relevant humanities indexes through OCLC's FirstSearch service. While enormously useful, these databases to some extent replicate each other, and none of them yet offers substantial access to full texts of journal articles or full retrospective indexing to music periodicals prior to 1970. The marketplace for electronic indexing and electronic access to full texts of journals is changing rapidly, and subscription costs for these services take up ever-increasing portions of library budgets. I hope that, at some point in the not-so-distant future, vendors can learn to work with librarians to produce tools that provide both simpler indexing and enhanced access to music-periodical literature.

Did the education I received during the 1970s in my MLS (Master of Library Science) program prepare me fully for the challenges that I face every day? Yes and no. It would be absurd to assume that any graduate program can "complete" one's education, particularly in these times of enormous technological changes. Continuing professional development and outreach to colleagues through networks and library organizations are absolutely essential. I worry about the future of our profession, however, when so many library schools are de-emphasizing the "library" component of their programs and highlight the "information" component. I am sometimes visited by library-school students who express interest in being music librarians but have not taken any courses in cataloging or music bibliography. Learning how to design web pages (taught in many library schools) does not, in my view, replace a professional education that includes knowledge of the structure of library catalogs as well as of major reference works in our discipline.

This said, technology has positively influenced every aspect of my working life and that of my colleagues. Most of us cannot imagine doing our jobs without e-mail and web resources. Automated library catalogs and the availability of electronic reference databases have transformed the nature of research work and of librarianship.

Just as it is likely that the nineteen individuals who attended the first MLA meeting in 1931 would be surprised (and, we hope, pleased) to see what our libraries look like today, it is also likely that none of us can envision what libraries will look like seventy years hence. Nevertheless, it is our responsibility to preserve and build upon our existing collections. I hope that many of the volumes on Juilliard's shelves, some of which were here seventy years ago, will still be available in their physical form seventy years from now. I expect that the catalogs that we use to access these materials will have new interfaces, interfaces that fully integrate print and electronic resources of all types, from both the local collection as well as remote digital libraries. Audio and video will be transmitted over networks, and library users will be able to access information in a variety of media from various locations.

I also trust that the Music Library Association, which will celebrate its 140th anniversary in 2071, will remain the primary organization that music librarians turn to for professional support. I look forward to working with my colleagues as we encounter challenges and opportunities in the years ahead.

NOTES

[1] For a complete chronology and detailed description of the development of music libraries in the United States, see Carol June Bradley, *Music Collections in American Libraries* (Detroit: Information Coordinators, Inc., 1981). The development of the Music Library Association is chronicled by Bradley in "The Music Library Association: The Founding Generation and Its Work," *Notes: Quarterly Journal of the Music Library Association* 37/4 (June 1981): 763-822.

[2] Music Library Association, Inc. Constitution and By-Laws, Article II: Purposes.

[3] Bradley, "The Music Library Association," 770.

[4] See Carol June Bradley, "Building Collections" in *American Music Librarianship: A Biographical and Historical Survey* (Westport, CT: Greenwood, 1990), 9-68.

[5] The MARC format for machine-readable cataloging of monographs was adopted in 1969; the MARC format for music was adopted in 1976. For a detailed description of developments in music cataloging, see Ralph Papakhian's article on "Cataloging" in "Music Librarianship at the Turn of the Century," *Notes* 56/3 (March 2000): 581-590.

[6] RISM was founded in 1952; RILM in 1966; RIdIM in 1971, and RIPM in 1988. All of these projects are sponsored jointly by the International Musicological Society and the International Association of Music Libraries.

[7]The first edition of Sir George Grove's *Dictionary of Music and Musicians* was published 1878-1890 in four volumes. The fifth edition, edited by Eric Blom, was published in 1954 in nine volumes.

[8]See Bradley, "Music Library Association," 770.

[9]Vincent H. Duckles, "The Place of Gramophone Recordings in a Music Library," *Reader in Music Librarianship*, ed. Carol June Bradley (Washington, D.C.: Microcard Edition Books, 1973), 265.

[10]An excellent summary of current copyright issues for music libraries is provided by Mary Wallace Davidson in her article "Copyright" in "Music Librarianship at the Turn of the Century," *Notes* 56/3 (March 2000): 598-604.

[11]An excellent summary of current preservation issues is provided by John Shepard in his article "Preservation" in "Music Librarianship at the Turn of the Century," *Notes* 56/3 (March 2000): 574-580.

[12]Ruth Watanabe's article was published in *Notes* 38/2 (December 1981): 239-256; Mary Wallace Davidson's article was published in *Notes* 50/1 (September 1993): 13-22.

[13]Juilliard was founded in 1905 as the Institute of Musical Art.

Born in New York City, pianist **Gary Graffman** studied at the
Curtis Institute in Philadelphia with Isabelle Vengerova before
making his debut with the Philadelphia Symphony. In 1948 he
won the prestigious Leventritt Award, and for the next three
decades he performed throughout the world as a concert artist;
with conductors such as Leonard Bernstein, Zubin Mehta, Eugene
Ormandy, and George Szell, he also recorded for Columbia (CBS)
and RCA such works as the concertos of Tchaikovsky,
Rachmaninoff, Prokofiev, Brahms, Chopin, and Beethoven. In
1979, however, Graffman seriously injured his right hand. Since
then, in addition to performing works for the left hand alone, he
has taught at Curtis; in 1986 he became the Institute's director
and in 1995 its president. Graffman is the author of a memoir, *I
Really Should Be Practicing*, as well as popular articles on non-
musical subjects. He holds honorary doctorates from the
University of Pennsylvania and The Juilliard School; the City of
New York awarded him its Handel Medallion; and the
Commonwealth of Pennsylvania bestowed upon him its
Governor's Arts Award in recognition of his varied
accomplishments, including his "leadership of Curtis."

❦ Will Classical Music Remain a Vital Force in Our Culture?

GARY GRAFFMAN

An earlier version of the following article appeared in the Directory of the Association of
Performing Arts Presenters *(November 1993).*

NOWADAYS virtually every discussion about the business of music
bemoans the decline of American orchestras, audiences, and the state of
serious artistic endeavor.

Although similar complaints have echoed through the ages, I think it's
safe to say that Beethoven, like television's Energizer Bunny, marches on. It
is true, though, that society's enthusiasm for cultural activities waxes and
wanes during the course of any era. The pendulum swings back and forth, and

at this moment, the swing appears to be moving away from those of us who care deeply about the arts.

I have been stimulated to write this essay by an article in *The New York Times* (Edward Rothstein, 11 July 1993) describing some conclusions reached at that year's annual meeting of the American Symphony Orchestra League. Because of the 1993 recession and because some orchestras were indeed doing much worse financially than in other years, panic had apparently set in and suggestions were made for changes in format that, in effect, would enable our now "elitist" symphony orchestras to be all things to all people.

Warning its constituents that the American orchestra had become "irrelevant to its surrounding community," a League proposal suggested that orchestras begin to reflect more precisely "the cultural mix, needs and interests of their communities" by programming more pop, jazz, and cross-over music. That trend continues today.

I believe that trying to enlarge the scope of a symphony audience by sandwiching an Andrew Lloyd Webber medley between Haydn and Stravinsky is as ludicrous as interpolating a David Letterman routine into a production of *King Lear*. Subscribers to the Royal Shakespeare Company would no more be pleased than those who sit through *King Lear* in order to see their favorite actor.

Part of the worry about declining symphony audiences, I suspect, is that orchestra administrators, carried away by their successes in the recent past, have come to expect that the potential audience for so-called "classical" music is limitless; as a result, musical activities have gradually been stretched beyond the demand. But demand for this kind of music is—and, I believe, always will be—quite finite.

In any culture, at any time in history, interest in the arts has been evinced by only a small minority of the population. It is neither a necessity for physical survival nor an instinctively inspired human response. In most cultures, this interest has been an acquired taste, like the appreciation of good wine or olives. And while, in the best of all possible worlds, everyone would have an opportunity—in fact, would be expected, through compulsory education in arts and aesthetics—to learn about fine things like wine, olives, and the best in music, it is unrealistic to imagine that all of them would necessarily develop an enthusiasm for Romanée St.-Vivant, purple Alfonsos, or cello recitals.

I wonder whether much of the current concern about the financial decline of many arts organizations is not actually a shortsighted view, somewhat like worrying over a depressed real-estate market by studying only what happened to it during less prosperous years. If symphony-orchestra administrators today compared their present situation—which is considered "bad"—with the state of the same orchestras around, say, fifty years ago, I think they'd realize they were actually way ahead.

When I started out as a performer in 1949, the number of American orchestras that played—and, therefore, that were paid—for fifty-two weeks a year was strikingly insignificant. (In fact, the Boston Symphony may have been the only one.) Many major orchestras played seasons of no more than twenty weeks; this season extended from October to April, and summer concerts were few. The salary of an orchestra musician was not a living wage. And since there were fewer concerts than now, opportunities for soloists were a fraction of what they are today. I doubt whether any string quartets other than the Budapest made a living playing concerts. And there were certainly no contemporary or early music ensembles making livings as performing groups. The possibilities for performers today—even during "bad" times (and bearing in mind that, no matter what the cultural climate may be, it's difficult to make a career as a musician)—are undoubtedly greater than when I was a fledgling pianist.

And the audience for "classical" music is, at its most sparse, far larger nowadays. After all, New York now boasts two large concert halls (totalling about 5,600 seats) that are in use almost every night throughout the year. (Thanks to air-conditioning, summer is no longer off-season.) In 1949 New York had only one 2,760-seat concert hall, and very few performances sold out. Yes, Horowitz did, and Heifetz, and Rubinstein. But for the performances of many artists now considered legendary, readily available "student coupons" entitled anyone—not only students—to attend for practically nothing. I often remember sitting in a half-empty Carnegie Hall and listening to Philharmonic concerts conducted by Bruno Walter, Artur Rodzinski, and Dimitri Mitropoulos. But in those years (when the administrative staff consisted of about three executives and a couple of assistants and secretaries), marketing experts were unheard of, and nobody expected the world to beat a path to Carnegie Hall. Empty seats were more or less taken for granted, and Beethoven went marching on.

Today, when the administrative operation of a major orchestra resembles that of a huge international corporation (or perhaps even the government of a medium-sized monarchy), most of the marketing techniques employed—the selling of the symphony—have nothing to do with the original purpose of the symphony being sold: that of presenting the finest music, played in the best and most skillful manner, for an audience that wishes to listen. In the desperate search to find a way for orchestras to be all things to all people, these artificial gimmicks, with their continual emphasis on "relevance," succeed only in lowering the standards for everyone.

I believe that those of us who are involved in performing great music have to approach life with the conviction that, as long as such music exists, there will always be people (albeit a minority) who will want to hear it. Our job, then, is to continue that tradition and make no compromises. There is no real point to being in this field unless one strives to be "best" and "the most skilled"—which happens, by the way, according to my dictionary, to be the definition of "elite."

A native of Clay Center, Kansas, **Marnie Hall** began studying the violin at nine and the saxophone a year later. While completing her undergraduate degree at the University of Kansas, she played for four years in the Kansas City Philharmonic; later she earned her Master's degree at the Manhattan School of Music, where she studied with Raphael Bronstein and Artur Balsam. In 1972 Hall founded the Vieuxtemps String Quartet, an all-women ensemble. Her participation led to *Woman's Work*, a two-disk anthology she produced in 1975 on her own Gemini Hall label. As engineer/producer and executive director of Leonarda Productions, Inc. (aka Leonarda Records), Hall has been responsible for two dozen phonorecords and more than twenty-five CDs.

ॐ A Proposal for Artist-owned Recordings and a University-based Music Distribution Network

MARNIE HALL

I WAS invited to write this article after an essay of mine appeared in the November 1999 issue of the *CMS Newsletter*, entitled "The Music Industry: A Proposal for Change." The object of that article, and of this one, is to initiate a discussion of how we might turn around the music business so that the people making the music—the composers, performers, and colleges and universities that fund their projects—get something in the way of financial return.

I recognized long ago that, with few exceptions, the people making the money in the music business were not the musicians themselves; rather, they are the publicists, sound engineers, managers, administrators, and the many others who found a way to make the music business a lucrative one. Although this article will focus on recordings, many of the ideas presented can also apply to sheet music, books, videos—virtually anything for sale.

The Quest for Content and Intellectual Property

Today, all the talk is about content (rights to pictures, music, etc.). Microsoft is buying up content. Tower Records executives are worried because they don't own content. Movie studios have merged with major record companies, acquiring content. And then there is distance-learning content. Colleges, universities, and musicians should get in on the ground floor in this near-universal effort to own and control content.

Content is all the rage because it can be used in so many different ways and because its owners will be the successors to traditional record stores, with digital downloads replacing storefronts. Music can be sold or licensed in the form of sheet music, CD and DVD recordings, Internet presentations, and textbook supplemental recordings; it can be used in commercials, games, and media such as television, video, films, and CD-ROMs.

I read an article in the *New York Times* about distance learning that brought up questions about ownership of electronic rights to lectures. Traditionally, universities own the patents to research done on campus, but professors keep royalties from their textbooks, even if based on course work. With the potential income from distance learning so great, colleges and universities are reassessing their policies.

For-profit companies funded by venture capitalists have sprung up, signing deals with Columbia, Stanford, Carnegie Mellon University, the University of Chicago, and other prestigious institutions, offering them revenues and company shares. If projections are correct, "the University of Chicago could earn $20 million in royalties alone from the venture over the next five years. (Payment to participating professors has not yet been set.)"[1] Williams College is reviewing another offer that could bring in more than $250,000 a year per course.

University Participation

Don't universities, collectively, have the expertise to produce and market distance learning lectures as well as videos, recordings, and textbooks? If not, what's missing? It is certainly within the legal purview of not-for-profit educational institutions as well as for-profit ones. Many university presses already engage in such activities. If you can produce and sell your work, there is no reason why you cannot retain ownership of the content and the physical product itself.

Since the Internet can distribute text, sound, and moving images; colleges, universities, and musicians should investigate the possibilities that this medium can offer. By working with other departments—science, history, art, etc.—we could produce compelling Internet "learning capsules." There is room for endless creativity in this field. We might even make learning itself more a part of popular culture.

Sales of recordings used in conjunction with textbooks yield far greater financial rewards than recordings sold by themselves. Unfortunately, record companies are paid very little—a tiny fraction of what master tapes cost to produce—from licensing such recordings to outside publishers. The profits now accrue to textbook publishers and CD companies, usually special-products units with major recording firms, that assemble the tracks from various tapes and do the manufacturing.

Textbooks are the easiest product to market because firms know exactly who their potential buyers are and how to reach them. If there is any money to be made by people in music, those people must retain ownership rights not only to original recordings but also to recordings licensed for other uses. And unless individuals want fee dictated to them by outside distributors, they need to be able to *sell* these products as well. To accomplish this best, musicians need to set up a distribution mechanism that will serve not just one but many universities as well as their faculties, non-affiliated serious composers, and performers.

The Need for a Drastic Overhaul

Although composers and performers want to manufacture CDs, sales of all but the most commercial recordings have plummeted as independent stores have been replaced by chains and the market glutted with product. A recap of some of the points I made in the *Newsletter* calls attention to the need for major change.

Sales Income: At the present time CD retail stores in the largest cities that have the most extensive classical selections order only one or two copies of each new classical release—that is, unless the artist has an international reputation, the composers are well-known, and the recording boasts a major label. Stores do not automatically reorder, even if the CD sells out the next day.

➡ Advertising costs for small record labels always exceed revenue generated by the advertising. Some magazines even demand *quid pro quo* in the form of advertising to review recordings.

➡ With few exceptions (artists placing consignment items in local stores), chains will not buy from small companies. While large record companies have their own sales forces, small companies must use distributors that take about 33% of the wholesale price and pay companies only $6.50-7.00. As for library sales, small companies that incur advertising costs often see their mark-up diminished when libraries place orders with library distributors instead of directly with the record companies.

➡ Stores are reluctant to carry CDs containing works by more than one or two composers, since placement in stores is more difficult. Some distributors will not carry labels that list too many collections in their catalogs. However, in cases involving new music, direct sales to consumers instead of distributors increase when a group of composers and a single genre are represented.

Funding:

➡ Only a handful of foundations support recordings.

➡ Very few corporations fund recordings in whole or part, since their contributions are geared toward image advertising. They prefer to give to major arts institutions, to radio and television, and to local charities where they have employees.

Radio and Royalties:

➡ Recording companies and musicians receive no broadcast royalties; royalties go to music publishers, composers, and lyricists for intellectual property, not to performers. However, under a new law, digital radio must provide some sort of compensation for performance (as well as the means to record CD-quality music directly from radio).

➡ Most American radio stations either have no budgets for recordings or spend their limited budgets on CD subscriptions to Sony, BMG, and other major labels. Most of the time broadcasts *do not* generate sales. Although the same music selections played over and over in the pop music field creates followings for bands, this is seldom the case in classical music. Syndicated shows playing in a hundred or more localities do not seem to make a difference, even for smaller independent labels. After all, *music is free* twenty-four hours a day on the radio, and many recordings cannot easily be located in stores.

I often lament that the music business is not more like the art world, which attracts individual investors and drives up the price of art. Musical instrument collectors, on the other hand, drive up the price of violins. I don't rule out attracting investors, but they would need to invest in individual products, not the proposed distribution mechanism (itself probably a not-for-profit entity).

Distribution Systems: New Versus Old

The future will probably see both for- and not-for-profit recordings, depending on financing. CD funding by foundations may well go to non-profit labels, while CD funding by investors will almost certainly go to for-profit labels. Any excess revenues received by nonprofit labels may be funneled into recording funds for new projects.

Setting up an alternative distribution system involves three factors: order processing, storage/shipping, and publicity/advertising. The order processing division should provide, among other things, an online order form, credit-card access, and links to web sites for each company or individual with products being distributed. Off-site web pages could provide more extensive information than ordering sites, including audio samples, detailed product descriptions, and bios.

Order processing can be done by schools with work programs run in conjunction with classroom studies. Those of us who would like to establish artist-owned recording operations might start with clients who would do their own shipping, such as record companies and self-published composers, even before warehouse and shipping facilities are available. Eventually, with digital downloads, it may not even be necessary to store inventory or ship.

If we decide to distribute to retail chains, we may need to abandon certain types of distribution (i.e., selling to other distributors), at least in the beginning, in order to set up an alternate system. It is necessary to build up a large, exclusive catalog of recordings and any other product line we want to sell to make it worthwhile for retail chains to order directly from us, bypassing middlemen. There are certain anti-trust regulations that specify that, if you sell to one distributor, you must sell to all other distributors in that class; therefore, it would be best to sell only to retailers, not wholesalers or retail one-stops, in order to establish ourselves as wholesale distributors as well as distributors to consumers.

One way to build up our recording catalog quickly would be to become a distributor for many small record labels, especially if they are unhappy with their current distributors (and that may be the majority of them). Distributors don't sell that many recordings, and since they must accept unlimited product returns as a condition for doing business with chains, payments to record companies are often a year or more in arrears. We should be able to impose 1) our own ground rules on chains; and 2) restocking fees (even if modest ones) as well as 3) penalties for accepting product returns with store stickers and broken plastic cases.

We need our own broadcasting network. If only universities with radio stations would set some criteria or goals for their stations and ask them to play more American music, new music, vocal music, classical music, and jazz! Can we encourage university stations to program more of this music? Should music schools and music departments have their own digital radio stations? Internet audio samples? We need to promote what we want to sell.

Universities already have markets in place: their own libraries, faculty members, and lists of concert subscribers. Many colleges and universities have their own radio stations, publicists, and alumni newsletters; these could provide the publicity necessary to help get our venture off the ground. While nonprofit radio stations cannot carry advertising, they can announce recordings produced and made available by nonprofit organizations: the Public Radio Source, for example.

We could also work with other organizations, helping them distribute our products. Arts organizations could sell their favorite recordings at concerts, and all sorts of people could leave recordings on consignment in various types of stores. Some organizations and associations might either donate newsletter advertising space or take commissions from sales (instead of charging us for advertising). They might mention our web sites; if customers mentioned them when ordering from us, commissions could go to the organizations and associations involved. Professional societies like the National Flute Association might prefer payments to recording funds they administer. Universities might prefer vouchers for music-library purchases.

Even not-for-profit organizations with missions unrelated to music or education could receive commissions; they would need only to claim such commissions as taxable unrelated business income on IRS Form 990-T. This can be done without jeopardizing their tax-exempt status as non-profit organizations as long as the taxable portion were acceptable as provided by the tax code.

If musicians, composers, and the universities that fund their recordings are able to retain ownership rights to recordings and publications, would that undercut the record companies we hope to use as distributors? Yes, it probably would, but such companies are already being undercut by other companies— oftentimes independent audio engineers or CD manufacturers—that offer online distribution and pay musicians decent percentages of every sale they make. A number of people at traditional record companies provide services (recording, editing, graphic design, and publicity), and while they almost always charge for these services—except publicity, which may or may not come out of the fees artists pay—often they work at far less than going market rates. There must be a way to compensate people underpaid if recordings are not released on their labels. Artists using university distribution networks might hire such people and also agree to royalty splits with them.

Quality Control

Our success will be curtailed if we record all kinds of music indiscriminately and assume that customers will simply take what we give them. Instead, it is important to set up several different record labels or categories, each with some sort of identity representing different musical tastes. These might include new music categories representing avant-garde, adventurous, highly accessible, and mixed styles as well as orchestra, opera, standard classical, historical, jazz, instrumental, vocal, world, ethnic, various mixed styles, women composers, minority composers, and background music. The purpose of these record labels or categories is to help customers find the music they want, not to ghettoize performers or composers. Choice of record labels or categories would be largely up the artists themselves. The labels would not necessarily have these names, but would somehow reflect the tastes of the people selecting artists and repertoire for each particular label.

We need to set criteria for selecting musical material for each record label and category, a job done by A&R (Artists & Repertoire) people. There are several possibilities here:

➡ Several individuals, each with sole discretion to accept projects for one or more categories or labels.

➡ Several individuals acting as a committee to accept or reject projects for one or more categories or labels.

➡ A&R people at existing record companies who accept or reject projects for their own labels that are distributed by our network. (These people need not be excluded from the two entries above, and actually might be very good choices.)

Artists who present projects for evaluation could send their home recordings to A&R people, specifying which label (in order of preference) they might wish finally to record with. If evaluation tapes did not pass muster with the A&R people representing an artist's first choice of label, the artist could elect to present it to the second label, and so on, paying a fee for each evaluation. (We also need people to evaluate sound quality once master tapes have been produced.)

One job for A&R people would be to offer suggestions to composers and performers prior to making master tapes (as record companies presently do) by listening to home recordings, whenever possible with the performers who will make the actual recording. How composers are combined on a single disk is an important consideration; different pieces, much like movements within a piece, can enhance what becomes before and after. These people might also suggest titles and marketing strategies.

Funding and Marathon Recording Sessions

It is much easier to interest foundations, corporations, and individuals in funding concerts than in paying for recordings. Organizations tend to perceive recordings as commercial; they fail to realize that selling recordings and charging admissions fees to offset production costs are similar situations. Also, recording sessions are not often social events, and there is little interaction between the public and record-company personnel. However, we could have some success if colleges and universities were to become involved, especially if revenues from sales of recordings were to be used to establish recording funds and if vouchers could be used to enable libraries to expand their collections.

Funding could also be increased by including recordings in budgets for festivals and concerts, with recording sessions scheduled to follow such events. These should be marathon sessions to cut costs. Don't pay engineers to come in for a day or two; record for a week or a month whenever possible and watch costs drop! Record several CDs at once and record the same genres back to back to cut down on set-up time. A list should be maintained of approved recording projects and venues all over the country; scheduling should take the entire continent into consideration.

Finding Recording Spaces

Of utmost importance is locating colleges and universities with auditoria suitable and available for recording sessions. Such spaces are in short supply. Arrangements could be made to use such facilities; payment might even be made "in kind" (e.g., offering master classes by visiting recording artists and technical people).

How to make successful recording? The following suggestions may be useful in determininng the availability of suitable recording spaces in individual areas, institutions, or communities.

Making Recordings

Choosing a Recording Space: Most professional recording studios are acoustically "dead"; they're built for recording vocals, rhythm, strings, etc., in separate sessions and for mixing tracks together with reverb added at the end. Classical music and other musics recorded in live settings for later editing should be recorded in halls with beautiful, "live" acoustics, rooms in which echos have time to come back over a period of time.

Separate playback rooms such as recording booths, green rooms, office spaces, or sacristies for producers and engineers to monitor the sessions are desirable. Whenever possible, these rooms should resemble living rooms, so that recorded sounds will suggest home playback environments. Smaller playback rooms will usually work, too. Check the acoustics in these room as well as in the halls themselves; if it is too "boomy," the recorded sound may be too dead or "dry," since much of the ambiance comes from the playback rooms themselves.

Halls and Sizes: The more sound you have, the bigger hall you need. A hall seating 300 might accommodate several small-sized groups but might not be good for brass and other loud instruments. A hall seating 500-600 is usually better. Halls in the 1,200-seat range are often good, too. Spaces that are not box-like are preferred. Are there balconies? Vaulted ceilings? Is the space broken up in other ways? Are the walls too close together? Recording venues should *always* have high ceilings.

Reflective Materials: Check out reflective materials. What are the materials in the ceilings, walls, and floors? A combination of wood and plaster is usually good. Too much stone will produce bright, harsh sounds. Is there too much carpeting? Carpeting in the aisles is usually ok, but if it is under the seats too, it is almost always too dry. Clap and sing as you walk around any given hall. You don't want "clapback"; eliminate halls in which your claps come back to you as distinct, repeating claps. (Such halls are especially disastrous for recording percussion instruments!) What are the decay times? Two to three seconds is generally good. How smooth is the decay? Does it come back suddenly, or does it taper off? Even if it the echos sound a bit loud, a given space may work.

Noise: Always check for noises before you choose a place to record. Sit down and listen carefully for them. Is there street noise? Airplane traffic? Hum from lights? Noise from nearby rooms? Noise when it rains? Noise from elevators? From cooling systems in water fountains? Is there a noisy heating or air-conditioning system? Do blowers go on and off? (*Be sure* to ask someone to turn on the blowers so you can hear them.)

Most noise is much more evident on headphones, so always do a headphone check before you record. Some noises can be edited or filtered out, but noises with broad bandwidths, such as those made by blowers, are extremely problematic: one has to filter out so many frequencies, then try to add back other frequencies to enhance the sound. This can be *very* costly and time-consuming.

You may be forced to record when blowers, heat, and air conditioning are turned off, turning them on during breaks. Be sure to find out if maintenance personnel are available and can turn off blowers and transformers for your space without affecting other spaces or buildings. Also, find out how long it takes for personnel to come after you call them. If you have to turn off the heat, how long does it take to heat up the hall again?

Music-department administrators may be convinced that recording spaces are available during semester breaks, but be sure to check with maintenance staff, too. Once I scheduled a recording session and arrived during a break, only to find the auditorium in question being painted.

Last, but certainly not least, check any instruments that come with the hall. Would it be wise to bring in better instruments? Does the hall restrict the choice of tuners or movers for its instrument? Has the condition of any instrument changed since you last played it? Do the piano pedals creak?

Optimizing Space and Furnishing Variables: Stages are not always the best choices for positioning performers within halls. Walk around the auditorium, church, or synagogue you've booked and sing. Do you get more resonance in the middle of the room? The corner? Corners can give you the advantage of greater and more varied distances for reflected sound to return. If you record using a stage, sitting in front of its proscenium often helps.

Check your position in relation to the walls, particularly the back wall that acts as a sounding board and affects the bass the most. Position yourself in several places. You can often tell which is better when you play. Also, have someone listen as he or she walks around the hall while you play. You might want to use boards to reflect sound; see if they help general conditions or instruments such as the French horn.

If you are in a really dead hall with an unresonant piano, placing a large board on the floor directly against the back of the piano in an upright position behind the hammers will add resonance. I once used a piece of plywood approximately 4 feet wide and 8 feet tall and also placed a microphone in the room at some distance from the performers to create ambiance. In that case and in all cases when I am looking for places to put microphones, I walk around until I find the most resonant spots, ones that amplify sound and have the best blends of brilliance and sweetness. I check vertical positions too by squatting gradually (listening in the process) and standing on chairs (gradually bending my knees and, of course, listening in the process). Height, as well as distance, can make a big difference.

Opening exit doors leading to stairs and hallways often inproves sound; so if no one else is using the premises, try opening and closing them. Open doors contribute to smooth, gradual decay. Also experiment with opening and closing curtains.

A wooden floor under performers is usually best. Consider laying wood planks on non-wooden floors. A hall that is small and over-resonant is probably the only exception to this rule; in such halls you may wish instead to lay carpet, bedding, towels, or piano covers under or around some of the performers, in an area near them, and/or in various places in the hall.

How much of your sound seeps from the recording space to the playback room and visa versa? Some seepage may not matter; it may even help. For comparison's sake, do a test take with speakers blaring and another monitored only with headphones. You should always hear and approve a playback of test takes before starting a session. Once the sound is set, engineers and producers are less dependent on speakers to monitor sound, so the option exists of turning down the volume or using headphones if sound seeps too much from room to room.

Awkward or old-fashioned metal music stands and such can change the sound of your group. Watch out!

Pianos: I happen to find the sound emanating from nearly all pianos most pleasing when I am sitting at a 45-degree angle from the edge of the piano closer to the pianist's right hand, or when I am sitting half way between upstage and stage right with the piano in normal concert position. Bear in mind that the piano itself can be angled; in that case determine the 45-degree angle using the piano itself instead of the hall. I tend to place my left microphone (i.e., stage right) somewhere in the 45-degree line, determining distance by backing up from the piano and listening.

Piano lids should always be either wide open or taken off in order to avoid a muffled sound. Top notes can sound especially displeasing in recordings. When setting the sound, have the pianist play as loudly as possible in the low, high, and middle registers. You may need to move microphones back or record at lower volume levels to avoid unpleasant hammer sounds. Also, check the thickest passages (i.e., in terms of overall texture and pedal use) to test for muddiness.

When recording solo piano music, have the pianist play some scales from the lowest to the highest registers and back. Listen to the scales on both headphones and speakers; if the bass comes mostly from one channel and the treble from the other, with the sound rolling back and forth between speakers, you've got a problem! Adjust left and right microphone placement, or see if a central mike feeding both left and right channels takes care of the problem. I generally use a center mike in any event.

Microphones: It goes without saying that expensive, professional microphones are the ones to use. Never use a limiter (something television recordists are especially prone to do). Be careful engineers don't add EQ or "sound equalization" (which increases or decreases the volume of various frequency ranges) or anything else without your knowledge. You will probably not want to use EQ, but if you do, it might be to enhance the sound for a single microphone, such as a vocal soloist's microphone. I *do* use EQ in post-production situations if I think I can enhance sound, but I almost never use it in recording sessions. In settings familiar to you, such as post-production facilities you use regularly, you can make better judgments as to the sound you want. The same goes for reverberation. It is better to add it in studios than during recording sessions.

Try to obtain direct access to microphones as often as possible. To add resonance to instruments such as cellos, find uncarpeted wooden podiums if you can. If you're recording a vocal quartet, you might want something to give added height to the shortest singer. You may want to use baffles when recording percussion so that the sound does not "spread" all over the room. To lessen key noises on instruments such as flutes, place the microphone more above than in front of them. Be aware that some instruments may radiate low, middle, and high frequencies from their various parts.

Placing microphones in live, acoustical settings is one thing; placing them in studios is another. You may want to pick up the ambiance of the room by placing mikes farther back. Don't place mikes under or inside pianos or on top of violins or other instruments. Because low frequencies have longer sound cycles and high frequencies shorter ones, mikes will capture more high frequencies close up and more low frequencies farther back. Dynamic range also diminishes as microphones are moved farther back; this means that overall levels can be increased if mikes are placed farther back; this creates a more nearly seamless sound, one that doesn't tend to jump out as much in the loud passages.

On the other hand, diction and brilliance are enhanced with closer miking. Don't place mikes too close to singers with loud dynamic ranges, though—or, if you do, be sure to turn down the volume for those microphones when feeding sound to mixers. You may want to use directional microphones, but even omni-directional microphones record louder when aimed directly at sound sources than at an angle; for best results, experiment with the angle, or direction, of each microphone.

You might wish to use one or more room microphones placed back a bit in addition to microphones placed close to the musicians. In auditoria, room microphones are often placed in front of the first row of seats or as far back as the third row, but everything depends on the hall. Most producers and engineers who record classical music prefer fewer microphones, but this too will depend on given rooms and sizes of performing groups. Many chamber works and solo performances are recorded using only two to four microphones.

And remember: moving microphones as little one to three inches almost always makes a discernable difference.

Rehearsals: If you have a sound booth and recording equipment already on hand, you may be able to arrange a rehearsal in the hall itself while someone sets the sound. Make sure you determine the sound you want before the actual recording session begins; do this either at the beginning of the session itself or during a rehearsal (and recheck the sound in the latter case). It can be a good idea to take a well-engineered CD recording of the same ensemble you plan to record with you to the recording session. Your engineer may prefer that recording on DAT tape, so ask in advance. Use it to compare and check the ambiance; presence (energy, also related to closeness); high, mid and low registers; balance; and stereo/spatial imaging of the sound you plan to record. Watch the left (upper) and right (lower) channels of the recorder. How is the balance between left and right channels?

Can you visualize the stereo imaging, i.e., the position of the performers, in your own test takes? Can you visualize the size of the space just by listening? Is it small? Large? Does the amount of echo match the size of the hall? If you are able to make a test tape of the sound check, listen to that tape or a CD copy in a familiar setting. If you are out-of-town, at least listen to it in a location other than the recording space itself.

Ask the engineer if he or she has done a mono check for phase. S/he should be familiar with this procedure and should also check DAT machines' error correction rates well in advance of recording and send them in for repairs if necessary.

Sound check your loudest levels, then set recording volume about as high as you dare to get the best possible resolution using the largest number of digital bytes. Someone should always monitor the volume meters during recording and alert you if distortion occurs in loud passages. If it does, play some softer takes of the spot.

When you are ready to record, put tape under the musicians' chair legs or music stands. Do not change positions once that tape is in place. At the end of the first session or during breaks the engineer or producer should measure the position of *everything* in relation to a fixed place in the hall such as a corner or wall outlet. Included in such measures should be microphone positions, heights, and angles as well as the positions of musicians and piano legs (the taped marks). Once in a while you end up doing a patch session and need that information.

Recording Strategies: It is usually best to record in sections; this makes it easier to remember what you liked and didn't like as you record, and it gives the producer more time to make notes of things. Plan your sections in advance and look for tempo changes and pauses that might indicate stopping places. With digital editing, you can edit many, many places, but not everywhere. A difference in loudness of peddled passages in the piano is often problematic, and it can be difficult or impossible to edit passages where the loudness of the voicing in a chord varies from one take to another; take peddled passages and sustained chords into consideration. Some instruments are also more difficult to cut into than others; don't plan to edit in the middle of a cymbal crash or bass drum decay.

Mark your score and parts with measure numbers for each movement. Measure numbers make it easier for the control room to communicate precisely with you, and they are also useful for identifying segments during editing. "11 after J to 3 1/4 after K" is too long when you can refer to the same measures as "42–67.25."

The engineer has the option of keeping the tape running, of stopping it, or of pausing it between takes, which will automatically put ID numbers on the tape. Pausing too long is not good for recording equipment, so if you plan to stop or engage in a discussion of more than a few sentences, tell the engineer to stop the tape. Because stopping, starting, and slating takes (calling out take numbers) requires time, begin again even if you have one or even several "false starts"; your engineer or producer will note them as such and will not need to reslate. You can always do several short takes in succession without having the engineer or producer reslate; s/he will call the takes "T66a, 66b, 66c" or whatever. Let the sound die down before you play, however, and warn the engineer to "keep rolling" if stopping or pausing the tape between slates.

Do *not* stop for most mistakes unless you need to correct a specific note or measure after doing several complete takes of the section. Stopping is extremely time-consuming. Your producer should note mistakes (and successes!) as you record, keeping track at the same time of measures not covered. Get about three good takes, then cover only those measures not up to snuff; record a few measures on either side of each fluffed passage so your editor can get in and out. Some producers and conductors insist on many takes, but three will often do, especially if financial resources and recording time are limited.

When you start recording a section in the middle of a piece, always back up several measures. Never start cold on a place you want to edit unless there is dead silence preceding the passage; the echo in the hall carries over, and the sound will change if you have a cold start. It often takes four or five measures before you find your tempo (although a metronome will help), so begin before and play past the passage you want to edit out. Even doing this between movements helps, since part of editing is determining the time that should elapse between movements. Do not make noise, talk, or put down your instruments during this time. Room tone takes time to edit, too, so do yourself a favor and remain quiet following takes; don't talk immediately before them either. Don't forget to wait for the engineer's slate to die down before beginning to play.

§

I grew up in the 1940s and 1950s, a time when the big-band era still held sway and there were high-school bands throughout the nation. I love the sound of traditional instruments, and our high school still has its orchestra, marching band, and concert band. But computers and synthesizers are changing our lives forever. Is there a way for the musical community to embrace the new age and meet some of the many challenges we face? Will live performance as we know it become a thing of the past? Will fewer performing skills be required with the overlaying of musical tracks and unlimited number of times one can input musical notes? Or will improvisation and performance come together once again, as in past centuries?

Perhaps one way to keep traditional sounds alive and to promote so-called non-commercial music is to integrate them into the fabric of everyday life. The best way for the ideas presented here to succeed is to have as many artists and universities involved as possible. Each will contribute in some way to the overall success of group venture. It's up to you! I'd love to work with some other people on this.

NOTE

[1]Jacques Steinberg with Edward Wyatt, "Boola, Boola: E-Commerce Comes to the Quad," *New York Times* (13 February 2000).

A native of the Midwest, **John Kander** studied at the Kansas City Conservatory, Oberlin College, and Columbia University. After working as a pianist for off-Broadway shows, he made his Broadway composer's debut with *A Family Affair*—a venture that introduced him to producer Harold Prince and lyricist Fred Ebb. Together, Kander and Ebb wrote *Flora, the Red Menace* followed by *Cabaret, The Happy Time, Zorba, Chicago,* and—most recently—*Steel Pier*. Among Kander's most successful songs are "New York, New York" and "All That Jazz," both of which have been featured in motion pictures. Kander's honors include Tony and Grammy Awards for *Cabaret, Woman of the Year,* and *Kiss of the Spider Woman*. A member of the Musical Theater Hall of Fame, Kander lives in New York City.

John C. Tibbetts, associate professor of theater and film at the University of Kansas, holds a doctorate in interdisciplinary studies. Tibbetts served for four years with the Army Security Agency and later worked as a broadcast producer for KXTR-FM Fine Arts Radio and KMBZ News Radio, as an on-air host for KSHB-TV, and as a fine-arts reporter for KCTV (CBS). He has written about music for the *Christian Science Monitor* and the Monitor Radio Network as well as for Voice of America and National Public Radio. Tibbetts's publications include more than 250 articles for *The American Historical Review,* the *Journal of American Culture, Film Comment, Notes,* and the *American Record Guide*. Among his books are *American Theatrical Film, Dvořák in America,* and (co-edited with James M. Welsh) *The Encyclopedia of Novels into Film*.

❦ And the Music Goes 'Round
An Interview with John Kander

JOHN KANDER and JOHN C. TIBBETTS

W HEN asked to recall the most memorable experience of his long Broadway career, composer John Kander sidesteps song hits like "New York, New York," the smash premiere of *Cabaret* (1965), and his 1998 Lifetime Achievement Award from the Kennedy Center. Instead, he cites affectionately his most recent show, *Steel Pier* (1997), written with longtime collaborator Fred Ebb. Undaunted by the show's mixed critical reception, its failure to win a single Tony—it received eleven nominations—and its subsequent cancellation, Kander remains characteristically philosophical. He remembers that *Flora, the Red Menace* (1965) was a flop on Broadway before its 1987 smash-hit revival; and that *Chicago*—the hottest show on Broadway in 1999—was a critical and popular failure when it first opened more than twenty years ago. Kander is confident that *Steel Pier* will also eventually find its audiences.

"I still love that piece," he says of *Steel Pier*, a bittersweet tale of an unusual love affair set against the backdrop of a 1934 dance marathon in Atlantic City. "It's the polar opposite of *Chicago*; it's the most romantic thing Fred and I have written. The critics expected us to do something along the lines of that dance marathon movie, like *They Shoot Horses, Don't They?* But Fred and I didn't want to do that."

A line from *Cabaret* comes to mind: "One day it's kicks / then it's kicks in the shins."

For more than thirty years the team of Kander and Ebb has repeatedly pursued its own offbeat path. "We like something a little off-center, a bit bizarre," Kander admits.

Consider the sleazy Kit Kat Club in *Cabaret*, a metaphor for a world poised crazily on the rim of the Nazi Abyss. Or consider the milieu of the 1930s American Communist Party movement in *Flora, the Red Menace*. Or the sensational murder trial in *Chicago*, or prison life and homosexuality in *Kiss of the Spider Woman*. Certainly there is nothing commonplace about Kander and Ebb's two new collaborations: musical stage versions of Thornton Wilder's 1942 Pulitzer Prize-winning play *The Skin of Our Teeth* (a time-travel fantasy complete with singing dinosaurs!) and of Friedrich Dürrenmatt's 1956 expressionist revenge drama *The Visit*. "Their musicals may be set in Germany, Greece, or South America," notes commentator Ethan Mordden; they "may defy Fascism and flirt with death. But at the center of their art lies a love of the talent-take-all wonder of entertainment."[1]

Indeed, Kander and Ebb have earned their spurs as the most enduring and popular composer-lyricist team working today in the American musical theater. Many of their contemporaries have ceased writing, like Jerry Herman and the songwriting teams of Jerry Bock and Sheldon Harnick, Charles Strouse and Lee Adams, Harvey Schmidt and Tom Jones. Stephen Sondheim is still active; but, as Mordden observes, Sondheim and "the musical as entertainment" seem to have temporarily parted company. "[Sondheim's] questing genius has driven him first into opera and then into cameos, deliberately self-limiting, the musical as drive-by."[2] In contrast, Kander and Ebb have never lost their desire to write the kind of musicals that no one else seems to do today: shows in which people *make it*, in which youthful verve and joy triumph over despair and mortality (even if it takes a fantasy sequence, as in *Kiss of the Spider Woman* or *Steel Pier*, to achieve that ultimate transcendence; still, "Things work out, you're sure to find / When you leave the world behind"). That is why their new works, as well as the revivals—call them "reconstructions"—seem to be gaining increasing relevance and resonance with the approach of the new millenium. Impresario Harold Prince, who has frequently worked with the team, minces no words: "The work Kander and Ebb have done in the theater is extraordinary. They're as good as it gets."[3]

John Kander is shy of the press. He avoids first-night premieres and loathes being in the spotlight. He and Ebb have never had a press agent. "I think each public appearance knocks one day off the end of my life," he moans. However, he has consented to several interviews with me over the years, perhaps out of loyalty to a fellow Kansas Citian. He meets me at his brownstone on New York's upper west side, near Central Park. Kander is casually dressed in white sweater and slacks. His trim figure, thick shock of white hair, and smooth, unlined face belie his seventy-two years. He has just returned from Fred Ebb's apartment, he says, about four blocks away, where they are working on *Over and Over*, the highly anticipated musical version of *The Skin of Our Teeth* mentioned above.

"Projects like these take years," says Kander, ushering me up the quaint spiral staircase to his third-floor workroom. "When *Steel Pier* opened, it was after more than three years of work and eight weeks of workshops. After such a long time writing, it's really a thrill to watch something finally coming to life. It's a great moment."

Kander frequently peppers his conversation with that word, "moment." For him it has a special meaning, referring to that privileged instant in any show when words and music suddenly conjoin in a burst of harmonious expression.

Kander's music room is an agreeable clutter of posters, memorabilia, keyboards, and racks of recordings and audio tapes. A horned helmet, attesting to his Wagnerian interests, frowns down from a wall. A plaque certifies that "Dr. John Kander" received a doctoral degree from Oberlin

College in 1951. A piano sits nested among a collection of computer equipment and keyboards. Open closets display scores ranging from Mozart to Cole Porter. A tiny monitor perches above an exercise bench (so he can watch operas while undergoing the Daily Dozen, he confides). Decorated pillows lie scattered across a couch, each inscribed with the name of one of the Kander and Ebb musical shows. And a proclamation from the Mayor of New York City declares that the Kander and Ebb song, "New York, New York," is the official song of the Big Apple.

On the Roland electronic keyboard rests some music bearing the cryptic word "Finale." Kander informs me "Finale" refers to a computer program that allows one to notate directly into the computer. "Actually, I've been working with a computer for a long time," he explains. "When the Finale software first arrived, it seemed like a new guest that I had to get to know, to relate to. I had to make it feel at home." He began using it during a revival in 1987 of *Flora, the Red Menace*, when a computer expert friend from Yale taught him the program. Just now, Kander confides, he's fine-tuning *Over and Over*. All he has to do is punch in instructions about the key signature of the tune and what its metronome marking will be. Then he teases out a melody, plays it back, and adjusts the tempo. After that he works Ebbs's lyric into the program. The results print out between the musical staves, the syllables properly aligned with the notes.

"I especially enjoy the ease with which I can make corrections," he adds, after demonstrating the process. "Making a clean score used to be too awful a chore. I would find any excuse—even cleaning the house—to avoid it. Now, with the computer, it's very easy. It also means I can save every mistake I make, including any changes in the lyrics."

§

John Harold Kander was born in Kansas City, Missouri on 18 March 1927. "My ties to Kansas City were, and are, very strong," he says, relaxing on his couch, holding one of those exotic pillows on his lap. "I go back there at least three or four times a year. I'm still very close to my brother Ed. He didn't join the Kansas City Lyric Opera until he retired from the food brokerage business. Then he got into the opera world, thinking at first it would just be a part time thing. Well ..." He spreads his hands. "You know how *that* goes!"

"I was brought up in a house at 4335 McGee, right across the street from the Kansas City Art Institute. My parents were both from Kansas City. I started playing piano when I was about four. You could say I *found* the piano on my own. Fortunately, my family loved music, too. My father sang and my grandmother and my aunt played piano. Soon my aunt took charge and did something marvelous that I'll always remember: she placed her hands over mine, and we made a chord together. That did it. I started plucking out tunes when I was six.

"My teacher was a woman named Lucy Parrot. She lived about four blocks away, and she looked a little like the Wicked Witch of the West. She was eccentric, but looking back I realize she was a wonderful teacher and had great enthusiasm. She had a recording of Wagner's *Tristan und Isolde,* and if I had a good lesson, she would give me cookies and a glass of goat's milk and would play it for me. It's very hard to explain to you how exotic those moments were for me. There I was, sitting in this dark house with this hawk-like woman feeding me goat's milk ... and listening to Wagner. I guess I was afraid of her, but she stirred something in me."

John Kander (right) with Fred Ebb

Kander pauses to gesture toward the many recordings and audio tapes of Wagner operas that are strewn everywhere about the room. "Oh, yes," he explains, "I kept hearing more Wagner as a kid and all through high school. There was Mabel Glenn, the head of the Music Department of the Kansas City public schools—they don't have those sorts of positions any more, because of cutbacks—who would come to school once a week and play music and talk about it; and one day she came and played something I had never heard in my life (I was about twelve or so). It was the opening of the Third Act of *Götterdämmerung*, the Rhine Maidens' last scene. I was fascinated by it. I remember taking a streetcar to the Public Library to ask her to tell me more about the music. She lent me the records, and I took them home. So you see, Lucy Parrott and Mabel Glenn made me a confirmed Wagnerian from then on.

"Years later, at the Conservatory, I studied with pianist Victor Labunski. But I never approached the piano as an end to things. The piano, to me, was always an instrument to do something *else* with. I had a good ear and could play it; and I could get through parties that way. Eventually, I earned a living with it: during Basic Training I played at the Officers Club on Saturday nights to make money; and I played in a whorehouse in Shanghai to keep warm (it was very cold there!). After the war I went to Oberlin College, wrote some shows, then to Columbia to do graduate work. I got an assistantship in the opera workshop there (which meant coaching singers and playing scores). I think it was apparent by then that I was committed to music."

That commitment, however, has always been divided between the worlds of the popular show and the operatic stage. "Classical music was what I generally listened to, and what I still particularly enjoy. That's what really involves me. I was still kind of musically schizophrenic at Columbia, not sure in what direction I was going. Douglas Moore was the head of the Music Department there, and he and his family became my great friends, sort of my New York family. Douglas confessed to me one time that during World War I he had written a lot of popular songs. If he had it to do all over again, he said, he'd choose instead to write for the theater, for Broadway. I've always remembered that as a kind of 'legitimizing' moment for me. Sometimes with a very simple song, if it turns out well, I'll get some sort of fulfilled feeling that must be similar to somebody writing fine opera.

"Meanwhile, I was writing a lot of chamber music, some orchestral music and, while at Columbia, a terrible opera: a one-act thing called *Da Capo*, a watered-down-everybody-I-ever-heard sort of thing. I indulged in through-composing, the sort of thing I would later do during some of those emotional moments for ensemble in *Kiss of the Spider Woman*. My own neurosis, I guess, when I was writing *Da Capo* was being *too* conscious that I was 'writing opera.' I just didn't do it very well; I had much too much reverence for the form. Now I prefer to reserve that feeling for when I go to concerts and the opera."

Kander says he did not skip anything on his way to a musical career. After leaving Columbia in 1954, he spent nine years in the trenches: coaching singers, playing for auditions and show rehearsals, conducting in stock, working as a pianist in stage productions like *The Amazing Adele* and *An Evening with Beatrice Lillie* and composing dance arrangements for Broadway and television shows. "By the time I had done the dance music for *Gypsy* and *Irma La Douce*, the theater community knew me. It's not a class-oriented community, by the way. I was known as a professional and had access to everything. When the time came to do a musical, Hal Prince heard a piece I had done called *Family Affair*—about the obstacles family members put between two young people who want to marry—that I had written with James and William Goldman in 1962. Hal wanted to direct it. In fact, it was the first thing he ever directed. We've worked together many times since."

At this time Kander met the man who would become his longtime friend and collaborator, lyricist Fred Ebb. Five years his junior, Ebb was a New Yorker brought up in the Lower East Side. At that time Ebb had been writing material for nightclub acts and the satirical television series, *That Was the Week That Was*. His first stage musical, *Morning Sun*, for which he had written the lyrics, had recently failed after only a few performances.

"We liked each other almost right away," says Kander. "Freddie likes to say our neuroses complemented each other. We started working together immediately. It was as if we were pregnant all the time. We wrote fast. The very first hit song we had was 'My Coloring Book.' That was one of the only times Fred came to *my* house, by God, and he had an idea for a comic song for Kaye Ballard. But because I was in a bad mood, or something, I didn't want to be funny; so I suggested we try it as a ballad. Barbra Streisand turned it into a hit.

"But Freddie and I are very, very different people. He's a cynical New Yorker and I'm a sentimental Midwesterner. The main thing I can say is that things I'm afraid of, Fred is not; and vice-versa. Our pleasures are quite different. Classical music does not interest him at all. We have mutual friends, but not mutual close friends. But when we're in a room working together, we improvise together. We can both be very thin-skinned with other people, but together we can say anything without getting upset. When we're together, we create a third person. If there is a 'secret' to our success, it might be that 'third person.' The best time of all with us is the writing. It's after you finish writing the score that it turns to work. Sometimes things get improved working with a director, producer, choreographer, and a cast, but you're always fighting to preserve the original dream."

In May 1965, three years after "My Coloring Book," Kander and Ebb opened their first Broadway show, *Flora, the Red Menace.* This musical dramatization of Lester Atwell's novel *Love Is Just Around the Corner* tells a Depression-era story of the love of an idealistic young fashion designer for her boyfriend, Harry, a member of the Communist Party. When the love affair—and the politics—turn sour, Flora is kicked out of the Party. "When Freddie and I revived it in 1987, we altered its generally light, cartoonish style and mood to something more serious, something more akin to a 1980s sensibility," says Kander. Although the original presentation ran only eighty-seven performances, it has special significance because it earned a Tony Award for nineteen-year-old Liza Minnelli (the youngest performer ever to win that honor), who would go on to become Kander and Ebb's "signature" star.

"*Flora* opened, and it was not successful," admits Kander. "But Liza Minnelli got a Tony out of it, which was great. And I've always been fond of the song, 'A Quiet Thing.' Hal Prince told us that no matter what happened after the opening, we'd get together at his house to talk about the next show. And that's exactly what happened. Practically the day after the opening we started talking about *Cabaret.*"

Based on John van Druten's 1951 dramatization of Christopher Isherwood's "Berlin Stories," *Cabaret* opened in 1965 and ran for 1,165 performances. It garnered eight Tony Awards, including Best Musical and Best Score. Critic Walter Kerr described it as "a marionette's-eye view of a time and place in our lives that was brassy, wanton, carefree, and doomed to crumble."[4] When Bob Fosse brought it to the screen, the role of Sally Bowles was given to Liza Minnelli, while Joel Grey repeated his performance as Master of Ceremonies.

"That show did everything for us," says Kander. "We were accepted as professionals. We must have written sixty songs for *Cabaret.* But for the film version we were working under contract, and we had no control of the thing at all. Our one stipulation was that if anything new were written for it, Fred and I would be the ones to do it. We never went to Hollywood, nor were we involved with the film that much. One thing I do remember was that Bob Fosse needed a different kind of 'Money Song.' The original 'Money Song' was a big production number for the emcee and lots of girls. But Bob wanted a number just for Sally Bowles and the emcee. That new song is a better 'moment' than the original, and we incorporated it into the 1987 revival."

Among Kander and Ebb's subsequent Broadway shows were *The Happy Time* (1968), which starred Robert Goulet as a French-Canadian photographer nostalgically recalling his early family life in the 1920s and 1930s; *Zorba!* (1968), which adapted Michael Cacoyannis's 1964 feature film *Zorba the Greek* for the stage and presented Herschel Bernardi in one of his best stage roles; *Chicago* (1975), based on the 1942 William Wellman film *Roxie Hart*, about a publicity-seeking murderess; the Tony-Award-winning *Woman of the Year* (1981), a Lauren Bacall vehicle based on the eponymous George Stevens/Katharine Hepburn/Spencer Tracy film from 1942; *Kiss of the Spider Woman* (1992), adapted from the novel by Manuel Puig and the Hector Babenco 1985 film version; and *Steel Pier* (1997), set amid a 1933 dance marathon in Atlantic City. Meanwhile, revivals of *Chicago* and *Cabaret* have been tremendous successes on Broadway—perhaps because what seemed like flip cynicism in 1975 has become topical in the 1990s of celebrity trials and tabloid journalism.

Kander talks most affectionately about the shows that fell by the wayside, like *The Rink* (1984), a musical drama that deals with the estranged relationship between a mother and her daughter. Another failure was *70 Girls 70* (1971), which ran for only a few weeks. "*The Rink* is just a piece waiting to have its day, I think. It was our first collaboration with Terrance McNally. It was a step forward for us. It was adventurous and emotional. It has always reminded me of that line about circus life, 'I love you, Honey, but the season's over.' When you're working together with a cast on a piece like this, it's the most intimate life possible. You're all in love with each other. You have to be, because these are the only people you're going to see for a long time; and it's all very, very emotional. And then it opens. And even though you stay friends, there's this kind of 'Oh, hi...' thing later. *The Rink* and *Kiss of the Spider Woman* are the two shows from our earlier years I'm closest to. They are so full-out in their emotions, where people are allowed to feel, very deeply.

"Another show, *70 Girls 70*, was a rowdy, very low-brow piece based on an English comedy called *Breath of Spring*, which was later filmed as *Make*

Mine Mink. The critics would not let us do that. The subject of naughty old ladies who turn to a life of crime didn't work for them.

"The favorite for Fred, I think, would be our first staging of *Chicago* in 1975. That's because it's peppy. Fred told me his idea of a perfect score is something without a single ballad in it. I tend to be much more drawn to things that are more lyrical and emotional, like *The Happy Time* (1968), which also has 'moments' I really care about. I prefer songs like 'Dear One' or 'You Can Never Shame Me' and 'Sometimes a Day Goes By' (from *Woman of the Year*)."

Kander began composing film music for Harold Prince's *Something for Everyone* (1969). With Ebb he also wrote new numbers for Fosse's film version of *Cabaret*, although, ironically, the film's eight Academy Awards took no account of their work. That was remedied by the Academy in 1975, when the showstopper "How Lucky Can You Get," sung by Barbra Streisand in *Funny Lady,* was nominated for an Oscar. Two years later Kander and Ebb scored with another hit: "New York, New York," from the Martin Scorsese film of that name; and still another with "All That Jazz," from Fosse's film of the same name. Later Kander collaborated with director Robert Benton on several films, notably *Kramer vs Kramer* (1979) and *Places in the Heart* (1984); and he composed scores for such TV-movies as *An Early Frost* (NBC 1985), the first network show to address the issue of AIDS. In 1991 librettist David Thompson, director Scott Ellis, and choreographer Susan Stroman created the Kander and Ebb revue *And the World Goes 'Round.* Both men were elected into the Songwriters Hall of Fame in 1985; in 1991 both were inducted together into the New York Theater Hall of Fame.

Kander and Ebb share a general distaste for socializing and party-going. Most of their time together is spent on their shows. After working separately on their respective musical and lyrical efforts, the two men gather in Ebb's kitchen over sandwiches and coffee. They speak in a kind of code. They look for those "moments," as they call them. When they talk of "fixing" a work, they refer to solving the many problems of integrating music and staging.

"Then we move into another little room where I'll sit at the keyboard and try out a tune or a rhythm, while Fred messes around with a phrase or a quatrain. He can improvise in rhyme and meter the way I can with a melody. Ninety-five percent of our output has been written in that fashion. There's no way of predicting how fast a song will come. Once at Fred's house somebody challenged us to write a song between dinner and dessert. 'What do we write about?' asked Fred. 'I don't care much,' I said. Well—that was our title, 'I Don't Care Much'! We wrote it in fifteen minutes, and Barbra Streisand recorded it. By contrast, the song 'Gotta Learn How Not to Be Where You Are' in *Kiss of the Spider Woman* took lots of work, at least seven or eight versions.

"I think the best time for us is the writing. After the score is finished, then it turns to work. Then you have to fight with the director, producer, choreographer, and cast to preserve the original dream. Fred and I were among that last generation of show people—like Stephen Sondheim, Sheldon Harnick, and Jerry Herman—who were allowed to fail sometimes and still continue in careers in the theater. We feel a kind of guilty debt to young writers now, and we try to help them with workshops and public exposure for their work."

§

Like so many prominent Kansas Citians before him—composer Virgil Thomson, painter Thomas Hart Benton, and animator Walt Disney (to name only a few)—Kander carries with him the cozy values of neighborhood and family, no matter where he goes.

"In some ways New York is much more neighborly than my native Midwest," he says. "It's a warm city, and every time friends come here and stay at a hotel in midtown and race from one event to the other and see the panhandlers, they ask me, 'How do you live in this place?' I tell them New York is the reverse of what they think—that it's really a terrific place to live but a hard place to visit. Where I live, it's almost like a commune, where everybody knows everybody else. I'm a five-minute walk from Lincoln Center, fifteen minutes from Carnegie Hall. The cleaners are at the corner, the supermarket two blocks away, and delis and restaurants everywhere." He admits he doesn't go downtown much anymore, unless it is to the rehearsal stages at 890 Broadway or to the theaters that have presented his shows—especially his beloved Broadhurst on 44th Street, where *Cabaret* opened. Kander still has a special fondness for the West Village where, on his occasional visits he gets "very nostalgic and a little homesick." He says it is "like a village, a self-contained community." By contrast, the East Village, the area he knows least, is like a foreign land. "I always feel I need a passport when I go there."

I ask him if he feels his work belongs to a vanishing tradition in Broadway show music.

"I try not to think that way. I'm too selfish for that. I just try to write what pleases me and not worry about traditions and such. I try as much as possible in my whole life to do things that I find fulfilling and, consequently, pleasurable. I don't think in a historical way. There isn't a day in my life that I don't realize how lucky I am. I'm lucky to have spent so much of my life doing something I enjoy and that I seem to be good at. I'm lucky to be living in this house and have the friends that I do. To live in this neighborhood. It's not a matter of counting your blessings, but of being very, very aware of how you live, every minute of your life. It's all very well to have something in lights or to have somebody say, 'Oh, gosh, you wrote that?' But it's just as important to go to the cleaners and the supermarket and to *live* somewhere. It's very important to me. Just like Zorba says: It's important to live like everything is happening to you for 'the first time'."

In recent conversations *Over and Over* (formerly *The Skin of Our Teeth*) is still very much on Kander's mind. He and Ebb are currently dividing their time between it and *The Visit*, a macabre, expressionistic tragi-comedy about a vengeful woman's destruction of the man who had wronged her.

"We've been working on *Over and Over* for about three or four years now. If you have that much reverence for it, you don't want to screw it up! And I hope we don't. We'll stay with the time-travel idea and the people talking to the audience. It all sounds very strange, I admit. But, you know, the best opera libretto I can think of is a play that didn't quite work on its own and needed music, and that's *Pelléas et Mélisande*. But Debussy made a masterpiece of it. Now, *Skin of Our Teeth* has never been as popular as other Thornton Wilder pieces. That may be because it too was a piece that needed another element (and maybe a new title like *Over and Over*). We had a staging early this year [1999] at the Signature Theater in Arlington, Virginia, just outside Washington, D.C. It was a good experience, although some critics managed to get in. I don't know why they *must* come early like this. It's like reviewing a fetus. So I just have to keep my eyes on the material and not pay attention to them. We detected some problems that we're addressing. We need to have another production—maybe in Alaska, free of the critics! Eventually, we'll look toward a full production.

"Meanwhile, we have a December [1999] deadline for a rehearsed reading of *The Visit*. We're aiming for a New York production in the fall of 2000. Concentrating on that has taken most of our energies lately. Barry Brown, a producer, came up with the idea. As soon as he suggested it, I said yes. Terrence McNally said yes. Angela Lansbury said yes. We all said yes! But now the glamour part is over, and it's time to get to work."

Meanwhile, for John Kander, the music is everywhere. He cannot escape it. He laughs at the time he was out walking one snowy night in Greenwich Village, and he heard from inside a saloon the strains of The Most Famous Song in the World, "New York, New York." Kander recalls: "The singing was so raucous that I stopped in my tracks and went over to look through the windows. There they were, a whole bunch of people just screaming out, '*Start spreadin' the news, I'm leavin' today...*' Then, somebody inside spotted me peering through the window. He shouted out to me, 'Come on in, you old fool!' Well. I fled into the night. Once you've written a song like that, it's gone. And if you're lucky, it now belongs to others—no matter how badly they sing it!"

NOTES

[1]Ethan Mordden, "Celebrating America's Love of Show Biz," *New York Times* (13 April 1997), 4.

[2]Ibid.

[3]Quoted in Richard Harrington, "Life Is a Cabaret, Old Chum," *Washington Post* (3 June 1993), C4.

[4]Quoted in David Ewen, *New Complete Book of the American Musical Theater* (New York: Holt, Rinehart & Winston, 1970), 62.

William Kearns is Distinguished Professor Emeritus at the University of Colorado, Boulder, where he also served as associate dean for graduate studies and director of the American Music Research Center. Kearns received his doctorate at the University of Illinois in 1965; previously he taught at The Ohio State University and was principal hornist in the Columbus Symphony Orchestra. He is the author of *Horatio Parker, 1863-1919: His Life, Music, and Ideas* (1990), as well as articles and papers on aspects of American music, folk music, historiography, and aesthetics. A member of the steering committee that established the Rocky Mountain Chapter of the College Music Society, Kearns served as president of that organization from 1988-1990. He has also served the Sonneck Society for American Music (now simply the "Society for American Music") as editor of its newsletter, as a member of its board of directors, and as its vice-president.

❦ American Music Historiography Yesterday and Today

WILLIAM KEARNS

What Is Historiography?

"Historiography" has a number of different but related meanings; their common thread is the thinking *behind* the writing of history. Sometimes historians' philosophies, intentions, or prejudices are overt and stated in their prefaces, or they are easily discovered in the organization of their works. In other writings the basic assumptions are covert, although these histories may have, at first glance, the appearance of truth or complete objectivity. An awareness of the historian's underlying thinking is of vital concern because all historical writing carries the bias of its author.

One of the most influential historiographical works in the twentieth century is R. G. Collingwood's *Idea of History*.[1] The first four parts of the book are a history of historical writing, beginning with the Greek historian Heroditus and ending with Benedetto Croce, the Italian Idealist philosopher and historian with whom Collingwood has been closely identified; the fifth and last part contains seven "epilegomena" that categorize Collingwood's philosophy of history. In the present brief essay I shall use Collingwood's ideas as a touchstone in examing historiographical writings about music generally and American music specifically. I shall draw upon the thinking of Warren Dwight Allen, Charles Hamm, Leo Treitler, and Joseph Kerman about music historiography, and H. Wiley Hitchcock, Robert Stevenson, and Richard Crawford about American music. In conclusion, I offer some suggestions about possible courses that American music histories might take in the twenty-first century.

Collingwood's view of the history of history is evolutionary. The early Greek historians simply recounted tales, many of them part myth, from oral history. As following generations set their stories in writing, a body of literature emerged from which later historians drew. Collingwood refers to uncritical dependence on previous historical writing as "scissors and paste" history. Many of the ideas about the past that we now take for granted developed very slowly: our increasing sense of the remoteness of our past, our oneness as human beings, and, on the other hand, our distinctiveness as ethnic groups and nationalities. During the eighteenth and nineteenth centuries a "scientific" history emerged, characterized by the recognition of historical writing as a specific discipline, the increasing amount and variety of historical evidence made available through archeology, paleography, and other scientific procedures, and increased emphasis on reflective and critical thinking.

Collingwood's major contribution to historiography is the masterful way he formulated principles for historical writing. In the epilegomena he makes some of his most startling pronouncements that elevate historical knowledge over that of science, even philosophy itself. History is the only means of "knowing thyself"; it goes beyond science, which seeks the "outside" of things, to discover the "inside." "History is present," for historians must always reformulate their questions about the past in ways meaningful for the present. And their constructions must always be, to a degree, "imaginative," because someone must fill in the missing parts of the past, those that exist only in fragments. Historians are like detectives who ask questions and find answers that, in turn, lead to new questions; their fields of investigation are controlled by the kinds of questions they ask. Collingwood's most startling assumption is that historians who have gathered sufficient evidence and reflected on it are capable of "reenacting past thought." From all the evidence at their disposal "scientific" historians construct a story of the past, and the competent historian's *idea* of the past is as close as we can get to the actual past itself.

General Music Historiographies

A major study in the historiography of music is Warren Dwight Allen's *Philosophies of Music History*.[2] Part I of this two-part volume surveys 317 histories in chronological order of their writing; Part II deals with philosophical issues pertaining to the writing of history—origins, continuity, development, progress, evolution, sequential patterns—and how these issues are handled in the histories of music. Allen was particularly critical of how much historical writing during the nineteenth and early twentieth centuries was dominated by evolutionary theory to the degree that composers and their works were often treated simply as points in a progressive chain rather than items of interest in themselves.

Joseph Kerman's *Contemplating Music*, a survey of post-World War II writing about music, contains chapters on music history, theory, criticism, ethnomusicology, and historical performance.[3] Although the book is not intended to be historiography, it offers some salient historiographical observations. In the chapter on history, entitled "Musicology and Positivism, the Postwar Years," Kerman describes most American musicology as following the precepts of nineteenth-century German historiography: first, ascertaining facts by means of positivistic or scientific procedures; second, discovering laws derived from these facts.

Most American musicologists, Kerman feels, have been locked into the first phase and too timid to venture beyond, either to discover general laws or offer valid criticism in their subject areas. The latter is Kerman's special interest. Among some exceptions is an American study, William Austin's *Songs of Stephen Foster from His Time to Ours*,[4] described as rich in several contexts: biographical (Foster's life), social ("singing in mid-[nineteenth] century America"), ideological (the role of "pathetic plantation songs" in the abolitionist movement), and historical ("that these ... songs with their ... false image of slave life, came to be regarded by the end of the century as Negro folksongs").[5] Kerman describes Austin's work as an "extended inquiry into the meaning of [Foster's] vernacular tradition," and Collingwood might find Austin's analysis to be as close as we can get to antebellum thinking about Foster and his world.[6]

Leo Treitler is to general music historiography what Richard Crawford (see below) is to American music historiography. Both have written extensively in their respective areas. Treitler's *Music and the Historical Imagination* is an anthology of his articles on historiography published in various periodicals from 1966 through 1988.[7] His book shows Collingwood's influence throughout: the use of "historical imagination" in the book's title is also the subject of a Collingwood epilegomenon, and the titles of some chapters ("The Present as History" and "What Kind of a Story is History?") resonate with Collingwood's language. Finally, Treitler acknowledges Collingwood to be the "sharpest and most provocative" historiographical thinker and offers a summary of the epilegomena from the latter's *Idea of History*.[8] The musical analyses that Treitler makes throughout the book are faithful to the principles found in the Collingwood's epilegomena. They are both richly contextual and attempt to get at the thinking behind the composition. Like Kerman, Treitler calls for a critically oriented musicology that has become increasingly apparent in American music studies during the past twenty-five years.

In a short article, "Some Fugitive Thoughts on the Historiography of Music,"[9] Charles Hamm codifies new thinking about music historiography in the late twentieth century. As Kerman and Treitler have done, Hamm urges emphasis on contextual study of art works rather than their existence as "autonomous" objects only. He is also critical of the present manner of defining historical periods through stylistic analysis of compositions, thus treating them as independent of their context. Hamm suggests that style analysis cannot account for the plurality of twentieth-century music. Rather than establishing the modern era at 1900, we might instead define it as the "electronic" era beginning in the 1920s and 1930s. The electronic period has made possible a wide variety of music, vastly increased its production, and widened its dissemination. These features, more than style, are the defining criteria.[10] Hamm makes four "observations" about how quality might be perceived in such a pluralistic era:

> qualitative ranking of [different] musical genres is intolerable; music ... that does not make use of electronic media ... must not be judged inferior because of this; evaluation of music might focus on dissemination and reception [rather than composition]; each listener perceives [and values] each piece of music in individual fashion.[11]

Although these observations are the logical result of pluralism, society as a whole probably would not abide by them. Arguments will continue to be made for the superiority of one genre over another; certain genres will be challenged for both musical and ethical reasons; perception and judgment are unlikely to become completely individualistic and, thus, solipsistic.

American Music Historiography

About the time of publication for his own history of American music,[12] H. Wiley Hitchcock delivered a paper entitled "Nationalism and Anti-Nationalism in American Music Histories" at the 1968 Yugoslav-American Seminar on American Music.[13] Hitchcock noted the tendency of Italian, French, and German historians to tout the art music of their countries as superior to that of all others;[14] however, he felt that most American historians have taken the "anti-nationalistic" position of degrading their own art music, treating it as derivative. According to Hitchcock, English influence in the United States during the eighteenth and early nineteenth centuries was replaced by German authority and the equating of German with "cultivated" music as the latter influence increased throughout the nineteenth century. Serious American composition, however, either wasn't worth talking about or was at best far behind that of Europe. To assert any sort of individuality for American music, historians would have to abandon the usual "great composer-masterpiece" formula of European histories and find another rationale.

Hitchcock cites Gilbert Chase as establishing a new basis for writing American music history, partly through the inspiration of Charles Seeger—who, in 1950, called for a more inclusive look at music history beyond the fine-art tradition to that of primitive, folk, and popular traditions.[15] Also, as early as 1916, Oscar Sonneck, a figure who looms behind all American music historiography,[16] had called for "a history of American musical life."[17] These alternatives have governed much American historical writing in the latter part of the twentieth century. Hitchcock assessed Chase's *America's Music*[18] as

redressing the balance in American music historiography between concern for the tradition of fine-art music—virtually the only tradition dealt with [however, apologetically] by earlier writers—and the traditions of primitive, folk, and popular music.[19]

But Chase pushed further and "like any good revolutionary ... devalued American fine-art music"; whereas, Hitchcock, in his own history "attempted to be more moderate."[20] Chase's position eventually became more tempered by the time of the third edition of *America's Music* (1987).

When in 1969 music historian Robert Stevenson presented the Louis C. Elson lecture at the Library of Congress,[21] he borrowed "Philosophy" from the title of Allen's historiography but specified American music history as his topic. The constraints of a lecture caused Stevenson to demur from making a chronological survey of the histories to that date, as Allen had done for Western music history. Instead, Stevenson went directly to basic questions that a historian should ask about content—the scope of American music, types of musical activity, the music's value, the public for such music—and about methodology—the historian's reliance on primary and/or secondary sources, and his or her attitude toward teleology. Concerning American music's scope, he found major differences between Latin American and North American historians, with the former searching for aboriginal origins but sometimes failing to cover recent events, and the latter beginning as late as the European colonization of the New World and moving quickly to the present. Regrettably, Stevenson found much of Collingwood's "scissors and paste" writing in American music histories; however, he pondered the question of how much primary source material historians can examine critically when their subject is as vast as the entire history of American music. In the historian's selection of material for discussion, the question of value arises, and the historian's "taste" is bound to be a factor. Stevenson stated his own preference for catholicity: "a philosophy that extended hospitality to all sorts and conditions of men, including even composers of pieces like 'Narcissus,' 'the Lord's Prayer,' 'Sobre las olas,' 'Cielito lindo,' and 'La golondrina'."[22]

Another prominent historian of American music has carried out the task of examining in detail American music histories, as Allen had done for music histories in general. In the opening chapter of his book *The American Musical Landscape*,[23] Crawford looks at each of the major histories of American music, beginning with George Hood's *A History of Music in New England* (1846). Buttressed by approximately thirteen pages of documentation, including many content footnotes, Crawford's chapter is the most extensive historiographical study for American music to date.

As Hitchcock had done earlier, Crawford describes a shift in emphasis for American histories as occurring at mid-twentieth century. His terms for the dichotomy in historical writing are "cosmopolitan" (basically emphasis on the art music tradition that we share with Europe)[24] and "provincial" (emphasis on popular and folk music arising from or identified with various regions of the United States). Again, Gilbert Chase's *America's Music* (1955) is named as marking the change, and John Tasker Howard's *Our American Music*,[25] the leading history of the 1930s through the mid 1950s, ended a line of more-or-less cosmopolitan histories that began with late nineteenth- and early twentieth-century writers: Frédéric Ritter (1893), W. S. B. Mathews (1889), Louis Elson (1904), W. L. Hubbard (1908), and Arthur Farwell and W. Dermot Darby (1915).[26] These histories differ vastly in their inclusiveness and emphases, as Crawford shows, but they all accept the premise that art music should be at the pinnacle of culture. A few histories from the early nineteenth century[27] and most since that of Chase have followed a provincial bent by looking at other-than-art music for essential American qualities.

In *The American Musical Landscape* Crawford goes into considerable detail in outlining the new areas of music that Chase brought to our attention, including southern folk hymnody, Anglo-American folk music, Afro-American spirituals, blues, ragtime, and jazz. These heretofore had been either omitted or merely appended to American music histories. Neither Hitchcock nor Crawford points out that Chase's celebration of provincial musics is as European in origin as our art-music tradition, for Chase's thinking can be traced back through a line of European thought to that of the eighteenth-century German philosopher and philologist, Johann Gottfried von Herder, who believed that "the essence of a nation's character ... can be discovered in the folk tradition of its people."[28] Like Herder, Chase distrusted the art tradition as a desirable aspiration for a national music unless that *genre* took into account a direct association with folk culture. In the United States the strongest assertion of folk culture was to be found in subcultures such as those of blacks, Native Americans, and rural whites. Thus, for Chase, American art music that ignored these subcultures was not only simply derivative of Europe but also lacked the vernacular base that *any* art music should have.

Another strongly provincial history that Crawford examines is Hamm's *Music in the New World*,[29] the content of which is limited to music that has undergone change from its European roots or originated in the United States. Hamm goes beyond a discussion of music and composers to take in, as Crawford notes, the "uses" of music (performers, listeners) and an "acceptance of the music market place as a fact of American musical life."[30] Thus, the historical treatment of successful commercial composers such as

Irving Berlin is no longer left to popular-music hagiographies but drawn into the arena of serious historical discussion.

What conclusions does Crawford make in his survey of a dozen or so American music histories? Although he found something admirable in each, he remarked: "Historians of American music have yet to agree what the history of American music is." What is lacking, he finds, is a tradition, "a certain musical repertory ... centered on fundamental issues, subject to changing interpretations and approaches."[31] Crawford suggests that these issues should deal with the influence of the Old World, the ingenuity of the New World, their intersection, the role of aesthetics, geography, commerce, criticism, popularity, and the relation of a musical canon to history.

In the Preface to *The American Musical Landscape*, Crawford lists the assumptions on which the book is based:

> It is a viewpoint that tries to take Old World musical practices (especially European) into account, that encompasses both "cultivated" and "vernacular" traditions [a division that he finds useful in Hitchcock's *Music in the United States*:], that looks beyond composers to the contributions of performers, that distrusts music history written free of economic considerations, and that holds the United States to have enjoyed a vital, distinctive musical life for more than two centuries.[32]

Unlike other American musical histories, Crawford's book brings the tradition of historical writing into discussion and builds on it.

Much in Crawford's historiographical chapter, indeed, the premise of the entire book, follows Collingwood's principles. Crawford's statement that *The American Musical Landscape* is not a "nationalist polemic" but an attempt to understand ourselves fits Collingwood's concept that the purpose of history is to know both the "inside" as well as the "outside" of things, the better to "know thyself."[33] Crawford's comment, "As one's vantage point moves, the meanings of facts often change,"[34] matches Collingwood's belief that historical writing must be pertinent to the time in which we live. Crawford's sympathetic treatment of early histories such as Ritter's *Music in America* (1883) and Elson's *History of American Music* (1904) reflects Collingwood's insistence that historians must exert a rigorous imagination in reconstructing the past,[35] for Crawford seeks to understand *why* these historians, especially Ritter, attacked the provincialism of earlier histories and defended so vigorously cosmopolitanism, now often treated as mere "colonialism." ("In the time of Ritter and Elson, music in the cultivated tradition was still struggling for a secure foothold.... Their apparent empathy for the genteel ... has sometimes led us to see them as doctrinaire supporters of Europeanized taste when in fact they were advocates of a more diverse American musical life."[36]) Finally, as Stevenson had done before him, Crawford's emphasis on asking fundamental questions about American music history[37] complements Collingwood's concept of historical knowledge as reflective thinking[38] and the latter's methodology of historical writing by advancing from one question to another.[39]

Toward a Framework for Understanding American Music History in the Twenty-first Century

The United States will enters the third millennium as an even more diverse culture than in the past. Collingwood would point out that historians need a perspective to fit our generation. We might consider the progress that music historiography, specifically American, has made toward "knowing ourselves." The reflective thinking that Collingwood stressed has become increasingly apparent, particularly Allen's probing into the uncritical application of evolutionist theory to music history and Kerman's and Treitler's suggestion that music history move beyond its positivist phase to address issues of significance and meaning. Hamm has challenged our usual way of defining historical periods and making value judgments in an age dominated by electronic media and mass communication. The historiographers of American music have called not only for a more inclusive treatment of American music, embracing popular and folk as well as art music, but also for a more extended consideration of "musical life," including performance, reception, and business. Beyond these matters of scope, Stevenson and Crawford have offered valuable suggestions about methodology, particularly the use of source material and the framing of proper questions to address, and about the building of a historiographical tradition for American music.

§

For the remainder of this essay, I will address two fundamental, related issues for the writing of American music history. The first is a reconsideration of our cultural base from America-versus-Europe to one that is Euro-American. The second is greater emphasis on aesthetics in historical writing, particularly in examining our art music.

Although Crawford found American music histories to be disparate in both scope and methodology, he states that they united on one basic tenet: all "take Europe as a starting point" and "agree that the U.S.A. is a European colony."[40] Crawford's bipolar adjectives, "Cosmopolitan-Provincial," the basis of his review of American music historiography, defines American music in relation to that of Europe. Words such as "colony" and "provincial," which have a precise political meaning, can be misleading when extended to cultural ideas. Thus, the premise that we have been subservient to Europe culturally is too sweeping to apply indiscriminately in surveying our entire musical culture. Our political status as a colony was eliminated over two centuries ago. For a time, we continued to be both dependent on and independent of Europe culturally (witness the tension in psalmody of the Federal Period[41]), but the United States was beginning to "catch up" with Europe, even surpass it in some musical aspects, during the nineteenth century. For example, Theodore Thomas considered his orchestra superior to those in Europe,[42] and, today, the United States's performing and educational institutions, even its composers, are generally on par with those of Europe. Haven't we been for some time a part of one large Euro-American culture, one which in many respects is becoming a world culture? The contrasting of America with Europe may be useful as a premise for our earlier history, but a better concept for the late nineteenth and most of the twentieth centuries would be to think of ourselves culturally as one greater Atlantic community.

A Euro-American concept would place a different perspective on the nagging, evasive problem of defining "American" as opposed to "European" music. Bipolar historical writing is strewn with failed definitions. American music historians too often have started with the assumption that their task is to suggest qualities that are "American" and then make procrustean efforts to measure the composers, music, and musical activity that they recount fit these predispositions. For example, a recent history of twentieth-century American music asserts "experimentalism" to be "an American tradition,"[43] starting with Ives and Cowell, but what about the European experimentalism which predated or parelleled that of these composers?

Even Crawford's carefully considered approach to the issue of bipolarity—"For the cosmopolitan school, technical mastery and the acceptance of European forms and aesthetic principles.... For the provincial school, originality, experimentation, eclecticism"[44]—is problematic. Who would deny our cosmopolitan composers these provincial values, and, on the other hand, our provincial composers cosmopolitan values? Certainly much of our musical activity—composing, performing, listening—has nothing to do with our citizenship or even our ethnicity. Creativity, skill in manipulating an instrument, and depth in perceiving a composition are activities that are basically human, and we cultivate them to varying degrees as individuals. Of course, our environment, including our ethnic backgrounds, shapes how we compose, play or sing, and listen, but it is a funnel through which these activities are directed. And this environment has been Euro-American for some time.[45]

Such a Euro-American concept would change our manner of evaluating our composers. The postulate that seems to place "derivative" composers beneath "original" composers simply because of the geographic basis of their style sources would no longer be adequate. Walter Piston will be no less an "American" composer for being a master craftsman, and Harry Partch, no more, for being an innovator. Both work in an art tradition that is Euro-American (in spite of Partch's attempts to circumvent much Western music history).

Turning to the role that aesthetics should play in the writing of history, a recent emphasis has been on "musical life" in America, an aspect that Oscar Sonneck had called for near the beginning of this century. He might be surprised at the direction some authors have taken, however, for terms such as "sacralization" and "highbrow-lowbrow" have become focal points for explaining the popularity of classical music in the United States.[46] Sacralization suggests that our hunger for musical masterpieces is like our search for God. In rummaging through the past, one can discover descriptions of music that are hardly discernible from religious discourse. The term is used to demonstrate a sociological phenomenon, the increasing cultural rift in nineteenth-century America between the upper and lower classes. Classical music becomes a property of the "highbrows" to the exclusion of the "lowbrows."[47] Sacralization, however, cannot explain our affinity for "serious" music as a pinnacle of human expression. Instead we must look at other areas of aesthetics.

Confronting aesthetics will be difficult for many music historians, who usually give the subject a salutatory but casual treatment. By the mid-eighteenth century, when the sea change in music aesthetics occurred, the writing of music histories along nationalistic lines was already established, and the two issues—aesthetics (music as an art form) and nationalism (music as a part of a culture)—continued to be conflated or, at best, murkily separated. The profound difference in the way we came to view music was the result of the shift in aesthetics from the proposition of *art as imitation* to that of *art as expression*, particularly of feeling or emotion.[48] Such an attitude was conducive to the increasing popularity of instrumental, or "absolute," music, and a corresponding aesthetic that treated such music as valuable *by virtue of its lack of words or "meaninglessness."*[49]

Treitler's analysis of the "Andante" movement from Mozart's Symphony No. 39 in E-flat Major, K. 543, is an illustration.[50] Treitler concentrates on Mozart's *musical* narrativity by explaining how the work unfolds both within the conventions of sonata form and in the individuality of Mozart's treatment. As a historian, he searches for the way that eighteenth-century theorists of absolute music might have heard it, as an unfolding of mental activity (expressiveness) in musical sounds. The aesthetic principles for absolute music came to be applied to *all* classical music, even art songs, choral music and opera.

Throughout the past two centuries both philosophy[51] and psychology[52] have structured fairly elaborate systems of explaining musical activity, thought, expression, and feelings as purely musical (absolute) *or/and* as imbued with myriad associations. Nationalism is such an association. As valuable as it might be to the appreciation of a composition, it remains associative rather than fundamental. Aaron Copland skillfully blended both musical qualities and associative ideas related to the American experience in many of his compositions, which has made them among the most popular in twentieth-century America. Much of the music of Samuel Barber, on the other hand, has remained popular and no less respected without such associations. Popular, folk, and ethnic musics are, on the other hand, saturated with associations to the degree that writers have only recently delved seriously into their purely musical aspects.

Future historians writing general histories of American music will, of course, embrace the large amount of writing now being done about our popular and our many ethnic musics, but they will also have to give serious consideration to our increasingly rich art-music tradition. A new cosmopolitanism could emerge based on various cultural groupings that have existed and now exist in the United States. It will be neither an attempt to "cath-up" with Europe nor a means of counteracting provincialism, as Crawford has suggested for our earlier cosmopolitanism. Its aesthetic principles will include those of looking deeply into music and its unfolding, whether the activity is composing, performing, or listening. The new cosmopolitanism will also address music's strong associative power to engage

213

in so many aspects of our personal and social lives. The latter will include our family, local, regional, national, and worldwide associations. Future historians might see art music's potential to fulfill our deepest intellectual-emotional needs, and popular and ethnic musics as enriching our lives through their numerous activities and associations. In the United States, where cultural diversity is recognized and practiced so intensely, the task of future American music historians will be doubly complex, for our music has for many different people many roles that need to be sorted and defined.

NOTES

[1]R. G. Collingwood, *The Idea of History*, ed. Jan van der Dussen (New York: Oxford University Press, 1994). Collingood (1889-1943) was an English philosopher who wrote extensively in the areas of metaphysics, epistemology, ethics, and aesthetics. He was also a historian and specialist on Roman Britain. *The Idea of History* draws on both his work as a practicing historian and his thinking as a philosopher. It is an outgrowth, in part, of his lectures on history, given at Oxford University during the late 1920s and 1930s. It was first published posthumously in 1946 and has been in print ever since. The most recent revised edition, edited and with an introduction by Dussen, also contains Collingwood's lectures from 1926 to 1928.

[2]Warren Dwight Allen, *Philosophies of Music History: A Study of General Histories of Music, 1600-1960* (New York: American Book Co., 1939). A paperback edition published by Dover in 1962 won Allen's volume wide circulation; for this edition he wrote a five-page preface surveying briefly major historical publications for the 1940s through the 1960s.

[3]Joseph Kerman, *Contemplating Music: Challenges to Musicology* (Cambridge, MA: Harvard University Press, 1985).

[4]William Austin, *"Susanna," "Jeanie," and "Old Folks at Home": The Songs of Stephen Foster from His Time to Ours* (New York: MacMillan, 1975).

[5]Kerman, Contemplating Music, 176-177.

[6]Kerman, *Contemplating Music*, 177; Collingwood, *The Idea of History*, 215.

[7]Leo Treitler, *Music and the Historical Imagination* (Cambridge, MA: Harvard University Press, 1989).

[8]Ibid, 42-44.

[9]*Charles Hamm*, "Some Fugitive Thoughts on the Historiography of Music," *Essays in Musicology: A Tribute to Alvin Johnson,* ed. Lewis Lockwood and Edward Roesner (American Musicological Society, 1990), 284-291.

[10]Although the idea is more specified in Hamm's article, it is suggested on a broader scale in Walter Wiora, *Die vier Weltalter der Musik* (Stuttgart: W. Kohnhammer, 1961), published in English as *The Four Ages of Music*, trans. M. D. Herter Norton (New York:

Norton, 1965). The Fourth Age is described as "The Age of Techniques and Industrial Global Culture" and covers the twentieth century.

[11]Hamm, "Some Fugitive Thoughts," 290-290.

[12]H. Wiley Hitchcock, *Music in the United States: A Historical Introduction* (Englewood Cliffs, NJ: Prentice-Hall, 1969).

[13]Hitchcock, "Nationalism and Anti-Nationalism," *Papers of the Yugoslav-American Seminar on Music*, ed. Malcolm H. Brown (Bloomington: Indiana University, 1970), 199-208.

[14]Ibid, 200.

[15]Ibid, 205.

[16]See Richard Crawford, "Sonneck and American Musical Historiography," *Essays in Musicology: A Tribute to Alvin Johnson*, 226-283. Although Sonneck never wrote a general history of American music, his books and articles about the subject and his methodology have been a guide and inspiration for all scholars in the field of American music.

[17]Hitchcock, "Nationalism and Anti-Nationalism," 205.

[18]Gilbert Chase, *America's Music: From the Pilgrims to the Present* (New York: McGraw-Hill, 1955; rev. 3rd ed. [Urbana: University of Illinois Press, 1987]).

[19]Hitchcock, "Nationalism and Anti-Nationalism," 207.

[20]Ibid, 207.

[21]Robert Stevenson, *Philosophies of American Music History*: a pamphlet published for the Library of Congress by the Louis Charles Elson Memorial Fund (Washington, D.C., 1970).

[22]Stevenson, *Philosophies of American Music History*, 13-14.

[23]Crawford, "Cosmopolitan and Provincial: American Music Historiography," *The American Musical Landscape* (Berkeley: University of California Press, 1992), 3-37.

[24]The term "cosmopolitan" had been used previously by Joseph A. Mussulman in *Music in the Cultured Generation: A Social History of Music in America, 1870-1900* (Evanston, IL: Northwestern University Press, 1971), 32 and Chapter VII.

[25]John Tasker Howard, *Our American Music: Three Hundred Years of It* (New York: Crowell, 1931; rev. ed. 1939; 3rd ed. 1946; 3rd ed. [with supplementary chapters by James Lyons] 1954; 4th ed. [published as *Our American Music: A Comprehensive History from 1620 to the Present*] 1965). See also John Tasker Howard and George Kent Bellows, *A Short History of Music in America* (New York: Crowell, 1957; 2nd ed., 1967). Karl Kroeger, who prepared the bibliography for the 4th edition, said that Howard affirmed his purpose to have been a chronicler rather than a historian of American music.

[26]Frédéric Louis Ritter, *Music in America* (New York: Scribner, 1883; new ed., 1890; reprint, New York: Johnson, 1970, and New York: Franklin, 1973); *A Hundred Years of Music in America: An Account of Musical Effort in America during the Past Century*, ed. W. S. B. Mathews (Chicago: Howe, 1889; reprint, New York: AMS Press, 1970); Louis C. Elson, *The History of American Music* (New York: MacMillan, 1904; rev. ed.

1915; rev. 1925 by Arthur Elson; reprint, New York: Franklin, 1971); *History of American Music*, ed. W. L. Hubbard, with introductions by George W. Chadwick and Frank Damrosch = Volume 4 of *American History and Encyclopedia of Music* (Toledo: Irving Squire, 1908); *Music in America*, ed. Arthur Farwell and W. Dermot Darby = Volume 4 of *The Art of Music*, ed. Daniel Gregory Mason (New York: National Society of Music, 1915).

[27]George Hood, *A History of Music in New England; with Biographical Sketches of Reformers and Psalmists* (Boston: Wilkins, Carter, 1846; reprint, New York: Johnson, 1970); Nathaniel D. Gould, *Church Music in America* (Boston: A. N. Johnson, 1853; reprint, New York: AMS Press, 1972).

[28]Gene Bluestein, *The Voice of the Folk: Folklore and American Literary Theory* (Amherst: University of Massachusetts Press, 1972), 10.

[29]Hamm, *Music in the New World* (New York: Norton, 1983).

[30]Ibid, 31.

[31]Crawford, "Cosmopolitan and Provincial," 3-4.

[32]Crawford, "Preface," *The American Musical Landscape*, x.

[33]Collingwood, *The Idea of History*, epilegomenon 1, 213-215.

[34]Crawford, "Cosmopolitan and Provincial," 1.

[35]Collingwood, *The Idea of History*, epilegomenon 2, 247-249.

[36]Crawford, "Cosmopolitan and Provincial," 32.

[37]Ibid, 33.

[38]Collingwood, *The Idea of History*, epilegomenon 1, 215-217.

[39]Collingwood, *The Idea of History*, epilegomenon 3, 281.

[40]Crawford, "Cosmopolitan and Provincial," 6.

[41]See Richard Crawford, "'Ancient Music' and the Europeanizing of American Psalmody, 1800-1810," *A Celebration of American Music: Words and Music in Honor of H. Wiley Hitchcock*, ed. Crawford, R. Allen Lott, and Carol J. Oja (Ann Arbor: University of Michigan Press, 1990), 225-255.

[42]Ezra Shabas, *Theodore Thomas: America's Conductor and Builder of Orchestras, 1835-1905* (Urbana: University of Illinois Press, 1989), 107, 219.

[43]Kyle Gann, *American Music in the Twentieth Century* (New York: Schirmer Books, 1997), xv.

[44]Crawford, "Cosmopolitan and Provincial," 7.

[45]I am addressing our classical tradition primarily. The United States has an extensive history of African-American influence in its folk and popular music traditions and to some extent in its classical tradition. Asian musics have recently and will probably increasingly become influential in American music.

[46]See Lawrence W. Levine, *Highbrow/Lowbrow: The Emergence of Cultural Hierarchy in America* (Cambridge: Harvard University Press, 1988). Levine deals with the arts in the United States generally and has had a major impact on the sociology of music.

[47]Ralph P. Locke offers an effective criticism of Levine's book in "Music Lovers, Patrons, and the Sacralization of Culture in America," *19th Century Music* (Spring 1994): 149-173.

[48]A succinct account of the history of aesthetics can be found in DeWitt H. Parker, "Aesthetics," *Encyclopedia of the Arts*, ed. D. D. Runes and H. G. Schrickel (New York: Philosophical Library, 1946).

[49]John Neubauer, *The Emancipation of Music from Language: Departure from Mimesis in Eighteenth-Century Aesthetics* (New Haven: Yale University Press, 1986), elaborates on this change. Italics and quotation marks are mine.

[50]Treitler, "Mozart and the Idea of Absolute Music," *Music and the Historical Imagination* (Cambridge, MA: Harvard University Press, 1989), 176-214.

[51]Monroe C. Beardsley, *Aesthetics from Classical Greece to the Present: A Short History* (New York: MacMillan, 1966), offers a good overview. Edward Lippman, *A History of Western Musical Aesthetics* (Lincoln: University of Nebraska Press, 1992), examines the interaction of musical ideas and philosophical aesthetics.

[52]Hans Kreitler and Shulamith Kreitler's *Psychology of the Arts* (Durham, NC: Duke University Press, 1972) is a synthesis of the numerous contributions of a century of psychology to theories of the arts. Current work in the psychology of music can be found in *Psychomusicology*, a bi-annual journal of research in music cognition.

An associate professor at Omaha's Creighton University and chair of that institution's Department of Fine and Performing Arts, **Marilyn Kielniarz** holds three degrees in organ performance from Northwestern University as well as a Certificate in Dalcroze Eurhythmics from Carnegie Mellon. Active in many different areas of music, Kileniarz has concertized, won prizes in European and American performance competitions, and served as a musician for several Protestant churches and at least one synagogue. A member of the Nebraska Arts Council, she appears as a keyboardist with the Omaha Symphony. In her capacity as director of Creighton's Javanese Gamelan ensemble, she makes regular trips to Indonesia. Kielniarz belongs to the Board of Directors for the American Guild of English Handbell Ringers, serves as chair of that organization's Publications Department, and chairs Area VIII (Illinois, Iowa, Kansas, Missouri, Nebraska) on behalf of the Guild's membership.

❦ Challenges and Visions
Reflections on American Church Music

MARILYN A. KIELNIARZ

To some, it may seem a bit incongruous that an individual like me would choose to reflect on American church music. Although I claim a solid history of church-music employment and hold advanced degrees in organ performance and sacred music, I now spend my days happily engaged in collegiate-level arts administration, ear-training instruction, and Indonesian gamelan. I have left the world of weeknight choir practices and Sunday morning worship behind me. Even though I haven't bronzed my organ shoes, I have taken a furlough from the trenches of sacred music.

To be honest, my situation is scarcely unique.

The last years of the twentieth century find the profession of sacred music in decline. Many of my colleagues have opted to leave church employment in search of such tangibles as greener financial pastures, competitive employee-benefit packages, reduced evening and weekend work assignments, concrete evaluative instruments, improved employee-support mechanisms, and sustained career growth. For many of us, it has become increasingly difficult to justify pursuing careers that can scarcely support individuals, much less families. Put it another way: our artistic souls simply cannot be satisfied if our bodies—and spirits—lack nourishment.

Local newsletters of American Guild of Organists chapters testify to the fact that there seem to be more organ jobs than organists to fill them. Yet national statistics document decreasing enrollments in collegiate and conservatory church-music training programs. Many talented music students never even consider entering church music as a profession, opting instead for more "practical" career paths such as computer science, medicine, and law. As a result, dedicated full-time academic positions in church music have been and continue to be redefined or lost to retirement.

Artistically, church musicians have not always been successful in reconciling their visions with those of their faith communities. At the same time, American denominations have become increasingly diverse in their memberships, and many congregations have redefined their musical tastes through contemporary means of expression that reflect advances in music technology and a broadened "consumer base." No wonder classically-trained organists increasingly feel pressured to provide musical offerings that may sound more like popular entertainments than worship tools. As one colleague of mine remarked, "Our offering plates fill to the brim whenever I present happy, peppy music." Issues of economy extend beyond those of programming, however. Congregations today seem less often eager to justify costs associated with aging church organs, especially when roofs or decades-old boilers need replacement.

Although it boasts centuries of excellence in design and construction as well as some of the greatest composers and performers of history, the "King of Instruments" is more and more often orphaned by the institutions it has served. And highly-trained professional organists more and more often find they offer something their churches are no longer able to appreciate, much less afford. Artistic approaches carefully honed through years of higher education and practical experience are coming to be considered "snobbish," "old-fashioned," and even "boring"—and this by well-meaning, influential, generally amateur church-music critics. An example: a group of elders in a Lutheran congregation I once served gave voice to the sentiment: "We want to hear more Bach, more of our heritage." When I supplied "more Bach," however, this was what I heard: "Is that really Bach? Bach doesn't sound like that!"

Anecdotes like this one aren't limited to churchgoers. Unfortunately, a litany of similar responses—coupled with meager salaries, competition for resources, and unwieldy hierarchical management structures—have taken their toll: increasingly, musicians have left congregations or, in extreme circumstances, the profession itself.

§

Given these sentiments, you might think I have nothing positive to say about the future of American church music. But I do. I see brightness as well as darkness ahead. I don't believe the profession is destined for extinction.

It cannot be denied that many of our churches are changing their approaches to the practice of faith within a contemporary, highly diverse society. A vast majority of Americans profess the importance of spiritual pursuits, yet many of them no longer belong to traditional or "mainline" denominations. Consequently, church music is no longer limited to the sounds of pipe organs and SATB choirs. During this past year's Easter weekend, for instance, Christian congregations in eastern Nebraska listened to everything from Moravian trombone ensembles to West African drummers. Services incorporating traditional Latin plainchant were offset by "jazz Easters." My own community also boasted a full schedule of post-Passover observances, daily prayers at our local mosque, pujas at our local Hindu temple, meetings of the local Buddhist sangha, and Native American sweat-lodge ceremonies. The new century shall witness a veritable world of spiritual expression throughout the Midwest; many successful church-music programs, particularly those associated with "mainline" denominations, are already demonstrating a variety of artistic approaches, coupled with excellent examples of contemporary expressions.

Church musicians can no longer satisfy the needs of their congregations merely through proficient performances of historical Western European organ and choral literature. Centers dedicated to preparing church musicians— whether affiliated with specific faiths or defined as college/conservatory professional programs—are developing and offering curricula far more inclusive and creative than were widely available to members of my generation. Today, counterpoint exercises co-exist with discussions of Indian ragas. Developments in music technology open exciting new possibilities for the preparation, production, and presentation of sacred music. Students may still purchase organ shoes and batons, but they also buy handbell gloves, drum sticks, and fakebooks. Innovative training programs recognize the need to prepare students for successful professional relationships with a variety of age groups; they offer classes devoted to early childhood development as well as to older adults. Moreover, innovative veteran musicians strive to incorporate basic educational philosophy into church work. The motto is becoming: "Meet your people at their level and, by way of skill and specialized training, raise them to a level similar to your own."

A few students, of course, still wish to specialize in organ performance. Highly proficient mentors continue to share this centuries-old craft with those destined to carry it well into the new century.

That things have largely changed, however, does not mean change is merely plunging us downhill. Today, philosophical discussions and approaches that might previously have fractured communities of practitioners may now provide opportunities for reconstruction. A case in point is that of the organ world's twentieth-century "Baroque revival." Enthusiasm associated with the rediscovery of European Baroque principles has extended to changes in organ-building, in literature selection, in performance practice. Even after decades of heated discussion, positive and negative opinions about "revival" issues still surface occasionally in *The American Organist*'s "Letters to the Editor." Between initial explorations and the establishment of "authentic" Baroque practices, a cadre of veterans has emerged—experts possessed of practical experience, and capable today of offering opinions and judgments unthinkable even twenty years ago.

Today's music students anticipating church careers are also better equipped to assume pro-active, meaningful roles in matters concerning their own employment situations. Advocacy organizations—the American Guild of Organists is perhaps the most familair to musicians, but several individual demoninations have their own—strive to provide increased insights into the practical world of sacred music. Future church employees appear also to be approaching their prospective careers with less idealism and a keener awareness of challenges. To be sure, the number of full-time, well-paid music-ministry positions are limited. Gone are the heady days of old-fashioned, "Lord will provide" mentality. On the other hand, improved understanding of contemporary society and all its challenges is creating smarter, savvier church musicians. And, although the Church may be eternal, its employees are discovering that temporal success involves a little applied Darwinism: happy retirement is directly linked to carefully considered social adaptability.

Many church musicians are excellent managers, and more than a few have been able to move into positions as academic administrators. Large, successful church-music programs require their directors to juggle several choirs and sizeable numbers of participants, to keep track of multiple interactive schedules, and to plan and document complex budgets. Too, their programs must appeal to diverse consumer bases. Regardless of size, successful music ministries are capable of ongoing programmatic developments and evaluation as well the effective management of resources and a very real sense of shared ownership. Personally speaking, any triumphs I may be credited with in academic administration are probably grounded in my years as the director of a church music program.

I believe academe must shoulder some responsibility for the future success of American church music. We cannot prepare our students for positions more appropriate to 1920s Protestant America than those that exist today. Prospective music ministers deserve honesty in career counseling and full disclosure of employment trends. Curricula must address the artistic, spiritual, and social needs of America's diverse publics. As educators, we must continue to demand excellence while challenging ourselves and our students to develop broad-based conceptions of sacred music. Despite our lofty goals, we must have patience as we teach our students about music's abilities to be more than simple entertainment, something capable of inspiring both intellect and soul. Above all, we must have the courage to effect change when it becomes prudent to do so.

Now for a confession: my opening paragraph contains some falsehoods. I am still involved with sacred music. Sunday morning may still find me at an organ console assisting my *congregation du jour* with its solemn worship. Even though I've exchanged a full-time church job for life in the Ivory Tower, I still consider it a privilege to guide others musically in corporate worship. I also hold a leadership position in the American Guild of English Handbell Ringers, an organization that has maintained a strong, fifty-year-long connection with the Church.

Furthermore, I am engaged on a weekly basis in the study and performance of a unique, spiritually-based type of music. For some people, this music presents a problem: it doesn't hail from the West, and it certainly isn't grounded in the traditions of any religious denomination I've served in the past. I am a student of Central Javanese gamelan. Among its many forms, I have discovered this music's ability to inspire and stimulate spiritual reflection—an ability made stronger by its very nature as a form of artistic expression, one produced by a community of participants. Over the years, Javanese mentors have contributed greatly to the feelings and sensitivities I hold for music as an art form. My ongoing experiences with gamelan and Javanese culture have added greater depth to my spiritual and musical development; they've also taught me something about the great variety of artistic expressions that can nourish the soul.

I believe American church music of the twenty-first century will enjoy a bright future as it fully embraces the rich diversity available throughout "spiritual song" of all kinds. Its practitioners, however, must address a challenge as old as the field itself: the need to establish a respectful, positive coexistence between various lofty and diverse music traditions. These traditions have often been perceived as mutually exclusive, making it difficult for music professionals, their co-workers, and those they serve to share a commonality of artistic appreciation.

It is the responsibility of highly trained church musicians, as well as of the Church itself, to search for and nurture excellence within a broad musical spectrum. Sharing responsibility for a successful future, the Church must also provide a fair and honest place for musicians to work, and it must demonstrate as much concern for the welfare of its musical employees as it showers upon its other faithful servants and followers. I expect the coming years will show us vibrant new approaches to full partnership with sacred music's rich legacy. Gifted musicians will continue to lead, challenge, and inspire others in their work as artistic ministers. With this vision in mind, I think I'll wait to bronze my organ shoes.

Ann Kilkelly is professor of Theatre Arts and Women's Studies at Virginia Tech. She completed her undergraduate work at the University of Minnesota and took her doctorate in English at the University of Utah, where she also studied theater and dance. Kilkelly has held positions at the University of Kentucky and Transylvania University. A master teacher and rhythm tap performer, she has published poetry and prose in *Women and Performance: A Journal of Feminist Theory* and other periodicals as well as poetry in *The American Voice*; with historian Mary Neth she is completing a book entitled *Tapping the Margins*; her performances include shows at New York's La Mama Theater and the Kennedy Center, Washington, D.C.; and her collaborations with composer Zae Munn have been widely performed and have received several prizes in women's choral competitions. Kilkelly holds a Senior Fellowship at the Archive Center of the National Museum of American History.

❦ Foot Notes
Tap in the Twentieth Century

ANN KILKELLY

If It's Serious It Must Be Funny, or: What's a Nice Girl Like You...?

On the eve of the millennium I found myself onstage at La Mama Theatre on the lower East Side of Manhattan singing, tap dancing, and playing the ukulele while dressed in a pink satin corset, bunny ears, and a tattered crinoline.[1] The song was "Ukulele Lady," a 1925 tune with lyrics by Gus Kahn and music by Joe Henderson. My partner Carol Burch-Brown and I dressed like appropriating, Duane Hansonesque tourists, with allusions to Josephine Baker and Arthur Godfrey. Our comic set, "Songs of Our People: The Tourist," also included Irving Berlin's "What'll I Do," performed as a warbling duet of voice and snorkel. The sexist, racist, colonialist, and entirely charming "Ukulele Lady" featured an interpolated passage from "Malagueña," played by Carol on the soprano uke and accompanied by me using mouth castanets and a large gold pom pom that shook appealingly. The dance combined many vernacular and eccentric steps, a Stanley Brown soft shoe, and improvisation.

That a fifty-three-year-old white female feminist academic would land in this circumstance at a point of *maturity* in her career is indicative of the pleasures, ironies, and complications of the jazz-tap idiom as I have experienced it. The dance is music of the streets, of immigrants and working-class migrants, of Ireland, Africa, of African Americans and many others. It is intellectual and "low brow," "high" art and entertainment, esoteric and wildly popular, essentially comic and poorly understood. Its complexities embody American cultural history, but they are also the confusions and contradictions of my creative and scholarly life.

The essay that follows interweaves stories and observations from my life as a tap dancer with stories, analyses, and appetizing tidbits from and about other dancers who were and are my teachers.

§

As a
middle-class
formerly heterosexual
white
woman
with a Ph.D. in literature
living and working at Virginia Tech
in Blacksburg, Virginia, USA,
of working-class Irish and Cockney English
small-town
upper Midwest
(They called us "Black" and "Shanty" Irish
when we wanted to be "lace curtain")
heritage,
whose Mother was
a flapper turned housewife
whose Father was
a factory worker who became a time-study engineer
one grandmother a pie-making suffragette;
the other the proprietor of a boarding house.
One grandfather a logger, then a gentleman farmer;
the other a Golden Gloves Champion boxer and plumber,
It is no surprise that I am a tap dancer.

Child Star Meets Feminism

One of my earliest memories is trying to reproduce the sound of horses' hooves, the ones that galloped under that one tree in Saturday westerns. Then my mother brought home a pair of tap shoes from the rummage sales she ran at our church. The shoes were gilded gold, had huge bows, and were much too small, but I wore them anyway, though they pinched unmercifully. In them I could reproduce not only the horses but also dance in the image of all the girl-women I longed to be: Ginger Rogers, Debbie Reynolds, Tinkerbell. And in the living room my mother and I danced, during the hours between the time my father went to work at the factory and the time he came home for lunch. It was our secret, our pleasure—the Charleston, the Cakewalk, the Black Bottom, which she said wasn't nice and, slapping her fanny, did it anyway.

> *Gertrude "Ma" Rainey, the first of the Classic Blues women, sang and danced the famous Black Bottom. The song says, "I'm gonna show you all my big Black Bottom; it'll put you in a trance."*

But the pleasure of this dancing with my mother in our living room began to adjust itself into the feminine form I saw on TV and in the TV when I danced alone in front of it, an early model with a reflector screen strapped to its front. The screen sent back my legs significantly elongated, my body appropriately obscured.

> *I remember Spike Jones, Julie London, Doris Day, Ginger Rogers, Ann Miller, the Mills Brothers, the Ames Brothers, Louis Armstrong, Perry Como, Bill "Bo Jangles" Robinson, Shirley Temple, Donald O'Connor, Hoagie Carmichael, the June Taylor Dancers, Arthur Miller, Kate Smith, Sarah Vaughan, Ella Fitzgerald, Pat Boone, John Bubbles.*

Common Wisdom

Ned Wayburn, a Broadway choreographer of the 1930s, wrote the following description of his "business" as a dance teacher:

> It is necessary that every feminine form be as near perfect as possible in order to attract they eye of the audience as well as the ear. In our school we make it a business to produce beauty, neither sentiment nor art enters the question. It is purely a commercial proposition with us. Audiences will not come to the box office with their money to see some ugly misshapen girls on the stage. Therefore it is up to me to make it right.[2]

A Couple of Traditional Tap Steps

A rudiment of tap, the time step, used to be taught to be a percussion accompaniment to other players. The old dancers taught it by sound. Make these sounds with your feet:

A. Thanks for the Buggy Ride (repeat 6 bars with 2 bar break)
   Thank you for the Buggy Ride (with flap)
   Thank you very much for the Buggy Ride (with shuffle)
   Where shall we go for a Buggy Ride? (with double shuffle)
B. The BS Chorus consists of an audience-pleasing set of flash steps, including travelling time steps, crossover steps, one footed wings, over-the-tops, and trenches. The dancers always said, "And BS doesn't mean Bachelor of Science."[3]

Higher Education

In graduate school I kept my dancing in the closet, believing my studies sublime and my tapping ridiculous. I received a Ph.D. in English; I studied the great literature of the Western tradition: all men, almost all white. At the same time I danced, going from the cavernous gymnasium where a hundred or so of us struggled with pull backs and wings and time steps to "I Want To Be Happy." After that I spent hours in my library carrel pouring over Blake's *Proverbs of Hell* and Northrop Frye, and, as time wore on, Dérrida, Artaud, Brecht, and others.

As I began my career as an academic, I discovered feminist literary criticism and brought my dancing out of the closet. I began to understand my difference from the models I had been studying, and I began to note and analyze the absence of women from my education. I found Virginia Woolf, Jane Austen, Sylvia Plath, and Christina Rosetti. Then Toni Morrison, Margaret Atwood, Alice Walker, Nikki Giovanni. Then more and more dances and old dancers. And the longer I danced, the more I came to understand that the dances that gave me so much pleasure, taught to me by women, came first from black men and women who were rarely rewarded or recognized in the cultural ivory tower. This is still true.

Tapping the Margins

First you lay down some iron, then you start cooking — Brenda Bufalino

In jazz idiom, "laying down the iron" means to establish a groove; "cooking'" to stay in it until it heats up and yields a potent mixture of shape and surprise. Who gets to lay it down, who can put a foot down, and who does the cooking have been questions circulating around jazz and jazz dance with great intensity in recent years, although they are hardly new.

Tap is both marginal and mainstream; its history is saturated with racial and class stereotypes and marked by appropriation; its "masters" are male and mostly black, yet it is a form now practiced in large numbers by white women. Its history is oral and pedestrian and, to date, largely uncollected.[4]

Academic criticism in dance and movement tends to comment almost exclusively on forms derived from Western European traditions, most notably modern dance and ballet. The vernacular—and, in some sense, also indigenous—tradition of American tap dancing goes largely unnoticed in dance and performance criticism. Recent books by Susan Foster and Sally Banes, for example, theorize choreography in postmodern and social-contextual terms, but rarely is a tap dancer treated seriously or included as representative of a genre.

Recent texts about black dance largely ignore tap, though for very different reasons: they concentrate either on traditional African dance or African forms as modern choreographers incorporate them. Moreover, critics of tap have been at pains to claim their subject dead or dying, while its proponents constantly insist on its revival or renaissance. Few other forms are so constantly subjected to murderous intent and resuscitation. Perhaps tap dancing is simply the "undead."

The scholar who writes about tap dancing struggles with a tension between the need to celebrate or reclaim artists whose works are badly underacknowledged and the need for ongoing discussions, both theoretical and critical, about tap's position in the United States today. A few excellent books on African-American dance have come out recently, including Jacqui Malone's *Steppin' on the Blues,* but even this book doesn't include women performers or gendered analyses. Cheryl Willis's work, still in a mostly unpublished Temple University dissertation, documents a number of African-American women dancers through oral history, but it is far more celebratory than analytical, especially insofar as it treats the complex intersections of race and gender.

Jazz-tap dancing is tied to jazz music and the history of black America, although its roots are not exclusively African-American; Irish jig dancing and Lancashire clog dancing also fed into its development, just as European musical forms fed into jazz in the early part of its history. Other influences include Native American, Jewish, German, Polish, and every "lower" group in late nineteenth- and early twentieth-century America.

Tap took its rhythmic propulsion and syncopation from African-influenced forms like sand and buck dancing and patting Juba; its upright body position, musical phrasing, and the use of wooden shoes or taps incorporate Celtic forms. Many of the percussive dance traditions that fed into tap are rooted in poverty and struggle and born of the need for cultural or national identity asserted in the practice of particular steps. The contemporary successes of *Riverdance* and *Bring in Da Noise: Bring on Da Funk!* demonstrate that this is still true. The history of these forms needs to be focused on the relationship of national identity, politics, and dance.

Tap also emerged from the streets and the backrooms of bars and jazz clubs. The great dancers were primarily men, as well as a few women who had little or no access to formal education (much less training in formal dance academies). They worked on vaudeville circuits, danced for coins on the streets, entertained in hotels, small clubs, and theaters on extensive touring circuits around the country.

That tap is "show biz" *and* associated with immigrant and working-class people *and* Hollywood suggests the complications of class in the form.

> *Of course, intellectual effort is routinely thought to be distinct from the world of entertainment. The critical theorist and the teacher operate in a realm of "high" culture; the jazz musician operates in a lower cultural orbit. The separation between "high" theoretical discourse and "low" jazz entertainment reinforces a political stratification built not only on racial and professional lines of exclusion but also on a less visible inability to imagine the common circumstances that they share.* [Merod, "Resistance to Theory," 53]

In the 1920s tap and other vernacular jazz forms like the Charleston moved to Broadway in all-black shows, then into white shows and Hollywood movies, where it "whitened" even more and became more visual than musical. Broadway history and the heavily inscribed heterosexual romance of the 1930s and 1940s combined with class distinctions; racism contributed to an aura of the known, the popular, the trivial, the meaningless that has kept tap dancing from being fully recognized. Stereotypically, tap is *utterly* meaningless: it suggests mindless, formless fun, the rattle of exotics and little girls like Bill Robinson and Shirley Temple—one of America's first "acceptable" interracial couple (not unlike Miss Daisy and her chauffeur).

Stereotypes abound, often commented on by dancers. You can always "tap your troubles away," as the song tells us. "I want to be happy," sings Jane Goldberg, "but I just feel crappy"; and she complains about what most tappers know: that it takes a lifetime of work and dedication to the form to become a really strong dancer and that tap dancers are anything but happy. Brenda Bufalino also counters this misconception in her introduction to her *Cantata and the Blues.* "Have you ever known a happy tap dancer?" she asks. "Tap dancers are philosophers—and what's the reason they're philosophers?" ... she pauses for effect ... "It's because they're always broke. They're always sitting around asking themselves *why?* Why am I so broke?"

Cunningly, Bufalino centers her "joke" in the bottom line of economic reality. Entertainment tap is "business," one that since the 1950s has produced fewer jobs than dancers. The problematic position of tap in American culture is also centered in its "popular" or "entertainment" connection, in its relative absence from the concert stage and the history books. It has been constructed as easy, the cultural production of naïve or primitive people, manifested in glibly artificial show biz. Many black artists lived as entertainers, finding the form "available" in a culture that legitimized only "arts" to which they had no access. The consignment of tap to show biz neatly reinforced exclusive and bigoted practices in performance without revealing their racist agaenda.

Misconceptions about tap and tap dancers are sometimes also fed by a romance perpetuated by the dancers themselves. Honi Coles introduced the "Coles Stroll" or the "Walkaround," he said repeatedly, to demonstrate that "if you can walk, you can tap dance," Eddie Brown habitually encouraged his sweating, struggling, and frustrated acolytes by saying, "You see, it's easy. You can do it; you're doing it! That's right!" The conscious intention, of course, is encouragement, but the "expression"—as Brown called it—is not "natural" in any conceivable way; like any musical activity, it requires something like ten hours a day of practice for ten to fifteen years to produce a soloist. Everybody who taps seriously knows this, and yet the romance is perpetuated. To be sure, tap also demands improvisational skill, an appearance of naturalness, the persistence of discovery within a set structure. Disturbingly, this conscious presentation of ease can be read as the mindless happiness imaged in the static grin of the minstrel performer: a representation that effaces or renders invisible the performer's individual identity. Understandably, this association has been repugnant to some black dancers: it calls to mind slavery and struggle and devastation of identity. The result is irony and loss.

But tap dancing is also—as many dancers have pointed out, John Bubbles and Chuck Green among them—musical and subversive, comic and profound.

The feet are musical instruments, capable of producing rhythms so complex that they are difficult or impossible to score. Like other forms of jazz music, tap dancing contains elements of resistance in its essential forms and in the community it both expresses and creates.

Because of these complications, tap dancing is also a performance site of great (if contested) power, because the rhythmic essence behind and inside the visual performance anchors it to codes of resistance and subversion.

Scholars of jazz music, especially the blues, often suggest that a part of the origin of jazz was to express and conceal simultaneously. W. C. Handy said that "the Blues started behind the plow," connected to labor on plantations, where the call-and-response pattern of work songs could pass information through double entendre, insuring that it would escape the white master's notice since he assumed slaves incapable of subtlety and, therefore, of metaphor.

The origins of tap are also improvisational. It is standard practice to lay down a time-step rhythm and elaborate it in a break. In bebop dancing and jazz-tap the time-step pattern broke and stretched out into subtle and complex rhythmic lines. Willis echoes a fairly common sentiment among bebop players: that the move from swing and big-band sound to bop was an attempt by African-American musicians to resist cultural appropriation. This has also been a fairly common idea among jazz musicians.

In tap language or text, what someone "has got to say" is set out in deviation from set patterns. There is a premium on individual style, on what stretches or goes to the limits of the set structure while still staying inside it.

The idiom, the foot notes, can simultaneously create a sense of ease and simplicity and carry subversive intent. Improvisation, scatting, making it up inside a set rhythmic structure—these constitute a kind of dialectical play between stable structure and performing subject. Yet, despite its artful complexity and its obvious pleasure, the reception of tap has often meant that the romance of "naturalness" and ease has fed into existing racial stereotypes. Such stereotyping perhaps was part of the apparatus that allowed white choreographers simply to appropriate the moves of the old dancers, since they were 'nothing' anyway, just "raw" or "natural" material.

Leroi Jones (Imiri Baraka) suggests in *Blues People* that blues-based forms are perceived as primitive because they are based on another musical scale, one not appreciable to the "trained" Western ear. If dance is marginal to performance discussions, tap is all but invisible in dance criticism and often the object of contempt in "serious" dance schools. Typically, dance classes that include barre exercises derived from ballet, that concentrate on turns, leaps, and difficult adagio routines, are described as "technical." Tap is non-technical, non-serious, "fun."

For the female tap dancer the traditions of vernacular movement and tap are also problematic because of the encoding of female sexuality, particularly black female sexuality. As Jane Goldberg once quipped, "It's about what happens when she gets into his pants, i.e., his shoes." Like most African-based movement, vernacular jazz and tap movements originate in the pelvis and lower body, although the whole body is involved. Tap dancing is insistently earth referential; the ground or floor is part of the instrument (unlike ballet, which strives toward the air, to leave the body altogether). Vernacular movements that call attention to the eroticism of the female body, like the Black Bottom, the Charleston, and the Suzi-Q, were wildly popular but received by guardians of public morality as obscene and outrageous. Moreover, some feminist readings suggest that the frank eroticism of such movements must insure the objectification of female performers.

Black feminist critic Hazel Carby, however, provides a most provocative argument about the blues in her article "It Jus Be's Dat Way Sometimes: The Sexual Politics of Women's Blues." Although Carby's subject is classic blues singers, the argument can be readily applied to tap dancing, a related form. Speaking of the female blues singer, Carby describes the representation as a "struggle over sexual relations," against objectification and towards the reclamation of women's bodies and desire. She describes the blues as "an alternate form of representation, an oral and musical women's culture that explicitly addresses the contradictions of feminism, sexuality, and power."

Ma Rainey and Bessie Smith sang songs explicitly about unmasking and undressing the male: "You low down Alligator, watch me sooner or later. Gonna catch you with your britches down." Carby focuses on the lyrics of blues songs, but the dance supports this idea even more directly. For instance, Ma Rainey's famous "Black Bottom" openly asserts her power to control the spectator. She sings, "I'm gonna show you all my big black bottom; it'll put you in a trance." If we apply Carby's notion, the gyrations of Ma Rainey's hips accompanying the text of her song "situates the singer at the center of a subversive and liberatory activity."

It is clear that characteristic vernacular movement is frankly pleasurable; it is offered in a spirit of defiance rather than sexual invitation or tease. Moreover, while it is characteristic of white Christian culture to read pelvis movement as lascivious or at least as sexual, in many African cultures, where vernacular jazz movements mostly originated, this is not necessarily so. In fact, according to Marshall Stearns, in some African cultures partners touching each other in a ballroom partner dance would be considered obscene, inappropriate for public viewing. In much African movement, pelvic rotation suggests fertility and celebration; the pelvis is considered sacred, not the occasion or site of mortal sin, but the center of natality. It is tempting to speculate that the status of dance in American culture can be directly related to the location of individual body movements, and that the translation of those movements into the quotidian contexts in which music and dancing occurred reinforced both Puritanical notions of sexuality and intensified the objectification of the dancer. While the dances and songs themselves contain angry and very humorous and coded attacks on oppressors and oppression, they are not unproblematically celebratory or meaningful. Such forms do, however, contain complex traces of their origins and of multiple cultural values that may be drawn on by contemporary performers.

Despite the subversive potential of jazz forms and movements, it is a long way from Ma Rainey to Ginger Rogers. The black vernacular traditions of jazz may suggest the potential for subversive performance, as I have suggested; on Broadway, the chorine, the perfect feminine form—duplicated again and again—asserts the opposite.

In both traditions reception objectifies and boxes in the female body. Nothing is lower than tap dancing and no one less visible in it than women. Ironically, in the years since tap presumably "died" on Broadway (the general consensus of male tap dancers is that Agnes DeMille killed it with *Oklahoma!*), tap has experienced "feminization" in the proliferation of professional dance schools like Barbara Ann's School of Dance. This is a historical phenomenon that needs to be understood and examined. I suggest that, when tap lost its mass appeal and status, it became available to white, middle-class women, and that the emphasis of this particular appropriation, if appropriation it was, had little to do with the jazz basis of the form. In such schools young girls might be offered classes in tap, "acrobatic," ballet, or jazz dancing; but the point was and is not to prepare a healthy body for its own pleasure or for the capability of expression. The point is for girls to grow into, to put on, the invisible tutu of femininity, the metaphorical high heel.

> *I learned to dance first in one of those schools,*
> *dressed up as a doll in a clear plastic wrapper.*

**Ann Kilkelly (second from left), adjusting to the
"metaphysical fate of femininity"**

This feminization of tap inspired Gene Kelly to say, in 1964, "Dancing
is a man's business altogether, but women have taken it over." Kelly's
attitude, shared by some black male masters, is that women cannot and should
not perform solo or do the essential "flash" and acrobatic body steps (e.g.,
pull backs and wings, over the tops, and pulling trenches). Eddie Brown often
said that women didn't have the "expression," even though nearly all his
protégé(e)s were women. Even the women who learned from the old teachers,
like Brenda Bufalino, might have learned differently because of prevailing
ideas about who could and should do what in dance. Elsewhere I have written
about Bufalino's frustration with teachers who never taught her such steps.[5]

The notion that tap is a male form persisted and persists, despite the
fact that the overwhelming majority of white and black students of tap for
many years have been women. Now that tap is experiencing another revival,
now that the authority of "master" dancers is being re-established (even as
the last of them are dying)—again, often through the agency of women—

racial ownership is claimed and disputed even as women are still largely excluded. In fact, in a 1998 article in the *Village Voice*, Itabari Njeri actually blamed white women for the exclusion of black women from tap because, as Njeri claims, they pursued male dancers in order to have sexual relationships with them! Again, disputing this point with historical evidence (which the article completely lacks) is the subject of another, much longer text. Few dancers would deny the omnipresence of racism in the daily experiences of men and women in jazz; they knew and know it well. Yet they also know that music and dance often constitute a world in which dancers and jazz artists, all outsiders insofar as the "real" world is concerned, can bond in many ways. There are many stories of exclusion, bigotry, and systemic cultural racism experienced by black men and women dancers, but serious critical race theory has not yet taken a good look at the dance. Sexism, racism, and class bias continue to obscure the necessity for incisive analysis, leaving profound social binaries intact. Sadly, those practitioners of an endangered form who might be allied are instead experiencing deep rifts with each other. Social change seems unlikely to result.

There seems to be a staggering array of conflicting systems for the female tap dancer to negotiate, a performance world where gender systems intersect unpredictably with racial and class constructions. The female tap soloist must navigate in a situation where her right to constitute herself as a subject will be questioned on every level, her opportunities to work will be limited and often attached to a dominant male "partner," and she will be seen as an entertainer, not an artist. If she is black, she may aspire to the elevated status of "hoofer," *à la* Dianne Walker, but she will have to move between ownership and denial in a tradition that has had black women soloists— soloists that have, largely, disappeared.

> *Juanita Pitts, Cora LaRedd, Dorothy Salter, Jenny LeGon, Irma Young, Dorothy Dandridge, Lois Miller, and many many others.*

Racial identity claims often produce outright refusal to deal with questions of gender, and, as Angela Davis has made clear in her recent book on the blues, class usually manages to drop out of the analysis altogether. The aggressive, competitive demands of solo performance, which among men may have originated in a spirit of creative play, now double as fighting for available gigs, as Tap Festivals create the phenomenon of "Masters." Women's status in this context is highly contested and threatens to undermine the future health of the form.

Choreography

Women soloists, present throughout the development of tap but rarely acknowledged, build performances in ways that allow tap dancing to comment on their own marginalization in the form and to appropriate the production of sound for their own pleasure and critique.

Brenda Bufalino sets most of her dances into a context that, using spoken monologue to introduce each dance, challenges and resists patriarchal limitations on her claim to the subject position. Here is part of the text, the introductory monologue, for *Cantata and the Blues*:

> The question is, "How can I be if I can't be everything?"
> Stripped of my influences I am nothing.
> And the influences are all the cultures that sang their way into my mind and heart.
> My Mother sang me the blues she sang summertime sweet and sorrowful,
> My Mother sang me the hymns she sang in church sometimes, sweet and joyful,
> It was all the same to me—
> Touched my heart colored my skin every which way,
> Freckle-faced and buck-toothed I didn't know I'd have to choose
> Between a cantata and blues someday—
> There was a time I thought it was all mine.
> I didn't know that if I opened my mouth to speak someone would cut out my tongue as if I stole the song from him,
> I thought my dance was everybody's dance,
> Not a chance that what I wanted to be was not free to be, which was all of them that lived in me.
> Bach, Count Basie, Chopin and Ellington, why not Gilbert and Sullivan and Cab Calloway too,
> Cantatas *and* the Blues.

The shape of the dance movement shows multiple influences in its musical structure and accompaniment. Bufalino dances in 3/4 time with a blues feel, a light, airy, tapped melody line, and lyrical torso and arm movements suggestive of ballet. She dances the "cantata" over the blues line in her body and feet. Her costume is a white suit, a reference to the male figure, but often in the performance she pulls it back at the waist to reveal the action of her hips, a frank acknowledgement of the strong hip movement from jazz vernacular. She incorporates the *jetté* from ballet, but her flat shoes take the focus from the visual line of the foot into the sound of the tap, thereby commenting on ballet through tap, asserting cantata *and* blues.

The stated subject of the dance is the cultural encodings that simultaneously fill and empty the female performer—"stripped of my influences I am nothing"—despite the stubborn assertion that she will have "the cantata and the blues." The intersecting meanings of tradition cited earlier all but insure that her dance will not be "free to be all of me which is all of them that lived in me." Although Bufalino has been accorded master status, for much of her career critics saw her only as Coles's protégée, denying that her dance is hers at all. I have elsewhere written how "Too Tall, Too Small Blues" came about because Honi Coles once said Bufalino couldn't do anything on stage that wasn't him. He did not say that she couldn't *perform* anything that he hadn't taught her, which may be mostly true for dancer-protégés of masters; he said she could only *be* him. The 1989 Creative Residency at the Boulder Festival was designed to preserve Coles's choreography, an appropriate and important move because of his disabling stroke and because only a few years remain in which to preserve his generation's dances. At first, however, Bufalino was proposed to teach the movement as Coles's assistant. As his "feet."

Critics have variously read her dance as too sexy (before she changed to the suit); now they sometimes describe her as inappropriately aggressive, her costume as too male. Rusty Frank's recent book *Tap!* has a great variety of interviews and honors Bufalino in the commentary, but the photos are amazingly strange—she appears as 1950s sex kitten, beatnik, and prom queen; they are interesting both because they are so stunningly unlike her and because they possess only ironic power. The pictures do not show Bufalino as a tap dancer.

Bufalino's creation of the American Tap Dance Orchestra was a conscious attempt to shape tap's development and stage a broader choreographic vision, substantially resisting the traps and restrictions of the solo mode.

While her orchestral dances do not comment as overtly as her solo pieces on feminist issues, their polyrhythms, their pop jazz references, the voices of all those taps deeply and directly embody her influences. Such dances are in some ways stronger assertions of her subjectivity, because they are not psychologically motivated or personality centered. Moreover, the use of multiple dancers and simultaneous different rhythms decenters the authority of the master performance and its implications, and focuses the dance on the pleasure of complex syncopation. Bufalino might not have the "correct" shoe, but she has a closet full of them. Her move away from self-referential solo pieces to orchestral suites moves to dismantle the idea of authority in the received tradition while still preserving jazz-tap's character.

Dancer Jane Goldberg calls herself "the ultimate protégé" and uses the anxiety of influences to create a comic, monologic tap-rap that comments constantly on the female body in performance. Her "Rhythm and Schmooze" begins with an acknowledgement of pleasure: "I like to talk [she is tapping], I like to tap; I like to tap while I talk. I like to talk about tap." She smiles disarmingly—her hair is curly; her dress cites femininity as constructed in the 1940s, low cut to reveal breasts, incorporating hip- and waist-defining skirt. The tap-rap and the title of the piece can be seen as ironic reflection on tap tradition: "The Tap Goddess Speaks" is comic precisely because, given the class, gender, and racial constructions of tap, it's absurd to imagine a small white woman in a dress possessing tap power, absurd that the power of a goddess figure might be built into a low-status activity like tap dancing (one, nonetheless, owned by males). Goldberg's "rap" style seems free and easy, is improvisatory and relaxed, obviously pleasurable, but her sense of time, her manipulation of steps belies skill and sophistication in the form. In this way she also humorously comments on virtuosity by seeming to throw it away. This has not made her popular among dancers who, in recent years, have increasingly laid stress on technical prowess.

Goldberg connects the conflicting claims of ownership of tap—"so finally I just say that the Jews started tap." The audience laughs, their laughter expressing an understanding of the absurdity of the claim. To laugh in this instance, as we laugh at the idea of tap goddesses, forces recognition of race, class, and gender lines we all understand. Goldberg's piece also foregrounds politics. Thus she describes her early involvement in tap: "I got into tap because I was seeing spiritual enlightenment. They said, 'you must liberate the ground on which you stand'." Again, laughter devolves upon the absurdity of pairing so "meaningless" an activity as tap with grave notions of enlightenment—and delight: because it is true.

Like Bufalino, Goldberg struggles with reception; although she sees herself as carrying on the traditions of old dancers in the comic structure of their pieces, the foregrounding of feminist issues threatens the authority of male dancers. Although Goldberg, according to one Philadelphia headline, "saved tap dancing from death" in her BY WORD OF FOOT festivals in the early 1980s; although she created the Sole Sisters, an all-women's tap show; although her work has involved not only dancing but, often, helping dancers survive rather than be totally erased in the performance world—nevertheless, she is rarely seen at tap festivals or acknowledged as an important historian. The film *Tap* clearly passes the tap tradition from male to male—from Sandman to Gregory Hines to Savion Glover. The Shim Sham Girls (Dianne Walker, Dorothy Wasserman, and Jane Goldberg) remain peripheral; the lead female actress couldn't even dance, but was chosen for visual effect. Her function was to marry Hines and his dancing, and in that way carry on the tradition. Men produce; women reproduce. Gregory Hines has received primary credit for raising the public's consciousness about tap dancing although women teachers, black and white, have kept the form alive.

In the Broadway hit *Black and Blue*, Dianne Walker was honored as the only female tap soloist and designated a "Hoofer"; nevertheless, she was constrained by an impossibly scanty costume and high heels, despite the elegant and lyrical sophistication of her solo. In the same production blues singer Carrie Smith was pinned to a disk; blues diva Ruth Brown was suspended on a trapeze dressed like a bird, four men holding down her gigantic white tail. Women pinned to sets, chorus women dancing in boxes, jazz soloists in short, skin-tight, sequinned, panniered *boxes*! I suspect the energy of female jazz artists may be too dangerous to let loose on stage. This is, of course, tremendously ironic in an all-black show intended to celebrate black artists.[6]

The crux of the matter is this: many of us who love tap dancing see it as significant, see its exclusion from dance and theater discourse as a function of the racism and elitism that, in earlier years of this century, kept jazz out of the conservatories. I think some of these issues are being addressed and that general reception will acknowledge race and class discrimination. I think a feminist analysis less likely.

MORE GHOST NOTES: A Performance Piece

Upstage right two chairs face out toward the audience and sit angled so that they appear to be watching the performances. Near them a wooden hat rack holds a bright red chiffon dress and a checked man's sports coat in a conservative pattern.

Ann enters and looks at the chairs, then addresses the audience:

This is my Father's coat.
This is my Mother's dress.
His dark houndstooth;
Hers red chiffon.
He was the slender Irish dancer elegant but ugly in his cups;

She was the Cockney scrubwoman given to strong language and large
 gestures.
These feet are his.
These shoulders are hers.
Though he was the flower,
She bought the dress a short time before she died.
Thin, fashionable for the first time in her final illness, she bought this flame of
 a dress, fire-engine red,
A color hard and bright as nail polish, embroidered chiffon and taffeta, a tiny
 belt—a very good dress.
Once she wore it in the living room, in the morning, and she taught me the
 Charleston.
When she died, propriety prevailed and we buried her in appropriate gray
 linen—another good dress, better than she would have chosen in life.
His coat came from Rothchilde's in St. Paul, a few years later
The very name came from a world to which we didn't, and could never,
 belong, given the lingering smell of turf and cabbage in our muscle
 memory
Always thin, he had grown thinner though still upright and handsome, silver
 hair catching the light, looking almost happy as he contemplated the
 good fabric, the nice fit
And he bought me lunch at the St. Paul Hotel

I ate a California burger and he drank white wine
It was the most delicious food I had eaten
His coat, like her dress, for a time cloaked his invisible decline in memory
Joe and Margie Kilkelly dancing in the Crocus Park ballroom
Down by the river where the poor kids could go
Fine and handsome
They cut a rug
They waltzed in time
Before the dress, before the coat
Before me.

I hang the coat on a hanger to see its shoulders grow broad again;
I drape the red heart of a dress on a chair.
If you listen, really listen, you can hear their dance in a rustle of fabric, their
 last visible breaths.

Ann walks to coat rack and puts the coat on a hanger, dances with it briefly, then drapes it on one of the chairs. She picks up the dress, holds it against herself, then carefully places it on the other chair, clearly touching the coat in some way. She moves away slowly to "My Wild Irish Rose." The dance continues in 3/4 time and gradually moves away from the chairs. The music slows and changes to a blues with a minor-mode feel. The blues moves into a more up-tempo, swing-feel passage, and the dance becomes fast and bright. The blues and waltz come back in and the piece ends on a few lingering notes. Ann bows to the chairs and slowly exits, turning.

If It's Serious It's Got to be Funny

At the turn of the twenty-first century I am no longer able to perform without consciousness of my own and tap dancing's racialized, gendered, overly class-determined, multi-ethnic, and hyper-heterosexualized history. I know that these meanings have been written on and in my body long before I understood that I have always, already, been positioned. I wonder whose body dances, what color the steps are, if the drum knows who plays it. In bunny ears, ukulele, tap-shoes, and an overabundance of aging pink fabric and flesh, I imagine myself performing and possibly, just possibly, resisting the boxes available to deny me or others a full voice.

NOTES

[1]The show was *Milking the Millennium*, directed by Laraine Goodman; it took place from 30 December 1999–14 January 2000.

[2]Richard Kislan, *Hoofing on Broadway: A History of Show Dancing* (New York: Prentice-Hall, 1987), 53.

[3]Honi Coles, Ernie Smith Dance Film Collection.

[4]Despite the general lack of collected material available for study, there have been significant projects in collecting oral histories and records of tap dancers. Delilah Jackson in New York and the Women's Tap Project in Philadelphia have collected and presented much information about Black women in the form. Cheryl Willis's 1991 dissertation also assembles a great deal of information. Historically, Marshall and Jean Stearns wrote the first and still in some ways most thorough study of American vernacular jazz. The Ernie Smith Film Dance collection at the Archive Center in the National Museum of American History contains a large quantity of film footage that has been transferred to video tape.

[5]Ann Kilkelly, "Too Tall, Too Small Blues."

[6]Kilkelly, "Ghost Notes": performance piece, Blacksburg, Virginia, 20-22 March 1999.

ADDITIONAL SOURCES

Banes, Sally. *Writing Dancing in the Age of Postmodernism*. Hanover, NH: Wesleyan University Press, 1994.

"Brenda Bufalino's Blues, 'Too Small'?" *Women and Performance: A Journal of Feminist Theory* 3/6 (1988): 67-77.

Bufalino, Brenda. Unpublished Interview. Colorado Dance Festival, 1988.

Cantata and the Blues: live performance, Lexington Opera House, Lexington, Kentucky, 1984.

Desmond, Jane C. "Embodying Difference: Issues in Dance and Cultural Studies." *Meaning in Motion: New Cultural Studies of Dance*, ed. Jane C. Desmond. Durham and London: Duke University Press, 1997.

Foster, Susan Leigh. "Dancing Bodies." *Meaning in Motion: New Cultural Studies of Dance*, ed. Jane C. Desmond. Durham and London: Duke University Press, 1997.

Goldberg, Jane. Unpublished Interview, New York City, July 30, 1988.

Jazz-Heritage Series: unpublished video of live performances by Tap Dancers Honi Coles, Jimmy Slyde, Steve Condos, and the Jazz Tap Ensemble, National Museum of American History, Smithsonian Institution, Washington, D.C.

Jenkins, Henry. *What Made Pistachio Nuts? Early Sound Comedy and the Vaudeville Aesthetic.* New York: Columbia University Press, 1992.

Jones, Leroi. *Blues People: The Negro Experience in White America and the Music That Developed From It.* New York: Marrow-Quill, 1963.

Kislan, Richard. *Hoofing on Broadway: A History of Show Dancing.* New York: Prentice-Hall, 1987.

Malone, Jacqui. *Steppin' On the Blues: The Visible Rhythms of African American Dance.* Urbana and Chicago: University of Illinois Press, 1996.

Merod, Jim, "Resistance to Theory: The Contradictions of Post Cold-War Criticism (with an Interlude on the Politics of Jazz)," *Critical Theory and Performance*, ed. Janelle C. Reinelt and Joseph R. Roach. Ann Arbor: University of Michigan Press, 1992.

Placksin, Sally. *Jazz Women: Their Words, Lives, and Music.* London and New South Wales: Pluto Press, 1985.

Showcase Performance of American Tap Dance Orchestra: live performance, New York City, 1991.

Smith, Ernie. Jazz Dance Video Collection. Archive Center, National Museum of American History, Smithsonian Institution. [The collection of 321 film transfers contains clips of film, television and live jazz and tap dance from 1898 to the 1970s.]

Stearns, Marshall, and Jean Stearns. *Jazz Dance: The Story of American Vernacular Dance.* New York: Macmillan, 1968; reprint New York: DaCapo, 1994.

Woolf, Janet. "Reinstating Corporeality: Feminism and Body Politics," *Meaning in Motion: New Cultural Studies of Dance*, ed. Jane C. Desmond. Durham and London: Duke University Press, 1997.

A native of Mississippi, Riley B. King—today much more widely known as **B. B. King**—made his professional debut as a blues singer in 1948. In the 1950s, after the release of "Three O'Clock Blues," he became a national celebrity; in 1956 alone he and his band played an astonishing 342 one-night stands throughout the American heartland. King's celebrated performances include his appearances in 1967 at the Montreux Jazz Festival and his 1969 tour with the Rolling Stones. During the 1960s, 1970s, and 1980s he recorded more than 100 blues singles and albums. In 1990, the same year he joined Ray Charles as part of the Philip Morris Superband world tour, King received the Songwriter's Hall of Fame Lifetime Achievement Award; he also boasts eight Grammys, the Presidential Medal of the Arts, and Kennedy Center honors as well as four honorary doctorates. B. B. King is widely considered the foremost and most popular blues performer in the world today.

Another native Mississippian, **William R. Ferris** studied at Davidson College before taking his doctorate in folklore at the University of Pennsylvania. During the eighteen years that preceded his 1997 appointment as chairman of the National Endowment for the Humanities, he served as founding director of the Center for the Study of Southern Culture at the University of Mississippi, Oxford. Ferris's publications include his books *Blues from the Delta* and *Mississippi Blues* as well as the sound recording *Highway 61 Blues*; he has also served as a consultant for such films as *The Color Purple* and *Crossroads*. Among his distinctions are the Charles Frankel Prize in the Humanities, the American Library Association's Dartmouth Medal, and—like B. B. King—membership in the Blues Hall of Fame.

𝒲 The Blues—Past and Future
An Interview with B. B. King

B. B. KING and WILLIAM R. FERRIS

The following interview took place on 2 January 2000 as part of the "American Voices" presentations at the "Millennium on the Mall" celebration held in Washington, D.C., and sponsored by the Smithsonian Institution. The interview was introduced and moderated by Stephen Yussum, Director of the Anacostia Museum and Center for African American History and Culture, Washington, D.C.

B. B. King and William R. Ferris

The transcription that follows has been edited for punctuation. For reasons of clarity, a few passages have been edited or omitted. Edited passages are indicated either by ellipses or square brackets. Audience responses and other events are indicated by square brackets and italic type.

After introductory remarks by Yussum, Ferris and King began speaking.

FERRIS: ... It's a great honor to be here. It's been quite a series of programs that the Smithsonian and others have done. We've heard lots of people reflecting on the twentieth century and America's contributions to the next century. But B. and I have been talking, and I think this has been the century of the blues as the great American music, the music that has shaped twentieth-century musics from jazz and country to gospel, to classical music, to poetry, literature, and the visual arts.

Each of us this afternoon is incredibly privileged to be in the presence of the single most important blues artist of this century. A man who, decade after decade, has shaped the blues, has reinvented himself as a musician and [reinvented] the blues. From his earliest recordings on Beale Street to his most recent performances, no one can parallel or match the contributions of the King of the Blues, Mr. B. B. King! [*applause*]

KING: Thank you, Bill; thank you, ladies and gentlemen. I am happy to be here today. Over the weekend I maybe had a little bit too much air. So I'm a little hoarse today, but my fingers are in pretty good shape.... I don't know really where I'm going to start at, other than to say that [I'm ready].

FERRIS: Let's start at the beginning, down at Itta Bena, Mississippi, where the Southern crosses the Dog....

KING: That's right!

FERRIS: That's where the sound started. Let's talk about your first memory of the blues.

KING: Well, this really goes back a bit, Bill. My dad said that I was born near Itta Bena, which (the way he describes it) is between Indianola and Itta Bena, but I grew up knowing more about Indianola than I did about Itta Bena. Now my Dad's passed on, so: Indianola.

244

I first remember my mom and dad were divorced when I was about five, I guess, and [mom] took me back in the hills. Now to make a little sense, if I can: "the hills" we called [the area] from Greenwood going back past toward Tupelo, which is where Elvis was born.... My mother was very religious, and she used to take me to church when I was five or six years old. And I first didn't care to go so much, but I learned later that pretty girls would be at church. [*laughter*]

In the church we had a pastor named Archie Fair.... I now just [began] to like music because he played guitar in the church. My faith is the Church of God in Christ—"Sanctified," a lot of people call it. However, I wanted to be a musician. Even then I wanted to play and sing, but I didn't think in terms of blues music at all. It was all gospel. I wanted to be a gospel singer. I felt that I could be pretty good because I heard of a guy called Utah Smith, Rev. Utah Smith, and he played electric guitar, which was the first one I ever heard. I also had an aunt that bought a lot of records, like the kids do today. And the records she would buy were Blind Lemon Jefferson, Lonnie Johnson, Blind Blake, Reverend Gates, and people like that. But Lonnie Johnson always stood out. Now, today, Robert Johnson is very, very popular among the young people. Robert Johnson was very popular at that time. But he wasn't my favorite. I liked him, I thought he was good, but not my favorite. And I started to hear things. And usually, when I was a good boy, my aunt (who was my great, my mother's aunt) would let me play a Victrola, [a] phonograph, whatever you want to call it. It's a thing you wind up, then you set the needle and it would play these big thick 78 records. [Records] that, if you dropped [one] like that, you'd have to go back to the store again, because that one was gone.

Anyway, as I grew up a little bit more, we moved back to Indianola. I guess now I'm about fourteen, maybe, and I'd sit on the street corners in Indianola and play gospel music because now I'm a part of quartet called the St. John Gospel Singers, and I thought we were good. *Very* good. But people would come up and ask me to do a gospel song—they would request a gospel song—and when they did, I would play with all I had. And they would seem like they were very pleased, and then they would pat me on the head or shoulders and say, "That was good, son! Keep it up; you're going to be good one day." They would pat me again, but they didn't put anything in the hat. But people that would come up and ask me to play a blues song would always praise me highly, *but* they would put something in the hat! So now you can see why I decided to become a blues singer. And it actually started a bit from there, where I started to really want to pick on what was going on musically, and the blues seemed to do more for me.

We had at that time ... I didn't know the word "television," but we [also had] something called ten-cent vendors. Today they call them "soundies." A soundie was something that had a monitor that almost looked like a television screen, but it had a 16 mm film inside. And you put in a quarter, half a dollar—a dime would get you one [minute], a quarter would get you two or three maybe, a half dollar three or four. But you never knew what was coming up is what I'm trying to say. When you put your money in the machine, it would just start to play from wherever, from [where] the last program was that was shown, so you never knew what was coming up. So I just sat around and watched and hoped that someone would come and put money in. And that was when I had a chance to learn about Count Basie, Louis Armstrong, Duke Ellington—oh, gosh! I learned about many of the great people in jazz. Benny Goodman. And others I can't think of at the moment. When you get to be seventy-four years [old], your memory sort of leaves a little bit. (My son tells me it didn't just start.) I started to pay more attention to the blues and the other music that sounded bluesy. And that's the time that I really wanted to be a blues singer.

And later, as I got a little older in [19]43—I was eighteen years old—I got this letter from Uncle Sam, said, "We want you now." So that's when I heard T-Bone Walker. Prior to that time, there was Lonnie Johnson, Lemon Jefferson—"Blind Lemon," he was called. And then I heard of a guy I heard played electric guitar, jazz electric guitar: Charlie Christian. Fell in love with him. And when I went in the service, only for a short while, one of my buddies went overseas. He knew I liked guitars, so when he came back he brought records of a person named Django Reinhardt from the Hot Club in France. Fell in love with him. And later, lastly, another guy called T-Bone Walker. Ha ha! if I'da been a girl, I'd try to marry him. [*laughter*]

So that's the beginning of it, and that's how it started, and from there I should say to now with many, many stops along the way. I hope I was able to make a little sense of what I'm talking about. I was in radio from [19]49-[19]55; they never did learn me to talk, but with Lucille [King's guitar] I feel more comfortable.

FERRIS: B., let's talk about one of the stops, when you went up Highway 61 to Memphis, the worlds of Beale Street and WDIA, and what happened with your music and with your life there.

KING: Well, I'd never heard the word "superstar." But before I left Mississippi, I come to find out I was a superstar, whatever that is. Tractor driver, that is. In my area in the Delta, tractor driving paid the best salaries: twenty-two dollars and a half a week.... You laugh if you want, but it was big money to me, big money. And that takes me back to the street corner again... [What musician was] making $22.50 a week? And I must say I was a very good tractor driver. You know, it's something that you're proud of. People think that, because you're a farmer and you're on the farm, [you're not important,] but you can be proud.... There are many things that you take pride in, picking cotton, for instance. You know, I could pick 500 lbs. a day. Ha! I thought I was great. And then I graduated to tractor driving and, hey! you could steal the girls. Well, I'm sorry, but that was a big part of it. I've always been crazy about the girls.

It was nine tractors, and we would go from ... I don't remember how many acres of cultivation it was, but you'd go from one end of the plantation to the other, and we did all the plowing. However, on the street corner some Saturday evenings I would make $40-$50, which was more than I'd made all week driving a tractor. That was another thing that motivated me. I asked my group, the Quartet, if we could leave from Indianola and go to Memphis, because in Memphis they had music stores, recording studios, and they had many of the facilities that I knew about but I'd never seen. Each year, when we gathered our crops—"gather your crops" means you finish picking cotton, and pull usually what little corn [there was]. Cotton was king then.... [Anyway,] each year we would always lose; we would never have any money. So the guys would say, "No, not this year; wait til next year." So we did that two or three years, and then finally I said, "If you're not going, I'm going anyway." So that's when I hitchhiked from Indianola, Mississippi, to Memphis, Tennessee, on a produce truck. I had $1.25. Some people say I had $2.25, but it was not. It was $1.25. [*laughter*]

I hitchhiked with this person and helped [him] deliver produce from Indianola all the way to Memphis, and when I got there, I had a cousin—the only person in the family that ever made fame that I know about in the music business—named Booker White. Booker worked in a place where they make tanks. When I use the word "tanks," I don't mean the ones that shoot at you; I mean the ones they put underground at service stations where they put fuel in it. So [Booker] got me a job there. I heard about a guy called Sonny Boy Williamson, who was number two, that is. There was one prior to him, but this one I used to hear every day while I was on the plantation. He would broadcast from over in Helena, Arkansas, and the title of the program was *King Biscuit Time with Sonny Boy Williamson*. Anyway, to make a long story short, coming in for lunch—and in Mississippi at noon we called it "dinner"; see, all you hip people called it lunch, but for us it was dinner—so, you'd get at home midday, noon, and at 12:15 Sonny Boy Williamson would come on the radio. It seemed to me kind of like, I don't know ... some of you I'm sure watch Bob Barker on *The Price Is Right*. It seems like you know him. It seemed like I knew Sonny Boy because I heard him so much. It just seemed like you could say, "Hey! how you doing, guy?"

So finally, when I got to Memphis, I heard that [Sonny Boy] was in West Memphis, so I went over there... I got over there [and] Sonny Boy was very tall. He had to be close to seven feet tall, and he looked like he could fight. And he looked like this, and I would be like the cat when the dog comes around. I said, "Sonny Boy?..." He said, "Yes?" and he looked straight at me as if his eyes was going to cut me. (And he would like to have a little taste [of alcohol] once in a while, and, when he did, his eyes would get red.) And he seemed like that to me, and his eyes were like that, so I felt a little funny when I asked him this favor. But they tell me: when you want something, go ahead and ask. And I said, "I would like to sing a song on your program, please." [*laughter and applause*] He said, "On my program?" I said, "Yes, sir." "Can you sing?" "Yes, sir." "All right; let me hear you." So I took my old guitar and I started to do a song called "Blues at Midnight," and he said, "That's pretty good." And he asked one of the guys to give him another drink, and then he called some of his buddies and said, "We're going put this boy on the air today." So they put me on the air, and I sang "Blues at Sunrise." And he called the place where he usually worked ... nowadays they call it "four-wallin'." I know a lot of you know exactly what I'm talking about. It means that whatever comes in the door, you can have it. That's four-wallin' today. A lot of people do that in Vegas now, four-wallin'....

Anyway, to make a long story short again: the lady that he worked for was named Miss Annie, and she had a place called the 16th Street Grill. So he asked Miss Annie that day after the broadcast, did she hear me play? And she said, "Yes." And he said, "Well, I'm going to send this boy down in my place tonight." He hadn't asked me anything, but just looking up at him, whatever he say, I would do. So I go to Miss Annie's place, and my job that night was to entertain the people that didn't gamble. (At that time West Memphis was almost like Las Vegas. Nearly every place had gambling places.) Now they had what we call a juke box: this is a player that played records, if you will. And my job was to keep the people happy that didn't gamble. And a lot of them was girls too. I guess, being young, they seemed to like me a lot, because I was young [too]. Homely looking ... a little more than now. [*laughter*] But somehow they seemed to take pity on me. [*laughter*] And I loved my job, so Miss Annie paid me $12.50 that night and told me that, if I could get me a job on the radio, as Sonny Boy had, she would give me this job six nights a week. Room and board [and] $12.50 a night, and I started figuring in up, and I ain't never had that kind of money in my life.

So I just heard that time that there was a new radio station named WDIA. Two young entrepeneurs, Mr. Pepper and Mr. Ferguson, had just bought this. First, it was a country and western station; they played country and western only. But now they were an all-black-operated station, so I had heard about it. I went over there, I had to walk 8-10 blocks to get to it from the bus stop (got wet on my way there, it rained). And I noticed this big black man sitting in there, and I could see his mouth going, and I had heard about radio and this big red light was on, so I figured he was recording. I stood at the door, and I looked like a dog when he is very hungry. So, finally, he saw me and he came up and said, "What can I do for you, young fellow?" And I said, "I'd like to make a record, and I'd like to go on the radio." And he looked at me and laughed, and his name was Professor Nat D. Williams, but everybody called him "Nat D." So he called his boss, Mr. Ferguson. Mr. Ferguson came out and looked at me, and he said, "You want to make a record?" "Yes, sir." "You want to go on the radio?" "Yes, sir." "Well, we don't make records, but maybe we could use you on the radio. We got a new product coming out called Pepticon." Now, over in West Memphis, my friend who just put me on the radio was advertising a project called Hadicol. Both are tonics, supposed to be good for what ails you. So [Mr. Ferguson] says, "Can you write a jingle?" "Yes, sir! ... What's a jingle?" [*laughter*] So when they gave me an idea what was going on, this what I came up with [*singing*]:

> Pepticon, sure is good.
> Pepticon, sure is good.
> Pepticon, sure is good.
> You can get it anywhere in your neighborhood.

He said, "Yeah, well, take it." So that's how I got on radio.

And this is 1949. I stayed with them until [19]55, but during that time I did start to record. My first record that I made was there in the station. [The station] didn't make records, but there was a company out of Nashville called

Bullet. And Bullet brought portable equipment, and they set it up in Studio A, and I did finally record there. And then they went broke. That shows you how good my record was.

But that's how I got started—actually got started—from there. And then finally I got lucky. Ike Turner ... I don't know if some of you have heard that name ... But Ike to me was nothing like they portrayed him to be in the movie [probably a reference to *What's Love Got to Do with It?* (1993)]. I still like the guy. I like him today. I like Tina too, and I think she's a tremendous artist.... Anyway, Ike Turner was working for the Behara Brothers out of Los Angeles. And I had met Ike prior to then. He was kind of like an A&R man: that's a person that would look up talent for you that [you] are not familiar with... So he introduced me to the Behara Brothers. And we made several records, and then finally we made one called "3 O'Clock Blues," and that was my first hit. And from there we stopped many times on the way. [*applause*]

FERRIS: B., the only voice in blues that's almost as famous as yours is that of Lucille. Now I think we need to talk about here and let people hear her voice as well, and how she got the name.

KING: Well, I'll start with how she got the name, and then we'll see what we can get her to do.

Lucille is quite a guitar. In 1949, the same year that I went on the radio, I was playing one of those places, sort of four-wallin' as I say, over in Twist, Arkansas. Twist, for you that may not be familiar, is about forty-five miles northwest of Memphis, Tennessee. I used to play there quite often, especially in winter [when] it got cold, very cold. So ... they'd take a big garbage pail— picture in your mind this, magnified about a thousand times [*holding a glass of water*]—and half-filled with kerosene, as this water [glass] is. Then they would take something and light that fuel and set it in the middle of the dance floor. People would dance around it and never disturb it. I didn't have no problem with that because I could never dance anyway. But people dance, and of course today there is no way you could put an open container half-filled with kerosene [out on the floor] and get away with it. Shows you that you do a lot of things when you're young that you do think about when you're older.

However, one night two guys started to fight, and one knocked the other one over on this container. When they did, it spilled on the floor, and when it spilled it was already burning, so it looked like a river of fire. And everybody started to run for the front door. Reason for that, they would always nail up the back door, so people couldn't sneak in.... So when I got outside [too], I realized that I had left my guitar inside. Please believe me: in 1949 it was hard to keep a good guitar. They cost so much that you couldn't hardly afford one, and when you did get one, others would borrow it without your permission. And when they did that, they never brought it back. However, I went back into the building that was burning rapidly, and it started to collapse around my head. I almost lost my life trying to save my guitar. The next morning we found that these two men who were fighting were fighting about a lady that worked in a little night club. I never did meet her, but I learned that her name was Lucille. I named my guitar *Lucille* to remind me never to do a thing like that again. [*applause*]

So you are now looking at *Lucille XVI*. I have sixteen of them. Really seventeen; they made one for me on my seventieth birthday that had my picture on the butt of it. I don't take it out. I used to take it out and set it on stage, like Lucille is now, so it could learn what Lucille did. But I don't take it out anymore. But that's how it came about for real, and the reason I have so many—I'm sure somebody has a question about that—is, every time something goes wrong with it. They're good instruments, but like anything else they get worn on the neck a little bit. And I send it back to the company. Gibson, I say proudly, and loudly: *Gibson!* guitars. [*laughter*] And they always send me another one, and when they do, I play it. And when the other one is ready, they send that one back, but I never send the one back that they send me. That's why I have so many. Anyway, I want to thank you so much ... gosh! ... thank you for sitting here and letting me talk to you. I just love it! Thank you. [*applause*] So many more stops on the way, Bill.

FERRIS: B., you hear always about the blue note and what you've done with tremolo. Can you give us an example of what that really is on Lucille?

KING: Yeah, I think I can do that. When I first started to try and play like my cousin, Booker White, he was one of those guys that could use the bottleneck. I could never use the bottleneck or those pieces of pipe they'd cut off and put on their fingers. But I always liked the sound of it. And I was crazy about the country musicians playing on the steel guitar. Oh, man! if there's any music anywhere on earth, it had to come from heaven. To me. That's how nice it sounds.... [*turning on his amplifier*]

I used to also hear of the Hawaiian guitar players playing with the slide. My fingers, they're just stupid; they never work with my brains or vice versa.

To make it sound like that. So it was nothing that I was trying to do, like Ford knew when he was making cars: he knew what he had in mind.... But I didn't know what I had in mind. It just seemed to me that when I did this [*hitting a note*], it sounded good. [*beginning to play*]

Now a lot of the musicians are so well-versed (I guess that's a good word), and they would practice and practice. And practice makes perfect, I was told. I never did practice enough. I've always been very lazy when it comes to practicing physically. But usually I take the guitar and sit it over and swear at it in my mind and wonder why I can't do what I'd like to do with it. [*laughter*] But sometimes it just makes you get up and practice. So I guess I've practiced this so long [*playing*], it seems like it's a part of my nervous system. No, I'm serious. I used to see musicians play, and I could see certain things happening to them, and I wondered. Now I can't explain it, but it seems like ... if you've ever shot pool, you take the stick and shoot and if it ain't going exactly where you want it to, you just kind of [*gesturing*]. You know what I'm saying.... Well, that's kind of the way it is with the guitar.

So. I started to do [this; *playing*] and doing that to me is not quite ... I think they use the word "pizzicato," but I like for the guitar to kind of sing, sound similar to a human voice if you will. So when I'm playing, I hear it singing. [*playing*]. And I like to take each note as if somebody was measuring sugar or flour for you. You know, if you want six ounces, you want six ounces. So each note gets so much. (Am I making sense, I hope?) [*playing*] And I practiced that in my mind and physically. And that's how the tremolo began, thinking in terms of the bottleneck. And I can do it with any finger.

So gospel, country, jazz; I even recorded a little bit with Pavarotti.... So we can add a little classical with it too. I'm trying to say all of that makes up the blues of B. B. King. [*applause*] Thank you very much.

Now, Bill, if you'll pick up your guitar, maybe I can learn something today.

FERRIS: Being a folklorist, I always told my students that the real teachers for me were not in the universities. And, at the Endowment, I feel the same way that our great teachers are not within the ivory towers, but they're people who have come to knowledge—profound knowledge—in the ways you just described. I love to quote an African proverb that says: "When an old man or woman dies, a library burns to the ground." They are living libraries, and you for the blues and for many other things are such a library. Which is why we're all here to learn from you. [*applause*]

KING: Bill, I'm going to say it in the presence of our audience: you're a great man, and I thank you. [*applause*]

Ladies and gentlemen, getting back to the tonic that I used to broadcast for, if you will: Pepticon. I used to go out on the trucks with the salesman on Saturday afternoons and sit on the truck, and I would sing and play, and a lot of times I had no idea of the melody or melodic line that I was playing. But just playing. But I would notice that a whole lot of the older people at that time [were] the age that I am today. And they would buy [that tonic] like they wasn't going to make anymore. And I didn't know until about twelve years ago the reason: that it was 12% alcohol. [*laughter*] So I'm going to pretend at this time that Bill and I are sitting on the truck, selling Pepticon.

We are going to do it in [the key of] E? And I don't know what I'm going to do, but I'll do something, okay? Usually the blues; we may not know of a lot of the progressions and things that a lot of the learned musicians do, but one thing we are usually good with and that is the beat. This we call the beat. [*tapping his foot*] That is, the people that dance that don't know very much about music, don't care too much about anything else but keeping the beat, keeping the beat. We're not going to do it that fast, though. [*plays a song with Ferris*]

Now, some time ago I made a song called "The Thrill is Gone." [*applause*] I tell you what: I won't do it in the key that we recorded it in, because of my voice today. So let's try it in A. [*plays a bit*] I apologize for my throat. They say the good Lord gave us two of everything except the one we use too much [*laughter*]... so I guess I talk too much. [*playing and singing*]

> Thrill is gone,
> Thrill is gone away.
> Thrill is gone, baby,
> Thrill is gone away.
> You done me wrong, baby,
> Gonna be sorry some day.
>
> Thrill is gone,
> Thrill is gone away for good.
> The thrill is gone away, baby,
> Thrill is gone for good.
> I know I'll be over it all one day,
> Like I know a good man should.

Now I'm free, baby,
I'm free from your spell.
Free, free, free now,
I'm free from your spell.
Now that it's all over,
All I can do is wish you well.

[*standing ovation*] Thank you very much. Thank you.

YESSUM: We are going to try to have some questions and answers. But Mr. King taught me something: he talked about when you want something, you just ask them to do it. So I've asked B. B. King and Bill Ferris to do a favor for us. The nation's most important historian, John Hope Franklin, is in the audience today. [*applause*] Today is his birthday. So, please join B. B. King and Bill Ferris and all of us in wishing Dr. Franklin a happy, happy birthday. [*singing "Happy Birthday"*]

FRANKLIN: I'm just happy to be with my classmate [Bill]. We received honorary degrees together in 1997 at Yale University. [*applause*] You made reference to the fact that the university is perhaps not the center of certain activities. I can tell that on that occassion, when B. B. King gave a concert in Town Square in New Haven, no one was at the university.

YESSUM: Okay, now I get to try to moderate you guys asking questions of B. B. King and Bill Ferris. There are microphones in the aisle.... And I want questions, not comments.

QUESTION 1: How often have you gone back to the Church of God and Christ, and how have you been received there?

KING: I usually try and go back not only to my church but to other churches of the same faith every year. That's my faith, and I pray to God and try my best to live a certain way. I'm a blues singer, but that's the way I make a living. My aunt and mom and them used to be angry with me because they say it was the devil's music. But when I was plowing, they didn't say that. So my answer is: Every year, sir, as many times as I can.

QUESTION 2: What has been your reaction to all of the British musicians, starting in the [19]60s and beyond, who started to emulate your music, and which of those have you enjoyed the most?

KING: I was very happy; they made me very happy. I just wish I had more songs that they liked. But I think the Rolling Stones, I guess, would be the closest [to me], because they played a lot of blues things, bluesy things. We had another group, the Who. But you know we just can't bypass the Beatles.

QUESTION 3: How do you feel when you're considered to be such an historical icon and have people call you the best?

KING: No, I think I do that like I do reading the papers: I don't believe everything people say. I have to apologize a bit, I guess. I've played loud blues too long, and I can't hear so good sometimes. But no, I guess I'm glad that I've never believed. Well, let me put it this way: when I first left Mississippi and went to Memphis, I thought I was something else. Man, I could sing! But then I heard guys like Gatemouth Moore and Roy Brown, people like that. Then I found out I wasn't such a good singer after all. And then I heard guys playing like T-Bone and all the rest of them, and I ain't so good at guitar either.

QUESTION 4: The guitar players today—like Eric Clapton; Stevie Ray Vaughan; Eric Burdon, who played with Elvis Presley; and those musicians—are any of those musicians your favorite today? I was just wondering who might be some of your top three, four guitar-players today?

KING: Well, first let me say it this way: in my opinion, Eric Clapton is the number-one guitarist in rock and roll. Nobody is better, in my opinion. [*applause*] But there are so many great guitarists that play so well, that it makes my liver quiver. I tell you the truth: that I have never heard anyone yet that I didn't admire. My hat's off to them because each guy that spends the time that I know he had to do playing guitar [like that], my hat's off to them. The late Stevie Ray Vaughan was like a son to me. Eric Clapton is a good friend. But there are many others—George Benson [for example]. And I could just go ahead and name you so many of the great, great guitarists. I think that just knocks me out.

QUESTION 5: Could you tell us what you liked so much about Lonnie Johnson in particular, and could you demonstrate a little bit what his sound was like?

KING: I wish I could; I would've been playing like him. But to tell you a little something, the people that I mentioned that I like so much: most of them were guitar players but others weren't. For example, Louis Jordan, Bobby Hackett ... Johnny Hodges—they had a way of phrasing. They would take a note, and it would seem to me it was like a sword. [*playing*] To me it tells a story, it don't say that much, but ... [*playing*] He takes the time with what he's doing in his phrasing. Lonnie Johnson did that, and to me Lonnie Johnson was like a link between jazz and blues, gospel and jazz, country and you name it; musically he was that link between whatever kind of music was being played at the time. And I wanted to be like him, to record with people like he did. He recorded with Louis Armstrong, he recorded with Duke Ellington, Mahalia Jackson, another Lang (not Johnny Lang; Johnny weren't around at the time, but I can't think of the first name). I've been lucky and wanted to be so much more like him, I could never phrase exactly like I'm trying to explain to you. But that's what he did to me, it just seemed to go through me. I could just sit there and listen. There used to be a program on the radio, *Name That Tune.* "I can name that one in two notes." I could always name his in one note.

QUESTION 6: What's the single most important advice you could give a blues musician? And number two: what do you feel will happen in the near future in the blues?

KING: I would like to try and answer by thinking in terms of some young kids on the way to Carnegie Hall. They didn't know exactly the direction to go, so they saw several old fellows like myself sitting out playing checkers. So they said—these are young guys to the old people—"How do we get to Carnegie Hall?" A couple of them said, "Practice." [*applause*] I would say to the younger people: Practice. Believe in what you do. Get high off of your music and nothing else.

The other part of the question: what do I think about the blues and where it's going today? I've prayed many, many days and nights, hoping that it would be in the mainstream of music. That you could turn on your radio if you wanted, and you'd be able to hear not only some type of rap or jazz or country or gospel, but hear some blues too. And not [only] Saturday night after midnight!

QUESTION 7: My name is — and I worked with the late Congressman Sonny Bono... And one of our number-one issues is copyright. Having [copyright] last for your lifetime plus fifty [years]. Are these concerns that you have?

KING: Well, I think that we all like to get paid for our work. I know I do. So I'm very strong for your music being copyrighted and protected. I'd like it to be; that's the only way that we can survive. There was a time, I think, in the [19]20s or so, [when] you could grab it and play it and, Yeah! Hurray! I did that one. But it's much better today, but not where I think it should be, so I'm strong for it.

YESSUM: Can we give a real Washington thank-you to B. B. King? [*standing ovation*]

KING: Thank you. Thank you so much.

Born in Chicago, **Howard Mandel** is an independent journalist who serves as president of the Jazz Journalists Association and editor of its website <www.jazzhouse.org>; he also teaches "The Arts: Jazz" and "Roots of American Music" seminars in the adult degree program of New York University. After taking his bachelor's degree at Syracuse University, Mandel began writing for *Down Beat* twenty-five years ago and still contributes to that magazine, as well as to *Jazziz, The Wire, Musical America, Tower Pulse,* and other publications. The author of *Future Jazz,* he also produced the CD *Future Jazz: Breakthrough Tracks* (Knitting Factory Records). Among other distinctions Mndel is a two-time winner of ASCAP's Deems Taylor Award for music criticism.

❦ Jazz, Now and Always

HOWARD MANDEL

A FEW days before Christmas 1999 a *CBS Evening News* producer phoned me to ask, "What is the sound of the millennium?"

She knew full well that music doesn't change overnight, even on a night that loomed as large as New Year's Eve 1999/2000. "I suppose it has something to do with synthesizers," she continued, "and new ways to play them—something I'd guess jazz musicians are doing?"

"Sure," I volunteered. "Like Graham Haynes processing his trumpet over loops and samples (*Tones for the 21st Century*). Or George Lewis creating software for interactive improvisatory trombone/computer duet—I don't know of a recording of that, though. Or multi-keyboardist Joe Zawinul, whose ultrafunky Zawinul Syndicate I consider woefully under-recorded, in spite of *World Tour.*

"You see ..." she hesitated. She then admitted she'd just interviewed trumpeter Wynton Marsalis, and he'd told CBS that jazz at the beginning of the next century will sound a lot like it did at the beginning of the last one. Marsalis had also mentioned something about "globalization."

For almost twenty years now, Marsalis has been a jazz icon—and as these words are written, has issued fifteen wildly diverse recordings under his own name in the past twelve months. Included in this unprecendented feat—

organized, incidentally, by the Columbia Jazz A&R department in which Wynton's brother Branford had a prominent hand—are the following: *At the Octoroon Balls*, a string quartet; *Sweet Release* and *Ghost Story*, ballets for jazz orchestra and combo; *Reeltime*, an unused soundtrack commissioned for the film *Rosewood* (and featuring vocalists Cassandra Wilson and Shirley Caesar, pianist Marcus Roberts, and progressive country fiddler Mark O'Connor); and a bargain-priced seven CD-boxed set *Live at the Village Vanguard*, performed by the Wynton Marsalis Septet. Waving the centenary banner of Duke Ellington, Marsalis led Ellington's own Lincoln Center Jazz Orchestra on a world-wide tour in 1999 and ended the twentieth century on 29 and 30 December by premiering *All Rise*, a new symphonic work for a 100-voice chorus, the Lincoln Center Jazz Orchestra, and the New York Philharmonic conducted by Kurt Masur.

Nonetheless ... "Jazz next year will sound like it did a hundred years ago!" I asked the reporter, "What can Marsalis mean? Do you really think we're going back to John Philip Sousa's Marine Band and James Reese Europe? Ragtime and Irving Berlin, George Gershwin and Jelly Roll Morton? To New Orleans polyphony *à la* Louis Armstrong, Johnny Dodds, and the Original Dixieland Jazz Band? To African retentions handed down from slaves drumming in Congo Square? Bawdy songs from vaudeville, black Broadway and Harlem Renaissance revues? Riffing jazz troupes roaming the land by rail and car, finding dancehalls everywhere, like in the 1930s and 1940s?"

True, an enormous bounty of classic jazz, as well as "classical" and "folk" music, is available to us now; historic restorations transferred to CDs long ago impressed me with fidelity that refreshes ancient musical gestures, and editions brim with detailed documentation. See the end of this essay for discographical suggestions. True, I too indulge in the past—all hail expert remastering! But for Marsalis, the nation's jazz icon, to give us nothing to look forward to besides replays and reviews!

That's as bad as when someone asks me, "What's new?" Too often nothing memorable comes to mind. Consider some evidence of this deplorable trend: in a recent *Down Beat* list of top-rated 1990s albums, fully half were reissues, recorded originally between the 1920s and the 1970s.

Marsalis couldn't have been speculating that jazz will enter a phase of retrospection or regression, could he? Not while the music claims by right of association some of the most far-thinking artists on the planet!

Consider composer-conceptualist-alto saxophonist (and trumpeter-violinist) Ornette Coleman, whose gloriously quirky, dense, and joyful *Tone*

Dialing remains prophetic. Or consider Thelonious Monk (perhaps through *Solo Monk*. Jazz today has a pianist as original as Monk in the too-often overlooked veteran Andrew Hill, featured on Greg Osby's *Invisible Hand*; Hill's *Dusk*, featuring a brillaint younger septet, won critical acclaim upon its May 2000 release, and he seems poised for a productive run.

Consider master drummer Elvin Jones, as ferocious as when he played with Coltrane (*Live at Birdland*), as he is also when performing with intense pianist Cecil Taylor and with tenor saxophonist Dewey Redman (*Momentum Space*). And there are many other visionaries: composer George Russell, for instance—famed for writing "Cubano Be" and "Cubano Bop" for Dizzy Gillespie's jazz orchestra in the late 1940s, but still going strong as a composer, ensemble leader, and engineer (?) at the New England Conservatory. Or vocalist Cassandra Wilson (*Traveling Miles*). Or saxophonist John Zorn (*The Circle Maker*).

There is a pantheon of at-the-moment progressives such as Sonny Rollins—who, along with Jackie McLean, is among the most inspired surviving saxophonists of the 1950s. Rollins's best 1990s recording is *+3*; McLean's latest is *Nature Boy*. And trumpeters, including Jon Hassell (*Fascinoma*), Wadada Leo Smith (*Yo Miles!*), and Nils Petter Molvaer (*Khmer*)—all these artists extrapolate from the electronic innovations of the immortal Miles Davis that began back in the late 1960s.

Meanwhile, Marsalis remains top dog of the unplugged horn-players pack. It's worth noting that recording and releasing fifteen album-length projects in one year was simply impossible in 1899. Nor was it attempted even last year by any of Marsalis's fellow trumpeters: Jon Faddis of the Carnegie Hall Jazz Band (*Carnegie Hall Jazz Band*), Terence Blanchard (*Jazz in Film*), Dave Douglas (*Leap of Faith*), Roy Hargrove (*Crisol*), Tom Harrell (*The Art of Rhythm*), Nicholas Payton (*Nick at Night*), or Wallace Roney (*Village*).

Saxophonists, trumpeters, guitarists, keyboardists, bassists, drummers— most of the biggest and most active names in jazz live the music today not as it was *then* but as it is, no fooling, right *now*. In the last couple of years there's even been a strong reaction to jazz's 1980s neo-conservative Young Lions: the "ecstatic movement" of hardbitten urban free improvisers documented on such scrappy independent labels as Knitting Factory Records, Eremite, and Cadence or CIMP.

So, at the beginning of this, the twenty-first century, jazz is overwhelmingly inhabited, as it always has been in its best times, by rugged individualists who've had to fight to survive on the strength of their creativity and originality, by ultra-sophisticated artists who've devised hip lingos of their own. Wynton *can't* really believe jazz will sound like it did when it was brand new a century ago. Today, jazz people must of necessity be savvier and are, overall, better educated than the unselfconscious musicians of that distant, seemingly more innocent age. And that's not to call jazz musicians primitive, but America the less media-glazed.

Regarding Marsalis's reference to globalization: yes. Jazz is wide open, ready to embrace the globe's surprises in the on-rushing future. Maybe that's what Marsalis, who's currently thirty-eight years old, was trying to say. Way back when, New Orleans was a port city, open to all cultures, reveling in sound whatever its style. Jazz could serve as the New Orleans of the twenty-first century; it could be a cultural portal through which ideas from everywhere arrive and are assimilated, disseminated, and/or mixed to make even fresher sound.

Already we recognize Latin jazz, Afro-Cuban jazz, Jamaican jazz, Brazilian jazz, an English jazz scene, Dutch jazz, German free jazz, Australian jazz fusion, jazz in Japan, and jazz in the former Soviet Union, in South Africa, Mexico, and Canada, in Scandanavia, France, Italy, Spain, and Portugal. Jazz is beginning to seep out of the Middle East: consider Scandanavian electric bassist Jonas Hellborg's *Aram of the Two Rivers*, recorded live in Syria. Long ago jazz landed from outer space: the bumper sticker "Sun Ra is Alive and Well on Saturn" refers to that artist's catalog of once hard-to-get Saturn record albums, including *Nubians of Plutonia* (1974) and *Monorails and Satellites* of the mid-1960s, bountifully reissued on the Evidence label beginning in 1991.

Yes, Cuban-born and passport-holding pianist Gonzalo Rubalcaba (*Antiguo*) lives outside Miami now. Richard Bona, a bassist from Cameroon (*Scenes from My Life*) and the most charismatic debut artist on anyone's roster in a long time, is performing unheralded in Manhattan's downtown clubs. Canadian Diana Krall (*When I Look into Your Eyes*) is the belle of jazz romance. And Mongolian throat singer Sainkho Namchylak, who sounds like no one else on earth, performs with the London and Berlin-based Moscow Jazz Composer's Orchestra on *Let Peremsky Dream*. There's even jazz in Johannesburg, with *Smooth Africa* from Heads Up International proving that listener-friendly improvisation strikes a chord well beyond America's shopping malls.

"No, jazz never sounded like this before," I tell the *CBS Evening News* producer, sure I'm right and Wynton Marsalis is ... well, Wynton Marsalis. "It's completely different than it sounded in 1900, or 1930 or 1960, for that matter. And you can be sure it always will sound different, from now on!"

DISCOGRAPHY

Recommended Recordings

Classic early jazz:
Louis Armstrong Volume IV, Louis Armstrong and Earl Hines (Columbia 1989).
Original Dixieland Jazz Band, *The 75th Anniversary* (Bluebird 1992).
Johnny Dodds, *Blue Clarinet Stomp* (Bluebird 1990).
George Gershwin, *Gershwin Performs Gershwin: Rare Recordings, 1931-1935* (MusicMasters 1991).
Jelly Roll Morton, Centennial: His Complete Victor Recordings (Bluebird 1990).

Recordings by now guitarists:
Dave Fiuczynski, *Jazz Punk* (Fuzelicious 2000).
Bill Frisell, *Have a Little Faith* (Elektra Nonesuch 1993).
Jim Hall and Pat Metheny (Telarc International 1999).
Charlie Hunter Quartet, *Ready, Set, Shango!* (Blu Note 1996).
Pat Martino and Joyous Lake, *Stone Blue* (Blue Note 1998).
Vernon Reid, Elliot Sharp, and David Torn, *Guitar Oblique* (Knitting Factory Records 1998).
Marc Ribot y Los Cubanos Postizos (Atlantic 1998).
John Scofield, *A Go Go* (Verve 1998).

Recordings by now keyboardists and pianists:
Geri Allen, with Ornette Coleman Quartet, *Sound Museum* (Harmolodic/Verve 1996) and *Cyrus Chestnut*, (Atlantic 1998).
Dave Bryant, *The Eternal Hang* (Accurate, 1999).
Marilyn Crispell, *Nothing Ever Was, Anyway* (ECM 1997).
Larry Goldings, *Light Blue* (Minor Music 1993).
John Medeski, with Martin and Wood Medeski, *It's a Jungle in Here* (Gramavision 1993).
Myra Melford, *Above Blue: The Same River, Twice* (Arabesque Jazz 1999).
Andy Milne, *New Age of Aquarius* (Contrology Records 2000).
Danilo Perez, *PanaMonk* (Impulse! 1996).

Recordings by now bassists:
Charlie Haden, *Night and the City* (Verve 1998).

Dave Holland, *World Trio* (Intuition Music 1995).
Christian McBride, *Number Two Express* (Verve 1996).
William Parker and Alan Silva, *A Hero's Welcome* (Eremite n.d.).
Reggie Workman, *Images: The Reggie Workman Ensemble in Concert* (Music & Arts
    Programs of America 1990).

Recordings by now drummers:
Joey Baron, *We'll Soon Find Out* (Intuition n.d.).
Jack Dejohnette, *Oneness* (ECM 1997).
Roy Haynes, *Praise* (Dreyfus Jazz 1999).
Elvin Jones and John Coltrane, *Live at Birdland* (Impulse! 1968).
Max Roach, *M'Boom* (Blue Moon/MR 1992).

Recordings by Wynton Marsalis:
At the Octoroon Ball (Columbia 1999).
Ghost Story (Columbia 1999).
Live at the Village Vanguard, with the Wynton Marsalis Septet (Columbia 1999).
Reeltime, with Cassandra Wilson, Shirley Caesar, Marcus Roberts, and Mark O'Connor
    (Columbia 1999).
Sweet Release (Columbia 1999).

Futuristic concepts:
Richard Bona, *Scenes from My Life* (Sony 1999).
Ornette Coleman, *Tone Dialing* (Harmolodic/Verve 1995).
Jon Hassell, *Fascinoma* (Water Lily Acoustics, 1999).
Graham Haynes, *Tones for the 21st Century* (Antilles 1997).
Jonas Hellborg, *Aram of the Two Rivers* (Bardo 1993).
Andrew Hill, *Dusk* (Palmetto Records 2000).
Diana Krall, *When I Look into Your Eyes* (Verve 1999).
Nils Petter Molvaer, *Khmer* (ECM 1990).
Thelonious Monk, *Solo Monk* (Columbia Legacy 1992).
Sainkho Namchylak, *Let Peremsky Dream* (Leo Lab 2000).
Greg Osby and Andrew Hill, *Invisible Hand* (Blue Note 2000).
Sun Ra, *Nubians of Plutonia* (reissued on Evidence 1991).
_____, *Monorails and Satellites* (reissued on Evidence 1991).
Dewey Redman, *Momentum Space* (Verve 1998).
Gonzalo Rubalcaba, *Antiguo* (Blue Note 1998).
Wadada Leo Smith, *Yo Miles!* (Shanachie 1998).
Smooth Africa (Heads Up International 2000).
Cassandra Wilson, *Traveling Miles* (Blue Note 1999).
Joe Zawinul and the Zawinul Syndicate, *World Tour* (Zebra 1998).
John Zorn, *The Circle Maker* (Tzadik 1998).

Mainstream now:
Terence Blanchard, *Jazz in Film* (Sony Music 1998).
Dave Douglas, *Leap of Faith* (Arabesque 1998).
Jon Faddis, *Carnegie Hall Jazz Band* (Blue Note 1998).
Roy Hargrove, *Crísol* (Verve 1998).
Tom Harrell, *The Art of Rhythm* (BMG/RCA 1998).
Jackie McLean, *Nature Boy* (Blue Note 2000).
Sonny Rollins, *+3* (Milestone 1996).
Wallace Roney, *Village* (Warner Bros. 1998).
Nicholas Payton, *Nick at Night* (Verve 1998).

Dale A. Olsen is professor of ethnomusicology and director of the Center for Music of the Americas in the School of Music, Florida State University. He holds degrees from the University of Minnesota and took his doctorate in ethnomusicology at the University of California, Los Angeles. Olsen has lived, worked, and researched as an ethnomusicologist in Argentina, Brazil, Chile, Colombia, Peru, Paraguay, and Venezuela; he has also performed as principal flutist with the Philharmonic Orchestra of Chile. In addition to holding other positions with professional societies, he is currently serving as president of The College Music Society (1999-2000). Among his publications are *Musics of Many Cultures: Study Guide and Workbook* (now in its third edition) and *Music of the Warao of Venezuela: Song People of the Rain Forest*; the latter volume won the Alan Merriam Prize. During the 1990s Olsen was recording review editor for *Ethnomusicology* and, with Daniel Sheehy, co-editor of *The Garland Encyclopedia of World Music*, Volume II (republished in part as *The Garland Handbook of Latin American Music*).

❦ Globalization, Culturation, and Transculturation in American Music

From Cultural Pop to Transcultural Art

DALE A. OLSEN

A TERM used frequently in late twentieth-century musical and social science scholarship is "globalization," which I define as a merging of influences from around the world. For ethnomusicologists (i.e., individuals who study the way musical processes originate, develop, and have an affect on societies), globalization exists on a continuum that includes many combinant gradations and variations.

Two processes that affect this continuum and may explain how globalization occurs in musical composition are what I call "culturation" and "transculturation." I define "culturation" as the concept of culture moving forward as a self-fulfilling process, including a type of unconscious, intentional, or spiritual glorification and continual (re)creation of one's own culture. I define "transculturation" as the process of cultural transference, or the influences of one or more cultures moving back and forth with another or other cultures (i.e., influences across cultures). Perhaps globalization could also be seen as the final result at the farthest end of the continuum, when cultural elements from many regions of the world appear to be blended together or seem to be sharing the same space.

The application of globalization and transculturation to the United States is not so unusual because in reality our nation is a microcosm of the world; many of its cultures, at least the major ones, are found within our borders. In America, for example, one can hear Chinese *pipa*, Japanese *shakuhachi*, Laotian *khaen*, Indian *sitar*, Iranian *tar*, Senegambian *djembe*, Guatemalan *marimba*, Brazilian *berimbau*, Mexican *guitarrón*, Cuban *batá*, Indonesian gamelan,* and indeed, nearly an infinite number of musical instruments, ensembles, and songs from almost everywhere in the world. These are "American" musical traditions because they represent large segments of our population at the beginning of the twenty-first century. Had the United States become a "melting pot" as our founding fathers envisioned, one might be able to speak of an "American music" today. The United States, however, became instead a "salad bowl," consisting of people of many ethnicities, representing many cultures, and performing many musics. In the twenty-first century we must speak about American musics, rather than American music.

This idea, of course, is not new, and most American academics realize that the musical expressions of our country are varied. Some of the realizations, however, are slow in coming. On 31 December 1999, during the PBS day-and-a-half presentation entitled *Millennium 2000*—a presentation that featured musical and dance performances from around the world and around the clock—Leonard Slatkin, conductor of the National Symphony Orchestra, was interviewed by Todd Mundt of PBS. Mundt asked this question of the Maestro: "The twentieth century was an American century—you think of the music of Aaron Copland and Gershwin. Now that we're ready to enter a

---

*[Of the names of these exotic instruments, only "gamelan" has entered the American musical vocabulary; for that reason it is not italicized, either here or elsewhere in the present volume. – Eds.]

new century ... [What will be] the sound of the twenty-first [century]?" I jotted down Slatkin's reply:

> Over the course of the [past few] hours, what we have heard is the American influence worldwide. People have taken their own music and adapted it to American musical styles. If I had to look in a crystal ball, I would think we're going to begin to see the influence of other world cultures come into play in music in this country. Even as we hear music of India, Taiwan, Sri Lanka, wherever it happens to be, somehow it's sounding a little more indigenous to our country than it used to; so I think a more melding of cultures and a combination of styles will be what to look for in the next ten to fifteen years anyway.

I believe Slatkin was referring to the ears and minds of the masses when he talks about musical perception in the United States; and I hope he is right. In the minds, pencils, computers, and performances of American composers, however—and also among academics—the influences of other world cultures have come into play for many decades, including in the music of Copland and Gershwin. (Had Mundt given it some thought, I'm sure he could have come up with more recent composers to represent American music in the twentieth century.) In the lead article in the first issue of the *College Music Symposium*, for example, Wilton Mason discussed multicultural awareness and stated, "We are now in rapid communication with every part of the globe ... we have ourselves proven receptive, as never before, to ideas and impulses from abroad."[1] Thus, globalization and transculturation are not new concepts, but more people in the United States will be aware of their implications in the twenty-first century than ever before.

My application of the term "culturation" to our nation is perhaps a new concept. In the history of Western music, and certainly of American music, the term "nationalism" is used to describe the concept of glorification of one's nation through music, although terms such as "naïve nationalism," "romantic Americanism," and "exotic romanticism"[2] tend to cloud the issue. I use "culturation" to mean the process of cultural continuation or culture moving forward. It can perhaps be viewed as a cultural fulfillment or glorification similar to nationalism—not in the political sense of nation, but in the cultural sense of a group of people who share particular ethnicities, behaviors, and values; thus it is a type of insider phenomenon, whereby a person of a particular ethnicity creates something for his or her own ethnicity. Within our shores are numerous groups of people who regard themselves as culturally and ethnically homogeneous, and while many of them are "peoples" in their own right, hegemony keeps them from having political power in the dominant society. The largest groups within this category are Native Americans, who are descendants of America's first immigrants. Culturation is a concept that helps us to understand Native American pop and art music as composed by Native Americans. In both areas of musical composition (i.e., pop and art) culturation is an important concept among marginalized Americans.

In this essay I shall address several aspects of American musical expression that represent what I broadly call "musical globalization" (i.e., along the globalization continuum) during the twentieth century and into the twenty-first century. I will also answer Mundt's question by looking into my ethnomusicological crystal ball during my conclusion. By following my subtitle, "From Cultural Pop to Transcultural Art," I will briefly point out some globalized and culturated trends in pop music in the United States and then briefly discuss twentieth-century global, cultural, and transcultural American art music, ending my essay with a look at the compositional styles of five representative global, cultural, and/or transcultural American composers for the twenty-first century: David Ward-Steinman, Takeo Kudo, Alex Lubet, Brent Michael Davids, and Michael Bakan. These are five American composers whose styles and philosophies are quite different from each other. There could have been dozens (perhaps hundreds) more about whom I could write similar sketches, women as well as men; the difficulty is in identifying them.

Global and Cultural American Pop Music

One of the types of pop music that derives much of its inspiration from non-Western sources is often called "world music," which should more correctly be termed "world music pop." This is an East-West-North-South fusion music that is mostly non-European influenced jazz or jazz-pop. John Schaefer writes the following about this type of globalized and transcultural music in his book *New Sounds*:

> The merging of Orient and Occident, one of the most consequential developments in this new music, is a direct product of the technology of recordings and jet-age travel. The results are known by such labels as "World Music," "One-World Music," "Fourth World Music," "Earth Music," or any number of other terms.[3]

Some of the examples discussed by John Schaefer are former and present popular music and jazz groups or performers such as the Paul Winter Consort, Oregon, John Coltrane, David Amram, and Mickey Hart. Schaefer concludes with the following words:

> For the average listener, the real value of World Music is ultimately the exposure it gives to non-Western sounds. Most of us have little contact with the music and instruments of Brazil, or India, or Ghana, as part of our daily routines. But like the Europeans in the time of the Crusades, many Westerners are now discovering, to their considerable surprise, that a number of other highly developed musical cultures do exist, and that some of them are more ancient and, in the case of rhythm, even more complex than Western music.... Of all the new styles that have appeared recently, World Music is perhaps the most successful at crossing— or ignoring—musical and cultural boundaries.[4]

Another type of globalized and transcultural music that has importance in the United States is pop music that originates among cultures that are not part of the dominant Euro-American or African-American cultures. For example, American pop music groups consisting of or including composers, arrangers, and musicians from Brazil, China, Egypt, Ghana, India, Japan, Senegal, and other countries often make extensive use of their own traditional instruments, rhythms, scales, and timbres, creating complex musical expressions that go far beyond the experimentations of American and European pop-music groups that incorporate non-Western elements. The California-based Asian-American pop group Hiroshima, for example, consisting mostly of second- and third-generation Japanese musicians, incorporates Japanese koto, shakuhachi, and taiko drums into their otherwise Western-sounding ensemble. Los Lobos, a California-based Chicano pop group incorporates many Mexican instruments into their ensemble. They play American genres such as rhythm-and-blues, funk, and rock, Mexican genres like mariachi and Tex-Mex, and many fusions that incorporate styles from both sides of the Rio Grande.

The largest group included within this type of globalized music in the United States, however, is Native American, whose pop music has developed much like other pop musics in the United States except for the blending of traditional Native American melodies, instruments, and aesthetics with rock, country, or new age styles. Native American rock and country bands, vocal groups, solo singers, instrumentalists, and other performers come and go as with pop music everywhere; styles discontinue and others take their places.

Brent Michael Davids, a Native American composer and scholar, very perceptively explains these Native American trends:

> Personally, I think that any music created by Native Americans today is "Native American" music. In fact, I think only a Native American can create that music—whether it be classical, traditional, experimental, some other kind of mix or a new hybrid. There are so many new kinds of Native American music! There are bluegrass fiddlers, Cherokee Baptist choirs, rock bands, waila bands, classical composers, electronic composers, opera singers, orchestra performers, folk singers, blues artists, rap musicians and of course "traditional" singers and flutists. Whether these genres make use of our "traditional" indigenous techniques or not, does not negate them as meaningful Native American music in my opinion. However, it does raise a set of vital questions. There are obvious traditional influences in any indigenous music today and not-so-obvious ones. On one hand for instance, a Cherokee Baptist choir may sing in the Cherokee language from a hymnal with Cherokee characters in it. On the other hand—the musical tones, the 16th-Century counterpoint, the avoidance of parallel motion in perfect fifths, the figured bass, the "roundness" of the vocal singing style, the use of SATB (Soprano, Alto, Tenor, Bass) and regular metered rhythms (4/4 and 3/4)—all constitute music derived from a culture not "historically" Native American. Yet, these choirs are singing contemporary "Native American" music! Therefore, I think the most crucial issue facing any indigenous composer today is one of self-evaluation and self-critique. After all, what methods should we use to create our own music? Where does this criteria [*sic*] come from? Are these techniques derived from "traditional" life or a synthesis of non-traditional life? Which is better and why? When should we use traditional songs in our music and when not? These are some of the questions central to any composer today—in other words—what does our music really mean?[5]

All Native American pop composers probably wrestle with those questions of culturation (and "acculturation" or change from the outside). Some of the culturated Native American groups and singers interested in blending their native traditions with other American styles and who I shall now discuss are Buddy Red Bow, Cherokee Rose, Keith Secola, Joanne Shenandoah, and R. Carlos Nakai.

Buddy Red Bow, a Lakota Sioux who tragically died in the late 1980s, made a culturated recording entitled *Journey to the Spirit World* (1983); it incorporated traditional Lakota singing with rhythm-and-blues and synthesizer styles of the times. Like other singers, Buddy Red Bow always used his music as a means of teaching others about Native American ways, and protest was often a part of that teaching. His fusion style was a part of his interest in reaching out to Native American youth.

Cherokee Rose recorded a number of her compositions in a rhythm-and-blues/country style in 1993. Her "Black Irish Indian" from her album *Buckskin* is based on her own words about her ethnicity:

> I am a Black Irish Indian
> But you don't know about me
> Cause nobody ever taught you
> Your true history
> You think it's a simple matter
> One side white, one side black
> In our fear and ignorance and paranoia,
> It's knowledge that we lack.
>
> I got an Irish slave owner's blood
> Running through my veins
> Caused by the African woman he loved
> My father got his name
> I got the blood and spirit of the Indian deep within my soul
> My mother's Cherokee grandmother
> Was a princess, I am told.

As a sensitive poet and skilled songwriter, she has a powerfully personal style that portrays her as a culturated musician. Moreover, she deeply expresses her cultures through a medium (country-western) ethnically neutral in her case, that is, it is neither Irish, African-American, nor Native American.

Keith Secola is Ojibwe, although he is interested in the breadth of Native American expressions from the Southwest to the Midwest. His most famous composition is "NDN Kars" (later rerecorded as "Sun of Indian Car"), a humorous song about a young man (himself) going to a powwow in his car held together with bumper stickers. The cultural context is a contemporary Native American powwow, the medium is country music, and the message is the humorous reality of owning an old car. Another of his compositions, an extraordinary culturated and contemporary soundscape, is "Rasp," which includes such traditional instruments as a rasp (a serrated stick that is scraped while placed on top of a drum, believed to imitate the sound of a bear coming out of hibernation), a bullroarer (a whirled wooden blade that buzzes, believed to be the sound of spirits), a drum, and a flute as well as traditional southwest singing, all gradually merged with electric guitar.

Joanne Shenandoah is an Iroquois pop music composer, arranger, and singer characterized by an eclectic style that has moved from an earlier country music idiom to a more recent new-age ballad style. In the former style is her CD *Once in a Red Moon* (1994), which features her compositions accompanied by contemporary instruments and Plains courting flute. In the latter vein, she joined forces in 1995 with Peter Kater on piano and synthesizer and Kazu Matsui on Japanese *shakuhachi* (bamboo flute) to produce a recording with an easy listening, light jazz, latin, new age, yet deeply profound sound. Entitled *Life Blood* (1995), the compact disk features Shenandoah's songs that are heartfelt arrangements of traditional Haudenosaunee ("Longhouse People")-Iroquois songs, transformed into new creations with Kater's and Matsui's improvisations. Particularly noteworthy is the song "Life Blood," a traditional fish dance that features Japanese *honkyoku* (traditional *shakuhachi* music)-like effects by Matsui and creative jazz solos by Kater, all to the beat of latin percussion. Shenandoah's 1995 creations are both transcultural and cultural because they bring together several musical heritages (jazz keyboard, traditional *shakuhachi*, and Afro-Caribbean percussion) as vehicles with which she represents her Native American culture through original song melodies and texts.

R. Carlos Nakai is a Navajo-Ute musician who performs his own compositions on the Native American flute known generically as "courting flute." As a composer and performer, he has displayed an unparalleled interest in globalization and transculturation, along with his native culturation. He has performed his compositions and improvisations with Japanese musicians who play *kôtsuzumi* and other traditional drums from *nôgaku* (music for *nô* drama), *shakuhachi*, and other Japanese instruments; he has improvised and recorded with American jazz musicians, such as Paul Horn and Jim Pepper; he has musically experimented with several innovators in new age styles, such as William Eaton, a creative instrument-builder and performer. This year two of his 1999 recordings were nominated for Grammies (*Inside Monument Valley* and *Inner Voices*). While the Native American courting flute lends itself well to new age music because of its plaintive tone, Nakai has also used the instrument to perform jazz, first in his 1980s combo Jackalope and his R. Carlos Nakai Quartet of the 1990s. While he jokingly refers to the musical style of Jackalope as "synthacousticpunkarachiNavajazz," Nakai takes a more serious attitude in 2000 when he expresses his feelings about the Eurocentrism and Afrocentrism of modern American music: "[America] is not really developed as a culture.... You [European descendants in the United States] are no longer living in Europe. ... You are us now. It is time for you to start learning how to be in our land."[6]

Four Global and Transcultural American Composers of the Twentieth Century

During the twentieth century in the United States, a number of composers can be considered global and transcultural, at least with regard to some of their compositions. Like most American composers, their compositional styles often vary because their sources of inspiration vary. In this brief survey I will consider four musicians who have probably been discussed in all the textbooks dealing with music in the United States during the past century: Henry Cowell, Harry Partch, John Cage, and Lou Harrison. I will merely look at them through my ethnomusicological lens.

Henry Cowell (1897-1965).

One of the first composers in the United States to look beyond the Western Hemisphere for inspiration, and thus become global and transcultural in my opinion, was Henry Cowell. According to Gilbert Chase, Cowell's first transcultural experiences occurred during his adolescent years growing up in multicultural San Franscisco, where music in the Chinese community fascinated him. Later he studied at the University of California, Berkeley, where he was greatly influenced by Charles Seeger, one of the most systematically transcultural thinkers of the twentieth century (and also one of my ethnomusicology professors at UCLA in the 1970s).[7]

It was his experiences overseas as a cultural attaché in Iran and Japan, however, that introduced him to the musics of cultures outside of the American and European mainstream. One of his compositions that I have particularly enjoyed performing is *Toccanta* for flute, cello, piano, and nontexted (vocables only) soprano. Influenced by the rich musical tapestries or arabesques of Persian music, with microtonalities and instrumental melismas, the composition is perhaps inspired by a traditional ensemble consisting of *nay, kemanche, santur,* and female vocalist.

A prolific composer who created over one thousand compositions, Cowell also wrote prose that explained his ideas. In 1933, for example, he penned an essay entitled "New Horizons in Music," in which he stated, "Western and Eastern arts must come together on an equal basis."[8] While just a small number of his works adhere to this idea, his multicultural vision influenced many younger composers.

Harry Partch (1901-1974).

Perhaps more experimental than global and transcultural, Partch chose to create his own musical instruments to achieve his desired sound. Nevertheless, the results of his creations and his music often resemble multicultural soundscapes.

Chase writes the following about one of Partch's most multicultural compositions, "Even Wild Horses," subtitled "Dance Music for an Absent Drama" (this is the third section of a large work entitled *Plectra and Percussion Dances*, composed between 1949 and 1952): "Musically, it is an ethnic potpourri, including Partched versions of the samba, rumba, naniga, conga, 'Tahitian Dance', and 'Afro-Chinese Minuet'!" To summarize his compositional style, Chase states that "Partch's main concern was always with 'the quality of vitality that makes a culture significant'."[9] Yet "Even Wild Horses" is one of his only compositions that makes direct references to particular non-Western sounds. However, perhaps Partch's blurring of culture by incorporating his own melodic and percussive creations provides us with a glimpse of the future of globalization, at least in a sonic sense.

John Cage (1912-1992).

Like Cowell, who was Cage's teacher, and Partch before him, Cage wrote only a handful of pieces that can be called global or transcultural. Yet, besides those that reveal elements that can be scientifically described as non-Western, practically the entirety of his musical pallet is global and transcultural in its inspiration. His early piano piece *Dream*, for example, although reminiscent of Satie, Cowell, and even Debussy, also sounds Indonesian because the pelog scale is constantly used, although it merges into other scales and dissolves as an Eastern impression. The pelog scale and others also influenced Debussy and many composers with impressionistic or post-impressionistic tendencies.

Likewise, Cage's *Sonatas and Interludes* (1960) for prepared piano often display timbres similar to Indonesian gamelan music, although Cage himself wrote the following about them: "The *Sonatas and Interludes* are an attempt to express in music the 'permanent emotions' of [East] Indian tradition: the heroic, the erotic, the wondrous, the mirthful, sorrow, fear, anger, the odious and their common tendency toward tranquility."[10] This is a surprising quote by the composer because no common instrument in India produces the gamelan-like timbre achieved in Cage's works for prepared piano; only the *jaltarang*, a set of tuned bowls, slightly resembles the soundscapes produced in the *Sonatas and Interludes.*

Lou Harrison (b. 1917).

Like John Cage, Harrison also studied with Henry Cowell and also worked with Harry Partch. Unlike his more senior colleagues, however, Cowell has made a conscious effort throughout his life to incorporate Asian elements into his compositions. A number of his works, including the *Suite for Solo Violin, Piano, and Small Orchestra* from 1951, are scored in such a way as to sound Indonesian. As Chase explains: "And it is these instruments that manage to evoke the sounds of Indonesian gamelan music, mainly by featuring piano, celesta, and harp."[11] To achieve the precise sound he desired, however, Harrison, like Partch, created his own instruments. Harrison's instruments, however, were replicas in iron of those found in a Javanese bronze gamelan ensemble.

While these composers are but a fraction of those in the United States who were aware of and interested in globalization and transculturation during the twentieth century, they are certainly the pioneers. In our country today, at the threshold and into the twenty-first century, are many composers who have continued what these masters began and who have expanded the concepts of globalization and transculturation, both sonically and technically. I now present five of them who I consider musically and creatively to be innovative and compelling.

Five Global, Cultural, and/or Transcultural American Composers for the Twenty-first Century

While many composers in the twenty-first century are creating music and musical performance events affected by globalization, culturation, and transculturation, I have selected the following five to provide a glimpse of the great diversity that is possible in the present age: David Ward-Steinman, Takeo Kudo, Alex Lubet, Brent Michael Davids, and Michael Bakan. This section of my essay is based on my interviews and sometimes personal experiences with them and their music. In addition to requesting personal information from them, I presented each of the composers with the following interview topics:

describe your composition studies;

describe your employment history as a composer (or during the times
  you compose);
explain how your interest in composition began;
describe your compositional style(s);
discuss your global, cultural, transcultural, or other philosophical
  motivations as a composer;
describe two (or more) of your compositions that you consider
  representative of you as a global, cultural, or transcultural
  composer;
describe your feelings about your place (influence, future, etc.) as an
  "American" composer for the twenty-first century; and
provide any additional comments that are relative to this study.

All five composers received the introductory pages of this essay, including my definitions of specific terms and explanations of how I employ them.

David Ward-Steinman (b. 1936).

With an undergraduate degree from The Florida State University and graduate degrees from the University of Illinois, composer David Ward-Steinman is professor of music and Composer-in-Residence at San Diego State University. Ward-Steinman has unique and visionary approaches to scholarship, teaching, and composition, making him a profound communicator interested in bridging cultures. In the scholarship category, he has written several books, including *Toward a Comparative Structural Theory of the Arts and Comparative Anthology of Musical Forms* (1989), in which he describes, interprets, and compares the ways musics from a number of cultures are constructed. In addition to teaching composition, he spearheaded a program in comprehensive musicianship at the university level that teaches about musical styles, theories, genres, and cultural contexts from traditions around the world. His compositional styles, which are quite varied, include a large component that is global and transcultural.

Ward-Steinman has composed a number of works for what he calls "fortified piano," a combination pun on the term "pianoforte" and a way to distinguish the techniques involved from Cage's "prepared piano." Fortified piano is achieved several ways: by playing directly on the strings with brushes, fingers, or mallets; by laying objects on the strings, such as sheets of paper, sticks, and rulers, and then sounding the strings in the usual way with the keyboard; by adding material elements to the strings, like in prepared piano; and by playing normally. The sounds achieved in such compositions as

Sonata for Piano Fortified (1972) and *Intersections II: "Borobudur" for Fortified Piano and Percussion* (1989-1990) are strongly reminiscent of Balinese and Javanese gamelan orchestras.

Intersections II: "Borobudur" for Fortified Piano and Percussion was inspired by the composer's visit to the eighth-century Javanese temple, Borobudur in 1989 as he writes: "The composition reflects the monument's impact on the composer, who witnessed both sunset and sunrise over Borobudur, and draws heavily on gamelan sounds—Balinese as well as Javanese."[12] While the work does not include actual instruments from a Javanese gamelan, the fortified piano and variety of Western percussion instruments are imitative of a Javanese gamelan's subtle sounds. The work is transcultural in that Ward-Steinman effectively creates and allows the listener to travel across Western and Indonesian soundscapes through the use of a variety of Western and modified Western musical media.

A composition commissioned by the San Diego State University for its faculty quintet-in-residence (Arioso Wind Quintet) is *Night Winds*, composed in 1993. While five musicians make up the ensemble, in this composition they are required to play many other instruments from non-Western cultures, such as bamboo flute, clay ocarina, *didjeridu*, Aboriginal rhythmic sticks (or Cuban claves), and other sound makers and whistles. The composer explains that "these are used to create some of the atmospheric 'night-wind' sounds—not only wind-sounds but wind-borne sounds as well."[13] The effect of this composition is one of globalization (cultural blending, at the end of the globalization continuum) rather than transculturation because many different sounds from a variety of cultures are blended together to create an atmosphere rather than provide a conduit from one culture to another.

Takeo Kudo (b. 1942).

Takeo Kudo is a *nikkei* (i.e., person of Japanese ancestry) composer and *shakuhachi* player, a professor of theory and composition, and a former Music Department chair (1993 to 1998) at the University of Hawaii at Manoa. He holds an undergraduate degree in music education from the University of Hawaii, an M.A. in ethnomusicology from the University of Hawaii, an M.M. in music theory from Indiana University, and a D.M.A. in composition from the University of Miami. As an ethnomusicologist he has conducted research in Japan on the *shakuhachi* bamboo flute, and is an advanced player.

Many of Kudo's compositions since 1971 are transcultural because he brings together Japanese and Western elements. In a personal interview with me, conducted in March 200, he explained that his recent compositional style (since 1971) has centered on the musics of Asia, principally Japan, with which he asserts his ethnic roots as a *sansei* (i.e., a third-generation Japanese; his grandparents were born in Japan). Kudo made this awareness not through his grandparents, however, but through Barbara Smith, one of his ethnomusicology professors at the University of Hawaii. He explains his compositional style in these words:

> I realize that I am gaining more and more attention through my works that grew out of Asian influences. Initially (early 1970s), I embraced concepts found in Japanese music, such as elastic beat, breath phrases, use of silences, and so forth. Since then, I've come to feel that this kind of pursuit can play a part in "homogenizing" traditions. While my attraction to musics of other cultures is genuine and may cause me to embrace certain musical gestures and features, I now [in 2000] try as much as possible NOT to incorporate the aesthetics or mind-set of the foreign culture but, instead, to look upon myself as a thoroughly "Western" composer in a world-conscious and sound-accessible environment. In this way, I don't think of myself as a "world music" composer even as I admit to a long-standing interest in foreign cultures. I am a product of Western training in a decidedly Western tradition and I accept wider influences simply as a consequence of living in an age where technology enables direct exposure(s) to other (interesting!) cultures. Even as I consider myself fortunate to have daily access to ethnomusicological research and to be able to compose in as "multicultural" an environment as will be found anywhere else under the U.S. flag, I am no more "ethnic," I think, than (e.g.) eighteenth-century composers who were enamored of "Turkish" music, or late nineteenth-century composers who fell sway to the Indonesian gamelan—meaning, I use WHATEVER happens to generate (inspire?) musical form. At this point in my output, parallels to "non-Western" music exist simply because of a long-standing use of certain gestures and expressive devices found in musics of other cultures which have become part of my vocabulary.

Because of his *shakuhachi* background, several of his compositions are written for solo shakuhachi or shakuhachi and orchestra. Kudo's most-performed work is *Into the Tranquil Circle* for solo *shakuhachi*, string orchestra, harp, and percussion, composed in 1986 and revised in 1995. In this work he uses a meditative model:

> [My meditative model is] a circle, outside of which the frenetic activity of daily existence could be heard, and the inside of which utter calmness was experienced

at its very center. In this piece, I tried to keep each element (solo instrument and orchestra) distinct—the shakuhachi utilized musical gestures clearly derived from Kinko-ryū honkyoku, and the orchestra was decidedly "Western" in its musical expression (i.e., not trying to "imitate Japanese music").

Into the Tranquil Circle has been performed by Kudo himself, in concert with a number of orchestras in the United States.

One of Takeo Kudo's most recent compositions is *Let Freedom Ring*, composed in 1998 for symphony orchestra and traditional Japanese percussion instruments. It was specifically composed for Kenny Endo, *taiko* artist. Music critic Ruth O. Bingham describes the work with these words:

> Inspired by the internment of Japanese during World War II, Kudo composed a work about "the indomitable human spirit ... that perseveres through adversity." The result was an extended crescendo in three sections that explores the conflict of being Japanese-American in a time when Japan and America were at war. Kudo represented that conflict through contrasting themes ("My Country 'Tis of Thee" and "Kimigayo," the Japanese national anthem), scales (diatonic and pentatonic), keys (through bitonality), and moods (reflection vs. agitation).[14]

The Japanese percussion instruments employed by Kudo in this work include *kô-tsuzumi* (a small shoulder-held drum used in *nôgaku*), *shime-daiko* (a medium-sized drum), and *ô-daiko* (a large drum weighing over 350 pounds). Each instrument represents a particular theme in the symphony's program. Kudo explains that the drumming represents "the human heart yearning to be free."

Alex Lubet (b. 1954).

With graduate degrees in composition from the University of Iowa, Alex Lubet is the Morse Alumni Distinguished Teaching Professor of Music at the University of Minnesota in Minneapolis, where he teaches composition and music theory. He is also an Adjunct Professor of American Studies, an author, lyricist, playwright, poet, and a performer who has developed the Blended Cultures Orchestra, a multicultural improvisation ensemble whose repertoire includes compositions and musical performances by African-American, Chinese, Ghanaian, Greek, Hawaiian, Hmong, Japanese, Jewish, Korean, Latino/Caribbean, and Ojibwe and Parsi musicians, dancers, actors, storytellers, and poets. Lubet's compositions include innovative cultural, transcultural, and globalized works for Jewish ritual, musical theatre, dance, and concert.

Lubet has had a career-long interest in encounters between cultures, especially since his graduate school years. He has taught in Bolivia, Poland, and China, and his compositions have received over three hundred performances on six continents. He makes extensive use of musical and extramusical influences from beyond the European tradition. Since 1982 Lubet has incorporated various strategies into his compositions, such as elements of improvisation and performer choice (where performers given a broad range of expressive responsibilities). Because of the particular performance demands of many of his works, he has developed several performance groups (such as the University of Minnesota New Music Ensemble and the Blended Cultures Orchestra) that specialize in his type of music and similar compositions by other composers; his most recent projects have been in collaboration with artists from many different cultures.

Some of Lubet's compositions include *Iris of Light*, for koto ensemble; *Alyssa in Bali*, for gamelan; *And the Walls Come Tumbling Down*, a dance-drama chronicling relations between African- and Jewish-Americans; *The Wise Men of Chelm*, a klezmer musical for children; *Bosnia Blues*, stagework (script by the composer) with Jewish and blues musicians and live electronics; and *African Sabbath*, for vocal soloists, chorus, and jazz and African instrumentalists. In addition, many of his compositions can be performed with nearly any variety of instruments and voices. *Putting Our Differences Together*, for example, has been performed by one musician playing Native American courting flute, Japanese *shakuhachi*, and European silver flute; *Putting Aside Our Differences* has been performed by two musicians playing Chinese *er-hu* and Japanese *shakuhachi*; and *The Alyssa Permutations* has been performed by an orchestra of diverse world musical instruments.

The Alyssa Permutations was composed in 1987 and revised in 1990. Named for his daughter and deriving its theme from the letters of her names, the composition is many things, according to the composer in a personal interview conducted in March 2000:

> *The Alyssa Permutations* is a gamelan piece, a koto piece, and a composition for any combination of instruments, especially instruments from around the world. It is a fairly small work that includes lots of improvising, and it can be done by many different performing forces. It was created with the intention that the widest possible cultural representation of forces can perform the piece.

The Alyssa Permutations has received over fifty performances.

African Sabbath is a large work that was composed in 1998. It is an arrangement of a famous Jewish liturgical melody and is not a concert piece; rather, it is intended for Jewish worship: "African Sabbath is a setting of the Jewish Friday evening liturgy of the reform movement in Judaism, principally in a West African style." It has been performed by a large ensemble that included the following groups and musicians: selected members from the West African Music Ensemble from Macalester College, directed by Sowah Mensah from Ghana; members of the Blended Cultures Orchestra; the Temple Israel Choir; and two cantorial soloists. Because this composition is intended for a Jewish ritual, it is what I call a cultural work; the fact that it includes cantor, Jewish choir, and African percussion, however, makes it transcultural as well.

Bosnia Blues is a combination of Jewish vocal music, blues, and live avant-garde electronics. In his interview Lubet explained that "its first version was written in 1993, and there are versions that exist all the way up to 1999. Because it is a theater piece, I've had to make new versions of it for every production." Inspired by the Jewish Holocaust, Lubet added:

> The piece is written from the perspective of an American Jew who witnessed the terror of Bosnia from afar as an echo of the Holocaust. Because of who I am, I wanted to use American musical expressions in the piece. Therefore, I wrote it for cantor, blues singer, slide guitar, and narrator; sometimes it also includes other electronics and other blues musicians. This is also a very big work, and there are many different versions of it. It runs anywhere from forty-five minutes to two hours. One of the things I think is most important about this piece is its total lack of symbolic notation, traditional or otherwise. The music is described exclusively in verbal cues, to accommodate oral tradition performers—Jewish- and African-American—who haven't always been fluent in Western notation. I felt it was a huge breakthrough for me to successfully convey my ideas to musicians who don't read Western notation, as even so many performers on "non-Western" instruments do.

About his feelings of globalization, Lubet states:

> I don't work in Western art music venues very much. My compositions and my ensemble are usually heard in places other than formal concerts and our audiences don't generally identify with or even care much about "classical" music. Many people with whom I've collaborated for years don't think of me as a classical composer and probably think of me first as an instrumentalist, bandleader, or concert producer, despite my other life as a composition professor with a

substantial number of widely performed works in traditional notation. I just don't really exist in the Western art concert-music world.

But more than being merely globalized or transcultural, Lubet also considers performance as an aspect of his compositional process:

> My pieces are always real collaborations with the performers. I compose pieces in which the process of putting the work together, from the time that I conceive it through rehearsal, is all tremendously important. I think about the experience my performers have, what they are going to learn from doing the pieces, everything.

In addition to being performer choice compositions, the recent works by Alex Lubet are large-scale performer collaboration pieces that are both cultural and transcultural musical encounters.

Brent Michael Davids (b. 1959).

Davids is a young internationally recognized composer of Native American heritage (his mother is English, his father Mohican); as a member of the Mohican nation pertaining to the Stockbridge-Munsee Tribal Community in Wisconsin, his Mohican name translates as "Blue Butterfly." Davids holds undergraduate and graduate degrees in composition, respectively from Northern Illinois University and Arizona State University.

Often combining elements of Native American tribal music with Western compositional techniques, Davids has composed for and been performed by a wide range of ensembles, including the Joffrey Ballet, Kronos Quartet, National Symphony Orchestra, New Mexico Symphony Orchestra, Chanticleer, and other organizations. His repertoire also includes Native American songs and instrumental works grounded in indigenous America, incorporating native flutes, drums, Apache fiddle, and other instruments (or their substitutes from the Western instrumentarium). Some of his compositions include parts for himself as performer on quartz crystal flutes of his own design. He has also composed for film, and he is a strong advocate for the employment of Native American composers for films about Native Americans.

Davids is a cultural composer because he upholds the ideals of Native American culture through his compositions. For him, this is a great responsibility, as he himself writes:

As a Mohican, the music I compose must bear up under the weight of tribal scrutiny. Creating music that empowers the tribe—to the betterment of our many nations—obligates us as indigenous composers! As a Mohican "composer" I know that Native American song is a gift and Native American music is a responsibility.[15]

One of the ways he achieves this is by creating new tonalities and incorporating old and new Native American musical instruments into his soundscapes, as he explains:

Besides inventing new tonalities, I can see the possibility for indigenous composers to make the orchestra sounds themselves more "Native American" somehow. The instruments themselves might be performed less as instruments and more as talking sticks ... singing reeds ... pounding heartbeats ... rustling winds ... warming voices ... shooting thunder and breathy whispers.... Ever since [1987], the search for new sounds has captured my imagination, and my instruments have often turned out to be as fascinating to me as children.[16]

On the other hand, Davids is also transcultural, as he incorporates Western concepts into his compositions and deftly moves back and forth from Native American to Euro-American styles, as he explains: "[As] an accomplished composer, I have spent many years studying Western European music theory and composition, supplemented by independent investigation and comparative study of indigenous music."[17] He gives this advice to other Native Americans interested in composition:

Getting trained is a significant achievement for any composer! It's good to learn as much as you can about everything and not be afraid of a formal music education! It's been my experience anyway, that a formal education will not make you forget your own musical voice. In fact, the more training you get, you'll begin developing a greater musical vocabulary to express yourself with! One more practical thing ... look for a teacher that has a diversity of students. If a teacher's students come away from their lessons with compositions that all sound the same—like little replicas of the teacher—that's not a good teacher to choose. Look for one who encourages your own voice and creativity.[18]

Davids' largest composition is *PauWau: A Gathering of Nations*, subtitled "a day in the life of a powwow." Composed in 1999-2000, it is a symphonic and choral experience with a traditional intertribal powwow narrator. Davids explains, "just as one hears the master of ceremonies at a powwow, his voice is heard throughout the symphonic work as well—to direct, explain, announce and entertain." Joanne Sheeny Hoover, music critic for Albuquerque's *Sunday Journal*, described the premiere of *PauWau* at the University of New Mexico in the following words:

> If New Mexico Symphony Orchestra conductor David Lockington has long wanted to present something that could only happen in this state, he certainly achieved his goal Friday night. UNM's Popejoy Hall was transformed into a Native American celebration for the world premiere of Mohican composer Brent Michael Davids' work "PauWau: A Gathering of Nations".... Skillfully calling upon his Native American resources and his western classical training, Davids did both traditions proud in his first symphonic journey. Based upon the typical events of a powwow day, the work is divided into 15 movements. (PauWau is the old spelling of the word). In addition to a symphony orchestra and chorus, it used a powwow emcee and the unique sounds of Davids on his crystal flute, plus a group of Native American dancers. Davids cleverly had the emcee verbally define the structure of the work, calling out each of the movements, from the opening "Welcome" and "Sunset" through various dances and songs to the final "Grand Exit." The part was filled with engaging warmth and flair by the veteran powwow master of ceremonies Sammy "Tone-Kei" White, Kiowa from Oklahoma.[19]

Davids is truly a cultural and transcultural composer, author, scholar, and music advocate for the next millennium. One of his greatest interests is communication, not only within his own Native American world, but also across cultures, especially between Native Americans and non-Native Americans. While he writes "I have come to know that indigenous people determine the meaning of their lives on their own terms, and music is one way of working it out,"[20] he also realizes that music is one of the best ways to bridge the many cross-cultural communication canyons within the United States.

Michael B. Bakan (b. 1960).

Michael Bakan received a B.M. degree from the University of Toronto in percussion performance and M.A. and Ph.D. degrees from the University of California, Los Angeles (UCLA), in ethnomusicology. At both schools he also studied Western composition, and at UCLA he studied cross-cultural composition with Elaine Barkin and film scoring with David Raksin. As an undergraduate student he composed works for percussion ensemble, electronics, and jazz ensemble, and as a graduate student he composed additional works for jazz ensemble.

As a percussionist, Bakan has performed and recorded with leading jazz, classical, and world-music artists. He has conducted extensive research in Bali and Indonesia, and is one of the world's leading experts on the genres of gamelan *beleganjur* and gamelan *gong kebjar*, publishing a book entitled *Music of Death and New Creation: Experiences in the World of Balinese Gamelan Beleganjur* (1999). He formerly taught ethnomusicology and Balinese gamelan in the College of Musical Arts at Bowling Green State University, Ohio, where he directed the college's Kusuma Sari Balinese Gamelan orchestra. He is currently associate professor in the School of Music at The Florida State University (FSU), where he teaches ethnomusicology and directs FSU's Balinese Gamelan Ensemble, Sekaa Gong Hanuman Agung.

Bakan has composed numerous large works for Balinese gamelan orchestras, including *Gesuri Variations* for gamelan *gong kebyar*; *Ke 'Tut Dua* for Balinese gamelan *beleganjur*; *Unyai* for electric guitar, flute, double bass, and gamelan *gong kebyar*; *Innocence* for electric guitar, viola, *shakuhachi*, bass, and gamelan *gong kebyar*; *B.A.Ph.PET* for hip hop scratch DJ (stereo turntable scratching), synthesizer, electric bass, and gamelan *gong kebyar*; and *Pepper's Jagul* for jazz drum set and gamelan *gong kebyar*. Creating new works for Balinese gamelan *gong kebyar* and gamelan *beleganjur* is a tradition in Bali, where composition competitions occur annually—this tradition has been a source of inspiration for him. Although Bakan did not pursue composition as a major in his post-secondary schooling, his first interest in ethnomusicology was to learn about non-Western cultures so he could compose music using different styles. Many of his works for traditional and popular Western instruments are derived from his understanding of non-Western cultures and also his interest in rhythmical complexities—a natural outgrowth of his background as a percussionist.

Bakan's talents and success in Balinese gamelan composition result from at least six factors: first is his belief that composing a type of music is one of the ultimate ways of understanding that music; second is his fulfillment of becoming bimusical (achieving musical fluency in two contrasting musical traditions); third is having a gamelan *gong kebyar* at his disposal at his places of employment since the doctorate (Bowling Green University and FSU); fourth is his interest in composing gamelan works so he can better teach certain musical concepts, such as the interlocking or hocket technique (*kotekan*) of Balinese music; fifth is his interest in musical synthesis; and sixth is his fascination with rhythmic complexity and its many combinations and permutations.

Perhaps Bakan's interest in musical synthesis is an outgrowth of his interest in teaching and dissemination. His unique characteristic of successfully fusing several traditions from Bali and America, for example, makes gamelan music more accessible to American students and audiences because it builds on what they already know: electric guitar, jazz improvisation, hip hop DJ turntable scratching, and so forth. This also makes him a transcultural composer in sort of a reverse way from how David Ward-Steinman and others incorporate non-Western elements into their composition. Whereas Ward-Steinman inserts gamelanesque melodies, textures, and scales into his Western music, one could say that Bakan inserts Americanesque ideas, including musical instruments, jazz improvisation, turntable scratching, and others, into his gamelan music. Before he had a gamelan at his disposal, however, the reverse was true, and gamelanesque ideas were incorporated into his compositions for jazz ensemble.

For his compositions, Bakan draws upon musical elements and musicians that are a part of his locale, as he explained in a personal interview last March:

> More than anything, what has influenced my approach is what's available to me at any given time, so you must look at the different pieces that I have composed over the years: for a while I was composing a lot of percussion ensemble stuff, because I was playing in a lot of percussion ensembles; then I was composing jazz-oriented things, because I was playing in some interesting jazz groups with musicians who could deal in rather adventurous musical things; and most recently that concept has taken me into the gamelan world, where I began by doing kind of intercultural jazz-based experiments with conventional Western instruments and applying Balinese musical concepts and techniques. And now, that has kind of turned around the other way so that, because I direct a gamelan and do ethnomusicological research on gamelan music, I am also composing for gamelan. Also, part of the underlying reason of why I compose the kind of music I do for gamelan is that I feel I will never compose in a truly indigenous Balinese style as well as the Balinese composers already do; therefore, I would rather do something different and bring in my different experiences with other kinds of music, and then synthesize them.

This latter concept is clearly seen in his most recent works for gamelan and other instruments. For example, *Unyai* and *Innocence* were written for gamelan and electric guitar because of his friendship with Wayne Goins, a former student at FSU and an accomplished jazz guitarist; *Innocence* also includes viola and shakuhachi because of his friendship with Pam Ryan and myself, all of us colleagues at FSU; *B.A.Ph.Pet* was written for gamelan and scratch turntable hip hop DJ Charles Tremblay, one of his former students and gamelan member; and *Pepper's Jagul* was composed for gamelan and drum set because of his admiration for jazz drummer Leon Anderson, another professor at FSU, who premiered the piece.

As a composer, Bakan is not interested in committing his music to score (although the parts for non-Balinese instruments are written in Western notation). He summarizes his feelings this way:

> I look at my life as a composer, so far, as a localized thing. I sort of think in terms of the musicians I know, those I would like to work with and for whom I could create some kind of shape into which they can fit their own creativity. I feel that to work at the local level and to nurture something at that level is a worthwhile venture. The last things I think about are whether there are any other groups that can play my music, and whether I should make my music available in notation. Composition for me is sort of a self-generated thing, and I am more interested in having people be able to listen to my music performed in the way I conceive of it, than I am in having other people perform it. I am not adverse to having other people perform my music; I just haven't found the time or energy to think about how I would notate many of the things I compose. Also, I try to create pieces that combine things that are composed with improvisatory elements, which might be hard to explain in score form.

To this end, Bakan has produced a compact disk of his music as performed by FSU's Balinese Gamelan Ensemble, Sekaa Gong Hanuman Agung, and guest artists.

Bakan's most recent composition is *Gending Beruang* (2000), which means "Song of the Bear." Its title is inspired by a little Winnie the Pooh bear that his infant son Isaac received as a gift from his aunt: "When you press its stomach it sings this stupid little song." When Bakan (the father) first heard the song, he was both startled and intrigued by it; thus, he decided to write a gamelan piece based on it. To do so, however, he had to "gamelanize" it to make it fit within the five tones of the gamelan gong kebyar. Then he began to compose many rhythmic permutations, taking the melody and breaking it into different cycles:

> You have basically a nine beat cycle, a twenty-seven beat cycle, and a forty beat cycle; nine comes from my birthday, twenty-seven is Isaac's birthday, and forty is the actual length of the melody. Then, forty minus twenty-seven is thirteen, and thirteen becomes a significant number for all types of other permutations. And so

basically you have the melody going through all these different things, and you have the gamelan divided into three separate gamelans, each with its own gong, each with its own interlocking parts; it becomes this incredibly dense and complex canon that just keeps changing. The relationship never stays the same because all the cycles are going on at different rates. But then, eventually, after 1,080 beats, it comes back around so that everybody is in unison again at the end.

This commentary gives us an idea of the composer's great interest in rhythmic and mathematical possibilities in music.

Percussive vitality, rhythmic intrigue, textural density, cross cultural synthesis, occasional humor, and unmatched originality are some of the characteristics of Michael Bakan's transcultural compositional style.

Conclusions

As I gaze into my ethnomusicological crystal ball and respond to Todd Mundt's question noted much earlier in this article, the music of the composers discussed above and hundreds like them are and will continue to create the sounds of the twenty-first century. These individuals of the present and future—as composers, some of them scholars, a few of them academics, and all of them communicators—are and will be America's composers of the twenty-first century. As musicians, teachers, administrators, and other people concerned about communicating ideas, our ears and minds are constantly being stretched wherever we are. Globalization, culturation, and transculturation are successful ways that certain composers of our time have introduced the world to new sounds, expanded our musical palate, and taught us that music and other aspects of culture have fewer borders and boundaries than ever before.

NOTES

[1]Wilton Mason, "Folk Music in a Changing World," *College Music Symposium* (1962): 33.
[2]William W. Austin, *Music in the 20th Century from Debussy through Stravinsky* (New York: W. W. Norton, 1966), 436; and Gilbert Chase, *America's Music: From the Pilgrims to the Present* (Urbana: University of Illinois Press, 1987), 266, 285.
[3]John Schaefer, *New Sounds: A Listener's Guide to New Music* (New York: Harper and Row, 1987), 113.
[4]Ibid, 122.

[5]Brent Michael Davids, "Four Classical Composers Talk Shop" [internet communication, 1995].

[6]James Ring Adams, "Indian Flutist Charms the Grammies," *Wall Street Journal* (18 February 2000): W15C.

[7]Chase, *America's Music*, 456-457.

[8]Cited in Austin, *Music in the 20th Century*, 439.

[9]Chase, *America's Music*, 600, 602.

[10]Cited in Louis Goldstein, liner notes for *Piano Music by John Cage* (Greensye Music, Greensye 4794 [CD], 1996).

[11]Chase, *America's Music*, 609.

[12]David Ward-Steinman, liner notes for *Borobudur-Prisms and Reflections: The Chamber Music of David Ward-Steinman* (Fleur de Son Classics, FDS 57935 [CD], 1999).

[13]Ward-Steinman, "Night Winds (Woodwind Quintet No. 2)": Program Schedule, Concert Programs & Notes, Abstracts (1998 Annual Conference of The College Music Society, October 22-24, San Juan, Puerto Rico), 16.

[14]Ruth O. Bingham, "Kudos for Taiko and Symphony," *Honolulu Star-Bulletin* (4 January 2000).

[15]Davids, "Indian Actors Are Not Enough: Indigenous Composers Empower Native Films," <http://www.inform.umd.edu/EdRes/Topic/Diversity/Specific/Race/Specific/Native_Ame rican_Resources/Books/comp/html>.*

[16]Davids, "Four Classical Composers Talk Shop."

[17]Davids, "Can You Taie a Feather on It and Call It Indian?"

[18]Davids, "Four Classical Composers Talk Shop."

[19]Joanne Sheeny Hoover, "New Symphony Reflects Heritage, Style," *Albuquerque Sunday Journal* (12 December 1999): F3.

ADDITIONAL REFERENCES

Bakan, Michael B. *Music of Death and New Creation: Experiences in the World of Balinese Gamelan Beleganjur.* Chicago: University of Chicago Press, 1999.

Davids, Brent Michael. "Can You Tie a Feather on It and Call It Indian?" [Internet communcation, 1996).

Horn, Paul, and R. Carlos Nakai. *Inside Monument Valley.* Canyon Records, CR-7020 (CD), 1999.

Loza, Steven. *Barrio Rhythm: Mexican American Music in Los Angeles.* Urbana: University of Illinois Press, 1993.

*[URL addresses cannot be hypenated; the "break" at the end of the first line of this address should not be taken literally, and the word "American" entered without interruption. – Eds.]

Machlis, Joseph. *Introduction to Contemporary Music.* New York: Norton, 1979.

Mielke, Bob. "An Appreciation" : liner notes for *Piano Music by John Cage, Louis Goldstein.* Greensye Music, Greensye 4794 (CD), 1996.

Musics of Multicultural America, ed. Kip Lornell and Anne K. Rasmusson. New York: Schirmer, 1997.

Nakai, R. Carlos. Liner notes for *Island of Bows.* Canyon Records, CR-7018 (CD), 1994.

Red Bow, Buddy. Liner notes for *Journey to the Spirit World.* Tatanka Records 9734741012 (CD), 1983.

Rose, Cherokee. Liner notes for *Buckskin.* Clearlight Music (cassette audio tape), 1993.

Secola, Keith. Liner notes for *Circle.* Akina 1992 (CD), 1992.

_____. Liner notes for *Wild Band of Indians.* Akina 202 (CD), 1998.

Shenandoah, Joanne. Liner notes for *Once in a Red Moon.* Canyon CR-548 (CD), 1994.

_____. Liner notes for *Life Blood.* Silver Wave Records SD 809 (CD), 1999.

In December 1999 **Jerold Ottley** retired as music director of the Mormon Tabernacle Choir. Earlier he sang in the Choir and served in turn as its associate and then its acting conductor; he also held an adjunct professorship of music at the University of Utah. After studying at Brigham Young University and the University of Utah, Ottley completed his doctorate at the University of Oregon. Prior to working with the Choir, he taught and conducted in the schools and churches of Salt Lake City, Utah, where he was born and raised. Among Ottley's honors are a Fulbright Study Grant to Germany, a Presidential Citation from Brigham Young University for "exemplary service to family, church and community," and the Utah Management Society's Distinguished Citizen of Utah award. His wife JoAnn, a soprano and voice teacher, holds the last two awards with him.

❦ A Case for Continuity

JEROLD OTTLEY

SEVERAL years of graduate school and a short sojourn as a university professor isolated me from some important musical realities. An appointment to the music directorship of the Salt Lake Mormon Tabernacle Choir* served as an abrupt reminder that an important segment of the potential audience for music holds a populist view of the art. Humorist Dave Berry expresses it this way: In matters of musical taste, everyone has a right to his or her own opinion, and yours is wrong!

Forced by this appointment to reevaluate my priorities, I undertook a study of the history of the organization and its audience. Much was discovered that opened my mind to both the wishes and the needs of the less musically sophisticated listeners who constituted a majority of our audience. As a result I committed myself and members of the Choir staff to listen carefully to audience comments. From them we learned that familiarity was an important factor governing most people's enjoyment of music, regardless of genre— familiarity either with a particular work, with the style of its composition and

*[More widely known simply as "the Mormon Tabernacle Choir" or "Tabernacle Choir" and so referred to below. - Eds.]

performance, or with some other element that allowed each listener to make a comfortable connection with the music. This attitude flew in the face of the serious musical world of the mid-twentieth century, the purpose of which seemed to be to destroy all that was familiar about music.

From the history of the Choir it was apparent that we would be obliged to perform a wide variety of works incorporating many genres and styles and that historical precedents would continue to influence the direction of the organization. Accordingly, we determined that, in spite of the many uncontrollable influences upon the Choir's life, we would guide the selection and performance of *all our music* with as much artistic integrity as circumstances allowed. We also promised to honor past accomplishments of the Choir even as we questioned the viability of some of its hallowed traditions.

Our philosophical focus was sharpened dramatically at the commemoration of the three-thousandth broadcast of the Choir's program, *Music and the Spoken Word*. John Burrows, Vice President of CBS Radio, observed that:

> I'm not sure you realize the magnitude of your accomplishment in terms of broadcasting history. The chances of a program that started on a national network in 1929 still being broadcast in 1987 are very, very slim. But you have done it. In fact, you are the only ones to have done it.[1]

Now, after more than seventy years of continuous network radio broadcasting, the Salt Lake Mormon Tabernacle Choir's program remains an unlikely survivor in the electronic media. Billed as the longest continuing radio broadcast in the world, *Music and the Spoken Word* continues to endure, a phenomenon that puzzles even the most astute industry observers. Despite network realignments, changes in broadcast technology, radical revamping of programming formats, and the intrusions of sporting events and paid advertising, the program continues to satisfy a loyal and proprietary clientele.

Although networks have preempted most programming of this kind, the Tabernacle Choir continues to broadcast weekly on more than 2,000 radio, television, and cable outlets. Even more remarkable is that these broadcasts are supported by the largess of broadcasters that donate public-service broadcast time. For many, *Music and the Spoken Word* has become a national institution; for others, it represents an ongoing conundrum. What is the secret to its success? How has it survived? Why aren't there other examples of this kind of broadcast longevity?

As steward of this broadcast for nearly twenty-five years, I was obliged often to justify its content and format. Interestingly, the first line of defense was against local producers who, in their concerns for the financial bottom line, have argued for change. However, the CBS radio network, the program's affiliate sponsor since 1932, has advised against tinkering with a format that has remained virtually unchanged for sixty years. The network noted that such tinkering usually leads to broader and sometimes radical changes. Historically tinkering is usually the precursor to a program's cancellation. Yet the network's defense of the broadcast seems enigmatic, because local stations are no longer obliged to accept all network programming. Today, more stations are privately owned than in the past; they now select their own formats and program content. Network affiliation has become merely a convenience that provides some programming too expensive to produce locally.

Historically, the Federal Communications Commission has required stations to provide a significant amount of air time for public service. In recent years powerful lobbies have succeeded in reducing that requirement. Local programmers now have the option of generating such programming without obliging themselves to accept network offerings. Regulators also stipulate that public service broadcasts must represent a balance of community interests, insuring the retention of dogmatic neutrality.

In this restricted milieu, the CBS radio network has maintained a commitment to a minimum of programming that represents cultural rather than commercial values. The network chooses to continue its support of *Music and the Spoken Word*, even though a majority of its affiliate stations have adopted formats that are not compatible. In fact, the majority of CBS affiliates no longer carry the program—and, as a result, it is heard on many more independent than affiliated stations. These changes in the broadcasting industry have required constant evaluation of the mechanisms for producing and distributing the Tabernacle Choir's product. Inevitably, these evaluations have centered on philosophy and purpose.

A program that attempts to perpetuate musical and social values in a society that generally eschews tradition is constantly in jeopardy. While the Tabernacle Choir is an arm of a specific religious institution, it has managed to retain a neutral position by presenting, as the verbal masthead of the broadcast states, "a program of *inspirational* music and spoken word." Given the concession that the portion of our society most interested in the broadcast is predominantly Judeo-Christian by tradition, the musical and verbal messages have been drawn from compatible genres. The musical repertoire, whether classical, sacred, patriotic, folk, or popular, is carefully screened for inspirational content without regard to specifically sectarian issues. Such an approach almost inevitably becomes populist in its attempt to cover a wide spectrum of potential listenership. The demographics of the Choir's surveyed audience indicate that its listeners are older, more established people who appreciate content that reinforces their more mature value systems. As a result, the program features musical literature more often nostalgic than contemporary. The spoken-word messages, however, tend to deal with present concerns and attitudes in daily life. The evidence is that the Choir's listenership seeks stability. They appreciate a program that is consistent and recognizable from week to week. They require something of consistency in a world frenzied with change.

(This discussion would not be complete without acknowledging the largess of hundreds of station owners and operators. Their support has been a major factor in the continued existence of *Music and the Spoken Word*. Their commitment of free air time reflects both the desires of their listeners and their own personal commitment to the philosophy of the program.)

The flagship station, KSL Radio of Salt Lake City, has anchored the program since 1932. KSL and its parent company, Bonneville International, have produced the program from its inception. Bonneville also introduced a parallel television version of the broadcast in 1962. Bifurcation of the program for radio and television greatly increased the technical burdens of production; creating a visually pleasing presentation from a relatively inanimate radio broadcast, however, presented a distinct challenge. Refinements in program content, timing, audio and picture quality, and the addition of complementary video footage have been some of the obvious results.

The Choir's participation in other ground-breaking media events has contributed to the continuing success of the radio program. As early as 1910 acoustic recordings were made by the Columbia Phonograph Company of New York, using two large horns to capture the sound on wax disks. Several 78 rpm recordings were produced for Victor Company of Camden, New Jersey, in the late 1920s and early 1930s, using the newest electronic equipment. In April 1940, Bell Laboratories demonstrated Harvey Fletcher's design for binaural (stereo) sound to an invited audience at Carnegie Hall. Included in the demonstrations were recordings by Paul Robeson, Leopold Stokowski (and the Philadelphia Orchestra), and the Salt Lake Mormon Tabernacle Choir and Organ. Recordings of the Choir made for this project resulted in two long-playing releases on the Columbia Masterworks label, which, in turn, led to one of the more successful collaborations in recorded history: that of Eugene Ormandy and the Philadelphia Orchestra with the Tabernacle Choir. The series of recordings that followed was so successful that Columbia Masterworks declared the Tabernacle Choir to be the largest selling recorded choir in the world.

Contributing to the film score that introduced Cinerama to the motion-picture world; televising a presentation of excerpts from Handel's *Messiah* from the Red Rocks Amphitheater in Denver as part of a Bell Telephone Hour broadcast; taking part in the first international television satellite broadcast from Mount Rushmore; winning a Grammy Award, two Platinum, and five Gold Records from the recording industry; appearing at Presidential inaugurations and other national events; performing on radio and television specials; and maintaining a consistent calendar of live concert performances at home and around the world—all these activities constitute a continuous stream of activities that have supported the Choir's record-setting broadcasts.

When one considers the speed with which our society has changed during the last seventy years, the survival of *Music and the Spoken Word* is unique. The Tabernacle Choir is in reality a dinosaur. Its nineteenth-century size, context, and artistic style seem so unfashionable by the standards and innovations of the twentieth-century music world.

If there is a secret to the Choir's success, however, it appears to be because it and its broadcasts are the antitheses of our societal penchants for change, innovation, and what we call "progress." There exists in every soul a need for consistency, for unchanging values that foster stability and continuity in our dash toward the future, for a modicum of ritual that anchors new ideas and trends to current reality.

Is fulfilling these basic human needs a justification for continuity? I believe it is. Present indicators predict that there shall indeed be a place for *Music and the Spoken Word* in the twenty-first century.

NOTE

[1]Taken from a tape recording of the ceremonies following the broadcast.

Frances W. Preston is President and Chief Executive Officer of Broadcast Music International (BMI), a music performing-rights organization representing more than 200,000 songwriters, composers, and music publishers. Preston joined BMI after working in the music and broadcasting industries in Nashville; she opened the firm's southern regional office there and led the organization to a position of preeminence in the area. Among other honors, Preston was named Person of the Year at the 1999 MIDEM conference in Cannes—the highest international award given to music industry executives. In 1999 she was named an American Broadcast Pioneer by the Broadcasters' Foundation and inducted into the Broadcasting & Cable Hall of Fame.

ও They're Playing My Song
Performance Rights in the Twenty-first Century

FRANCES W. PRESTON

IN the current climate of media mergers, transnational capital, and the digital downloading of MP3 files, we can easily forget that the music industry exists because of those countless individuals who struggle against many fierce obstacles in order to compose music the public will appreciate, even love, for years to come. Every songwriter worth the name hopes to create a hit, perhaps even (with luck) a standard—something their children and their children's children will continue to sing and enjoy. Hearing their material performed on the radio or television, or featured in films, or even played over the phone while being kept on hold is a validation of the songwriter's craft and the fact that music enriches our lives in many, many ways through many, many forms of performance.

Of course, not all songwriters count on becoming famous or having a hit record, but all of them hope at the very least they can earn a living doing the work they love. As much as anything, songwriters need to be compensated for their labors, to be assured that their work is protected from abuse, and to know that their music will be paid for by those who use it. From its founding in 1940 Broadcast Music, Inc. (BMI) has believed in the talents of songwriters and the need for their works to be protected. It all begins with a song! The music industry would not exist without songwriters, and BMI strives to insure that its members can have the kind of career that supports and nurtures their skills.

When BMI was founded in 1940, a number of songwriters—particularly those who created the roots music of our nation (blues, country, jazz, gospel, and folk)—did not receive adequate representation from existing performance-rights organizations. Over the course of the last sixty years, BMI has helped composers working commercially in these and other genres to market some of the most popular, influential, and ground-breaking music of the twentieth century. Insuring that the users of music compensate composers for their material has benefitted not only the creators and publishers who belong to BMI but also the public at large. Just think which songs might never have been written were it not for performance-rights societies like BMI. To name but one example, the most popular piece in BMI's repertoire, "You've Lost That Loving Feeling," written by Barry Mann, Cynthia Weil, and Phil Spector, has kept audiences enthralled for more than thirty-five years and for over eight million performances on the radio, in live concerts, in films, on television, and in countless public places where music plays a role in the environment. BMI artists have composed hundreds of other successful songs, but their careers would never have been as long or substantial were it not for BMI and the performance rights it administrates.

As we face the twenty-first century, songwriters and publishers are discovering many novel vehicles by means of which their works can be heard. The Internet has transformed the way in which information and entertainment reaches the public. Like the technologies that preceded it, the Internet offers new opportunities and creates new challenges. Because of the manner in which it works and the erroneous assumption some share that the information it contains should be available without cost, some individuals argue that no legal controls whatsoever should affect its users. Other individuals argue that one should be able to transmit any information in whatever manner he or she pleases, without compensating the owners of that information. In April 1995 BMI responded by licensing the Internet through OnRamp.com. This was the first license of its kind ever granted, and many more have followed. BMI assumes that songwriters and publishers should be able to treat digital technology as another money-making venue, and we assure our members that they will be compensated for their work.

As the next millennium begins, BMI recognizes that a new playing field exists in the arena of the mass media as a result of digital technology. We have, therefore, taken steps to insure our members that they will continue to receive timely and accurate earnings reports, a hallmark of BMI since 1940. New technologies help us perform those services in an even more efficient fashion. An example: in 1992 the BMI New Technology Strategy Group was established to assess the changing electronic environment and plot strategies for the digital era. Certain policies were instituted right away; thus BMI began accepting publishers' song registrations online. Two years later, in 1994, BMI launched the first music industry website: BMI.com. The following year we added to that site a searchable catalog of our entire song database, some 7,500,000 items of information. This material was also released in 1996 in CD-ROM format and is known as the BMI "Hyperrepertoire." In 1997 the BMIMusicBot was conceived as a computer search engine capable of locating sites on the web that use music and of creating profiles of the kinds and amounts of music they use. BMIMusicBot can process almost instantaneously information equal to that sought by more than two dozen Internet searchers working twenty-four hours a day, 365 days a year. In Spring 1998 BMIMusicBot was licensed to performance-rights organizations in Europe and the Far East in order to facilitate their tracking systems.

Obviously, BMI considers digital technology not only a tool in the creation of music, but also a tool for monitoring music use in an ever-changing technological environment. To that end BMI launched its most substantial initiative in 1999: the Horizon Project. The aim of Horizon is to institute programs that assure that our services will be available online, at the click of a mouse, to our songwriters, publishers, licensees, and partners in copyright organizations around the world. It insures that writers and publishers will be able to register new works via the Internet, receive information about their BMI royalties online, make direct deposits of royalty payments to bank accounts, and, through access to an exclusive, secured web domain, consult a catalog of their works, receive updated accounting information, make inquiries of BMI personnel, and even obtain significant professional discounts. Users of our music licenses are able to make online license fee payments as well as find out information about the material they employ through the "Hyperrepertoire." Film/TV producers and production companies can now file cue sheets electronically for any music licensed by BMI. These benefits make the use of the work of BMI writers and publishers simpler and more streamlined than ever before.

BMI has done other things to make sure we are productively connected to the global music industry. An example: as of June 1999 foreign royalty income comprised approximately twenty-five percent of BMI's total licensing revenues; that figure will increase in the future. In order to keep track of foreign royalties as accurately as possible, the world's performance-rights organizations have developed collectively a sophisticated digital network for registering and exchanging information. Called the "Common Information System" (CIS) Project, this network links member organizations' databases and websites in order to provide a search engine that can navigate between them. CIS has already helped create a unified global body of information about music.

On the domestic front, BMI supports those national legislative initiatives that have secured the protection of rights for composers and publishers for the full term of their copyrights. We applaud the Copyright Term Extension Act of 1998, named in honor of Congressman and recording artist Sonny Bono. The Act extends copyright protection throughout the seventy years that follow the death of any creative individual. BMI also applauds the protection of creative rights insured by the Digital Millennium Copyright Act of 1998. This significant piece of legislation prohibits acts designed to circumvent restrictions regarding copyrighted materials or to tamper with copyright management information online.

I'll say it again: it did indeed all begin with a song. Performance-rights organizations like BMI exist in order to insure that composers will be properly compensated for the use of their talents. The future of organizations like BMI seems assured. On the other hand, who knows what unforeseen changes the music industry may face in the twenty-first century? Or in what novel ways music technology may affect the creation, production, and consumption of music? Whatever the future may bring, music will continue to be an inalienable part of our daily lives. And BMI will continue to make certain that, throughout that future, composers and publishers can earn a living from music.

Born in New York City, **Bruce Boyd Raeburn** is curator of the Hogan Jazz Archive, Tulane University. Raeburn holds a doctorate in history from Tulane University and has also studied at UCLA and the University of Southwestern Louisiana. Among his publications are articles in *Jazz: A Listener's Companion, Southern Quarterly*, and *The Jazz Archivist*, as well as liner notes for *The Atlantic New Orleans Jazz Sessions*. Raeburn has presented papers dealing with New Orleans jazz to the Society for Ethnomusicology, the International Association of Jazz Educators, the Louisiana Historical Association, the American Library Association, the Salzburg Jazz Festival, and the Alabama Jazz Hall of Fame. Among his honors are certificates of commendation from the Mayor of New Orleans, the United States Department of the Interior/National Park Service, and the American Association for State and Local History.

❦ Confessions of a New Orleans Jazz Archivist

BRUCE BOYD RAEBURN

SOME people think I was bred for this job. As the son of a progressive big-band leader and a jazz vocalist,* my exposure to jazz in New York had been a foregone conclusion, but that jazz had been strictly modern. The route that led me circuitously from Manhattan to Nassau, Bahamas, to Los Angeles, to Lafayette, Louisiana, and then to New Orleans was a musical mystery tour that interspersed indigenous forms such as calypso, cajun, zydeco, traditional jazz, with the Top-40s fodder of the 1950s and 1960s (much like Bourbon Street today). All this had taught me to appreciate ironies and contradictions long before 1989, when I became curator of the Hogan Jazz Archive at Tulane University.

---

*Saxophonist Boyd Raeburn (1913-1966) led one of the most adventurous and contro-versial big bands of the 1940s and worked with Dizzy Gillespie, among others. Ginnie Powell toured and recorded with Jerry Wald, Gene Krupa, Charlie Barnet, and Harry James; she married Boyd Raeburn in 1946.

New Orleans is a city that celebrates eccentricity, and anyone who seeks to understand its music must learn to respect a parochial point of view. While working on a dissertation about the New Orleans revival and the awakening of American jazz scholarship, I realized that, among some purists, the possibility that the son of Boyd Raeburn and Ginnie Powell might become the curator of a New Orleans jazz archive was tantamount to Lucifer becoming the gatekeeper of Heaven. No wonder jazz historian Bill Russell was perplexed when he found Bunk Johnson listening to (and apparently enjoying) some of my father's recordings in Gene Williams's apartment during the Stuyvesant Casino gig in 1946. (Russell never could accept Johnson's desire to join the *avant garde* and did what he could to keep him focused on anachronistic playing styles.) When debates erupted about jazz aesthetics, it was the musicians who were usually caught in the crossfire, but they were invariably more concerned with making a living and having fun, wherever it took them. It was this attitude that attracted me to traditional jazz and the milieu that went with it.

§

When I arrived in New Orleans in 1971 to work on a doctorate in history at Tulane, I was not particularly aware of traditional jazz. Like most Baby Boomers, I had embraced rock and roll in the mid-1950s, but I was also open to more exotic fare. In the Crescent City, music will seek you out. Try visiting the French Market or the Treme without running into a brass band marching in celebration of Creole tomatoes, or Saint Patrick, or Terpsichore, or Death! The street processions are seductive, with "half-fast" rhythms aimed decisively at the groin, compelling movement, and then percolating up to the heart and head. The "second line" (the uninvited guests that everyone expects to show up) goads the band into becoming more daring and disruptive, chanting "let's go get 'em!" in unison or beating on bottles and cans as the parade picks up the pace. Brass, reeds, and drums converge and seem to explode, with musicians and dancers alike swooning as they move *en masse* down the asphalt bayous that pass for streets in New Orleans. Like Carnival, the brass-band parade enables maskers to become anonymous and get lost in the flow, and after the first one, I was hooked. Initially, converts to traditional jazz tend to respond on a visceral and emotional level. After a while, however, intellectual curiosity takes over. It takes patience and perseverance to reveal a complicated cultural and historical mosaic.

My guides were members of the Old Guard: Al Rose, Richard Allen, and William Russell. I met Al Rose, by proxy, first. His step-son Forrest was taking a course in American history from me at Tulane and came up after class with some photographs of my father and his in Philadelphia in 1946. "Dad left some more of these at the Jazz Archive. Dick Allen is holding them for you," Forrest said. I was intrigued and hurried over to the Archive the next morning, completely unaware as I walked through the door that my life was about to change.

Richard Binion ("Dick") Allen was a jazz pilgrim from Milledgeville, Georgia. Allen first visited New Orleans in 1945 while stationed with the Navy at Gulfport, Mississippi; he moved there four years later. He became active in the preservation efforts of the National Jazz Foundation (1944-1947), an organization that fell victim to its own catholicity when purism became fashionable in the Crescent City, then switched allegiance to the New Orleans Jazz Club (established on Mardi Gras Day in 1948). The Club's preservationist agenda emphasized homegrown talent almost exclusively. Allen's innate conviviality led to abiding friendships with many musicians, and he became a regular at dance halls such as Luthjens and the Moulin Rouge, as well as on the streets.

When Allen decided to pursue a master's degree based on interviews with pioneer jazzmen, William Ransom Hogan, then chairman of Tulane's history department, sought funding from the Ford Foundation to set up a research center instead. The Archive of New Orleans Jazz, established in 1958 and renamed for Hogan in 1974, three years after his death, was the result. (Allen never did complete his degree.) Hogan hired Bill Russell as the Archive's first curator, with Allen as his associate, and together they began tape-recording the life stories of several hundred New Orleans musicians, following the precedent Alan Lomax had established in his sessions with Jelly Roll Morton at the Library of Congress two decades earlier.

By the time I met Allen in 1977, he had been curator for about a dozen years. Unfortunately, his position was precarious because a movement within the university sought to replace him with a trained librarian. Nevertheless, his demeanor was relaxed and cheerful; after handing over the photographs Rose had left for me, he showed me some of the Archive's materials, including some copies of *Down Beat* from the 1940s with pictures of my father on the cover. It was a gracious welcome and, like any first trip to New Orleans, a prelude to future visits.

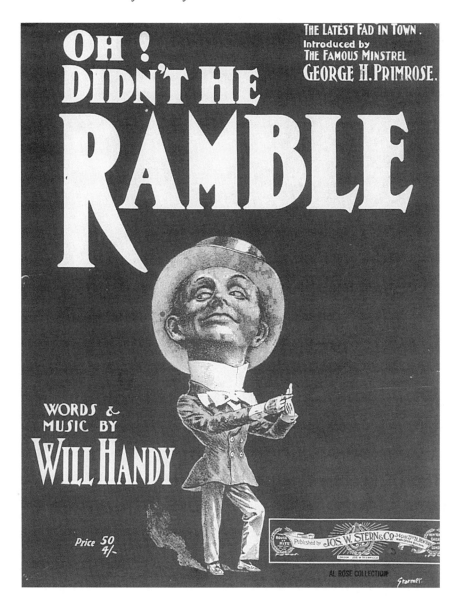

Cover for "Oh! Didn't He Ramble" by Will Handy
(New York: Jos. W. Stern & Co., 1902)
Actually composed by Bob Cole, J. Rosamond Johnson, and James Weldon Johnson,
three of the foremost early twentieth-century African-American song writers,
the song became a staple in the New Orleans brass-band jazz repertoire
and was recorded by Bunk's Brass Band in 1945.

Oral History Session
Bassist Alcide "Slow Drag" Pavageau tells his story to Dick Allen (left)
and Bill Russell (right) during an interview for the Archive of New Orleans Jazz (1958).

———————

At the time I had been discussing various dissertation topics with Henry Kmen in the History Department; his *Music in New Orleans: The Formative Years, 1791-1841* (1966) is a seminal study of New Orleans as a distinctive regional culture, but his sudden death in September 1978 meant cultivating new relationships. Bill C. Malone, whose *Country Music, U.S.A.* (1968) remains the standard text in its field, signed on as my graduate director, and, tangentially, Dick Allen became my ace in the hole. All roads now led to the Hogan Jazz Archive, and it was incumbent upon me to make the most of its collections.

Several months after my first meeting with Dick Allen, Al Rose invited me to his house on Bell Street for lunch. Rose's home was a mini-mansion complete with a small cinema and elaborately decorated with curios and furniture from Storyville, New Orleans's erstwhile pseudo-legal red-light district. (At that time Rose had recently played alderman Sidney Story in a B movie about the District and still looked the part.) As we sat down to sandwiches, he confided, "You know, your dad had some wonderful bands ... but, of course, what he played wasn't jazz." I had grown up with the idea that my parents had given their lives to jazz, sacrificing much for the cause ("thoroughbreds" was how Jon Hendricks had described them), and I was taken by surprise. Dizzy Gillespie had played with my father and was a family friend! What could Rose possibly mean? I felt ambushed but decided to hear him out. After all, Rose's reputation had preceded him: he had been a successful caricature artist and pupil of Diego Rivera, a Lovestoneite Communist, Trotsky's bodyguard, and possibly the first promoter to produce jazz concerts in the 1930s, at the Academy of Music in Philadelphia; his book *Storyville, New Orleans* (1974) had served as the blueprint for *Pretty Baby*, Louis Malle's new film, on behalf of which Rose worked as an historical advisor before falling out with Malle and suing him over purported inaccuracies. What Rose wanted was to impart to me the strict definition of jazz that had just been officially adopted by Moon Landrieu, the mayor of New Orleans—and it was my civic duty to listen!

According to this definition, jazz is "two or more musical voices improvising collectively in two-four or four-four time on any known melody and 'syncopating'." I had always thought of jazz as an infinitely elastic musical continuum, much like the proverbial elephant's trunk, so the idea of excluding most of what I considered jazz to be did not appeal to me. Nevertheless, an historical approach that began with the first identifiable jazz idiom—and did not refer to what came after—made sense. Later Rose and I listened to recordings of the Original Dixieland Jazz Band, Ory's Sunshine Orchestra, New Orleans Rhythm Kings, King Oliver's Creole Jazz Band, Clarence Williams's Blue Five, Armstrong's Hot Five, and Jelly Roll Morton's Red Hot Peppers, a didactic marathon that opened my ears to the burgeoning of the New Orleans idiom between 1917 and 1928. Rather than restricting my notion of what jazz was all about (as he had intended), Rose expanded it; he introduced me not only to the purist sensibility but also to LaRocca, Ory, Roppolo, Oliver, the Dodds brothers, Armstrong, Bechet, and

Jelly in context—a rainbow coalition that reflected the full diversity of New Orleans's "crazy quilt" demographics and their musical implications. In emphasizing "a place and not a race," Al Rose embraced a point of view that was not particularly welcome in later 1970s jazz studies and perhaps even less welcome in the Groves of Academe, where black history courses were being introduced to redress a traditional Eurocentric bias. Frank Kofsky's *Black Nationalism and the Revolution in Music* and Albert Murray's *Omni-Americans* (both 1970) had shown that the African-American musical experience could be interpreted in very different ways. With its roots in the blues, jazz was considered by both writers to be intrinsically black music. But Rose's point was not so much about distracting attention from the contributions of African-Americans as it was about attracting attention to the special features of music in the Crescent City. The term "African American" itself did not address the diversity of New Orleans's black community, composed as it was of many Afro-French Creoles, some of them *gens de couleur libres* with collateral Latino and Native-American ancestry.

This diversity often made "race" ambiguous. Consider the case of Edward Ory of La Place. Ory's father, Ozeme Ory, was descended from French emigrés; his mother, Octavie Devezin, was Afro-Spanish and Native American. Thus, the leader of the first black New Orleans jazz band to make a recording (the Sunshine Band recorded for Nordskog in Los Angeles in 1922) was mostly white genetically but lived as an Afro-French Creole. Unlike Jelly Roll Morton (Ferdinand Joseph LaMothe), who played down his Creole inheritance when he entered show business, Ory retained fluency in Creole patois throughout his life and factored it into his performance repertoire in songs such as "C'est l'autre Can Can" and "Eh la Bas." Conversely, Joe Oliver, an African-American from Abend, Louisiana, who worked for Ory in 1917, adopted Creole speech and mannerisms despite his Baptist upbringing because he found them conducive to promoting an image of refinement and sophistication in his musical endeavors. Race, ethnicity, and personality have often combined in unpredictable ways in New Orleans. These combinations themselves continue a *couture de metissage* tradition that dates from the French, Spanish, and African cultural matrix of colonial times, but jazz drove that tradition in new directions.

My own life may next have been driven by fate. In 1978 a newly-arrived graduate history student from the San Francisco Bay Area, Curtis D. Jerde, was entrusted to me for orientation. (He was a bass player and I was a drummer, so our professors assumed we would get along.) Jerde had just finished a master's degree in library science at Berkeley, and he was interested in writing his dissertation about the pre-history of jazz, picking up where Kmen had left off. Also new that year was S. Frederick Starr, a specialist on the Soviet Union and a clarinetist who became vice president for academic affairs at Tulane.

Starr and Jerde shared a passion for traditional jazz and formed a band, the Louisiana Repertory Jazz Ensemble, to explore forgotten aspects of the early New Orleans repertoire. The Rep did well, attracting enthusiastic dance crowds at the Maple Leaf Bar, and only mild surprise was expressed when Jerde became curator of the Archive two years later; Allen, incidentally, stayed on half-time as an oral historian, and I was invited to assist with plans for reorganization. In addition to his skills as a librarian, Jerde wanted to expand the Archive's visibility within the academic world through various outreach projects. The first of these projects was a collaboration in 1982 with the New Orleans Jazz & Heritage Festival called the Tulane Hot Jazz Classic, which included the Jelly Roll Morton Symposium. Among the participants in this event were Alan Lomax, Frederic Ramsey, Jr., Danny Barker, Lawrence Gushee, Al Rose, Dick Allen, and Bill Russell, and as part of the host team, I had an opportunity to interact with all of them.

"The Second Battle of New Orleans," as the symposium is sometimes called, revealed the fractious nature of traditionalists who argued over the African origins of jazz, research techniques and sources, and the credibility of Morton himself. As Jelly's biographer, Lomax tended to dominate the discussion, but at various points he was contradicted by Barker and Gushee, while Ramsey boycotted the proceedings, angered over a *faux pas* concerning accommodations. (Ramsey later relented, sharing a valuable reminiscence of Jelly's tribulations during the Victor recording sessions in 1939.) Allen, Rose, and Russell, on the other hand, engaged in symposium repartee with less aggression and more humor—the Big Easy approach.

It was a memorable meeting, and it served as my introduction to Bill Russell, who had been a composer of *avant-garde* percussion music in the early 1930s before he became enthralled with New Orleans-style jazz after hearing Morton's "Shoe Shiner's Drag." During the Depression Russell made a name for himself among "hot" record collectors for his ability to find rare records while travelling with the Red Gate Shadow Players, an itinerant Chinese puppet troupe—skills that earned him the title "David Harum of Jazz." Along with Charles Edward Smith, Russell became a traditional jazz purist, isolating the role of New Orleans pioneers in the origins and dissemination of that music. His contributions to Smith and Ramsey's *Jazzmen* (1939), a book considered by many to be the first viable history of jazz, elucidated the idiomatic development of the New Orleans style of collective improvisation and placed the emergence of jazz in a regionally distinctive cultural environment, much as Constance Rourke did with American humor. Then came Bunk.

Although the writings of Morroe Berger, Don Marquis, and Lawrence Gushee have since called into question Willie "Bunk" Johnson's credibility as a witness, Bill Russell never flagged in his dedication to Johnson, a sage trumpeter and raconteur. Russell had corresponded with Johnson while he was writing *Jazzmen* and became part of a collector syndicate that provided horns and a new set of teeth so that Bunk could make a comeback. In 1944 Russell founded American Music, a recording company, in order to document the performances of Johnson and other forgotten New Orleans stylists. After American Music got going, Russell spent less time writing and more time recording on location and managing Bunk's role in the New Orleans revival. Together with Eugene Williams, Russell expended considerable time, energy, and resources promoting Bunk's return and what he felt it represented—a reclaiming of authenticity in American music. Unfortunately, the experiment ended badly, with Williams committing suicide and Russell taking the blame for Johnson's fall from grace (the last the result of the trumpeter's own insouciance).

The schisms that divided traditionalists and modernists into hostile factions during World War II contributed to this fiasco, but they also galvanized support for the apotheosis of New Orleans jazz back home. The general recognition of jazz as an art form, as represented in histories such as *Jazzmen* and Rudi Blesh's *Shining Trumpets* (1946), meant that the nation's most "un-American" city could proclaim itself the wellspring of America's most prized and authentic cultural product (and reap the rewards *vis-à-vis* tourism). The ironic corollary was that modern jazz was rarely welcomed in the City That Care Forgot.

Bill Russell's relocation to New Orleans in 1956 set the stage for his appointment as curator of the Archive two years later. His reputation as the "Grand Lama of Jazz" (conferred by Fred Ramsey) did much to attract donations from the same stable of "hot" collectors that had sustained the awakening of American jazz scholarship in the 1930s and the New Orleans revival that followed. Oral history fieldwork (Russell's primary interest) continued, even as pioneer discographer Oren Blackstone and book collector

Robert George Reisner made substantial contributions to the growth of the Archive's collections. Of particular importance were donations from musicians, the first being the personal memorabilia of Dominic James LaRocca, a member of the Original Dixieland Jazz Band. Because of LaRocca's rather controversial views on the primacy of the ODJB's role in the creation of jazz, Russell asked Dick Allen to handle the negotiations; Allen's subsequent failure to win LaRocca's trust led to Bill Hogan's involvement to complete the deal. Scanty resources made purchases rare, but the band library of the John Robichaux Orchestra (1896-1931) and the Ralston Crawford photographic collection were compelling bargains, and money was found to purchase them.

After Dick Allen took over the Archive in 1965, Al Rose himself began to contribute sheet music, phonorecords, and photographs—the latter gathered during his collaboration with Edmond Souchon on *New Orleans Jazz: A Family Album* (1962); Rose remained a major donor and friend of the Archive throughout his life. Even after he gave up the curatorship, Allen continued to attract donations (including the bequest in 1984 by New Orleans Jazz Club official and attorney Harry Souchon), but Curt Jerde negotiated several significant gifts as well (including those of record collector Roger Gulbrandsen and drummer Ray Bauduc). Jerde also established a newsletter, *The Jazz Archivist*, to showcase the collection and circulate information about the Archive's activities.

The transition from Allen to Jerde signalled a shift of imperatives from collection development to access and preservation. I was fortunate to be exposed to contrasting styles of archival administration, each with its concomitant strengths and weaknesses. My jobs were many, and they required special tact and delicacy as I tried to serve as a buffer between Allen and Jerde, while learning from both of them. In time I worked my way up through the ranks, rising from student worker to part-time support staff member (working longer hours whenever grants facilitated special projects) and finally to "acting curator" when a tragic illness cut Jerde's administration short.

Following a national search I became curator in January 1989, with the proviso that I would complete my dissertation in history within two years or start work on a library degree. Preliminary research with Bill Malone to develop a topic based on my father's bands had led me to investigate the schisms of the 1940s in some detail, revealing the traditionalist ideology that had shaped early jazz histories. I decided to do my historiographical homework and write about how New Orleans came to be recognized as the "birthplace" of jazz and how these histories changed perceptions of the music at home. My appointment consolidated my disparate experiences as scholar and musician (a seemingly coherent strategy in retrospect) but also made it necessary for me to give up drumming until the dissertation was done. I had been touring the South with a rock band, Shot Down in Equador, Jr., the culmination of nearly two decades of musical activity that had included stints with guitarist Clark Vreeland and vocalist Becky Kury, a residency at the Playboy Club with Joan Harmon (one of Allen Toussaint's backup singers), a year with the legendary James Booker (the self-proclaimed "Piano Pope of New Orleans"), a one-shot session with Professor Longhair, and a lasting association with the Pfister Sisters (a close-harmony singing group modelled on the Boswell Sisters).

What I learned on the bandstand was that most New Orleans musicians had extremely eclectic tastes and took pride in their ability to perform beyond (or in spite of) categorical boundaries. Earl King, the definitive r&b guitarist, spent hours after each show talking about his admiration for Ravi Shankar; George Porter, Jr., the funky bass maestro for the Meters, could shine on "Bei mir bist du schön" with the Pfisters; and Booker's "Iko Iko"/"La Cucaracha" medley was impervious to categorization. Most early New Orleans jazz musicians carried business cards boasting their willingness to supply "music for all occasions," and they meant it. So much for purism. The common denominator uniting New Orleans music is the "fun quotient," the spiritual and emotional charge that quickens the heart or tickles the backbone, aesthetic qualifications notwithstanding. This was the insight I wanted to bring to the study of jazz historiography and the administration of the Archive.

It took three years for me to finish the dissertation, but that project gave me the perspective I needed to understand the challenges facing an archive dedicated to New Orleans jazz. The schisms of the 1940s had divided the jazz world into two diametrically opposed camps with competing theories about jazz as a vernacular cultural process, each with its own historiographical implications. Traditionalists believed that jazz was an authentic musical expression of American character, a paean to the possibilities of ethnic and racial diversity within a distinctive regional culture and that jazz was corrupted by commercialism when it entered the American mainstream. Modernists believed instead that jazz had evolved from the homespun to the sophisticated and that it had reached its epitome as art with the advent of bebop and progressive jazz.

In jazz studies these viewpoints have never been adequately reconciled, but since the mid-1950s the modernist perspective has been the dominant paradigm, especially among jazz educators whose students must contend with market conditions as they exist today. Thus, most jazz-history surveys of New Orleans conclude with Louis Armstrong's departure for Chicago in 1922, as if the Crescent City suddenly fell silent the second Louis stepped on the train. In fact, the untold stories of the Golden Rule Orchestra, the Reliance Bands, Sam Morgan's Jazz Band, the New Orleans Owls, John Hyman and his Alligator Stompers, the Eureka Brass Band, Celestin's Original Tuxedo Jazz Orchestra, and the Jones and Collins Astoria Hot Eight are reason enough to return to New Orleans. If I have learned anything in my eleven years as curator of the Hogan Jazz Archive, it is that we cannot be complacent about our knowledge of New Orleans's role in jazz history or about jazz history in general.

§

Trombonist Roswell Rudd recently lamented that "there are more missing pieces of jazz history than there are found pieces." His observation should encourage us to redouble our efforts to find some of those pieces. Consider, for example, the discovery three years ago of newsreel footage (with sound) of the Eureka Brass Band marching in the Zulu Parade on Mardi Gras Day 1929. The film shows members of the crowd on Canal Street making music for themselves while awaiting Zulu's arrival: Baby Dodds sashaying with a bass drummer in tow; a "convict" with a concertina setting his miniature counterpart to whirling; black shoe-shine boys tapping in counterpoint to a drum kit made of pans; and an impromptu cornet-kazoo duet spreading a ripple of dancing throughout the throng. Then the Eureka strolls by, pounding out the blues to a rapt audience. Everyone participates, regardless of class, race, or ethnicity.

Prior to this discovery the earliest document of a New Orleans parade band was an heuristic recording of Bunk's Brass Band made by Bill Russell in 1945 to demonstrate turn-of-the-century playing techniques. Although interesting, Russell's recording lacks context, and this is exactly what the newsreel supplies. Throughout the twentieth century the struggle facing jazz historians has been to convince the American people that they possessed an authentic culture worthy of respect and preservation, one that draws upon the full spectrum of our nation's diverse human resources and creates something uniquely American. In this goal traditionalists and modernists were united.

Today we can watch the Zulu newsreel and perceive how the universal is revealed in the parochial; we can revisit a moment when music mattered more than anything, if only for a little while. It is a suggestive scenario—the pandemonium and joy of mass catharsis on Canal Street—only months before the Great Depression. Our job now is to add this piece to the mosaic of jazz history, making sure that it is placed correctly, and then to find more.

New Orleans is a city that continues to backslide fearlessly into the future, its gaze fixed fondly on a checkered past. For those of us who study its musical history, the Crescent City's eccentricities invoke the power of irony to illuminate the variety of the American experience. In the century ahead the city's past will remain elusive, but perhaps a little less so; its music will surprise us, although maybe not as much as we would like; and its artifacts will deteriorate, even as we endeavor to preserve them. Embracing our past, we will still be doomed to repeat it but never the same way twice. Improvisation keeps both tradition and innovation alive as we invent new ways to be ourselves. Given what we know about the twentieth century, we can rest assured that life will not be easy in the twenty-first. But it should be fun.

Elizabeth C. Ramirez is director of the Theatre and Fine Arts
Department at St. Philip's College in San Antonio, Texas, her
home town. Ramirez was graduated from St. Mary's University
and holds graduate degrees from UCLA and the University of
Texas, Austin. She is a former vice president of the Association for
Theatre in Higher Education, a former Fellow in Dramaturgy at the
American Repertory Theatre at Harvard, and founder and former
director of the Chicano Theatre Program at California State
University, Sacramento. Ramirez's publications include
*Footlights Across the Border: A History of Spanish-Language
Professional Theatre* as well as numerous articles and reviews;
another book, *Chicanas/Latinas in Performance on the
American Stage*, is scheduled to be published by Indiana
University Press.

ℰ Cultural Outreach through Music in Community-College Education

ELIZABETH C. RAMIREZ

S T. Philip's College, the only community college in the nation designated both as an Historically Black College and as an Hispanic Serving Institution, celebrated its centennial anniversary in 1998.

A Community College's History

Founded by Bishop James Steptoe Johnson of St. Philip's Episcopal Church of the West Texas Diocese, the school began as a sewing school for girls; it had fewer than twenty students when it opened in a house located in the area known today as historic La Villita in downtown San Antonio.

Initially aimed at educating and training recently emancipated slaves of the post-Civil War era, St. Philip's swiftly broadened its mission and became recognized in the local African-American community. Notable women helped shape this vital resource in the growing city. Alice G. Cowen, a missionary with the Episcopal Church, for example, directed instruction from 1898 to

1900; Mrs. Perry G. Walker succeeded her in 1900. Perhaps the most renowned woman in the College's history was Artemisia Bowden, a teacher and the daughter of a former slave; she assumed leadership in 1902. Under Bowden's fifty-two-year leadership, St. Philip's evolved from a parochial day school into an industrial school and, ultimately, a fully accredited two-year college with a diverse curriculum.

A significant change occurred in 1917, when the school moved into an area east of downtown, one rich in African-American traditions and linked historically to that part of the city's population. An affiliation with San Antonio College and the San Antonio Independent School District (SAISD) in 1942 ended St. Philip's era as a private institution. Another change occurred in 1945, when St. Philip's and San Antonio College formed the San Antonio Union Junior College District under the direction of a newly formed board of trustees. By 1982 the District had become known as the Alamo Community College District.

In 1970 the Southwest Campus, situated in the west side of the city in an area primarily populated by an ever-growing Hispanic community, opened as a district extension center; it was designated as a campus of St. Philip's College in 1987. Today the Southwest Campus is home to many of St. Philip's occupational/technical programs. Other expansion sites include the Northeast Learning Center, which opened in 1996, and the Learning and Leadership Development Center, which opened in 1997 in collaboration with the City of San Antonio. Thus the College's presence extends far beyond its immediate location, and activities on the main campus generally draw audiences from a broad spectrum of San Antonio's diverse population.

Today there are four colleges in the Alamo Community College District, each striving to provide educational opportunities for the citizens of Bexar, the principal county, and surrounding counties. These institutions contribute to the economic, academic, social, and cultural development of the region; each serves as a center of academic excellence and technological advancement. The goals of these institutions include providing educational opportunities and establishing links with business, industry, governmental agencies, and community groups as well as with public school systems, colleges and universities. Another goal is enhancing the quality of life through public presentations in the fine arts and making facilities available for community use or joint sponsorship of events (together with increasing cross-cultural understanding and appreciation). Through two distinct outreach programs in the arts—the San Antonio Symphony Residency Program and the Music Advancement Program—St. Philip's has distinguished itself in accomplishing these broader goals. Its programs serve as representative examples of how community-college education can provide cultural enrichment and outreach for the surrounding community.

Music Outreach Programs

The Symphony Residency Program (SRP), a week-long outreach initiative that includes two midday chamber-orchestra concerts, one evening full-orchestra concert, and rehearsals open to the public, has provided students, faculty, staff, and community members access to world-class talent; it has also helped fulfill the College's and District's desire of promoting cultural enrichment. SRP also features master classes for students studying music at the College as well as educational study guides for teachers who bring hundreds of grade-school, middle-school, and high-school students to concerts and pre-concert lectures presented by recognized guest conductors, soloists, and other distinguished initiative participants.

As director of St. Philip's Theatre and Fine Arts Department, I manage SRP as well as chair its planning committee. Our collaboration with the San Antonio Symphony includes a college committee comprised of the technical director/auditorium manager, a public-relations director, several reservation clerks and ushers, a house staff, and a reception coordinator in charge of the final concert. A distinguished community member is often selected to serve as Honorary SRP Chair. The Symphony staff I work with includes the conductor, an operations manager, a public-relations director, a stage manager, and an education director who helps bring students of all ages to the main campus.

Since its inception in 1988, SRP's budget has increased from $15,000 the first year to $36,750 in 1999. Because of the unusually elaborate Centennial Celebration of 1998, the figure rose to $40,000. Most of this money pays musicians as well as special guests and/or performers. Publicity and a reception are expenses incurred by the St. Philip's president, who also serves as the Program's host; in-kind services, facilities, and personnel are also paid by the College. SRP reaches out each year to about 1,000 public-school students and 1,000 faculty, staff, students, and community audience members. St. Philip's Watson Fine Arts Center Theatre seats some 600 persons.

Through collaboration with the San Antonio Symphony, St. Philip's makes an important contribution to a community already rich in cultural history and traditions. Enhancing appreciation of music and providing college music students opportunities to interact with professionals are among the advantages of the Residency Program; through it, too, St. Philip's also contributes to arts education in the public schools and has at times contributed when the San Antonio Symphony was struggling to survive.

Besides SRP, St. Philip's also offers the Music Advancement Program (MAP). For the past five years the College, the San Antonio Symphony, and the San Antonio Independent School District (SAISD) have joined together as partners in this special music program. The MAP is an enriched music-education program for highly gifted and talented SAISD middle-school band and orchestra students interested in music development. The program targets economically disadvantaged minority students and provides them with an opportunity to receive concentrated, individualized music instruction and training from professionals in the field.

MAP instruction is offered at the College on Saturdays from September through May. Each year it provides full scholarships for sixth-, seventh-, and eighth-grade participants who receive private lessons, perform in ensembles, and take part in music workshops taught by College faculty, San Antonio Symphony musicians, and local professionals. MAP also seeks to foster discipline and encourage an appreciation of and participation in the performing arts for some of the city's gifted and talented youth, students who otherwise could not afford specialized music education and training. MAP is the only program of its magnitude and scope offered in the San Antonio area.

Since its inception MAP has served over 250 students. Participation is competitive; the selection process includes auditions and interviews. The program requires total commitment from both its participants and their parents or guardians. Designed originally to accommodate 40-50 students, MAP enrolled 48 students in 1998-1999; the ethnic composition was 79% Hispanic, 10% African-American, 4% Caucasian, 2% Asian-American, and 5% "other." In 1999-2000 the number of students increased to 64, because the Steering Committee recommended increasing the number of sixth-graders in order to insure continuity and consistency for this group.

MAP serves as one of the College's educational community outreach programs. St. Philip's recognizes that the future of the Program's students, whether or not they become musicians, largely depends on encouraging their talents. Through the efforts of our Music Unit, St. Philip's provides an enormous contribution toward that end.

Community Outreach and Diversity

Both the Symphony Residency Program and the Music Advancement Program have helped bring important figures to San Antonio, individuals who represent the highest accomplishments of minority members within their professions. Isaiah Jackson and Michael Morgan, two internationally recognized African-American conductors, have participated in the Symphony Residency Program; Carlos Miguel Prieto, a conductor from Mexico, has visited St. Philip's twice. These and other artists have brought with them important works from the repertories of their ethnic groups and have thereby introduced local audiences to a wide range of traditions. Guest composer Robert Rodriguez, for example, has introduced a Mexican-American musical tradition that has interested students of every background in his pieces. MAP students have performed in numerous venues within San Antonio; they have been recognized for taking part in the Cinco de Mayo city-wide celebrations that commemorate the city's Mexican heritage.

§

During a century of service, St. Philip's College has grown from a small school to an accredited institution serving nearly 9,000 students. Today, as a comprehensive community college, it offers day, evening, and weekend classes. Since 1898, it has educated and empowered students of various backgrounds. The music-outreach programs described above are only two of its many offerings, all of which exemplify the College's commitment to service. Through outreach activities and an emphasis on student and program diversity—issues of equal if not, perhaps, of greater importance for American culture in the century ahead—St. Philip's has made itself "A Point of Pride in the Community," a slogan by which it has long been recognized in San Antonio.

Across the United States community colleges have made valuable contributions to music education, cultivating an understanding and appreciation of music in both students and the broader communities they serve. St. Philip's College, a dynamic and innovative institution of learning, is recognized as a leader in education because of its people and programs. St. Philips values its role in preparing its students, campus, and community to meet the challenges of a rapidly changing world; its programs in music provide examples of how it is facing that challenge. My department's commitment to cultural enrichment and diversity has provided the surrounding area with a solid foundation on which we can continue to build, develop, and meet the community's education needs throughout the twenty-first century—and beyond.

SOURCES

Interviews with Mark Barnes, Historian of St. Philip's College, 1998-2000.

St. Philip's College Centennial Celebration Commemorative Program, Centennial Commission, St. Philip's College (1998).

St. Philip's College Catalog: 1999-2000 (Volume 99, No. 3 [July 1999]).

St. Philip's College President's Report (Centennial Edition 1998).

Historical Records of the Music Advancement Program and Institutional Advancement, St. Philip's College. Information provided courtesy of the Department of Theatre and Fine Arts; Richard Teitz, Director, Institutional Advancement; and Sandra Mayo, Dean of Arts and Sciences and former director of the Theatre and Fine Arts department.

Elliott Schwartz is Robert K. Beckwith Professor of Music at Bowdoin College, where he has taught since 1964. Schwartz has served as president of the College Music Society, vice-president of the American Music Center, and national chair of the American Society of University Composers (now SCI). With Daniel Godfrey he wrote *Music Since 1945: Issues, Materials, Literature*; with Barney Childs, Schwartz edited the anthology *Contemporary Composers on Contemporary Music*. His compositions have been performed by the Indianapolis Symphony, the Cincinnati Symphony, and the Minnesota Orchestra and at Tanglewood, the Library of Congress, the Bath Festival (England), De Ijsbreker (Amsterdam, Holland), and "Leningrad Spring" (Russia).; they have been published by G. Schirmer/Associated Music, Carl Fischer, Theodore Presser, and MMB/Norruth; CD recordings of them can be heard on the CRI, New World, Capstone, Vienna Modern Masters, Innova, and GM labels.

❦ The American Century
Remembering the Past,
Contemplating the Future

ELLIOTT SCHWARTZ

As these words are written, the twentieth century is nearing its close. This has been a remarkable one hundred years—and not least in the area of contemporary musical composition, which (at least in the century's second half) has been dominated by the United States. In fact, with the new millennium at hand, we find that American pre-eminence on the world new-music scene will probably remain entrenched over the next few decades.

It doesn't necessarily follow from this assertion that the United States is producing the most daring, exciting, or innovative concert music on the planet. Some might want to award that honor to Britain, the Netherlands, the Scandinavian countries, or Japan. Significantly, however, each of these particular musical cultures has embraced "American" values and correspondingly downplayed the traditional values of the central European (Austro-German or Franco-Russian) mainstream.

Two questions need to be addressed: how did the United States arrive at this position of prominence and what are the special characteristics of twentieth-century American music that have made such a strong impact internationally?

§

Of those two questions, the first may be easier to answer. The United States has risen to musical dominance on the world stage:

1.   by virtue of its unique geographical position, poised between Europe and Asia, and with increasingly large numbers of citizens who could trace their roots to Africa and Asia, creating a uniquely polyglot culture—an intermingling of many different rituals, perceptions of beauty, notions of time and continuity, and views regarding the function of art.
2.   by the great aesthetic (as well as physical) distance from the European art-music tradition. A century ago American isolation from the European mainstream was an accepted fact and assumed to be regrettable. Over the ensuing decades, however, that "isolation" was converted into a virtue, largely thanks to such innovative American iconoclasts as Charles Ives, John Cage, Henry Cowell, Harry Partch, and Conlon Nancarrow.
3.   by accident (!), responding to the political fortunes of Europe during the 1930s and 1940s, when many of Europe's most formidable composers, escaping the horrors of Nazi rule, immigrated to the United States. Béla Bartók, Igor Stravinsky, Darius Milhaud, and Arnold Schoenberg are but a few of the distinguished figures who spent the latter parts of their careers on the American side of the Atlantic. Note, however, that this particular wave of migration was merely one chapter in a continuing saga of European-American musical interaction during the twentieth century. Other chapters have included the phenomenon of Aaron Copland and other young American composers travelling to study with Nadia Boulanger in the years after World War I and the profound influence of the "New York School"—Cage, Morton Feldman, and Earle Brown—upon Europeans during the 1950s. As a result, American musical "isolation"—at first a handicap on the world scene, then perceived as an advantage—is now only a memory.

Answers to the second of our questions—defining musical qualities that are peculiarly "American"—may be less immediately obvious. From an early twenty-first century perspective, the American musical picture defies simple categorization. It is pluralistic, unsystematic, and lacks a single geographic center. Although a foreign visitor might assume New York City to be the centralized, dominant force (on the model of London or Paris), America's music life is surprisingly decentralized, with activity on both coasts as well as the Midwest and with a refreshing balance between large cities and smaller college/university communities. Los Angeles rivals New York as a media center; internationally renowned electroacoustic music studios are found across the nation, from Stanford University on one coast to MIT on the other. And, contrary to stereotype, the Midwest is surprisingly unprovincial. During Leonard Slatkins's tenure as music director, St. Louis had the nation's most "contemporary-minded" symphony orchestra, at least in terms of adventurous programming; the Twin Cities area of Minnesota has emerged as America's outstanding model of civic and community involvement in the creation of new music; important festivals take place in such unlikely places as Bowling Green, Ohio, and Iowa City.

Similarly, there is no single American stylistic center. The aesthetic range is multi-faceted and diffuse. And while many American composers share common concerns—including a history of involvement with electronic technology, interest in notational controls over performance issues, the use of pre-compositional processes, and continuing fascination with performance rituals (whether European or non-Western, acoustic or electronic, vernacular or "art"-derived)—they deal with these concerns in remarkably individual ways. The American new-music community, then, is notably open to stylistic diversity, tends to distrust dogma, and, on the whole, regards eclecticism as a virtue. To paraphrase a famous comment by Virgil Thomson: to compose American music, you simply need to be an American; then create any sort of music you want to.

§

Even so, a number of stylistic similarities begin to emerge from this array of individual approaches. In fact, one can discern a general pattern (or a quilt of related patterns). To begin with, many American composers have received their "inspiration" from models other than those prevalent in Europe. For example, the impact of Pierre Boulez, Iannis Xenakis, Olivier Messiaen, and Karlheinz Stockhausen upon the development of American composers pales in comparison with that of Copland, Cage, Ives, Elliott Carter, and Milton Babbitt. Schoenberg, Berg, and Webern have certainly been important influences, but often after having been first "filtered" through the personae of Babbitt, George Perle, and Donald Martino. In a similar vein, many Americans first came to grips with Stravinsky via Copland, Walter Piston, and Irving Fine. More often than we might imagine, our "primary sources" have been other Americans.

Issues of "continuity" and "focus" have been of special interest to many American composers. Quite a few have made a virtue of discontinuity: creating designs that focus upon violent contrast rather than repetition or a succession of discrete moments (slide-show imagery) rather than organic developmental growth. In this regard, it might be instructive to study Ives's *The Unanswered Question* (1906) and to compare its multiple exposures and overlapping levels with similar textural overlays in Cage's *Aria with Fontana Mix* (1960). Cage carries discontinuity even further than Ives, of course, since each of his two levels (solo singer and electronic tape) is itself a study in quick cuts, sudden changes, and violent juxtapositions.

In addition, both Ives and Cage are concerned with multi-directional focus (or, one might argue, lack of focus). *Aria with Fontana Mix* arrives at this through the juxtaposition of live performer and loudspeaker, and the three levels of multiple-exposure in *The Unanswered Question* reach the listener from widely separated performance spaces. From a totally different perspective, one might wish to examine the string quartets of Elliott Carter. Note that Carter's apparent rejection of discontinuity—replaced by its antithesis: a flexible, fluid super-continuity of narrative flow—is nonetheless often allied with an Ivesian use of multi-directional, antiphonal focus.

These are not isolated examples. On the contrary, many American composers are similarly concerned with issues of musical placement in space. The "space" may be physical, conceptual, or theatrical; the individual composer's fascination with "space" may stem from a concern with narrative flow, or acoustic directionality, or mystic ritual. But the issue of "space" has motivated American composers from Ives, Cage, and Carter to Pauline Oliveros, Henry Brant, and creators of electroacoustic "loudspeaker music."

Note, too, the American tendency to experiment with objects as well as ideas—to "tinker" on a grand scale—that has resulted in a rich legacy of instrument building (or re-thinking). Considering keyboard instruments alone, we have Ives's music for quarter-tone piano, the inner-string piano sonorities of Cowell, the prepared piano of Cage, Conlon Nancarrow's work for player-piano rolls, string bows applied to mallet percussion, George Crumb's use of chisels and soda bottles on piano strings, and the extended marimbas of Harry

Partch that divide the octave into 43 tones. Similarly, many American composers have extended the expressive and timbral ranges of a wide variety of orchestral instruments, often borrowing their techniques from the world of jazz. (Jazz phrases or the names of legendary players can be found as cues on written scores; thus Barney Childs writes on a string bass part "Slam Stewart").

Retaining vestiges of 1950s-1960s postwar avant-gardism, quite a few American composers make use in their work of chance operations, controlled improvisation (often involving graphic notation), a re-thinking of intonation, and aspects of ritual theater. These directions reflect a relatively anti-European stance—not surprising, given the degree to which Eastern influences (musical, religious and philosophical) have replaced many traditional Western models. There is also a uniquely American (as opposed to European) tradition supporting such activity—one that extends back to the pioneering work of Cage, Cowell, Partch, and Lou Harrison, and that was later exemplified in the music of Oliveros, Robert Ashley, Feldman, and Brown. In addition, one can sense in many quarters a desire to separate "complexity" from "difficulty"—to create rich musical textures, paradoxically, by using the simplest means possible. In such music—Oliveros's *Sonic Meditations* (1974) or Cage's *Apartment House 1776* (1976), for example—the "complex" fabrics result from composers' interest in sound-mass, states of density, or attention focus, rather than the rigorous, interrelated pitch-rhythm networks that characterize the work of Babbitt and Carter.

It could be argued, in fact, that American composition—of any historical period and within any stylistic context—has generally tended to be "simpler" in means and/or surface effect than the European mainstream of its time. (Many factors—political, religious, economic, sociological—may account for this phenonemon.) If one accepts the argument's premises, then one hears the music of William Billings, Anthony Philip Heinrich, and Edward MacDowell—or of Babbitt and Cage, for that matter—in an entirely new context. The stylistic changes that appear after their residence in the New World also mark the music of such major European figures as Schoenberg, Stravinsky, Bartók, Paul Hindemith, Ernest Bloch, and even Antonin Dvořák (!) and take on fresh meaning.

Minimalist (or "Process" or "Trance") music offers another prespective on the issue of simplicity. Inspired by a wide array of musical models—from Pérotin and Machaut to African drumming, contemporary rock, and electronic tape loops—minimalism became an important stylistic direction through the work of Americans Philip Glass, Steve Reich, Terry Riley, and John Adams. In such works as Riley's seminal *In C* (1964), Reich's *Different Trains* (1989), Glass's *Einstein on the Beach* (1976), and Adams's *Nixon in China* (1975), repetitive figurations—changing gradually over lengthy time spans—are wedded with surprisingly familiar long-range forms and "mainstream" harmonic gestures.

Note, too, those composers who, while not necessarily "minimalist," are remarkably single-minded. They focus upon certain areas of the musical fabric with admirable absorption, a stubborn "maverick" quality that has characterized many Americans from Ives onwards. In such works as his *Lucy and the Count* (1981), a re-telling of the Dracula story for string quintet, Jon Deak has ingeniously made his instruments "speak"—and in the context of wordless (or are they?) quasi-abstract narrative dramas. Tom Johnson, an American now living in France, has fashioned a unique style combining visual theater, a rigorous working-out of "process," and a genial, personal approach to music as game-playing. A number of Johnson's works have been recorded, including *Rational Melodies* (1982) and *Nine Bells* (1982), the latter requiring the performer to walk in prescribed patterns while striking bells suspended from the ceiling. Henry Brant, now approaching ninety years of age, has composed music of incredible energy and sonic brilliance that explores the infinitely varied uses of multiple (and simultaneous) performance spaces—a lifelong homage to Ives's *Unanswered Question*—as the touchstone of his musical inspiration.

As I have already suggested, the American musical scene is characterized by eclecticism. Individual compositions may also be eclectic, insofar as a broad range of stylistic influences—including traditional, tonal ones—affect the course of an individual work or passage. Not everyone finds merit in this approach; one music critic has referred to it in these terms: "we are treated to the composer as disk jockey. One discovers [the composer's] personality not in the music he writes, but in his tastes for the styles of others." On the other hand, a growing legion of listeners would argue that the most exciting American music being composed today—including works by William Bolcom, David Del Tredici, George Rochberg, and John Corigliano—falls into this broad "eclectic" category. For example, Bolcom's Second Violin Sonata (1985) interweaves the diverse idioms of ragtime, jazz-violin playing, and Palm Court style with that of taut, brittle "new music" techniques; Del Tredici's *Final Alice* (1981), one of the composer's many works based upon the Lewis Carroll "Alice" books, combines discordant, atonal passages, and

Ivesian multiple-tempi and eerie quasi-Theremin timbres with broad diatonic tunes and glowing orchestration reminiscent of Richard Strauss.

§

Any or all of the factors noted above—eclectic style juxtapositions, issues of textural density, degrees of pitch and/or rhythmic control, a fascination with alternative performing spaces and performance rituals, and minimalist concern for repetition and subtle change—have stimulated American composers to move in a uniquely electronic direction. Perhaps this results from a subconscious realization that the widespread post-1950 proliferation of tape recordings, long-playing records, and amplification systems has affected profound changes in our musical perception. To note but a few pioneering examples: the use of amplified heart beats in *Valentine* by Oliveros; Lucier's *Music for Solo Performer* (1982), with its electronic feedback of alpha-state brain waves; and the exploration of the performance-space as a unique, living "instrument" in Lucier's *I am Sitting in a Room* (1990).

Many works of the 1980s and 1990s have been especially provocative in their expanded concepts of "electronic performance." Laurie Anderson's *O Superman* (1981) can be heard on one level as a taut, minimalist alternation of two triads against a hypnotically repeating ground, but it also offers a virtuosic display of electronic illusions created by Vocoder, Casio, looping samples, multiple tracking, and the like. Anderson's text is also directly related to the pervasive sense of electronic ritual and illusion (she calls this "out-of-body experience") in everyday life; in this instance, an ominous foretelling of nuclear destruction is announced calmly over an automated telephone answering device—an ambiguity of reality and recording, past and future. A different kind of illusion is achieved by Charles Dodge in his *Any Resemblance Is Purely Coincidental* (1980) for piano and tape. The electronic part was digitally synthesized from a 1907 recording of Enrico Caruso singing "Vesti la Giubba." Hisses and scratches—and the orchestra—were removed by Dodge, who created entirely new melodic lines and dense choral passages with Caruso's voice. The piano soloist—whose part varies from a parody of the original Leoncavallo to angular, post-Webernian flurries—has therefore also been placed in the role of accompanist for an invisible singer who never appears on-stage (and who died many decades ago).

Finally, it is important to stress that many American composers are turning (or returning) to a strongly ethnic basis for their creative work. Composers such as T. J. Anderson, Alvin Singleton, Olly Wilson, and Carmen Moore have explored African and African-American artistic traditions and programmatic subject matter. These sources have often been combined with European ones, in a characteristically eclectic-American mix. Anthony Davis's opera *X: The Life and Times of Malcolm X* (1986) draws upon such diverse musical influences as Italian opera, African ritual, American popular music, minimalism, and the European postwar *avant-garde.*

Women composers are also increasing in numbers and in recognition; some of them have been motivated to identify with their sisters within organizations dedicated to the recording, publication, and promotion of women's music, others preferring to stand alone as creative figures in a (supposedly) sex-blind marketplace. In either case, there is no denying the importance of Joan Tower, Ellen Zwilich, Libby Larsen, Augusta Reed Thomas, or Thea Musgrave on the American musical scene. Surprisingly—or perhaps not so surprisingly—a number of women have excelled in the supposedly male domains of electronic music: consider Oliveros, Anderson, Jean Eichelberger Ivey, and Priscilla McLean, to name but a few.

§

Having reached this point in compiling a virtual laundry list of stylistic factors that characterize late twentieth-century American art music, can we hazard a few predictions about the American scene in the twenty-first? Perhaps if we let the immediate past and present serve as a rough guide for the future, I shall propose the following educated guesses:

1.   New compositions will be linked to emerging developments in technology, especially the technology that will be available in middle-class home "entertainment centers." Such music will be heard through the sound systems of sophisticated home computers; some works may ask the audience (at home in front of their terminals) to participate interactively in a work's performance.

2.   Paradoxically, there will also be a body of music involving no electronics at all: more accessible pieces, technically easy to play and most likely improvisatory. Designed for live performance by relatively untrained amateurs using acoustic instruments (perhaps even home-

made ones), such works will offer a significant "response" to overly virtuosic, highly technological art.

3. The blurring of distinctions among musical categories and styles (known to preceding generations as classical, jazz, folk, ethnic, and the like) will continue to accelerate. This process of stylistic "coming together" will take place with very strong encouragement from two distinctly different musical constituencies: (a) composers, and (b) recordings producers.

4. The changing demographic profile of the United States will see a corresponding increase in the impact of non-European cultures (especially those of Asia and Latin America) upon the traditional Western European base of art music, primarily in areas of texture, rhythm, pitch/intonation systems, and instrumentation.

5. The changes noted above will gradually influence the teaching of music (both methodology and content) at all educational levels from pre-school to university. Composition teaching, for example, will focus less on pitch manipulation within a tempered/twelve-tone octave and more on rhythmic patterning, timbre, and the creation of complex textures. Eclecticism (rather than stylistic consistency) and formal discontinuity (rather than organic development) will be qualities admired and emulated by younger composers. Students will examine uniquely twentieth-century approaches to musical form and "grammar" and will focus their attention on such figures as Jean Sibelius, Carl Nielsen, Stockhausen, Michael Tippett, Babbitt, Carter, and Boulez. Similarly, the theory curriculum will include style modulation (the twenty-first century equivalent of tonal modulation), with Ives, Gustav Mahler, Alban Berg, Peter Maxwell Davies, Alfred Schnittke, Francis Poulenc, William Walton, Benjamin Britten, Bolcom, and Rochberg as textbook models.

§

Enough crystal-ball-gazing, at least for the moment. The immediate present—American music at the start of a new century—is so fascinating that we don't really need to look into the future. We can only hope that composers of the United States maintain, and expand upon, the many strengths of their tradition: the brash, adventurous quality of American culture, its multiple ethnic and geographic traditions, its eclecticism, its expansive love affair with technology, its blurring of distinctions (whether stylistic, sociological or economic), and its limitless energy.

After a career as a college teacher and administrator, **Patricia A. Shifferd**, project director of Continental Harmony, joined the staff of the American Composers Forum. Born in Illinois, Shifferd was trained in sociology and anthropology; she received her doctoral degree from the University of Wisconsin, Madison, and her research and teaching interests have centered on community development, the role of the arts in society, sense of place, and the social aspects of environmental affairs. During her academic career she directed the Arts & Letters Series at Northland College, Ashland, Wisconsin, where she worked with performance and outreach programs; she also served as interim Dean of Academic Affairs. Her musical activities include singing in the Minnesota Chorale and work on behalf of a number of community groups.

❦ Continental Harmony
A Community-based Celebration of the American Millennial Year

PATRICIA A. SHIFFERD

Introduction

Continental Harmony (CH) is a millennium initiative of the American Composers Forum in partnership with the National Endowment for the Arts (NEA). One of only seven national millennium projects, CH is a new music program, consisting of fifty-eight community-based commissions and residencies, at least one in each state. The guiding principle has been to provide assistance and encouragement to local groups so each one could define a meaningful theme and way for its community to celebrate the millennium year with music. In addition, each composition has been written for local musical forces. This project is unique in its scope and in its "grass-roots" organizational structure. Forum staff-members serve as brokers, facilitators, and occasionally coaches in bringing the participating communities together with composers for their artistic partnership. CH is based on the organization's belief that local groups in small towns and urban neighborhoods have both the aesthetic judgment and organizational ability to carry out such a partnership. We have not been disappointed.

Butler County Arts Council

Presents

the World Premiere Performances of

"Heartland"

A Choral and Instrumental Tribute to Our Rural Heritage

by: Deborah Fischer Teason

Butler County Community Choir

with: Butler Co. Children's Choir • Carol Fuxa, Piano

The Czech Button Accordion Ensemble • The American Czech Brass Band

David C. Neely, Violin • The Ruth Nichols' Children's Art Project.

Conducted by: Keith Byrkit

May 5 & 6, 2000

St. Luke's United Methodist Church

David City, Nebraska

NATIONAL
ENDOWMENT
FOR THE
ARTS

A sample Continental Harmony program

Patricia A. Shifferd

In his provocative book *A Snake's Tail Full of Ants: Art, Ecology, and Consciousness*, British writer and artist John Lane proposes that the place of art in Western society needs to undergo a fundamental transformation. Lane's thesis is that in the modern age art has become disconnected from society, that "Art (produced by Artists) exists solely for its own sake ... and that it must be assessed in the manner we call 'aesthetic'."[1] While this has unquestionably resulted in the creation of masterful works, Lane argues, a tragic consequence has been neglect of the imagination and creative potential of ordinary people, with negative effects both on individuals and cultures.[2]

However, recognition of the responsibilities of the arts toward the broader civic culture is becoming more widespread. For example, Americans for the Arts and the Institute for Community Development and the Arts recently launched a major initiative, "Animating Democracy: Strengthening the Role of the Arts in Civic Dialogue."[3] Similarly, in the foreword to the new edition of his book on the community-arts movement, William Cleveland notes: "What started out seeming like a fairly contained universe has mushroomed into an ubiquitous presence in grant applications, community cultural plans, public agency initiatives, and thousands of new programs."[4]

Forerunners of Continental Harmony
at the American Composers Forum

While "arts-based civic dialogue" is seen by some as just emerging in music,[5] in fact the American Composers Forum has been contributing to this movement for some time. At present, the Forum is the largest composer-service organization in the country. Founded in 1975 by Libby Larsen and Stephen Paulus as the Minnesota Composers Forum, the organization adopted its current name and mission in 1995. The new name was a response to the fact that membership had grown to be nation-wide. The new mission, "to link communities with composers and performers, encouraging the making, playing, and enjoyment of new music," expresses the goal of reconnecting composers and their work with fabric of American culture. The staff of the organization believe that the results will be a widening of the audience for new music, more work for composers, and a general enrichment of our culture.

There are many ways to "link" music to community. Several Forum programs, both at the national level and in the ten Forum chapters,[6] help local groups find composers to write music that will be meaningful to them—for their community festivals and worship, for schools, civic groups, senior citizens. Often this means including residents in the creative process. The point is not that this form of art-making will or should replace that done in elite cultural organizations or by artists expressing their own inner voices. However, in the case of music composition, these venues are not sufficient to create a widening acceptance of new works and, hence, to expand opportunities for the large number of classically-trained composers who are at work in our society. This is especially true in the current funding climate— the decline in fellowships for individual artists and the increasing concern that the arts be able to demonstrate, not just assert, their value. While all may regret these developments, it is nevertheless the way things are at the turn of the new millennium.

Accordingly, bringing the work of composers into the service of community—defined as widely as possible—has been a central goal of American Composers Forum Executive Director Linda L. Hoeschler from the beginning of her tenure in 1991 as the organization's chief. For example, in the Upper Midwest and the Southeast, the Forum's Faith Partners program creates consortia of churches from diverse traditions. A consortium selects a composer to write music for each congregation and for that consortium's joint celebrations. The program's success has been especially great in rural areas, and the participating composers have found the experience to have a marked positive effect on their careers.

The direct forerunners of Continental Harmony include a 1992 stage production at Bemidji State University that brought together diverse portions of this rural Minnesota community to take part in the creative process and a 1998 pilot Minnesota Rural Commissioning Project.

In preparation for the latter effort, Forum staff contacted community-arts councils, festival organizers, and other presenters throughout the state to gauge the interest in making a new composition part of their community activities. This project laid down the basic structure that guides CH: community organizers themselves identify the occasion and theme for the projected work; a composer is selected from applicants by a community committee; that composer participates in residency activities in the area; and local musicians perform the completed work. In addition, although the Forum pays each artist's fee and travel, the host community makes a substantial cash or in-kind contribution to the project by hosting the composer and by mounting the performance. An artistic and financial partnership is thus established between the Forum and the site. Overall, this structure results in a higher level of community commitment to the success of the project than is sometimes the case with artist-driven projects.

The Rural Commissioning Project brought composers into three Minnesota communities. Carleton Macy wrote a work, *Grand Water Music*, featuring multiple local ensembles, for the dedication of the new Grand Marais Art Colony. For the annual Judy Garland Festival in Grand Rapids, Linda Tutas Haugen composed a song cycle based on poems written by Garland herself. And Larry Siegel wrote a choral work, *This Beautiful Valley*, for the HeritageFest in New Ulm.

The outcome of all this work was generally quite positive—two of the composers were later chosen to participate in other prestigious residency programs: the Meet-the-Composer's Rural Residency, and the Artists & Communities Millennium project administered by Mid-Atlantic Arts. One also became a CH composer. And Forum staff were able to learn from the occasional potholes these three projects hit how to create a smoother journey for composers and communities participating in CH. For example, Forum staff early on provided the organizers in the fifty-eight communities, many of which had never commissioned music before, with a guidebook outlining what to expect from the process from beginning to end.

The Development of Continental Harmony

With the approach of the year 2000, staff at the National Endowment for the Arts approached the Forum for ideas for suitable millennium projects. The concepts embodied in Forum programming—bringing composers into rural communities or other areas less likely to have access to new music— were attractive to the agency in light of the controversies with which they had recently been faced. In addition, the idea that each state should have a project seemed admirably appropriate for a national musical celebration of the millennium year. Thus from the beginning, Continental Harmony was directed especially toward smaller communities and urban neighborhoods.

At the same time, some members of the composer community and some staff-members at the agency were understandably concerned about what kind of outcomes such a project would produce, since the key aesthetic judgments were to be lodged with community people. The idea that communities would compete only with others from their own states, rather than on a national basis, seemed unfair or inappropriate to some. Another concern was whether the American Composers Forum would have the organizational strength to carry out such a big project. While in retrospect these concerns proved groundless, early 1998 was a time of both great expectation and some anxiety for staff both at NEA and the Forum. Would communities be interested?

Would they develop meaningful projects? Would composers be willing to write for the occasions and performers in rural areas and small towns? Would enough funds be found to fund the project so that all fifty states could be included?

Acting partly on faith and partly from a firm commitment to a community-based model of art-making, the Forum eventually convinced the NEA (and subsequently other major funders—the John S. & James L. Knight Foundation, the Rockefeller Foundation, the Land O'Lakes Foundation, the William & Flora Hewlett Foundation, and the Ecolab Foundation, along with the Illinois Arts Council, the Minnesota State Arts Board, and the Ohio Arts Council) that the concept would produce a notable celebration of the millennium.

As many musicians will recognize, the name of the project derives from a famous book of tunes: *The Continental Harmony* (1794), the sixth and final published work of William Billings (1746-1800). Billings was a colorful and independent figure, one who injected humor as well as excitement into his work. A self-taught artist who worked as a tanner before switching to music, Billings is now recognized as this country's first major composer and arguably its first professional musician. His influence was far-reaching: his war song "Chester," sung in scores of army camps, became a powerful propaganda weapon in the war of independence; it has been described as the "Marseillaise" of the American Revolution.[7]

Billings's attitude towards his art was characteristically American:

Perhaps it may be expected by some, that I should say something concerning Rules for Compositions; to these I answer that Nature is the best Dictator, for all the hard, dry studied rules that ever was prescribed, will not enable any person to form an air.... For my own part, as I don't think myself confin'd to any Rules for Composition laid down by any that went before me, neither should I think (were I to pretend to lay down the Rules) that anyone who came after me were in any way obligated to adhere to them.... I think it is best for every Composer to be his own Carver.[8]

The initial NEA partnership award was announced in St. Paul, Minnesota, in early June 1998 by newly appointed Endowment Chair, Bill Ivey.

The initial time-line called for the host communities to be selected before the end of Fall 1998, although in fact this proved impossible. The original schedule put great pressure on CH staff (I started work with the project in June 1998, and Robert Peskin arrived as Associate Director in

August) to set guidelines and produce and distribute a community invitation. Project staff wished to cast as wide a net as possible over all kinds of community organizations throughout the country. While preliminary database research had begun in early June, there was no nationwide listing of the kinds of groups that might be interested in the project. Therefore, primary reliance was placed on state arts boards and commissions to provide addresses of potential community partners; these lists were supplemented by as many sources as could be accessed, given the time constraints. By Labor Day 1998 some 12,000 brochures, printed in an attractive four-color format, had been mailed; the brochures requested that applications be postmarked by 2 November 1998. This schedule did not really allow enough time for communities to work on their applications, and CH staff extended the deadline upon request up to nearly Thanksgiving.

One issue, of course, was not simply the number of applications received, but whether organizations in every state would express interest. As the days of November passed, a frequent comment was, "Have we got anything from such-and-such a state yet?" In the end, state arts board staffs in two states were helpful in recruiting suitable community partners.

The selection of the host communities was done by a panel of five[9] that met in St. Paul in mid-December 1998. The panelists discussed and scored the 175 applications, identifying one community in each state that should be offered the project. In addition, the high quality of the applicant pool led the panel to identify thirty-two additional proposals that were judged excellent. The panel's recommendation was that these might also be included in the final project, should sufficient funds be found. Eventually, funds for eight additional projects were obtained, either through Forum efforts or the initiative of site organizers themselves. Thus, by the end of Summer 1999, the total number of projects had risen to fifty-eight.

By mid-January 1999 site organizers in the original fifty communities had, with assistance from CH staff members, developed a "job description" for each composer. These included desired themes, performers, occasions, and enough description of each community to evoke whatever aspects of landscape, history, or culture the hosts wished to communicate to interested composers. At the same time, CH staff developed a database of composers, using not only the Forum's membership, but also those of many other composer organizations. In addition, ASCAP and BMI made information about the project available to their composer-members. Thus, in February 1999 a brochure briefly describing the first fifty projects was mailed to approximately 5,000 composers, and a web site with extended descriptions was mounted. In addition to the expected scores and tapes, *vitae*, etc., applicants were asked to state how they would approach each project and explain their experiences with community-engagement efforts. Composers were asked to apply to no more than three project sites.

As the 1 April composer application deadline approached, staff began to be more and more curious about how many composers would apply, since there was no known precedent for a commissioning project of this scope. One staff member bet a skeptical colleague that at least 150 composers would complete applications. In fact, the skeptic lost that bet more than twice over! By 15 April, Forum offices were deluged with over 850 application packets from 350 composers. There was no place in the organization's small office suite to put the applications; thus another room in the building became a temporary "FedEx"-style sorting room. The applications were logged in, then boxed and shipped to the host communities.

Perhaps not surprisingly, the projects featuring orchestras—especially professional orchestras—received the greatest interest from composers. But each of the fifty projects received at least a few applications from which to select its artist. While CH staff provided the host site committees with extensive guidelines for the selection process, the final decision how to proceed was left to each community. In some places, all members of a committee reviewed all the applications. Some used a blind format (the identity of the applicants was not known to reviewers) until the finalists had been selected. In others, the music director or lead organizers made the first cut, while the full committee ranked the finalists. Site organizers were strongly encouraged to interview their finalists—in person, if possible. However, for many the travel expenses entailed were simply too great, so that telephone interviews sufficed. In all, the process was carried out with an enviable degree of professionalism, whether by arts organizations with paid staff or by those composed entirely of community volunteers.[10]

As is apparent from the list of projects appended to the end of this article, the Continental Harmony projects capture collectively much of the diversity of American music and culture at the end of the twentieth century. A suitable metaphor might be that the fifty-eight projects together create a musical quilt or tapestry representative of many, if not most, of the members of our society. There is orchestral music and choral music, chamber music and ethnic music, dance and musical theater, folk-inspired music and art music. The themes of the works fall into five general categories. The largest number are works that evoke a "sense of place"—of the landscape and its people. The other themes emphasize ethnic/cultural diversity, concern for family, women and youth, patriotism or broad social values, and music for its own sake.

Throughout Summer and Fall 1999, CH staff, community hosts, and composers launched the projects: letters of agreement were completed, residency activities began, negotiations as to exact instrumentation were carried out, staff visited sites, and the public-relations effort became much more active. And, of course, the process of composition got underway. In some cases, composers began work in their communities almost immediately—doing research, meeting community people and performers, searching for texts or engaging local people in writing texts, and so on. Composers worked with school kids, spoke to civic clubs, and interviewed senior citizens. They attended local festivals, worked with local writers, and toured the countryside.

Each composer's fee includes the commission and up to four weeks of residency activities. The Forum pays this (plus a travel allowance for travel to the site) in three installments: the first upon completion of the agreement; the second upon delivery of the score; and the third upon the premiere. Each host site makes a substantial financial commitment as well. Each provides housing and local arrangements for its composer during residency, absorbs all the costs of performance(s), and keeps a documentary record, including recording(s) of performance(s). This partnership assures commitment from the site to the success of the project.

At the national level, Continental Harmony staff worked to make sure the project would be recognized. It is, of course, difficult to attract the media's attention to the arts; this has also been true of CH, but perhaps for different reasons. For one thing, while the project as a whole is national, each project is local. For another, CH is a rather unusual arts project in that it does not involve elite performing groups in major metropolitan areas. To overcome this, a significant amount of time and money has been devoted to publicity; a public-relations firm, Foley-Sackett of Minneapolis, was engaged to assist in giving project materials an attractive, consistent, and professional look, to develop media contacts and follow-up, and to advise host sites on press relations.[11] In addition, state and national office holders and arts and humanities councils have been kept informed of progress. While it is certainly not the case that CH has become a household word, public-relations efforts of all project participants have resulted in quite substantial coverage of project events.

The culmination of these efforts was a contract awarded to Twin Cities Public Television by the Knight Foundation to produce a television documentary (to air on PBS early in 2001) about the project. By highlighting the process of engagement between composer and local people, this program will give American audiences insight into the ways in which art can and does flourish at the community level. In addition to the TV special, PBS will also launch an interactive web site in mid-2000. The activities accessible on the site will not only provide a series of sound and site portraits of all fifty-eight projects; they will also allow visitors to experiment with music and its composition. The purpose is not only to catalog this particular project, but to challenge the creativity of all who come to the site.

In addition to public relations, the national CH staff also concentrated on establishing partnerships in support of the effort. Two of the most notable results have been the designation of the project as an associate partner of the White House Millennium Council and an agreement by the Library of Congress to serve as the official archive for all materials generated by CH composers and communities.

Another significant partnership was established with the Rockefeller Foundation to evaluate and document the project as it unfolds. Staff at the Forum and the Rockefeller Foundation agreed that the scope of Continental Harmony provides an unparalleled opportunity to document the impact of these music projects on the many communities involved. Accordingly, an extensive multi-dimensional observation plan was developed to track the projects' progress in establishing or reinforcing community coalitions, in extending the effects of music beyond the concert hall and, generally, in bringing art into the service of wider community concerns.

The first of a nearly year-long series of premieres took place on 27 February in Grand Forks, North Dakota. The purpose of the Grand Forks Master Chorale's commission was to contribute to community healing in the aftermath of the disastrous Red River of the North flood that devastated the region in 1997. Composer Steve Heitzeg, well-known for writing music on environmental and social justice themes, prepared a three-movement work, *What the River Says*, that vividly captured images of rivers, both literally and symbolically.

The first movement, "Ask Me," a setting of the poem by Will Stafford, evokes a river under ice, its currents only temporarily hidden, and associated images of stillness and waiting. The second movement, "Belonging," with text from the poem by Alla Renee Bozarth, creates a sense of poignancy and loss, as well as ultimate hope of connectedness. The opening words, "The small plot of ground on which you were born cannot be expected to stay forever the same," resonate deeply with the people in the audience—not only because of their losses from the flood, but also because of the changes that have occurred in the region's farm economy as people have found it necessary to leave the land settled by their kin. The final movement, "Red River, Remember Me," is cast in folk style, using words written by Heitzeg himself as he drove through the high plains of North Dakota during his residency. Beginning with "You flow through the Dakotas north through Grand Forks to Pembina and weave your way to Winnipeg to rest in Canada. Floods and droughts, regret—things we can't forget," the lyrics go on to evoke images of the plains, its people, and its culture. While it is hard to know to what degree a piece of music can heal a community hurt by natural disaster, certainly the reactions of audience members, revealed through community feedback, suggest that the work will contribute to the healing process.

The Impact of Continental Harmony

As a project, CH has been designed to put particular emphasis on the community aspect of the American Composers Forum's mission: "To link communities with composers and performers, encouraging the making, playing, and enjoyment of new music." Defining each desired millennium musical project (and associated residency) and selecting each composer: these actions have been in the hands of local persons, with the Forum serving chiefly as a broker, advisor, and coordinator. From the beginning, the goal has been to encourage the strengthening of community structures and networks that will persist past this particular celebration and that may provide the basis for future local cooperation—not only in the arts, but also on broader issues of community concern. In other words, the goal of CH has been nothing less than contributing to the strength of civil society in numerous locales. Another important goal has been reconnecting the composer and the process of music composition with communities.

While the full impact of this project will not be known for some time—perhaps for years—early reports from composers and communities suggest that the project's goals will be substantially realized. Composers have found the welcome they have received to be inspiring to them musically. One composer established such a strong connection with the people and the landscape she worked with that she felt the need to produce a work of a very special nature. She was also led to reflect on her own roots; this had an important impact on her artistic work overall. While there are disadvantages to composers in working in community-based projects (writing for amateurs is one; writing site-specific music is another), it seems likely that, when CH is done, participating composers will have found the projects to be artistically gratifying. In addition, follow-up commissions and residencies, the new contacts, and the publicity will advance the careers of many.

Host organizations have found that their participation in the project has attracted interest in their work throughout their communities and beyond. They have attracted new supporters and new sources of funds. They have discovered organizational strengths that cannot but be helpful in the future. A member of one group from a very small community commented that, as group members prepared its grant proposal, they realized, "Hey! Even if we don't win, we really could do something like this ourselves!" And many have established cooperative relationships with other community groups that may be useful in facing important issues that will inevitably emerge.

The dictionary provides a definition of "millennium" along these lines:

Mil-len-ni-um: 1a: the thousand years mentioned in Revelation during which holiness is to prevail.... b: a period of great happiness or human perfection, 2a: a period of 1000 years, b: a 1000th anniversary or its celebration.

In our secular, materialistic society, 1 January 2000 brought more concern about computer software than about where we are and where we ought to be heading—about the values and behaviors that will help us assure the future strength of our families, communities, economies, and environments. But some more searching reflection on past, present, and future is appropriate at this time. While we of the American Composers Forum are not so bold as to claim Continental Harmony will usher in the prevalence of holiness (definition 1a), or "a period of great happiness or human perfection" (definition 1b), we hope that people in Parkersburg, in Farmington, in Cotton, in Omak and in all the other CH towns and cities will have been encouraged to consider how their communities might be renewed at this pivotal moment.

It might be argued that the best hope for building a sustainable future lies in the strengths that already exist in local communities all across the country—in the Ruidosos, the David Cities, the Gadsdens, and the Fitchburgs. Many of these communities have a tradition of people helping one other; these people also have the imagination and organizational experience that can be put to use to withstand the corrosive effects of mass culture. They have vibrant cultural traditions that can provide visions for adapting to the future. Finally, their direct experience with the cycles of nature may provide them with a transcending perspective in moving toward a sustainable society.

But making communities in which economy, culture, and environment are mutually reinforcing will not be easy. People will have to work together to identify with and celebrate the places they call home and to be creative in seeking ways to implement their visions.

That is why the arts are so important. The arts are essential to community identity and unity. Music—its creation and performance—is especially well-suited to this task. Composing, although it can be viewed as a completely individual activity, demands performers and audiences to be fully realized. And making music is a social activity. Community festivals and ritual observances are almost always marked by music, leading to a reaffirmation of basic community beliefs. Through music, communities recreate their histories in celebratory ways, often using texts that evoke the languages, landscapes, and cultural traditions of their citizens. Music can also evoke places and peoples far away, creating a vivid understanding of and empathy for the recurrent problems of life experienced by our fellow humans around the globe. And participation in music-making can be enjoyable and profitable for those with little or no special training as well as for professional composers and performers.

In his book *Gaviotas: A Village to Reinvent the World*, Alan Weisman relates the following anecdote: An international development team was working in a remote Indian village in Bolivia. When the team was about ready to leave, they offered the people a gift in gratitude for their hospitality. The elders responded:

"We know what we want to do with the money. We need new musical instruments for our band."
"Maybe," replied the Bank team spokesman, "you didn't understand. What you need are improvements like electricity. Running water. Sewers. Telephone and telegraph."

But the Indians had understood perfectly. "In our village," the eldest explained, "everyone plays a musical instrument. On Sundays after mass, we all gather for a concert on the church patio. First we make music together. After that, we can talk about problems in our community and how to resolve them. But our instruments are old and falling apart. Without music, so will we."[12]

More than one observer has noted that Western civilization appears to be on the cusp of a fundamental transformation. If this is so, then, of course, the role of the arts will also of necessity be transformed. To return to John Lane:

> If any transformation is to succeed, we will need to reverse the premises of our present world-view.... We will have to ... revision a sense of enchantment, revision the visionary function, revision our lost access to the magical world of archetypal myth and symbol; revision the role of art as a planetary healer, seek an integrated vision of the world.... What might this "art" of the future be like?... It has occurred to me that whereas we now accept (and celebrate) the separation of the Arts from daily life, the new paradigm may well relate the aesthetic dimension to other fields of human endeavor ... the future is likely to accept that the deepest essence of every human is his or her creativity.[13]

Whether such a transformation is imminent, many artists will certainly welcome opportunities to bring their creative energies into close connection with the lives of people in all kinds of communities. To quote once more from *Gaviotas*:

> People who dare to build a utopia use the same materials available to anyone, but they find surprising ways to combine them. That's exactly what composers do with the twelve tones of the scale. Like you, they're dreamers. In a dream you aren't limited by what is assumed to be permissible or possible.[14]

NOTES

[1]John Lane, *A Snake's Tail Full of Ants: Art, Ecology, and Consciousness* (Totnes: Resurgance, 1996), 10.

[2]Ibid, 25-27.

[3]<http://www.artsusa.org/>

[4]William Cleveland, *Art in Other Places: Artists at Work in America's Community and Social Institutions* (Amherst, MA: Arts Extension Service Press, 2000), xvii.

[5]Executive Summary in Barbara Bacon et. al., *Animating Democracy: The Artistic Imagination as a Force in Civic Dialogue* (Washington, D.C.: Americans for the Arts, 1999), 12.

[6]The Forum has local chapters in Atlanta, Boston, Chicago, Los Angeles, Minneapolis-St. Paul, New York City, Philadelphia, San Francisco, southern Minnesota, and Washington, D.C.

[7]David Ewen, *American Composers: A Biographical Dictionary* (New York: G. P. Putnam's Sons, 1922), 68.

[8]Ibid, 68.

[9]Panel members included Stephanie Ancona, New England Foundation for the Arts, Boston; William Cleveland, Center for the Study of Art and Community, Minneapolis; David Dzubay, University of Indiana, Bloomington; Alberto Rafols, Regional Arts & Culture Council, Portland, OR; and Lynn Adams Wilkins, Mississippi Arts Commission, Jackson. Wayne Brown, Music and Opera, National Endowment for the Arts, was a most helpful observer.

[10]The same process was repeated for the eight sites that were later added. In the interests of time, for the last three of these Forum staff used an e-mail call to composers rather than a print call.

[11]For its efforts on behalf of Continental Harmony, Foley-Sackett received numerous awards and citations from public relations professional associations.

[12]Alan Weisman, *Gaviotas: A Village to Reinvent the World* (White River Junction, VT: Chelsea Green, 1998), 5-6.

[13]Lane, *A Snake's Tail Full of Ants*, 160-161.

[14]Weisman, *Gaviantas*, 8.

Consult <http://ch.composersforum.org/> for additional information about Continental Harmony events.

APPENDIX
Continental Harmony Premieres, 2000-2001
All dates are 2000 unless otherwise indicated.

MONTH	LOCATION	DATE(S)	TITLE COMPOSER PERFORMERS [PROJECT SPONSOR, OCCASION]
February	Grand Forks, ND	27 February	*What the River Says* Steve Heitzeg, St. Paul, MN Grand Forks Master Chorale [Folk-on-the-Red]
March	Ann Arbor, MI	11 March	*Lokananta* Gabriel Gould, Ann Arbor, MI Ann Arbor Symphony & University of Michigan Gamelan

	Omak, WA	26 March	*Landscape Changing: A
			   Symphony for Okanagon
			   County*
			Andrew Teirstein, New York, NY
			Okanagon Valley Orchestra &
			   Chorus, Dayton Edmonds, and
			   Paul Steuermann

	Concord, NC	30 March	*Building Bridges* Ronald Nelson, Minneapolis, MN Cabarrus Children's Choruses [The Arts Experience]

April	Parkersburg, WV	8-9 April	*The Unknown Region: Journey of
			   Faith*
			Kenton Coe, Johnson City, TN
			College, Youth, and Children's
			   Choirs
			[West Virginia University,
			   Parkersburg]

	Miami, FL	15 April	*Migrants Journal*
			Lukas Ligeti, New York, NY
			Furcan Caribe
			[South Florida Composers Alliance;
			   Historical Museum of Southern
			   Florida; Sub-Tropics Festival]

	Blytheville, AR	28, 30 April	*Song for the Delta*
			Steve Cooper, Rogers, AR
			Blytheville High School Band;
			   community and school choirs
			[Ritz Civic Center and Arts Council
			   of Mississippi County]

MONTH	LOCATION	DATE(s)	TITLE COMPOSER PERFORMERS [PROJECT SPONSOR, OCCASION]
May	David City, NE	6 May	*Heartland* Deborah Fischer Teason, Hamden, CT Butler County Community Choir, Children's Choir, brass band, and accordions; David Neely, violin [Butler County Arts Council]
	St. George, UT	11-12 May	*Desert—Spirit—Valley* George Arasimowicz, Winfield, IL Southwest Symphony
	Plymouth, NH	11-12, 14 May	*Voices of the Lakes* James E. Clemens, Downers Grove, IL Friends of the Arts Youth Choir [Friends of the Arts Regional Arts Council]
	Santa Cruz, CA	13 May	*Glossary* Henry Brant, Santa Barbara, CA New Music Works
	Freeport, IL	17 May	*Song of the Earth* Patrick Beckman, Freeport, IL Highland Civic Chorale and Freeport High School Choirs
	Cotton, MN	17 May	*Cotton Cantata* Tyler Kaiser, Duluth, MN Cotton School Band and Chorus; children playing home-made instruments [Cotton Community Education]
	Kailua-Kona, HI	20 May	*The Channel* Christopher Roberts, Hawi, HI Kona Chorus & Orchestra
	Oakland, CA	20-21 May	*The Navigator Tree* Jaron Lanier, Sausalito, CA Handbell Ensemble Sonos, gamelan, and taiko
	Sacramento, CA	20-21 May	*Pictures of Years: Nianhua* Han Yong, New York, NY Camellia Symphony

MONTH	LOCATION	DATE(s)	*TITLE* COMPOSER PERFORMERS [PROJECT SPONSOR, OCCASION]
May (cont.)	Juneau, AK	26 May	*Glacier Blue* Evan Solot, Philadelphia, PA Bruce Paulson's LA Big Band; Linda Rosenthal, violin [Juneau Jazz & Classics]

June	Arkansas City, KS	2 June	*Carl Sandburg's Prairie*
			 Eugene Friesen, Townshend, VT
			 The Paul Winter Consort, Prairie
			     Wind Dancers, PrairieFest
			     Chorus, and Winfield Regional
			     Symphony
			 [Cowley Community College;
			     PrairieFest]

	Culver City, CA	4 June	*Portraits in Jazz* Thomas Oboe Lee, Cambridge, MA American Jazz Philharmonic
	Farmington, ME Livermore Falls, ME	15-16 June	*A Hill in the Country: Maine Suite* Alexis Alrich, San Francisco, CA Franklin Co. Fiddlers, U-ME Farmington Chorus, School Choruses, CH Chorus/Orchestra [Foothills Arts]

	New Haven, CT	18 June	*Convergence: Some Parades for*
			     Charlie's Dad
			 Neely Bruce, Middletown, CT
			 various ensembles
			 [International Festival of Arts &
			     Ideas]

	Jackson, WY	23 June – 30 September	*Petticoat Rules—the Jackson Hole* *Revue* Mary Murfitt, Ancramdale, NY and Pam Phillips, Wilson, WY Performing Arts Co. of Jackson Hole
	St. Paul, MN	24-25 June	*Descendants of the Dragon* Zhang Ying, Minneapolis, MN CAAM Chinese Dance Theater
	Edmond, OK	30 June	*Showdown on Two Street* Samuel Magrill, Edmond, OK University of Central Oklahoma Opera, Millennium Orchestra [Edmond Historical Society]

MONTH	LOCATION	DATE(s)	TITLE COMPOSER PERFORMERS [PROJECT SPONSOR, OCCASION]

July	Alto, NM	1 July	*Keepers of the Land*
			Jerre Tanner, Kailua-Kona, HI
			Paul Ortega, Los Romanticos,
			    Mescalero and Hispanic
			    Dancers, Chorus, and Orchestra
			[Spencer Theater]

	McCall, ID	3 July	*Breath of the Mountains*
			Linda Tutas Haugen, Burnsville,
			    MN
			McCall Chamber Orchestra &
			    Chorus
			[McCall Music Society]

	Wintergreen, VA	3 July	*From Time to Time* Anthony Iannaccone, Ypsilanti, MI Richmond Symphony [Wintergreen Performing Arts; Virginia Center for Creative Arts]

	Grand Canyon, AZ	4 July	*Guardians of the Canyon*
			Brent Michael Davids, Minneapolis,
			    MN
			Claire Hoffman, Brent Michael
			    Davids, Havasupai Dancers, and
			    other players
			[Grand Canyon Music Festival]

	San Francisco, CA	4 July	*Freedom Dreams*
			Jennifer Higdon, Philadelphia, PA
			San Francisco Lesbian/Gay Freedom
			    Band
			[Yerba Buena Center for the Arts;
			    Ol' Fashioned 4th of July
			    Alternative Family Picnic]

	Breckenridge, CO	4 July	*Nature's Universal Throne*
			David Heckendorn, Kew Gardens,
			    NY
			National Repertory Orchestra
			[Summit County Arts Council;
			    Breckenridge Music Festival]

	Wilmington, DE	4 July	*Delaware Rhapsody* Robert Macht, Baltimore, MD Delaware Symphony

346

MONTH	LOCATION	DATE(s)	*TITLE* COMPOSER PERFORMERS [PROJECT SPONSOR, OCCASION]
July (cont.)	Carmel, IN	4 July	*Liberty for All* James Beckel, Indianapolis, IN Carmel & Indianapolis Symphonies [Simultaneous performances in two locales]
	Scottsville, KY	4 July	*Three Songs: The Song of the* *Redeemed, We're Singing* *Heaven's Song, Heaven's* *Jubilee* Depp Britt, Nashville, TN Shape Note Singing Convention [Allen County Scottsville Arts Council]
	Takoma Park, MD	4 July	*Hallelujah, In Praise of Light* Lisa DeSpain, New York, NY Liz Lerman Dance Exchange
	Fitchburg, MA	4 July	*Raging River, Rolling Stone* Barbara White, Princeton, NJ Thayer Symphony & Fitchburg High School Band [REACH Fitchburg]
	St. Joseph, MO	4 July	*I Am St. Joseph* John Bisharat, Los Angeles, CA St. Joseph Symphony & Chorus & Sweet Adelines [Allied Arts Council]
	St. Louis, MO	4 July	*Bushy Wushy Rag* Phillip Bimstein, Springdale, UT Equinox Chamber Players [Crossroads School, Fair St. Louis]
	Carrollton, OH	4 July	*Suite Carroll County* Mona Lyn Reese, San Jose, CA Carroll County Chorale [Carroll County Commission for the Advancement of the Arts]
	Gettysburg, PA	4 July	*South Mountain Echoes* Robert Maggio, Media, PA Adams County Bicentennial Band [Adams County Arts Council]

347

MONTH	LOCATION	DATE(s)	TITLE COMPOSER PERFORMERS [PROJECT SPONSOR, OCCASION]

July (cont.)	Newport, RI	4 July	*Testimonies*
			Steven Newby, Everett, WA
			Northeast Chamber Ensemble &
			    Community Baptist Church
			    Choir
			[Salve Regina University]

	Sioux Falls, SD	4 July	*Spiritscapes: A South Dakota*
			    Cantata
			Bruce Roter, Albany, NY
			Sioux Falls Master Singers & Sioux
			    Falls Municipal Band

	Osceola, WI	4 July	*River Spirit* Craig Naylor, Kalispell, MT ArtBarn Community Chorus [St. Croix ArtBarn]

	Syracuse, NY	9 July	*Dance Mix*
			Rob Smith, Houston, TX
			Society for New Music & Mallets
			    Ensemble of the Syracuse
			    Brigadiers

	Missoula, MT	15 July	*Walt Whitman's Dream* William McGaughlin, New York, NY [International Choral Festival]

September	N. Charleston, SC	2 September	*Hope of a People*
			Evelyn Simpson-Curenton,
			    Alexandria, VA
			Project L.O.V.E. Parent & Child
			    Choirs

	Portland, OR	8-9 September	*Wood, Water, Wind* (W^3) Kenny Endo, Honolulu, HI Portland Taiko and other percussion

	New Orleans, LA	14, 16 September	*Citizen Soldier*
			Frank Proto, Cincinnati, OH;
			    libretto by John Chenault
			Louisiana Philharmonic
			[in honor of the National D-Day
			    Museum]

	Houston, TX	29 September	*The Continuous Life* Eve Beglarian, New York, NY OrchestraX [Diverse Works]

MONTH	LOCATION	DATE(s)	TITLE COMPOSER PERFORMERS [PROJECT SPONSOR, OCCASION]
October	Johnson City, TN	20-21 October	*Appalachian Harmony* Daniel Kingman, Sacramento, CA East Tennessee Children's Choir; Carlos Bendfeldt, guitar; Edith Dowd, contralto; Jane MacMorran, fiddle [Johnson City Area Arts Council]
	Carson City, NV	21-22 October	*A Land of Sun and Sage* Jim Cockey, McCall, ID Carson City Symphony & Carson Chamber Singers
	Fort Dodge, IA	22 October	*Landscape of Dreams* Jonathan Chenette, Grinnell, IA Fort Dodge Symphony [Blanden Memorial Art Museum]
	Madison, MS	22 October	*Traces of Mississippi* Anne LeBaron, Pittsburgh, PA Mississippi Symphony Orchestra, choir, & narrator [Madison County Cultural Center; The Millennium Festival]
November	Middlebury, VT	3 November	*Reflections of the Sky* Peter Hamlin, St. Paul, MN Middlebury Community Chorus, Middlebury College Choir & Harlem Spiritual Ensemble; Emory Fanning, organ [Middlebury College Bicentennial]
	Gadsden, AL	12 November	*I Am a Song* Philip Koplow, Covington, KY Etowah Youth Orchestras
	Piedmont, CA	12 November	*The Oh of Moon & Piano* Mark Winges, San Francisco, CA Piedmont Choirs
	Kennesaw, GA	17-19 November	*The Unsung* Eric Alexander, Acworth, GA Wings Dance Ensemble [Kennesaw State University]
2001	Oak Park, IL	27 January	*A Community Symphony* James Kimo Williams, Chicago, IL [Oak Park Area Arts Council]

MONTH	LOCATION	DATE(s)	TITLE **COMPOSER** **PERFORMERS** **[PROJECT SPONSOR, OCCASION]**
2001 (cont.)	Newark, NJ	11 March	*Jersey Polyphony* Raymond Torres-Santos, San Juan, PR Newark Boys Chorus & North Jersey Philharmonic Glee Club

Robert Sirota is director of the Peabody Institute of The Johns
Hopkins University. Sirota studied composition at Juilliard,
earned a degree in piano and composition from Oberlin, and took
his doctorate in composition at Harvard; among his principal
teachers are Richard Hoffmann, Joseph Wood, Earl Kim, Leon
Kirchner, and Nadia Boulanger. Widely known as a composer and
conductor of new music, Sirota has written solo instrumental and
chamber works as well as four operas, several musical theater
pieces, compositions for organ and choral ensembles, and
concertos for cello, organ, saxophone, and viola. He has received
commissions from the Empire Brass, The American Guild of
Organists, the Seattle and Vermont Symphony Orchestras, and the
Peabody Trio; and his awards include grants and fellowships from
the Guggenheim Foundation, the Watson Foundation, the
National Endowment for the Arts, and the American Music Center.
His music has been recorded on the Capstone label.

❦ Finding Our Way Back Home
Tonality in the Twenty-first Century

ROBERT SIROTA

FOR composers, the dominant discourse of the past century has been a
preoccupation with musical language. In this most metaphorical of arts, the
crisis of language has mirrored the existential crisis brought on in the West by
a century of protracted conflict and unprecedented destruction. The
movement toward an international style of composing following World War
II was born of the desire to repudiate the past, to create an art that reflected a
radically transformed world. In the 1950s and 1960s talented and articulate
composers such as Pierre Boulez, Karlheinz Stockhausen, and Milton Babbitt
set about to produce new music in no way identifiable with the past. For
Boulez, writing in 1952, there was only one answer, one true path:

I, in turn, assert that any musician who has not experienced—I do not say
understood, but, in all exactness, experienced—the necessity for the dodecaphonic
language is USELESS [emphasis his]. For his whole work is irrelevant to the
needs of this epoch.[1]

351

The third quarter of the twentieth century was to a considerable extent dominated by this kind of pronouncement in academic composition. It would be difficult to overestimate the power of Boulez's statement and its implications for the post-World War II generation of composers. It produced a strict orthodoxy against the "corrupting" influences of the past and in favor of the "new" ways of producing musical architecture. While it is certainly true that not all serious composers embraced this orthodoxy, it is fair to say that during this period most new music was described and defined in relation to it. Composers who wished to be taken seriously in academic and intellectual circles were expected to take a position, to stake out a territory, concerning innovations in musical language and their personal way of composing. A new composition that suggested traditional tonality simply wasn't taken seriously.

As a composer born in 1949, I am a member of the generation that made a transition from post-war hyper-modernism to the more eclectic and varied approaches to composition of the late twentieth century. In my own training, which took place in the 1960s and 1970s—first at Oberlin and later at Harvard (with a notable and exceptional year in between studying with Nadia Boulanger in France)—the belief in creating a new music that was completely objective and non-referential was already being combined with a growing nostalgia for the past. The mixed impulses—to create works that make reference to older music while, at the same time, sounding completely new in aesthetic surface and structure—produced experiments in "originality." Originality became the obsession of the age. By "originality" was meant the production of an art work in some significant way unlike any that preceded it. This preoccupation superseded other important aesthetic ideals, such as beauty, comprehensibility, or clarity of expression.

Composers of my generation were told repeatedly that the first task of writing a new work was to determine the "language" of that work. Since originality was paramount, composers considered many different models for musical discourse, including the following: serialism, total serialism, aleatoric procedures, minimalism, time-point composition, tropes, *Augenmusik*, *musique concrète*, microtonal music, extended tonality, polytonality, the use of tonal materials in non-functional contexts, the use of tonality as a structural basis with a highly free and dissonant foreground, the use of some elements of tonal language divorced from local or structural function, pastiche, music of indefinite pitch, and various combinations of all of the above.

Not surprisingly, most of the music written with these methodologies is not particularly original—certainly not in the way that, say, the wind writing in *Le Nozze di Figaro* is original, or that *Pierrot Lunaire* as a composition is original. This is because originality resides in the soul of the composer, in the composer's way of perceiving existence and translating it into sound. It has virtually nothing to do with methodology. The twentieth-century obsession with originality has been an expression of contemporary *Weltschmerz*. In our soul-sickness we continually mistook novelty for originality, mere sensation for true emotion, mechanism for causality.

In American music, the final quarter of the century witnessed an increasing concern with breaking this tyranny of pseudo-originality. At the vanguard of the counter-revolution was George Rochberg, who in 1972 wrote:

The desperate search in the second half of the twentieth century for a way out of cultural replication, i.e., being influenced by others, borrowing, leapfrogging, has let loose a veritable Pandora's box of aberrations which have little or nothing to do with art but everything to do with being "successful" historically or commercially. Even the critics, no longer willing to be left out or behind, have joined in the hue and cry for "the new"; they celebrate and rationalize it. Self-indulgence is now the rule. By a series of typical paradoxes only powerful creative spirits like Brahms, Mahler, Bartók, and Stravinsky have remained skeptical of everything but authentic values and, therefore, continue the process of cultural replication by refracting all previous music through their individual, particular natures.

What was advertised as the "exhaustion of tonality" at the end of the nineteenth century and described by historians, beginning typically with *Tristan* and tracing the demise through the new Viennese school, may simply have been an incapacity on the part of composers to continue to produce a viable tonal music which could stand comparison with the best work of the eighteenth and nineteenth centuries. Even if we grant the emergence of new perceptions and sensibilities, it does not follow that authentic values must be cast aside every time a new device or procedure is discovered. Culture, like time, its guardian, proceeds by slow accretion and eventually absorbs everything of value. By the same token nothing of value is ever lost. This is the only faith that a serious artist can live by, provided that he has made something worth preserving, even though he will never really know the fate of his work.[2]

Rochberg's remarkable essay was followed in 1973 by Leonard Bernstein's controversial Norton Lectures at Harvard, published as *The Unanswered Question*. The final lecture ends with a music Credo that hails what Bernstein characterizes as

the rediscovery and reacceptance of tonality, that universal earth out of which such diversity can spring....
    I also believe, along with Keats, that the Poetry of Earth is never dead, as long as Spring succeeds Winter, and man is there to perceive it. I believe that from Earth emerges a musical poetry, which is by the nature of its sources tonal.[3]

Around this time I began to teach composition—first at Boston University, then at Tanglewood, and subsequently at New York University and the Peabody Conservatory. My experience working with talented young composers has afforded me some insight into changing attitudes toward twentieth-century music.

In the mid-1970s and early 1980s, when I asked talented (and I stress the fact that they are talented) young composers to name composers they particularly liked and admired, they would frequently mention Igor Stravinsky, Béla Bartók, Arnold Schoenberg, Anton Webern and Alban Berg, as well as (occasionally) John Cage, Elliott Carter, Charles Ives, Karlheinz Stockhausen, and Luciano Berio. By the mid-1980s, as often as not, young composers would tell me of their devotion to Dmitri Shostakovich, Samuel Barber, and Aaron Copland—composers rarely if ever listed ten years earlier. By the late 1980s Second Viennese School composers were rarely, if ever, mentioned as favorites; and, while Stravinsky remained a perennial favorite, many new composers had been added to the list: George Crumb, John Corigliano, Philip Glass, Steve Reich, John Adams, and Christopher Rouse, as well as film composers John Williams and Jerry Goldsmith.

Clearly there has been a radical change in the taste and aesthetic direction of young American composers, and from what I have been saying up to this point, I should be pleased. But there are problems with this apparent sea-change. In an age that treasures its ironies, there is a great irony in the supposed "rediscovery" of tonality. The irony is that those who sought to decontextualize music, to create a new music that cuts itself off from the past, have succeeded beyond their wildest expectations: we are now looking at a generation of young composers who, for all their talent and technical ability, display a general lack of craft concerning the function of tonality as a basis for musical architecture. Like survivors of the Cultural Revolution, these composers have lost part of their history and are left with the task of reinventing what already exists.

Tonality, as a way of circumscribing musical architecture, is one of the great achievements of Western thought. The idea of tonality as the basis for constructing extended musical forms developed over centuries; it is a fluid and evolving concept, not a stable "common practice," as we were taught in music-theory classes. Tonal practice at the beginning of the twenty-first century incorporates decades of innovation and stylistic evolution, playing upon the listener's expectations of past music, and finding new contexts for familiar formulae and sonorities. Tonality is not just being rediscovered; it is in a continual process of being reinvented.

Unfortunately, many composers who are turning their attention to tonal materials have not mastered the higher principles of traditional tonal practice, and therefore lack the context to compose substantial music that either mirrors traditional practice or diverges from it in any coherent or systematic way. In a sort of "postmodern stress disorder" composers are experiencing a disconnect in thinking between the evocation of tonal materials in a composition and the working-out of the structural implications of those materials. The problem is analogous to the lack of skill in drawing from life that is increasingly prevalent in many contemporary visual-arts schools. The abstractions and constructions that result often reveal their creator's lack of direct experience with gestures and impulses learned from concrete shapes and forms. Similarly, in composition, because of the shift in emphasis brought about by the post-World War II academic cultures, we are witnessing a couple of generations of composers who have failed profoundly to integrate the principles of harmony and counterpoint into their creative consciousnesses. To many, traditional tonality is like Latin: a dead language, but the one from which most modern languages are derived.

If we accept the idea of music as a metaphor for human thought and experience, I believe we can also embrace the concept of tonality, in its broadest and expanding definition, as a compositional practice that seeks to define and traverse musical space. In "traditional" tonality the goal of any musical journey was to return home. In the twenty-first century, it may be enough for us to know, for the moment, where we are, and to have some idea, for the moment, of the possibilities where we might be headed. We may not know where home is, or we may not desire to go there. Or, we may not be going anywhere; we may even wish to deny the existence of anywhere to go! To deny the existence of the *memory* of these possibilities, however, and to use elements of tonal language without any reference to their richest implications—these seem to me acts of ignorance rather than of artistic discourse. Let us not confuse a lack of understanding with originality.

How are we to help young composers find their way in the language they have rediscovered? I believe those of us who have the responsibility of teaching composition must re-examine our methods and intentions. It is of little use to a young composer for her teacher to insist she find a distinct and new language for every work. We must return to teaching the basic principles that give life and meaning to a composition. Students need to discover how harmony and counterpoint work in their own musics. In order to do this, they should do what composers have done for many centuries: learn traditional harmony and counterpoint, learn how to analyze effectively the works of great composers, and then—most important—determine how these overarching principles apply to their own music.

More than once I have heard academic composers say that, in a sense, it is not possible to "teach" composition the way one teaches, say, violin. I agree with this statement only to the extent that every young composer comes to his teacher with a unique and distinct set of skills and needs. A great composition teacher is one who is able to help each student find the particular tools he needs to develop his own compositional voice. There is no room in this important business of teaching for the preconceptions and orthodoxies that impeded the flow of creativity in the middle of the twentieth century. As teachers, we have the responsibility to transmit the totality of our musical culture to our students. This is our challenge, and our privilege.

Finally, how we compose has everything to do with what we have to say. The recent past has witnessed a movement toward a more direct mode of expression. This reflects a renewed hunger to establish a stronger emotional and spiritual connection with the listener. As we reveal the yearnings of our hearts to our audience, we invite them to join us on a journey. When we succeed in connecting with our audience, we have found our way home.

NOTES

[1]Pierre Boulez, *Notes of an Apprenticeship*, trans. Herbert Weinstock (New York: Alfred A. Knopf, 1968), 148.

[2]George Rochberg, *The Aesthetics of Survival: A Composer's View of Twentieth Century Music* (Ann Arbor: University of Michigan Press, 1984), 235.

[3]Leonard Bernstein, *The Unanswered Question: Six Talks at Harvard* (Cambridge, MA: Harvard University Press, 1976), 424.

Jack Sullivan, director of American Studies and professor of English at Rider University, is the author of *New World Symphonies: How American Culture Changed European Music* and editor of *Words on Music: from Addison to Barzun*. Sullivan earned his doctorate at Columbia University; among his activities are appearances on National Public Radio and work on behalf of *Sweet Chariot: A History of Black Spirituals* for WNET television. Sullivan has written for the *New York Times*, the *Boston Globe*, the *Washington Post*, the *New Grove Dictionary*, *USA Today*, the *Chicago Tribune*, the *New Republic*, the *American Record Guide*, *Theory*, and many other publications. Sullivan's musical commentaries have appeared in Carnegie Hall's *Stagebill* and as liner notes for New World and Delos Records.

❦ Kurt Weill's Americana
The Open Road to the Future

JACK SULLIVAN

IT is possible, Michael Wood remarked (in a telephone interview with me on 10 September 1996), to idolize a country other than one's own. Indeed, that is what other countries are for. It is why people travel: to celebrate freshness, otherness, foreigness, as ideal states of being.

Since the mid-nineteenth century, when Hector Berlioz heard Louis Moreau Gottschalk play the piano, and Antonín Dvořák read Henry Wadsworth Longfellow's poetry, European composers have increasingly found this idealism in America, a New World where a lack of tradition and convention create continuing possibilities for renewal. Because music itself is an ideal state, less representational than the other arts, this idea of America has been embodied in its purest form by composers.

Every country has its own concept of national identity, but it is usually backward-looking, based on history and a notion, however imperfect, of a unified past. Only in America, as English expatriate Wood notes, is the self-perception "a picture of possibility. To be un-American is to be unfaithful to what the place might be." America has always been a melting pot, its sense of

357

identity complex and constantly shifting according to differing immigrant experiences and their fantasies of what the New World should be. The American Civil War, the House Un-American Activities hearings, the Civil Rights Movement, the Vietnam War protests, the South Carolina Confederate flag controversy, the Elian Gonzales crisis, and other tumultuously irreconcilable conflicts make clear that no single, stable concept of Americanism exists within the United States. America flourishes in spite of— indeed, because of—multiple ideas of Americanism and their vibrant if uneasy co-existence.

Europeans who come to America often have a clearer, fresher notion of Americanism than Americans do, if for no other reason than being in a position to compare the New World with the Old. As C. Vann Woodward puts it, Europeans have always regarded America as a "metaphor adapted to their uses."[1] Typical is the attitude of French émigré Edgard Varèse, who denounced "mummified" European tradition and said of his revolutionary New World symphony, *Amériques*: "I did not think of [this piece] as purely geographical, but as symbolic of discoveries—new worlds on earth, in the sky, or in the minds of men."[2] America was a place but also a subjective metaphor, a new world in the mind.

Because America is a nation of immigrants, Europe's discovery of the New World—in music, as in anything else—is really a rediscovery of itself in mysterious, half-recognizable forms. The split between innocence and calculation that Berlioz admired in Gottschalk is partly a self-revelation, the Old World embedded in the new. This American doubleness was fascinating to Europeans because it was enmeshed in their own identity. Europeans regarded artists like Gottschalk and Edgar Allen Poe as secret sharers who sailed to the New World and assumed mysterious new identities, personae rooted in European worldliness, but wilder and freer.

As the Old World rediscovered the New, the latter took its allure for granted or denied it altogether. Since Emerson, who warned of listening to "the courtly muses of Europe," Americanists have worried about New World identity being subverted by the Old, especially in music, where musical instruments, concert halls, and symphonic language are borrowed from European tradition. In a peculiarly defensive key, Americanists often downplay or fret about the New World elements in Dvořák, Darius Milhaud, Dmitri Shostakovich, Igor Stravinsky, Paul Hindemith and others, while hyping homegrown American music. They might as well relax—or as my students would say, they might as well chill; the influence came from America in the first place, demonstrating its potency rather than vulnerability.

While many American composers emulated European models, European composers were inspired by the very idioms these Americans shunned: spirituals, Indian motifs, popular music, Broadway, and revolutionary authors such as Poe, Walt Whitman, and Langston Hughes. These provided far more reliable markers of Americanism within the United States than anything on the American concert scene. Even Gershwin, admired by Ravel, Schoenberg, Tippett, and other Europeans as a genuine Americanist, was derided by many American intellectuals as un-American and un-musical, a dramatic example of America's inability to agree on what constitutes Americanism.

The consummate New World European was Kurt Weill. His assumption of American identity was not ambivalent or temporary, as was the case with Dvořák or Benjamin Britten, but passionate and consistent. Ironically and ultimately, it took the unstinting Americanism of Weill to point the way for American composers, many of whom abandoned vernacular culture for serialism and other European modes in mid-century, then embraced everything from F. Scott Fitzgerald to soul music a half century later, in an attempt to reconnect with an audience. In his Berlin-cabaret period, Weill created an America of the imagination. Jazz-infused operettas such as *Mahagonny*, *The Seven Deadly Sins*, and *Happy End* bring to life fantastical American scenarios and genres replete with cowboys, Chicago gangsters, and Salvation Army colonels. In his Broadway-Hollywood show music, Weill became a real American artist, a master of cross-over who took up where George Gershwin had left off setting the stage for Leonard Bernstein's *West Side Story*.

Like his fellow émigré Hindemith, Weill had a special affinity for Whitman, the poet of "The Open Road," of American egalitarianism and multiplicity. Whitman was a kindred spirit, a restless but joyful traveler, constantly on the move in both his art and personal life. "Of Manhattan the Son," Whitman was the poet of New York City, celebrating its diversity and electric energy. Unlike his colleagues in the press, who reacted with bitter hostility to foreigners flooding into New York, Whitman was an unstinting advocate of mass immigration. In flight from the Nazis and eager to renounce the crimes of their homeland, Weill and Hindemith rejoiced in Whitman's *Songs of the Open Road*, which explicitly rejected racism and nativism.

Whitman had another advantage: the all-encompassing humanity of his Civil War poems, could, without too much stretching, be yoked to the

American war effort. Gustave Holst, Ralph Vaughan Williams, and others had demonstrated that Whitman's *Drum-Taps* made eloquent vehicles for ruminating on the atrocities of the First World War and warning of a second. Weill and Hindemith, dusted them off again, this time as patriotic gestures in the fight against the Nazis.

Whitman sought to be all-embracing, and in his musical legacy he was spectacularly successful. He was all things to all composers, fulfilling the needs of experimenters like Carl Ruggles and traditionalists like Ned Rorem, and he was certainly all things to Weill. Always regarded as a radical, soon to be the model for Allen Ginsberg and the Beat Generation, Whitman allowed Weill to retain a vestige of his avant-garde past and still lavish the poems with an accessible style. Whitman had walked a tightrope similar to Weill's; he wanted desperately to be a popular entertainer as well as an artist, but to his great disappointment, he appealed almost solely to intellectuals. Weill was more successful in this regard: his music is as much at home in the cabaret, jazz bar, and Broadway theater as in the opera house.

Written between 1942 and 1947, Weill's Whitman songs are a bridge to his Broadway shows. Indeed, his most poignant Whitman lyric occurs in the love duet in *Street Scene*, which received its premiere in New York in March, 2000 as a concert suite. Although critics sometimes accuse Weill of imposing a breezy lyricism on Whitman's Civil War poems, the songs are closely in touch with their texts. As David S. Reynolds points out in *Walt Whitman's America: A Cultural Biography* (1996), Whitman emulated openly lyrical forms, especially Stephen Foster songs and the heart music of American families. The poems in *Drum-Taps* thus project a poignant optimism even in horrifying war scenarios. Weill's lyricism works against ugly subject matter just as Whitman's does, with the same life-giving tension. His humanizing approach anticipates that of Bernstein, Ned Rorem, John Adams, Craig Urquhart, Michael Tilson Thomas, and other American Whitmanians, individuals determined—as Whitman himself was—to reach into the hearts of a large general audience rather than a tiny academic elite.

Other European émigrés used Whitman as a vehicle for American identity, but few as successfully as Weill. Hindemith presented a Whitman setting to the judge at his immigration ceremony. He too had a vivid sense of Whitman as an indelible marker of Americanism in the United States. Hindemith later expanded this song into *When Lilacs Last in the Door-yard Bloom'd*, an austere epic that was received ambivalently at its premiere and has only recently begun to enter the American repertory. Hindemith was more convincingly American when living in Germany and dabbling in jazz; he never fully made the transition from an imaginary American identity to a real one, as Weill did.

A strikingly different kind of Whitman composer is represented by Frederick Delius. Like Dvořák, Delius was first initiated into the sublimities of American culture through black spirituals, Indian motifs, and American landscape. His other great American inspiration was Whitman, but he rejected the democratic, communitarian Whitman of Hindemith and Weill for a Whitman who was remote, nonconformist, and rabidly individual. It was Whitman's mystical individualism Delius embraced, not the "Divine Average" of the Poet of Democracy. Again, Whitman was all things to all Europeans precisely because his own Americanism was far from stable or unchanging.

The best-known passport to American identity was, of course, jazz and its related genres: ragtime, blues, swing, and Broadway. Here too, Weill was the most successful avatar of a long-standing New World European tradition. Bill Clinton, America's sax-playing President, recently declared jazz "America's classical music," but Europeans knew this from the beginning. Ravel, Satie, Schulhoff, Wolpe, Shostakovich, Walton, and dozens of others have written jazz-inspired pieces in a dazzling variety of styles. Indeed, Europeans often took jazz more seriously than Americans. It was Ernst Krenek who called jazz "the note of the times";[3] it was Ravel who said, "You Americans take jazz too lightly."[4] Weill went further than his European predecessors. Beginning with *Mahagonny* (1927), he used jazz as the basis for what he called a "new sound" that fundamentally altered his aesthetic rather than erupting in isolated works. Weill was not interested in imitating "real" jazz, whatever that meant; like Dvořák in his re-imagining of spirituals, he created his own sound based on the color and spirit of the idiom. Weill loved the mysterious doubleness of jazz, what enthusiasts call coolness, the disproportion between emotional fervor and cool exterior. Here again was the doubling of innocence and sophistication that Berlioz observed in Gottschalk and that the French admired in Poe.

And here again was the European fondness for mingling the dark side of the New World with the bright. Like Maurice Ravel in the *Concerto for the Left Hand*, Weill was happily obsessed with the sexier, more decadent aspects of jazz, the note of malevolence just under the sparkling surface. Europeans have always regarded jazz as a dangerous doorway to New World newness and freedom. Berlioz stated that the Gottschalk sound "cradles our disturbing and insatiable desire for the unknown;"[5] British novelist Geoff Dyer recently wrote that "there is something inherently dangerous" about jazz.[6] For Weill, the danger was real: the Nazis regarded his injection of jazz into the culture of Mozart and Wagner as deeply subversive. For Europeans, jazz was similar to Whitman's poetry in that it represented the democratic ideal, the ultimate Americanism: it was strikingly individual, yet reached out to everyone. The Whitmanian persona celebrates individual freedom, yet exists to embrace all humanity, just as the jazz player's most inspired solo improvisations grow out of an ensemble. This benevolent brand of Americanism, whether literary or musical, was seen by European émigrés as an antidote to hatred and totalitarianism.

American society had its own ugly injustices, of course, but for New World symphonists like Weill and Varèse, America was a state of mind that could be projected onto the most flawed realities. Weill declared that he felt like an American long before coming to New York. "Wherever I found decency and humanity in the world," he said, "it reminded me of America."[7] And wherever he heard jazz, it reminded him of a bliss unique to American culture: "Anyone who has worked with a good jazz band," he said in 1929, "will have been pleasantly surprised by the eagerness, self-abandon, and enthusiasm for work which one seeks in vain in many concert and theater orchestras."[8] This rare release of the self in the ecstasy of jazz was profoundly liberating during a time of war and holocaust.

Weill's final assumption of American identity came with his conquest of Broadway, a crossover triumph that prefigured the careers of "serious" American composers such as Bernstein and Stephen Sondheim. The Broadway show was specifically American and urban, a product of New York City's exuberant democratic materialism. To make it on Broadway, as Weill did in *Lady in the Dark* and *One Touch of Venus*, required a feel for American commercial culture, a day-to-day practical involvement in the show's production and run. Determined to make the New World ideal a working reality, Weill committed himself to this enterprise without ambivalence. His admiration for the Broadway musical and its most elegant practitioners such as Gershwin and Cole Porter paralleled his devotion to jazz: Broadway shows were entertainment of the highest order but also art. In *Street Scene*, with its depiction of a lower middle-class housewife struggling against spousal abuse, Weill went further than many American artists in fulfilling Emerson's call for an art that was truly American based on a direct rendering of ordinary life.

Weill's American career is summarized in the five haunting songs for *Huckleberry Finn*, a Broadway musical he launched with Maxwell Anderson just before his death in 1950. Weill's love of American literature is signaled by the singer repeatedly chanting "Mark Twain," like a mantra. Twain's greatest creation clearly had special meaning to Weill. Huck Finn is a survivor, a perpetual wanderer who searches for a home and finds it in motion—on the freedom of the raft and in the friendship with Jim, his African-American magus who is on the run from a racist society.

Weill always maintained that his Broadway shows were a logical continuation of his lifelong fascination with America, not something out of nowhere, certainly not a new Kurt Weill. There was only one Weill, a master of multiplicity and quick-change; this was not merely a stance but a reality, one that resulted in a dizzying variety of styles, identities, and genres. Weill was a creature of the New World from the beginning. Refusing to be defined by fashion or formula, he was always on the road with Whitman or on the raft with Twain. He existed in Whitman's eternal "Now," an uncompromising present moment that refused to look back or dwell on the past. For Whitman and Twain, looking back was spiritual death; for Weill, in flight from the Nazis, it was a literal one as well. "I don't take no stock in dead people," said Huckleberry Finn. Neither did Kurt Weill.

And neither do a growing number of European composers in the new millennium. Like their American counterparts, they are picking up where Weill left off, fervently embracing New World culture in a variety of genres: Elizabeth Liddle, who claims to have read *Moby Dick* hundreds of times and uses Melville's prose for a New World choral sound; Thomas Ades, whose *America!*, a dark New World Symphony written for the New York Philharmonic's "Music for the Millennium" concert, echoes Milhaud's *Christophe Colomb* (1930) in telling the Columbus story from the Indians' point of view; Robert Starer, whose exquisitely autumnal Whitman settings are part of the latest Whitman wave; Sophia Gubaidulina, whose spectral T. S. Eliot settings define a new Russian mysticism; Poul Ruders, whose colorful *Manhattan Abstraction* and *The Bells* renew the European fascination with American landscape and the American Gothic of Poe; Faradj Karajev, whose immersion in the New World covers everything from Emily Dickinson to George Crumb; Steve Martland, whose rock-inspired concert music is the newest kind of crossover; and Joanna Bruzdowicz, who prefaced her lyrical chamber piece *Spring in America* (1994) with a quotation from Sinclair Lewis: "Intellectually, I know America is no better than any other country; emotionally, I know she is better than any other country"—a chauvinistic gesture an American composer would never get away with.

Idolatry for a country other than one's own seems as popular as ever. In music at least, the object of adulation continues to be America.

NOTES

[1]C. Vann Woodward, *The Old World's New World* (New York: Oxford University Press, 1991), 83.

[2]Arthur Cohn, liner notes, *Amériques* by Edgard Varèse (Vanguard SVC 40 [1996]).

[3]Katherine H. Allen, liner notes, *Jonny spielt auf* by Ernst Krenek (Vanguard OVC 8048 [1993]).

[4]*A Ravel Reader: Correspondence, Articles, Interviews*, ed. Arbie Orenstein (New York: Columbia University Press, 1990), 390.

[5]Serge Berthier, liner notes, *Classics of the Americas* (Opus 30 9001).

[6]Richard Bernstein, "Jazz's Dark Forces and the Artists Who Love Them," *New York Times* (20 March 20 1996).

[7]Kim Kowalke, "Formerly German," *ACO Newsletter* (Winter 1999-2000).

[8]Kurt Weill, *The Threepenny Opera*, ed. Stephen Hinton (New York: Cambridge University Press, 1990), 166.

William Velez is president and chief operating officer of SESAC, a leading musical performing-rights organization. A former employee of BMI, Polygram Records, and ASCAP, Velez attended Fairleigh Dickinson University and received his law degree from Seton Hall; at one time he held an adjunct professorship in New York University's Music Business and Technology Program. Recently he has spearheaded the establishment of SESAC Latina, the first American-based organization dedicated exclusively to Latin music; he has also been responsible for directing SESAC's technological innovations, including the use of BDS digital pattern-recognition software and the MusiCode watermarking program for multi-media music tracking. Velez serves as a board member of the Nashville Shakespeare Festival and Nashville's Partnership 2000. His industy affiliations include the National Academy of Recording Arts and Sciences, the Nashville Songwriters Association International, the Copyright Society of the South, and Nashville's Leadership Music.

❦ Performing-Rights Collectives
Dinosaurs of the New Millennium?

WILLIAM VELEZ

THE business of licensing public performance rights in music is, for all intents and purposes, in its infancy in the United States. History (or folklore) has it that a group of composers dining in a New York City restaurant observed that that particular establishment was exploiting music for the purpose of enhancing the restaurant's atmosphere. Of course, it was happening at the expense of composers who were not being compensated and whose livelihood and incentive to create remained dependent upon such compensation. Ultimately, the situation led to the development of a not-for-profit clearinghouse or music-rights collective. This organization was founded in 1914, but it is still known and active as the American Society of Composers, Authors and Publishers (ASCAP).

Through ASCAP, writer and music-publisher members would be able to "police" the eventual public performance licensing in the United States of some 10,000 commercial radio stations, 1,000 local commercial television

365

stations, the major TV networks, and all of cable and satellite TV, as well as the Internet and the so-called general licensing segment. The latter consists of entities such as hotels, restaurants, bowling alleys, cruise ships, funeral homes, and live-concert venues, to name but a few. Conversely, these prospective licensees have avoided exposure to statutory penalties associated with the unauthorized usage of protected music (i.e., copyright infringement) by securing a public performance license from ASCAP in exchange for payment of a fee.

Regrettably, limitations of length prohibit a detailed account of the evolution of this industry. On the other hand, I can refer the interested reader to two outside references that do far more justice to the subject than I could hope to: John McDonough's short piece in the *Wall Street Journal* and Russell Sanjek's more extensive treatise.[1] Suffice it to say, the twentieth century proceeded to witness the establishment of two ASCAP competitors: SESAC,* founded in 1930 as a for-profit, privately held licensing organization; and Broadcast Music, Inc. (BMI), founded in 1940 as a not-for-profit corporation owned by broadcast interests. BMI was originally conceived with the goal of reducing the cost of performance rights licenses to music users via competition with ASCAP.

The United States remains one of several countries in the world that maintains multiple agencies conducting the business of public performance-rights licensing. This competitive environment gives rise to the two notable accomplishments associated with the industry in the twentieth century: 1) the growth, within less than a century, to what is now a billion-dollar industry; and 2) the maturing of this industry *vis-à-vis* the adoption of a "for-profit" mindset, the implementation of which may be the industry's saving grace as it anticipates significant challenges in the new millennium.

The first of these twentieth-century achievements is hardly miraculous when one considers that the industry started from "zero" and had no place to go but forward in terms of revenue growth. To trivialize this accomplishment, however, would be nothing short of heretical to the women and men at ASCAP, BMI, and SESAC. These men and women, albeit armed with significant ammunition in terms of a potent U.S. Copyright Law, have had to overcome persistent and stiff resistance from groups of music users who disrespect the notion that the owners of intangible, intellectual property are

---

*[Historically, "SESAC" was an acronym for the Society of European Stage Authors and Composers. Today, however, the organization is simply known as SESAC. – Eds.]

entitled to and must be fairly compensated for their creative efforts. The issue of growing resistance to the copyright law will be brought into sharper focus as this essay goes on to highlight threats and challenges in the new millennium.

The second of the century's notable gains is of heightened interest and importance: the adoption of a for-profit mentality in what has been a traditionally not-for-profit setting—both because it is late in its arrival and because it will ultimately make or break the industry in the future. "In my opinion, these challenges require that we adapt the best administration techniques available in the *commercial world*" [emphasis added] "Even though most of us are monopolies, *we have to behave as though there is competition out there. We must compete for our members' business because sloppy complacency breeds unwelcome competition*" [emphasis added].

Lest you believe that these quotes represent the utterances of Lee Iacocca or Bill Gates, try Frances Preston and John Hutchinson, CEOs of two of the world's largest not-for-profit performing rights organizations: BMI, and the United Kingdom's Performing Right Society Ltd. (PRS), respectively.[2] I rather doubt that research will reveal the existence of these sentiments from any "players" in the performing-rights community prior to the mid-1990s. To what, then, is this dramatic change attributable? The performing rights landscape in the United States serves as a case study for what has emerged as a global phenomenon.

First, prior to late 1992, there was still a pretense of competition in the United States. With ASCAP and BMI sharing in excess of 90% of the performing-rights market, no incentive existed for these goliaths to invest heavily to enhance operational efficiency. As late as the late 1980s, ASCAP remained particularly deficient in terms of computerizing its infrastructure. While BMI enjoyed a more progressive technological status (due, in part, to its shorter existence), neither ASCAP nor BMI evidenced a hunger for systemic technological improvements that might effectively have dismantled vested, decades-old performance monitoring and royalty distribution methodologies.

Enter SESAC.

Historically, SESAC has led a modest, yet healthy existence, surviving on the strength of repertory (largely devotional in nature) that was not particularly prized by ASCAP and BMI. The company was acquired in late 1992.[3] Its new management immediately embarked upon a strategic campaign that tied future success to SESAC's ability to utilize state-of-the-art technology both as a means of differentiating itself from ASCAP and BMI and as a vehicle for ultimately generating maximum revenue at minimum transactional cost.

In 1994 SESAC launched an unprecedented effort centered on an autonomous Latin music division. Essentially a performing-rights entity within a performing-rights entity, SESAC Latina developed into a laboratory for utilizing a digital fingerprint-recognition technology named Broadcast Data Systems (BDS). Armed with BDS, SESAC was able to approach the "holy grail" for songwriters and music publishers: a complete, twenty-four-hour census count of radio performances, as contrasted against traditional sampling methodologies. Arguably, of greater significance was the fact that SESAC Latina employed the same technology to fashion an unprecedented usage-based license for Spanish-language radio broadcasters and, thereby, replaced the traditional blanket-license format.[4]

The success of SESAC Latina led to the firm's expanded use from 1996 to the present of the technology across all mainstream radio formats. SESAC currently monitors in excess of 8,000,000 hours of radio programming annually, or about ten times more than ASCAP and BMI combined. (Note: ASCAP now supplements its customary performance-monitoring methodology with BDS as well.)

In 1998 SESAC became the first performing-rights organization in the world to enter into an agreement with ARIS Technologies (now the Verance Corporation) for the first-ever application of its MusiCode digital watermarking technology to performing-rights situations. Given the fact that MusiCode has now emerged from various industry trials as the preferred watermarking agent (not to mention a recent alliance reached between BDS and Verance that will facilitate deployment of a watermarking decoding network), things bode well for SESAC writers and publishers. Once again, these moves portend the likelihood that ASCAP and BMI will follow SESAC's lead.[5]

The point here is that, in terms of the U.S. performing-rights industry, vital gains in the technology arena have occurred as byproducts of a for-profit, business orientation focused upon innovation and efficiency. We need not argue the relative merits of particular technologies themselves. Let us stipulate that they do not constitute perfect solutions and that they have limitations when applied to performing rights administration. Nonetheless, they represent the best solutions available at the time. Barring reaction to the persistence and lead of SESAC (alas! out of competitive necessity), ASCAP and BMI would likely be stuck in 1990 instead of 2000. (Remember: a ten-year gap in today's digital environment represents an eternity.) In short, a for-profit mindset has driven long overdue technology advances in the twentieth-century American performing-rights industry. The for-profit approach to managing business continues to represent the industry's best hedge against some formidable challenges ahead.

The coming millennium might well be characterized as a good-news, bad-news proposition. Technology has unleashed untold new opportunities, especially via the Internet, for the creation, distribution, and usage of music. The last time performing-rights entities faced such potential for market expansion was during the advent of cable and satellite television. On the other hand, the new millennium will be fraught with problems, some familiar and some not; many or all of them could prove to be life-threatening to the performing-rights industry.

Old Reliables

1.   The existing Wall Street-driven business cycle will continue, directly or indirectly, to inhibit the creation of music. The music industry has experienced an age of "music men," followed by an age of lawyer CEOs. More recently, the investment bankers and the MBA crowd have become prevailing influences. The result has undoubtedly been greater corporate profits and higher multiples paid for acquisitions. Yet the impact of this approach has, apparently, also led to the "breaking" or development of fewer artists. There are fewer "adds" to radio playlists and, overall, a stifling of so-called "spec deals" involving talent development, because industry executives no longer perceive themselves as having the luxury of three-year or longer time-frames within which to achieve positive corporate financial performance. On the contrary, today the focus is on quarter-to-quarter results, and on talent or artists that exhibit almost immediate "bankability."

In the performing rights context, this augers poorly for continued support and/or subsidization of particular music genres such as jazz, classical, bluegrass, and folk, as well as some devotional music formats for which positive economic models have yet to materialize. On the other hand, as America's population shifts toward growth among its African- and Hispanic-American populations, things look

369

good for enthusiastic corporate support of R&B, hip-hop and rap, and Latin music.

2.   Calendar year 1998 once again witnessed detrimental legislation introduced and passed on both the state and federal levels. More particularly, the passage of the "Fairness in Music Licensing Act" proved to be anything but fair to creators of music and their representative performing-rights agencies. The legislation created a damaging legal precedent, with a licensing exemption granted to some restaurant and retail establishments for what amounts to commercial music use. This resulted in the erosion of a long-standing level of protection afforded to copyright owners.[6] It remains to be seen whether this defeat will embolden other music users to pursue similar legislative initiatives.

Emerging Threats
Some predictions:

1.   Historically, direct and source licensing have constituted rarely exercised options for writers, particularly television/film writers. This form of licensing bypasses continual writer compensation from ASCAP, BMI, and SESAC in favor of one-time "buyouts" of composers' public performance rights by production companies. Generally, each composer fares better by electing ongoing royalty payments from a performing-rights agency, based upon actual performance activity.

The new ingredient here is that, whereas production companies may not have muscled composers into accepting this type of licensing arrangement in the past, the complexion of the same companies has changed radically in recent years due to merger and acquisition mania. Today corporate entities such as Fox, AOL/Time Warner, CBS/Viacom, and Disney (to cite but a few examples) meld production, music publishing, and broadcast/cable outlets under the same roof. This integration creates incentive for a strategic linkage of corporate functions that have heretofore operated autonomously in an effort both to enhance revenue and to realize new economies.

In the past, composers have generally succeeded in uniting against efforts to impose direct or source licensing. Yet insatiable desires on the part of some of these conglomerates to enhance profits may pose renewed and serious threats to TV/film composers and, hence, to performing-rights agencies.[7]

2.   It appears that the nation, if not the world, may be headed down a path toward convergence. If this happens, home-television monitors may end up serving as appliances for delivering a range of services or functions such as entertainment "on demand," telephone access, personal computer and Internet access, and so on. Convergence appears to be only a matter of time; the nation is still grappling to conquer the requisite high-capacity wiring issues.

Should convergence become a widespread reality, it will call into question or, at the very least, complicate the traditional broadcast model that has served for decades as the bricks-and-mortar of the performing-rights market. At the moment, not enough is known about convergence models to warrant panic. In the absence of more concrete information, I remain cautiously upbeat about the ability of the performing-rights community to cope satisfactorily with technological, business, and legal issues associated with this development. If we play our cards correctly, convergence may even represent an opportunity for market expansion.

3.   The "traditional" blanket license may already be on life support, a victim of technological advancement. The performing-rights industry's ability to utilize, albeit belatedly, various performance-tracking technologies (e.g., digital-pattern recognition and watermarking) will ultimately lead to demands by music users for licenses based upon something approaching actual music use.

This is a damned-if-you-do, damned-if-you-don't scenario. If the performing-rights agencies balk at delivering this innovation, Microsoft, IBM, or the Telecoms may deliver it for us; they would then pose a serious threat to our continued viability. Accepting the challenge of technological innovation will be equally difficult, however, because large existing infrastructures (particularly those maintained by ASCAP and BMI) cannot be converted overnight, and conversaion will be expensive. This could lead to an historic consolidation of performing-rights organizations in the United States; or, perhaps, to the emergence of new alliances joining one or more existing performing-rights entities with new partners that have the capability of delivering value-added software/database management expertise or disproportionately large market share derived from overwhelming content.

Stated succinctly by Bernard Korman, ASCAP's former General Counsel of more than forty years,

I am aware of no persuasive economic or legal analysis demonstrating benefits to the public, to users, and to authors and their publishers as a group, in having more than one collecting society. More than one society means duplication of the expenses of licensing users and distributing royalties.[8]

On the other hand, Paul McGuinness, manager of the band U2, foresees a fragmentation of traditional music-rights entities:

A question I have to ask: What about the future? It is my strong belief we will be liberated by technological advances such as BDS and Soundscan, and will be able to track the performance of music to every last hairdressing salon. This means precise payments; there will be no reasons for inaccuracies. After all, when manufacturing, packaging and distribution are no longer part of the equation, record companies (as well as publishers) will be pure rights owners; maybe then they will each launch their own "rights societies" or perhaps even coalitions will emerge.[9]

It is ironic that, at the turn of this century, the most acute threat facing the performing-rights industry is the industry's propensity for adopting a complacent and even arrogant posture. As John Hutchinson, Chief Executive of PRS, aptly warns:

The business units operating in the music industry are going to have to change radically. And so are we, or we will be cut out of the future development of the business. We'll gradually lose the business like broadcasting, which requires a high-tech approach and will be left with the difficult stuff, like collecting license fees from hairdressers until someone finally puts us out of our misery. And then composers really will be threatened because their only option will be to accept a buyout for the works they create. And that really would damage creativity and the long term financial interests of composers and their families. But, we will have brought this calamity upon ourselves and them.[10]

It has been customary for American performing-rights organizations to distribute domestic performance royalties to writers and publishers after, roughly, six months from the date of actual performance. Monies derived from performances overseas may take up to two years to process and distribute. Once again, Hutchinson is right on target:

In the digital era a turnaround time of 2 days is a proven concept.... Why should our members wait longer when beyond the digital frontier all the information can be logged and in theory transmitted at the time of the transaction?[11]

Subscribing to Hutchinson's view, I envision a successful performing-rights business model emerging in the United States, one akin to the Charles Schwab approach in stockbroking. In other words: greater emphasis on efficient, high-tech service—thereby entailing lower transactional costs and real-time processing on both the licensing and royalty distribution sides, but with "no frills" in terms of budget-busting promotional activities such as elaborate award shows, nonproductive corporate sponsorships, and so on.

I cannot recall a time when prospects for the performing-rights licensing business have appeared both so promising and so perilous. Those who believe that collective administration is indispensable to the future of performing-rights licensing—and that it can make us immune from the threats cited above, may be in for a rocky ride as we plunge into the next millennium.

In the real-estate business the recognized mantra for success is *location, location, location.* If the performing-rights industry is to survive and prosper in the twenty-first century, it must draw upon recent experience and adhere to an approach incorporated in this mantra: *competition, entrepreneurial spirit,* and a *for-profit mindset.*

NOTES

[1] John McDonough, "The Serious Business of Popular Music," *Wall Street Journal* (4 October 1990). See also Russell Sanjek, *American Popular Music and Its Business: The First Four Hundred Years; from 1600 to 1984* (New York: Oxford University Press, 1988).

[2] Frances W. Preston, "Challenges and Prospects," an address delivered to the Confédération Internationale des Sociétés d'Auteurs et Compositeurs (CISAC) (Paris 1996). See also, John Hutchinson, "Can Collecting Societies Survive beyond the Digital Frontier?" an address delivered at Marche International du Disque, de l'Edition Musicale et de la Video Musique (MIDEM), Cannes, France; September 1998. Reprinted in its entirety in *Film Music* (September 1998).

[3] SESAC was purchased in late 1992 by Fredric B. Gershon, Ira N. Smith, Stephen C. Swid, and the merchant banking firm of Allen & Co.

[4] Traditionally, ASCAP, BMI, and SESAC have licensed music users pursuant to a "blanket license." In exchange for payment of a flat fee based upon a percentage of the user's revenue, the music user gains unlimited access to all musical works represented in the respective repertories of the licensing agencies. This licensing formula was deemed undesirable by owners of Spanish-formatted radio stations who craved payment of a lesser fee in exchange for access to a diluted repertory pool of primarily Latin music works.

[5] "Secure Digital Music Initiative Selects ARIS Technology," *Film Music Newswire* (15 August 1999).

[6]Bill S. 505, passed by both the House of Representatives and the Senate on 7 October 1998.

[7]Mark Holden, "Direct and Source Licensing of the Performing Right: The End of the Beginning, or the Beginning of the End?" *Film Music* (October 1998).

[8]Alan J. Hartnick, "Law and Entertainment," *New York Law Journal* (8 December 1995). The column featured reflections by Bernard Korman from a 1994 address sponsored by the Foundation for Copyright Promotion.

[9]Paul McGuinness, "Rights Battle Is Everybody's Battle," *Music Business International* 6/1 (February 1996).

[10]Hutchinson, "Can Collecting Societies Survive Beyond the Digital Frontier?"

[11]Ibid.

John White, emeritus professor of music at the University of
Florida, grew up in Minnesota; today he lives in Evergreen,
Colorado. White holds M.A. and Ph.D. degrees from the Eastman
School of Music as well as a Performers Certificate in Cello; he has
taught at Kent State University, Whitman College, and the
Universities of Michigan and Wisconsin. A composer as well as a
theorist, he has written works performed by the Cleveland
Orchestra, the Eastman Wind Ensemble, and the Atlanta
Symphony; his most recent book is *Theories of Musical Texture
in Western History*. In 1996 White held a Fulbright Research
Fellowship to Reykjavik; the following year he was made a
fellow of the American Scandinavian Foundation.

❦ Music Theory and Pedagogy before and after the Millennium

JOHN WHITE

COMPELLING as it is to speculate upon the future of so important a
subject, it is also daunting—a task to be approached with courage tempered by
humility. While retrospection is easier than prophecy, even here one must
remember that no matter how broad one's view, it is always colored by innate
proclivities, biases born of background, and individual differences fostered by
unique musical experiences from childhood and high school, from colleges and
conservatories of music, and from the adventures of graduate school and
after. Thus, "the more things change, the more they remain the same." I
don't know who first said that, but it applies as much to one's inner musical
life as to the qualities and propensities of a broad and multi-faceted national
musical community.

§

Music theory is a scholarly subject, practiced almost exclusively in
conservatories, colleges, and universities. It is research in the deepest and
most beautiful sense of the word, all the more so because it deals not only
with scientific matters, but, ultimately, with the warmth of the musical

experience: the creation, performance, apprehension, and comprehension of music.

That I am concerned primarily with "serious" concert music will be obvious from my background and from my musical persona as it has evolved over much of the past century.

My earliest contact with music theory took place in the "School of Musical Art" in my native town of Rochester, Minnesota. Every child who took music lessons at that school also took a weekly class in music theory; twice a week in the late 1930s, I walked a few blocks from my elementary school to take piano lessons or attend theory classes. The school occupied a comfortable red-brick building displaced a decade or two later by a large Catholic high school, Our Lady of Lourdes. That whole city block must have been owned by the Catholic Church because the School of Musical Art was operated by the Sisters of St. Francis, an order established in Rochester in the late nineteenth century in response to some sort of local disaster (a tornado, I think) that required the ministrations of many nurses and doctors—the same event, incidentally, that precipitated the founding of the Mayo Clinic. Apparently, the Sisters remained after the catastrophe to devote their attention to other good works, including the teaching of music.

As an elementary-school child in this theory class I practiced sight-singing and studied harmony at a more sophisticated level than some present-day freshman theory courses and all college-level remedial theory courses, the latter despised today by music students and theory faculty alike. I also composed at least one little piano piece for Sister Francis Claire, my piano teacher at the School of Musical Art. I didn't know it at the time, but that monastic musical environment may have resembled that of the medieval choir boys at the Monasteries of St. Gall, Cluny, and St. Martial's of Limoges.

Children's classes in music theory have been given for centuries, but rarely in American public schools; thus I saw at an early age that American music education was at best remiss and (as I learned later) at worst a blight on the musical community. I was never enticed by the pseudo-musical social attractions of marching bands, nor by later manifestations of popular groups such as swing or show choirs. Remedial theory courses would not exist today if American music education fulfilled its twentieth-century responsibilities.

Yet, to be fair, the public schools were, in a sense, the inspiration for my becoming a professional cellist. I think it was in third or fourth grade that the string supervisor for the Rochester Public Schools came to my school and put a violin in my hands. Priscilla Waggoner's hopes for me as a violinist lasted less than a year, however; one day she said to me, "John, you're no great shakes as a violinist—how would you like to try the cello?" She even brought along for me a full-size cello, an excellent student instrument my parents purchased for me later. I kept and played that cello throughout college and during my master's-degree work in 1954 at the Eastman School of Music. Later I acquired a better cello, and, like many string players, I continued to trade up over the years; today I own a fine eighteenth-century instrument.

In school I also sang and, thanks to my experience at the School of Musical Art, I was an adept sight-singer at an early age. In Rochester, Minnesota, I sang in the various choirs of the First Methodist Church, in the high-school choir, and in the Bach Society Choir directed by Orvis Ross, an excellent composer-pianist with whom I studied piano at a more advanced level. I was even a good enough tenor to sing Ralph Rackstraw in the 1949 Rochester High School production of *H.M.S. Pinafore* directed by Sidney Suddendorf. (Suddendorf had also encouraged me to compose some choral music, which he performed with his Rochester High School Choir.) During my undergraduate days at the University of Minnesota I pursued my love of singing and studied voice with Roy Schuessler; I also sang with James Aliferis's Chamber Singers. Although I continued choral singing and conducting throughout my career, I soon abandoned my aspirations as a solo singer (unknown audiences should be forever grateful).

Chamber music was also on my agenda. I was one of only two cellists in my home town capable of playing Mozart and Haydn string quartets; the other one was my cello teacher Stanley Gerlicher. In my senior year, however, I left him and made bi-weekly trips to Minneapolis to study with a cellist in the Minneapolis Symphony named Jess Melzer. Since Melzer was also cello instructor at the University of Minnesota, I enrolled as a freshman at that institution. I count myself lucky to have grown up in so rich a musical community. When I graduated from high school in 1949, my mentor, Orvis Ross, inscribed for me a copy of Goetschius's *Structure of Music*—a book I still pick up occasionally, mildewed and worn though it is.[1]

Although Percy Goetschius (1853-1943) represents the most conservative branch of of early twentieth-century American music theory, he was the only well-known American music theorist of his generation. That was partly because music theory, as a scholarly discipline, did not establish itself in the United States until much later. Early twentieth-century college music majors studied "harmony" and "keyboard harmony" rather than theory; sight-singing was taught as a separate course called "solfeggio." The systematic teaching of musical analysis was rare, even though the work of Donald Francis Tovey was becoming known and respected in the United States. The typical college-level course that pretended to address musical analysis was concerned primarily with pre-existing "forms" of music, rather than true analysis; hence the typical course title "Form and Analysis." Unfortunately, at the turn of the millennium, this situation has improved only slightly.

Surprisingly, Alfred Mann's 1943 translation of Fux's *Gradus ad Parnassum* (1725)[2] was the very first into English, the out-of-print English version of 1886 having been no more than a paraphrase. That a musicologist rather than a theorist was the translator of this major theoretical work was a symptom of the time; for as recently as the mid-twentieth century, music theory was still a branch of musicology. It was not until the late 1950s that music theory began to emerge as a scholarly discipline of its own; this was confirmed two decades later when the Society for Music Theory (SMT) was established in 1978. A year later *Music Theory Spectrum*, a journal religiously devoted to research in the scholarly areas of music theory, was launched as the SMT's official organ. Of course, the *Journal of Music Theory* had begun in the 1950s as a publication of Yale University, but its primary focus was and still is the history of music theory—*Journal* authors concentrate on discussions and translations of theoretical treatises and other aspects of music theory bordering on musicology. Today these are the two major American journals for publication of research in the field of music theory.

The establishment of SMT was a major step toward the recognition of music theory as a separate area of scholarly study and research rather than a portmanteau designation for teaching musicianship skills. Its founders were so conscious of this that pedagogy began taking a back seat to rigorous theoretical study. SMT conferences generally included a session on music-theory pedagogy; this was no more than a gesture, though, because the organization's primary concerns were the history of theory and music analysis. A predictable backlash produced the *Journal of Music Theory Pedagogy*, founded in 1987 at the University of Oklahoma. For a number of years I served on the editorial board of this journal; I have come to the conclusion, however, that the way music theory courses are structured today conflicts with a rigorous approach to theory as a scholarly discipline. Perhaps today's freshman and sophomore theory courses should be renamed; after all, they are *musicianship* courses.

Getting back to Goetschius: he wrote more than a dozen text books and numerous articles on various aspects of music theory and composition, based for the most part on precepts derived from classical and romantic symphonists, and a full-column entry commemorates him in the 1958 edition of *Baker's Biographical Dictionary of Musicians*. The most nearly "modern" composers that Goetschius embraced were Ernest Chausson (1855-1899) and Vincent d'Indy (1851-1931); Igor Stravinsky, Béla Bartók. *Les Six*, and the Second Viennese School—all contemporaries of his, whose music he could not have avoided hearing—made no impression whatsoever on the theoretical perspective reflected in his writings.

Goetschius strove to circumscribe and classify musical phenomena—a necessary activity for a theorist but one that can lead to canonic narrowness and pointless constraint. Goetschius was not above describing "the correct way" to use a given chord; it was he who gave us "the three forms of the rondo" so confusing to young musicians, who quickly realize that many wonderful rondos simply do not fall unequivocally into any one category. He considered the full diminished-seventh to be "the most wonderful chord in music" and viewed it as "the incomplete form of the dominant-ninth."

The latter idea was picked up by Walter Piston (1894-1976) in his *Harmony*,[3] an undergraduate theory textbook widely used as recently as 1978 in various editions. Indeed, *Harmony* was the theory text of choice at Ann Arbor when I taught there in the 1960s. At that time my colleagues included Wallace Berry and Paul Cooper, both of whom later made significant contributions to the literature of music theory. There was controversy over Piston's book, engendered perhaps by the fact that the chairman of the department at that time was John Lowell, an Eastman-trained theorist who championed the textbooks of Allen McHose, particularly *The Contrapuntal-Harmonic Technique of the Eighteenth Century*.[4] (The title was often given simply as CHT.) The chief difference between *Harmony* and CHT is the terminology for certain dominant-quality altered chords. Piston had coined the terms "secondary dominant" and "secondary dominant seventh" to describe chords such as a V^7 of V (or V^7/V), while McHose described the same sonority as a $II^{7\sharp4}$, apparently but not in fact ignoring the temporary tonicization of the fifth scale degree. The "$\sharp4$" referred to the raised fourth degree (e.g., F-sharp in the key of C Major). Both theorists sought to explain foreign tones in non-modulatory passages, but Piston's "secondary dominant" concept seemed also to point out the phenomenon of temporary tonicization without modulation. This terminology was extended to include secondary VIIs or VII⁷s that also temporarily tonicized scale degrees other than the tonic.

The whole concept can be carried too far. To use structuralist terminology, transforming dominant-tonic relationships (the VII-I concept) to other scale degrees works fine; using those newly tonicized scale degrees as points of departure for still other transformation borders on the absurd. At that point one should probably recognize a modulation, for descriptions such as "V of IV of VI" almost always lack validity. The chances are that, if the passage began in C Major, a transitory modulation to a minor or d minor has taken place.

I was thoroughly familiar with McHose's approach because his was my theory textbook when I myself was a University of Minnesota undergraduate. (We called CHT "The Green Bible.") My theory teachers there were Earl George and Paul Fetler, but later I studied with McHose himself at Eastman; he sat on my doctoral dissertation committee at the University of Rochester, and I used CHT in the 1950s during my first college-job stint at Kent State University. Nevertheless, I found it easy to transfer my allegiance to Piston—partly because, at that time, I was a lowly assistant professor at Ann Arbor, but also because I was easily persuaded that the secondary-dominant concept was preferable. A decade later *Harmony* had almost universally superseded CHT.

Another reason for this shift was that Piston drew on literature of all periods and all styles; McHose's drew much more extensively on the Bach chorales as models, although he also included many Renaissance and seventeenth-century examples illustrating the evolution of part-writing and also cited passages from Mozart and Haydn. In this sense McHose was a theoretical historian. An ugly rumor circulated that McHose used a statistical approach: e.g., that, in the Bach chorales, the VII triad appeared in first inversion 98% of the time and its third was doubled 95% of the time. Not so. Instead, McHose argued that one use was "usual," another "frequent" or "rare;" and he pointed out that "the majority of neighboring tones in combination with passing tones originate in the tonic harmony" or that, "on the whole, the rare altered non-harmonic tones are found as chromatic passing tones."

Notwithstanding this controversy, the student part-writing exercises I graded throughout the 1950s and 1960s were pretty much the same, no matter which book was used. They still are, for in spite of all the noise about transcending the canon and reaching beyond the so-called "common-practice period," four-part writing in eighteenth-century style persists today as the *sine qua non* in freshman and sophomore theory courses. Of course progressive theory teachers introduce more recent examples and even cite passages from the musics of other cultures; too, new technologies have changed the outward appearance of theory classrooms. Nevertheless, the primary objectives of sight-singing, part-writing, analysis, and keyboard skills remain substantially unchanged. Indeed, examining more recent textbooks like Joel Lester's *Harmony in Tonal Music*,[5] I find virtually nothing new. I'm sure authors like Lester would agree, for what *could* be new in such books; after all, the principles of tonal harmony remain unchanged. Lester uses Schenkerian graphs to explain harmonic background, and that's not a bad idea (although many theory teachers have found other paths to the same objective). Lester also presents many musical examples, all from the canon of Western music literature, however, and all from the eighteenth and nineteenth centuries. Thus, since the literature of Western music remains the primary basis for the study of music theory, the tonal prototype of freshman and sophomore theory courses remains the same.

Some late twentieth-century theory teachers have striven to reach beyond the canon and especially to transcend the so-called "common-practice period." Songs of Billy Joel, the Beatles, Simon & Garfunkel, The Carpenters, and so on, along with occasional examples of non-Western musics, began several decades ago to creep into theory classrooms and even into textbooks, but only as gravy; the likes of Palestrina, DiLasso, Bach, Mozart, Beethoven, Berlioz, Debussy, Ravel, and Stravinsky remain the meat and potatoes. My main objection to bringing rock, pop and "world musics" into theory classrooms is not one of quality (although I must say I generally agree with the late Barney Childs who was "dismayed by ... the flatulent tedium of rock"); for we all listen to some of this music, and pollution is not the problem. Rather, I feel that such material tends to dilute or water down course content, leaving less time and space for core literature. Because we live in the Western world, its cultural heritage should be, first and foremost, the basis for our higher learning.

I was fortunate in having Howard Hanson (1896-1981) as my dissertation director and adviser at the Eastman School of Music during my final year of doctoral study in 1959-1960, the same year his major contribution as a theorist appeared in print: *The Harmonic Materials of ModernMusic*.[6] Those of us who took Hanson's doctoral composition seminar were privileged to gain first-hand knowledge of this seminal theoretical work;

in my opinion it is one of the two most significant twentieth-century theory treatises, the other being *Technique de mon Langage musical* by Oliver Messiaen (1908-1992). I consider it noteworthy that both of these theorists, Hanson and Messiaen, were primarily composers and are best known in that capacity. Theirs is the tradition of Rameau—who, like other distinguished music theorists throughout history, came to this discipline as a composer.

Hanson's book is subtitled "Resources of the Tempered Scale," indicating that its author was exploring the compositional resources of all twelve tone scale (although not exclusively that of twelve-tone or other serial techniques). Hanson invented a system of labeling and analyzing all intervals in non-triadic sonorities: p = P4 or P5, m = M3 or m6, n = m3 or M6, s = M2 or m7, d = m2 or M7, and t = A4 or D5. This is the "interval-class system" promulgated a few years later by Allen Forte, who divested it of alphabetical letters in favor of Arabic numerals. On page 15 of *Harmonic Materials* there appears an "interval-class table" listing the number of half steps found in each interval, thus measuring the distance between the two tones of any interval in terms of the quantity of half steps. Counting the number of each type of interval in a sonority or group of tones—p, m, n, s, d, or t—leads to a descriptive label for that sonority or tone group, later known as an "interval vector." For the "heptad" shown below, Hanson would have arrived at the following label: $p^6 m^3 n^4 s^5 d^2 t$:

Hanson's system provided a new approach to the analysis of non-tonal or post-diatonic music, and it was picked up immediately by other music theorists. Yet his purpose in writing *Harmonic Materials* was more pedagogical than analytical; Hanson was a teacher who wanted to give his composition students a systematic method of harmonic organization. Perhaps the most important theorist who used his work as a point of departure was Allen Forte. In an article published in 1964 and entitled "A Theory of Set Complexes for Music" and in his *Structure of Atonal Music*,[7] Forte replaced Hanson's algebraic approach with a numerical approach derived from mathematical set theory. In Forte's procedure the sonority in Figure 1 would have been described by the following interval vector: 2 5 4 3 6 1 . Each of the six places represents one of the six interval classes starting with the smallest. Thus the sonority contains two intervals of the first interval class (m2-M7), five intervals of the second class (M2-m7), four of the third class (m3-M6), three of the fourth class (M3-m6), six of the fifth class (P4-P5), and one—a tritone—of the sixth class (A4-D5).

During the 1970s and 1980s Forte's set-theoretical approach dominated the analysis of atonal and post-diatonic music to such an extent that theorists almost forgot the whole thing originated with Hanson and his *Harmonic Materials*. Many theorists also seemed to have forgotten that pitch is only one element of music and that rhythm and timbre are just as important, especially in contemporary music. Indeed, so overbearing did this late twentieth-century preoccupation with pitch and harmony become, especially in the northeastern part of the United States, that a reaction was inevitable. In the 1980s books and papers devoted to the analysis of rhythm and sound began to appear, and there were spirited arguments at professional meetings between the proponents of set-theoretical and Schenkerian philosophies versus those who strove to include all musical elements in their analyses.

I distinctly recall one such argument at an international conference of the Society for Music Theory, held at the University of British Columbia, Vancouver, during the early 1980s—1983, I believe. Two well-known scholars presented a joint paper analyzing some music of Anton Webern using a set-theoretical approach, a paper that blatantly ignored all musical elements except pitch. Listening to these able and articulate scholars elucidating the arcane intricacies of their set-theoretical analysis, I sensed that the restless audience was ready to pounce. As soon as the question period was announced, I began by asking for a broader approach to analysis. I spoke at considerable length, and I remember that at one point I said, "This is not an analysis." When I sat down, the senior of the two presenters tried to poke fun at my comments by asking, "Would you mind repeating the question?" I was ready to do so because I had taken copious notes; instead, and immediately, one member after another of the audience rose in support of my comments and attacked the narrowness of approach of these two scholars. Finally the moderator, sensing a near-riot, called on Wallace Berry, host of the conference, in the hope that his voice would be one of mediation.

"I think we've exhausted this topic for now, can we change the subject?" the moderator asked.

Berry, however, said, "Well, I'm afraid I'm still on this topic. I agree with John's comments and would like to point out further that..." And the argument continued for at least another fifteen minutes while presenters and moderator sweated on the stage.

After that session I had coffee with one of the crest-fallen presenters who said ironically, "I guess it was a terrible paper, wasn't it?"

"No, it was a good paper," I lied, "but as analysis it didn't go far enough. Timbre and texture and sound are so important in all new music—even dynamics can be analyzed. Pitch is only one of many factors, and set-theory is only one way to approach it."

"Well," the presenter said, "people in the West just don't understand set-theory very well. I'll bet that only a few of them even knew what we were talking about. Theorists in the Northeast..."

"I think you're right," I interrupted, taking mental note of his parochial posturing. "I didn't understand everything myself." I went on to say that I thought they were using set-theory for its own sake, for the mathematician's delight in numbers and equations. What is fine as mathematics may have no place in music. Like so many other new systems, the value of set-theory was being obscured by overuse.

My opening question at the beginning of any class in musical analysis is to ask, seriously, "Why should musicians analyze music?" The purpose of musical analysis is to understand entire compositions, to explain their effect upon listeners in terms of apprehension and comprehension (and in the warm glow of the musical experience), and to help performers and conductors with their own interpretations.

I have reconstructed these 1983 SMT conference events as I remember them, and while there may be mistakes in the conversations, I've captured the gist of what happened; many American theorists remember that session as I do. Sessions like that one are exciting and good because the purpose of any professional conference—CMS, SMT or AMS—is to raise and confront issues. One should not sit on one's hands when a paper reader is making questionable statements nor when a dean or department chair is talking hogwash. The only time musicians need to be in agreement is when they are making music together. *Simulcantemus et semper auctoritatem dubetemus* (sing together and always question authority) is a good precept to follow at professional conferences—and it is a great motto for any music department.

Many of the scholars preoccupied with set-theory during and after the 1960s also became involved with Schenkerian analysis. This seems to have been an American infatuation. When the subject came up during my 1980s and 1990s visits to European conservatories, theorists and composers there seemed puzzled that so many Americans were disciples of Heinrich Schenker. Most European scholars had long ago dismissed him as an early twentieth-century figure whose graphic layer analysis was a valuable contribution to theory, but who was scarcely of real importance. Of course, a few prominent American scholars and musicians, notably Charles Rosen[8] and Eugene Narmour,[9] challenged the rationale of Schenkerism; perhaps because they weren't mainstream members of the music-theory community, theirs were voices crying in the wilderness.

I myself find Schenkerian graphs useful up to a point, but I also perceive serious logical problems—perhaps too arcane to discuss here—that led me to criticize Schenkerian theory in my own writings and to point out that Schenker's approach concentrates on harmony at the expense of all other musical elements, especially rhythm. Somewhere I also wrote about the simplistic nature of the *Ursatz*; the middle levels of Schenkerian diagrams are far more interesting and revealing. Finally, in the early 1990s I wrote two books and a book chapter (for which I produced several complete graphic analyses) that show what Schenkerian analysis can and can't do and point out ways it can be misleading.[10] I have also discussed Schenker the man, his limitations as a person (as manifested in his rhetoric), and some of the ways in which his personal traits affected his writings.

When I attacked Schenker, I attacked an icon, at least in the eyes of devout Schenkerians, and iconoclasts can expect to be attacked themselves. I received more than one angry letter from theorists, particularly with regard to the assertion that Oster, translator of *Der freie Satz*,[11] omitted significant portions of Schenker's prose because "they made Schenker look bad." In any case, I believe that the Schenkerian obsession has died down a bit. Twenty-first-century American theorists should be able to evaluate Schenker's work more objectively.

What else may happen in the realm of twenty-first-century American music theory? I think we shall see an increasing separation in the classroom of musicianship skills (i.e. freshman and sophomore music-theory courses) from the teaching of scholarly music analysis and the history of theory, as well as from "applied music." Some twenty-five or thirty years ago a movement called "comprehensive musicianship" attempted to integrate music literature, theory, history and performance into a single series of courses intended to replace traditional music-theory and music-history courses. This was a laudable undertaking, but it waned within a single decade because it tended to erode the identity and integrity of the various disciplines. Put it another way: while a good teacher of music history will touch upon some theoretical matters, and a good teacher of violin, voice, piano, or flute will do the same; these teachers will also be keenly aware of the breadth and depth of their own disciplines—an awareness that seems to be undercut by the "comprehensive musicianship" approach.

Theorists would like to see theory courses support the objectives of all music studios and classrooms, but most of them don't want theory to take over music curricula. Many performance teachers have been and still are concerned about the real value of theory and analysis. The late Millard Taylor once told me, "Courses in the analysis of music are a complete waste of time for performers." Taylor was a popular violin teacher of violin at Eastman for thirty-five years as well as an internationally known concertmaster and recitalist; he was also a good friend with whom I played a number of chamber-music concerts, so I knew him quite well and paid attention to his comment. On the other hand, I did not for a moment believe he was correct in condemning analysis courses. Eventually I came to the following conclusions:

There are gifted performers who possess or develop an approach to musical interpretation that, in whole or part, devolves upon an internal and perhaps subconscious process—a non-discursive approach. They cannot talk about this process and are often suspicious of those who can; nevertheless I believe that they, in their own ways (like Millard Taylor in his), "analyzed" music all the time, not only in rehearsal but also in performance. This was not something Taylor could discuss (much less write about), but I believe it happened. Perhaps, for him, courses in analysis would have done no good; on the other hand, he knew very well how music was put together, and his interpretive decisions were based upon carefully considered analytical judgments. That Taylor's analyses were non-discursive in nature makes them no less valid than those that appear in thoughtfully argued published treatises.

There are other fine performers, just as gifted, for whom a consciously rational and analytical approach to interpretation is the only way. Others lie somewhere in between. We are all different, and this is why every performance of every great work can and should be a new and interesting experience, even if we have heard that great work a hundred times before. Certainly courses in analysis can help most musicians, for the more music composers, performers, and scholars know, and the better they know it, the more likely they will produce something of lasting value.

In 1961 I was teaching at Kent State University (and very conscious of the fact that I was now "doctor"). It was then I received funds from Kent State to attend "The University Composers Exchange," a conference at the

University of Illinois. As a part of the conference Lejaren Hiller presented a session devoted to the Iliac Computer, the *Iliac Suite*, and the current state of computer music at Urbana. At one point in his talk Hiller remarked, "Someday we will be able to have computers extract instrumental parts from a full score and print them out!" I remember that remark vividly because, at that time, I was using a drafting table and an elaborate array of music pens, inks, templates, T-squares, and rulers—all the traditional equipment of a serious mid-twentieth century composer—to copy my own works. (I still have all that equipment and for some reason hesitate to dispose of it.)

In those days musical calligraphy was a required course for composers at Eastman; it was taught by Litchard Toland, who also ran Rochester Photocopy, the place where Ozalid prints of musical scores and parts were reproduced from translucent masters. First, however, translucent master sheets for all scores and parts had to be laboriously hand-copied in jet black ink—and this only after composers had produced pencil sketches of their scores. I took a certain pride in my manuscripts, but hand-copying was the unavoidable penance one paid for being a composer, at least until one could afford to hire a copyist. Some of my masters were dappled with rectangular, razor-cut holes, an attribute of *senza misura* passages that made the whole process much more fragile. My wife can attest that, until the late 1980s, I spent long, long hours at the drafting table, and there still is a lump on the last joint of the middle finger of my right hand produced by the pressure of the pen—an occupational deformity similar to the way my left index finger is permanently warped from many years of fingering extended positions on the cello. These are the physical marks of our art. That someday there might be faster and better ways of producing musical scores—this sounded to me and my colleagues of the 1960s like a miracle.

Yet Hiller's miracle came to pass: today I computer-typeset all of my music. Computers also enable me to copy, transpose, extract parts, and change fonts. Pressing the right buttons even lets me hear a sine-wave rendition of what I'm writing. Or, if I choose, I can enter music using an electronic keyboard, and my computer will instantly transform that music into professional-quality hard copy. All this is available even to composers who do not write computer music; for them—and I am not among them—more and more miracles are invented every day.

Obviously the computer will influence the music written by twenty-first-century composers. It will also affect the appearance of music-theory classrooms. As technological innovations become less expensive, computers and electronic keyboards will appear in every classroom—in some schools they are there already and have been for several years. Will music calligraphy become a lost art? I hope not, but I cannot help but realize that it is now rare for me to write anything by hand on a piece of music paper except when I am sketching; sometimes I even do my sketching at the computer. It would seem strange today to go to a store and purchase a package of music paper. Nor do I need to: I can now print blank music paper at my computer.

§

Near the beginning of this essay I quoted the adage "The more things change, the more they remain the same." I believe this will hold true for music theory as we enter the twenty-first century. Of course there will be superficial changes, many of them technology-related. And there may also be one important change I long for. As a beginning music-theory teacher in the mid-1950s I was surprised at the different backgrounds of my freshman students. A few had enjoyed private instruction in sight-singing, ear-training, keyboard performance, and even musical analysis; most of them had not. Clearly public-school music teachers were guilty of non-feasance, nor do I believe that music education as a discipline has improved much during the past half century. Many basic musicianship skills are more easily learned by children than by the young adults who knock on the doors of our undergraduate music departments—I know this from my own experience as a child at Rochester's School of Musical Art.

A few institutions of higher learning are beginning to identify potential public-school music teachers only at the graduate level; this insures that the undergraduate educations of educators are as rigorous as those of historians, performers, and theorists. I particularly recall the public controversy at SUNY Buffalo in 1997 when the administration abolished the undergraduate program in music education. Music was the last department on Buffalo's campus to follow this trend in teacher education. The vote within the department was fifteen in favor of abolishing music education, two opposed; three faculty members abstained from voting, and two were not present to vote. A heated editorial debate between a musicologist arguing in favor of the change and a professor of music education deploring it had appeared a few days earlier in the *Buffalo News*, and David Felder, department chairman at that time, had been quoted in the campus newspaper as follows:

Students who want to teach music will be in an excellent position to graduate from UB as music educators with strong performance backgrounds. They can receive a bachelor of music degree in performance or a bachelor of arts degree with a music major.[12]

Felder added that New York State Teacher Certification could more easily be acquired after students had finished their B.M. or B.A. degrees because by that time they would be well-prepared in the liberal arts and especially in music.

It is my hope that, by the end of the first decade of the twenty-first century, music education on the model of old-fashioned undergraduate teacher training programs will be offered nowhere or, at worst, only by the most backward institutions. When this happens the music teachers we send into our public schools will be much more highly qualified, capable of teaching sight-singing and other basic musicianship skills to children who are ready to learn. College freshman and sophomore theory courses can then be devoted to analysis, part-writing, keyboard harmony, and even counterpoint. These developments, together with higher admission standards, could make remedial theory courses a thing of the past. Music theory will then be able better to realize its potential as a profound and beautiful scholarly discipline.

NOTES

[1]Percy Goetschius, *The Structure of Music* (Philadelphia: Theodore Presser, 1934).

[2]Published as *The Study of Counterpoint from Johann Joseph Fux's Gradus ad Parnassum*, trans. Alfred Mann (New York: Norton, 1943; rev. ed. 1965).

[3]Walter Piston, *Harmony* (New York: Norton, 1941).

[4]Allen Irvine McHose, *The Contrapuntal-Harmonic Technique of the Eighteenth Century* (New York: Appleton-Century-Crofts, 1947).

[5]Joel Lester, *Harmony in Tonal Music* (New York: Knopf, 1982).

[6]Howard Hanson, *The Harmonic Materials of Modern Music* (New York: Appleton-Century-Crofts, 1960).

[7]See Allen Forte, "A Theory of Set Complexes for Music," Journal of Music Theory 8 (1964): 136-183; and in *The Structure of Atonal Music* (New Haven, CT: Yale University Press, 1973).

[8]See Charles Rose, *The Classical Style: Haydn, Mozart, Beethoven* (New York: Viking, 1972).

[9]See, for example, Eugene Narmour, *Beyond Schenkerism* (Chicago: University of Chicago Press, 1977).

John White

[10]See *Comprehensive Musical Analysis* (Metuchen, NJ: Scarecrow, 1994); *Theories of Musical Texture in Western History* (New York and London: Garland, 1995); and "Liszt and Schenker," *Liszt and His World: Proceedings of the International Conference Held at Virginia Tech, 20-23 May 1993* = Analecta Lisztiana, 3, ed. Michael Saffle (Stuyvesant, NY: Pendragon, 1998), 353-364.

[11]Published as Heinrich Schenker, *Free Composition* [Der freie Satz] = Volume III of *New Musical Theories and Fantasies*, trans. Ernst Oster (New York: Schirmer, 1979). Oster's translation is based on Schenker, *Der freie Satz*, 2nd. ed., ed. Oswald Jonas (Vienna: Universal, 1956).

[12]*Buffalo Reporter* 29/7 (9 October 1997): 5.

Born in Michigan, **Josephine R. B. Wright** is professor of music and The Josephine Lincoln Morris Professor of Black Studies at The College of Wooster. She studied at the University of Missouri-Columbia, the Pius XII Academy in Florence, Italy, and New York University; from 1994 to 1997 she served as editor for *American Music* and on behalf of the University of Illinois Press. Wright's publications include contributions to *The New Grove Dictionary of American Music*, an edition of Ignatius Sancho's compositions; with Samuel A. Floyd, Jr., she co-edited *New Perspectives in Music: Essays in Honor of Eileen Southern.* *Images: Iconography of Music in African-American Culture, 1770s-1920s*, a study she co-authored with Eileen Southern, will appear in print in the near future.

❧ Coming of Age
Reflections on Black Music Scholarship

JOSEPHINE R. B. WRIGHT

THE PRESENT state of scholarly research of African-American music history reflects positively upon the great strides we have made toward incorporating the contributions of black Americans into the history of music in the United States. From James Monroe Trotter's pioneering *Music and Some Highly Musical People* (1878), to Maud Cuney-Hare's *Negro Musicians and Their Music* (1936), to the hastily penned publications of the 1960s that were written to meet the demands of newly-established Black Studies programs, we have witnessed black music scholarship slowly mature and come of age at the close of the twentieth century, bolstered by a steady advance of new research and new research methodologies.

Eileen Southern set new standards and helped lay a solid foundation of scholarship for the discipline in the 1970s and 1980s through her numerous articles in academic journals and reference works, as well as her full-length tomes that reached and influenced thousands of readers—especially with her *Music of Black Americans: A History* (1971), now in its third edition, and her *Biographical Dictionary of Afro-American and African Musicians* (1982), which has served as a model for biographical references devoted exclusively to

391

musicians of the African diaspora. Rejecting a myopic historical approach, she explored fully the gamut of black musical expression in the United States, covering not only the evolution of ethnically-identifiable genres and styles such as the lined-out hymn, Negro spirituals, the blues, jazz, and gospel, but also exploring, among many topics, the history of blacks in art music, popular music, musical theater, the music recording industry, and music education. Through *Black Perspective in Music*, the journal she co-founded in 1973 with her husband Joseph Southern and edited until 1991, she created a forum that remained for many years the only scholarly venue that welcomed open submissions and published articles devoted to all aspects of music from the African diaspora.

In 1977 Samuel A. Floyd, Jr., founded the Institute for Research in Black American Music at Southern Illinois University-Carbondale, relocating it first in 1978 to Fisk University and later in 1983 to Columbia College-Chicago, renaming it the Center for Black Music Research. For more than twenty years CBMR has functioned as a resource center, repository, and national clearing house for investigators interested in black music. It has also published several important serials, among them the *Black Music Research Newsletter* (1977-1987), later continued as the *Black Music Research Bulletin* (1988-1990); the *Journal of Black Music Research* (1980–); the *CBMR Digest* (1988–); and *Lenox Avenue: A Journal of Interartistic Inquiry* (1995–).

Equally impressive has been the steady publication of reference tools that have increased the breadth and depth of our knowledge about African-American music and helped bring control to its literature. Included in those noteworthy contributions are Dominique-René DeLerma's four-volume *Bibliography of Black Music* (1981-1984), Samuel A. Floyd, Jr., and Marsha Reisser's *Black Music in the United States* (1983) and *Black Music Biography: An Annotated Bibliography* (1987), and Eileen Southern and Josephine Wright's *African-American Traditions in Song, Sermon, Tale, and Dance, 1600s-1920: An Annotated Bibliography of Literature, Collections, and Artworks* (1990). The latter identified primary writings and artworks documenting the evolution of traditional black culture in the oral performing arts from slavery through the first sixty-five years of freedom.

Musical biography received a major boost in the late 1970s, 1980s, and 1990s when major music dictionaries and encyclopedias became inclusive and routinely began to publish entries about famous black musicians—notably, the sixth edition of *Baker's Biographical Dictionary of Music and Musicians* (1978), *The New Grove Dictionary of Music and Musicians* (1980), *The New*

Grove Dictionary or American Music (1986), and the *Harvard Biographical Dictionary of Music* (1996). Among recent dictionaries devoted exclusively to black musical biography, D. Antoinette Handy's *Black Conductors* (1995) and the *International Dictionary of Black Composers* (1999), edited by Samuel A. Floyd, Jr., should be singled out for their unique converage and superb scholarship.

The 1990s brought access to the Internet, revolutionizing how we researched music history by bringing selected references, library catalogs, and archival resources right into our homes and offices, creating virtually an extended library without walls. Today bibliographical information about newly published books and articles can be obtained by accessing such refereed electronic databases as FirstSearch, RILM, the RLG Union Catalog (RLIN), ProQuest Digital Dissertation (Dissertation Abstracts), or other configured databases available through public and academic libraries. The Archives of African American Music and Culture at Indiana University-Bloomington maintains an Internet Resources Catalog that is useful for beginners. Such resources were unavailable in the late 1970s and 1980s when I began researching black music—exploring, e.g., black European and American musical connections in such studies as "George Polgreen Bridgetower: An African Prodigy in England, 1789-99,"[1] "Das Negertrio Jimenez in Europe,"[2] *Ignatius Sancho (1729-1780), An Early African Composer in England: The Collected Editions of His Music in Facsimile* (New York: Garland, 1981), and "Black Musicians in England during the 18th and Early 19th Century";[3] female musicians in "Black Women in Classical Music: 1850-1930";[4] and music literature and criticism in "A Preliminary Bibliographical Guide to Periodical Literature in Black Music."[5]

Notwithstanding my own obvious enthusiasm for electronic databases, a word of caution is warranted about their use. Despite their convenience, accessibility, and accuracy for investigating music bibliography, they have their limitations, especially when researching early African-American musical topics, and are no substitute for developing solid musicological research skills. Most are programmed to report sources in print after 1959—some go back only as far as the 1980s. None systematically yield clues to the widely diffuse literature from bygone years that discusses black music and performance practice. That literature cannot be accessed on-line under the subject heading "Black Music," largely because of the scattered manner in which the American press disseminated information about African-Americans up through the second half of the twentieth century; see "A Preliminary Bibliographical Guide to Periodical Literature in Black Music."

Along another vein, a few general anthologies of art music have recently broadened the Western canon to embrace the black composer, a singular sign of progress in the democratization of American music. Thus William Grant Still, the dean of Afro-American Composers, finally made it into the third edition of the *Norton Anthology of Western Music* (1996), edited by Claude B. Palisca; Scott Joplin and Duke Ellington appeared for the first time in the eighth edition of the *Norton Scores* (1999), compiled by Kristine Forney; James Briscoe published selections by Julia Perry, Tania León, Undine Smith Moore, and Mary Lou Williams in his *Historical Anthology of Music by Women* (1987) and *Contemporary Anthology of Music by Women* (1997); and the forthcoming Volume 7 of Women Composers through the Ages (1996–), edited by Sylvia Glickman and Martha Furman, will contain selected arrangements of Negro spirituals by Eva Jessye (1895-1992), as well as compositions by two relatively unknown black women active at the turn of the twentieth century—Miriam E. Benjamin (active ca. 1889-1910), composer of Theodore Roosevelt's 1904 presidential campaign song, and Carrie Melvin Lucas (d. 1908), a popular vaudeville singer-entertainer.

Not surprisingly, the explosion of scholarly information has led some graduate programs to endorse black music research as a legitimate area for scholarly inquiry. Since the 1970s more and more academic institutions, both at home and abroad, have reported doctoral dissertations written on various topics in black music—in the United States, e.g., such prestigious schools as CUNY, Brown, Columbia, Harvard (which recently established an endowed chair in African-American music), Indiana, Ohio State, Stanford, and Wesleyan Universities as well as Northwestern University and the Universities of California, Michigan, Pennsylvania, and Pittsburgh; in the United Kingdom, the Universities of Keele and London, which maintain American Studies programs; in Germany, the Universities of Berlin and Mainz; and in Austria, the Universities of Graz and Vienna, where research of black American jazz history has gained an apparent following. While many of these dissertations were written in traditional music departments, a surprising number have originated in academic programs outside of music—for instance, American Studies, communication, education, folklore, history, literature, religion, sociology, and theater—which demonstrates the interdisciplinary nature of black music research.

Reflection upon past accomplishments gives one pause to consider the future needs of the discipline. As an educator, I have long been troubled (and puzzled) by the absence of published anthologies of music by black composers or of comparable companion CDs of recorded sound, similar to those compiled to accompany the *Norton Anthologies* or James Briscoe's anthologies of music by women composers; such anthologies are long overdue for instruction of African-American music courses within undergraduate curricula at our colleges and universities.

As a researcher, I remain equally troubled by the lacunae and underrepresented areas of research in the field. The first is a paucity of critical scores and recordings of music by black composers for study, particularly the works of composers of classical music. Only a few African-American composers of classical music in the late twentieth century have been successful in getting their published works before the general public—namely, Leslie Adams, T. J. Anderson, David Baker, Adolphus Hailstork, Ulysses Kay, Tania León, Julia Perry, Hale Smith, Alvin Singleton, Howard Swanson, Frederick Tillis, George Walker, and Olly Wilson. The compositions of many other prominent voices of the last century—e.g., Margaret Bonds, Will Marion Cook, Edmond Dédé, Harry L. Freeman, Mark Fax, Francis Hall Johnson, Undine Smith Moore, Clarence Cameron White, Henry F. Williams, or John Wesley Work III—lie dormant in manuscripts or in ephemeral editions; they really merit publication or reissue.

Further needs of the discipline lie in scholarly research and writing of solid regional histories of blacks in music. Such studies, as Doris McGinty (musicologist and emerita professor at Howard University, Washington, D.C.) and I have shown, can yield invaluable data for reconstructing the cultural history of black America, particularly during post-Emancipation; regional studies similarly often highlight the roles black women played during this period in nurturing musical erudition in their respective communities as African-Americans adapted to their newly won freedom (see respectively "Black Women in the Music of Washington, D.C., 1900-20," and "Black Women in Classical Music in Boston During the Late Nineteenth Century: Profiles of Leadership").[6]

In addition, more solid biographical studies should focus upon African-American musicians outside the popular entertainment industry. While admittedly the life histories of highly visible celebrities may guarantee publishers excellent returns on their investments, many of these studies contain sloppy, often erroneous writing, and they contribute little toward building a solid corpus of scholarship that documents from a historical perspective the diversity of African-American musical life—not just through the lenses of highly visible performers, but through the lenses of prominent black music educators, composers, conductors, lyricists, choreographers, writers about music, music editors, publishers, producers, promoters, and entrepreneurs.

Finally, though some influential musicological journals now accept and publish an occasional article on black music (e.g., *American Music*, the *Journal of the American Musicological Society*, the *Journal of Ethnomusicology*, and the *Musical Quarterly*), younger scholars need many more venues to publish their articles, monograph-length studies, and books.

NOTES

[1]Published in the *Musical Quarterly* 66 (January 1980).

[2]Published in *Black Perspective in Music* 9 (Fall 1981).

[3]Published in Rainer E. Lotz and Ian Pegg, *Under the Imperial Carpet: Essays in Black History*, (Crawley, UK: Rabbit, 1986), 14-24; notes, 286-290.

[4]Published in *Women's Studies Quarterly* 12 (September 1984).

[5]Published in the *Black Music Research Newsletter* (Fall 1986).

[6]Both published in *New Perspectives on Music: Essays in Honor of Eileen Southern*, ed. Josephine Wright with Samuel A. Floyd, Jr. (Warren, MI.: Harmonie Park, 1992).

Born in Tennessee, **Judith Lang Zaimont** is professor of composition at the University of Minnesota School of Music. A student of Hugo Weisgall and Otto Luening, Zaimont earned degrees from Queens College and Columbia University and taught for a time at the Peabody Conservatory. She has won grants and fellowships from the Guggenheim Foundation and the Alliance Française de New York (the latter for postgraduate study in Paris with André Jolivet), as well as from the Maryland and Minnesota state arts boards, the National Endowment for the Arts, and the American Composers Forum. Zaimont is creator and editor-in-chief of the Greenwood Press book series *The Musical Woman: An International Perspective*. Many of her works have been awarded prizes, including the Gold Medal of the 1972 Gottschalk Centenary International Competition, and First Prize in the International 1995 McCollin Competition for Composers.

❦ "A Closed Fist" from *Spirals*
for Violin, Viola, and Cello

JUDITH LANG ZAIMONT

Spirals received its world première on 7 May 2000 in Minneapolis at the Walker Art Gallery, Minneapolis, Minnesota.

T HE third of six movements of *Spirals*, "A Closed Fist" was commissioned for Ensemble Capriccio through a "Musical Celebration of the Millennium" grant awarded by Chamber Music America. A scherzo, it brings together new and old, partnering a palette of noise elements with pitches structured as a non-tonal inward coil, with just a hint of ragtime at the center. — Imagine a very young child exploring how consciously to make a fist, trying out different strengths of grip, then successfully throwing a few punches at the close.

The score begins on the following page.

A CLOSED FIST

from SPIRALS for String Trio

Judith Lang Zaimont

"A Closed Fist" from Spirals for Violin, Viola, and Cello

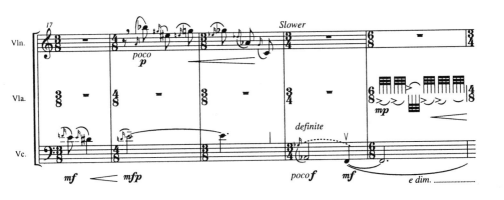

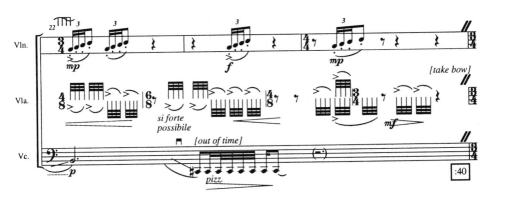

399

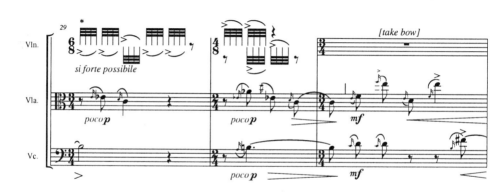

"A Closed Fist" from Spirals *for Violin, Viola, and Cello*

401

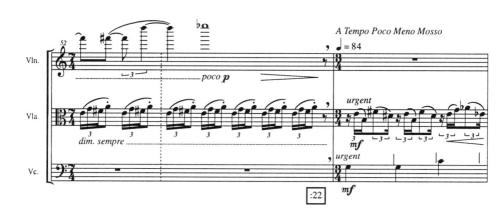

"A Closed Fist" from Spirals for Violin, Viola, and Cello

403

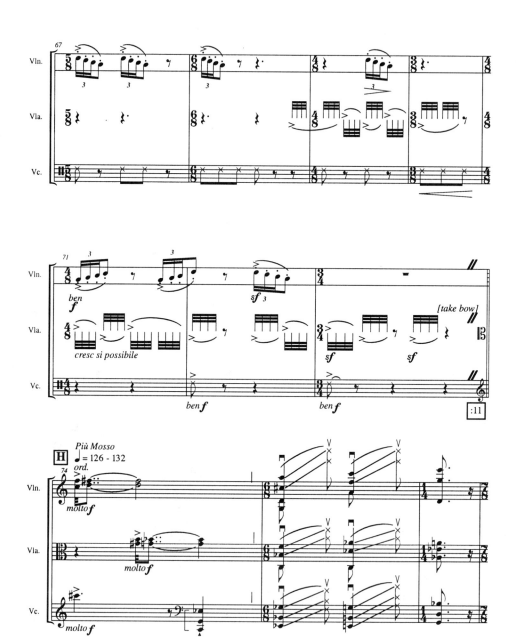

404

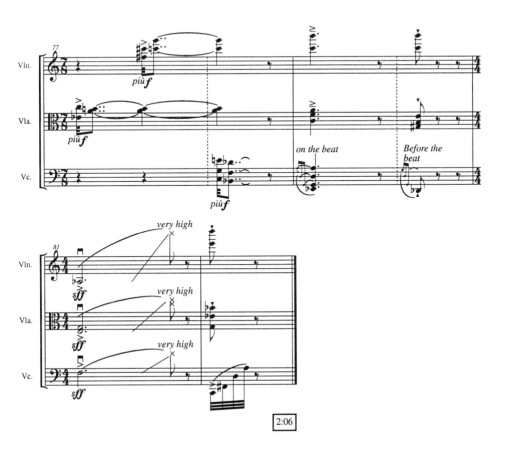

Index

Page number(s) in **bold italic** type refer to the texts of essays by individual authors; page number(s) in **bold** type refer to illustrations.
Institutional locations and editorial clarifications appear below in [square brackets]; names of authors, composers, or performers of books, compositions, and albums, as well as abbreviations and nicknames, appear in (parentheses).
Unless otherwise indicated, titles in *italic* type are those of daily newspapers; other periodical publications are so identified.

Reisz, Karel, 108, 111
Reliance Band, 311
"Return of the Son of Monster Magnet" (Zappa), 100
Revolver (Beatles), 95, 100
Reynolds, David S., 360
Reynolds, Debbie, 226
Rhodes, Phillip, 4
rhythm and blues (also r&b): *see* "blues"
Richmond Symphony, 346
RIdIM, 161
Riegger, Wallingford, 155
Riley, Terry [and works by], 324
RILM, 161, 166, 393
Rink [stage musical], 197
RIPM, 161
RISM, 161
Ritter, Frédéric, 208-210
Rivera, Diego, 305
Riverdance [dance show], 229
RLIN, 161, 393
Roach, Max, 131
Robert Shaw Chorale, 111
Roberts, Christopher [and works by], 344
Roberts, Marcus, 259
Robeson, Paul, 295
Robinson, Bill ("Bo Jangles"), 226, 229
Rochberg, George, 324, 327, 353
Rochester High School Choir, 377
rock and roll (also "rock 'n' roll"), 52, 73, 88-106
   analytical diagram of trends in, **92**
Rockefeller Foundation, 333, 337
Rodriguez, Robert, 317
Rodzinski, Artur, 171
Rogers, Ginger, 226, 233
Rolling Stones, 96, 255
Rollins, Sonny, 260
Romanticos, 346
Roney, Wallace, 260
Rorem, Ned, 360
Rose, Al, 302, 305, 307, 309
Rosenthal, Linda, 345
Rosetti, Christina, 227
Rosewood [motion picture], 259
Ross, Alex, 83
Ross, Orvis, 377
Roter, Bruce [and works by], 348

Rothko, Mark, 31, 33-34, 38
Rothstein, Edward, 170
Roue [motion picture], 108
Rourke, Constance, 308
Rouse, Christopher, 155, 354
Roxie Hart [motion picture], 197
Royal Philharmonic Orchestra, 108
Royal Scottish National Orchestra, 108
Royal Shakespeare Company, 108, 170
Rózsa, Miklós, 114
Rubalcaba, Gonzalo, 261
Rubinstein, Artur, 171
Rudd, Roswell, 311
Ruders, Poul, 363
Ruggles, Carl, 155
Russell, Armand, 149
Russell, Bill, 301-302, 307-308, 311
   photo of, **304**
Russell, George, 260
Russell, Ken, 108, 112
Ryan, Pam, 286

Saffle, Michael, *xiii-xvii*
Saint-Säens, Camille [and works by], 108
Salter, Dorothy, 235
Salzburg Festival [Austria], 23
Sam Morgan's Jazz Band, 311
San Antonio Independent School District [Texas], 314
San Antonio Symphony, 316
San Antonio Symphony Residency Program, 315, 317
San Diego State University [California], 276-277
San Francisco Bay Area Choral Archives, 120
San Francisco Bay Area Directory of Choruses, 120, 124-125
San Francisco Chamber Choir, 122
San Francisco Lesbian/Gay Freedom Band, 346
Sanjek, Russell, 366
Satie, Eric [and works by], 108, 274, 361
Saturday Night Club [Baltimore], 128
Scenes from My Life (Bona), 261
Schenker, Heinrich, 23, 381, 384-385
Schmidt, Harvey, 190
Schnittke, Alfred, 327

8 0 6 4